HONG KONG
AND
MACAU

FODOR'S TRAVEL PUBLICATIONS

are compiled, researched, and edited by an international team of travel writers, field correspondents, and editors. The series, which now almost covers the globe, was founded by Eugene Fodor in 1936.

OFFICES
New York & London

Fodor's Hong Kong and Macau:

Editor: Jacqueline Russell
Area Editor: Saul Lockhart
Editorial Contributors: Shann Davies, Harry Rolnick
Drawings: Ted Burwell
Maps and Plans: Pictograph, Jon Bauch Designs

FODOR'S

HONG KONG

AND

MACAU

1988

FODOR'S TRAVEL PUBLICATIONS, INC.
New York & London

ISBN: 0-679-01523-X
ISBN: 0-340-41840-0 (Hodder & Stoughton)

MANUFACTURED IN THE UNITED STATES OF AMERICA
10 9 8 7 6 5 4 3 2 1

CONTENTS

FOREWORD

Hong Kong is no quaint little backwater good for only a day's stopover or so. It is one of the world's largest cities, and by its human energy level probably the most highly charged. For dining and shopping it is a world-class magnet worthy of at least a week's exciting stay.

Macau, on the other hand, *is* a backwater, a step back in time and atmosphere.

The two—easily accessible to each other—make a potent travel combination, as political events promise to change radically the character of both places within the next two decades. Now is the time for a visit.

Fodor's *Hong Kong and Macau* is designed to describe and explain the area to you, and to help you decide, once you're there, what you want to do and where you want to go. We have therefore concentrated on giving you the broadest **range** of choices the city offers, and within that range to present **selections** that will be safe, solid, and of value to you. The descriptions we provide are just enough for you to make intelligent choices from among our selections, based on your own tastes and pocketbook.

While every care has been taken to ensure the accuracy of the information contained in this guide, the publishers cannot accept responsibility for any errors that may appear.

All prices quoted in this guide are based on those available to us at the time of writing. In a world of rapid change, however, the possibility of inaccurate or out-of-date information can never be totally eliminated. We trust, therefore, that you will take prices quoted as indicators only and will double-check to be sure of the latest figures.

Similarly, be sure to check all opening times of museums and galleries. We have found that such times are liable to change without notice, and you could easily make a trip only to find a locked door.

When a hotel closes or a restaurant produces a disappointing meal, let us know, and we will investigate the establishment and the complaint. We are always ready to revise our entries for the following year's edition should the facts warrant it.

Send your letters to the editors at **Fodor's Travel Publications, 201 E. 50th Street, New York, NY 10022.** Continental readers may prefer to write to Fodor's Travel Publications, 9–10 Market Place, London W1N 7AG, England.

FACTS AT YOUR FINGERTIPS

FACTS AT YOUR FINGERTIPS

 FACTS AND FIGURES. Both Hong Kong and Macau are small foreign enclaves on the southern tip of China. Hong Kong is the younger and larger of the two. Hong Kong Island was ceded to Britain in 1841, while the Kowloon Peninsula was ceded in 1860 and the New Territories and all 235 outlying islands were leased to Britain in 1898 for a period of 99 years. The lease expires at midnight, June 30, 1997, at which time sovereignty reverts to the People's Republic of China in the form of a Special Administrative Region whose economy and autonomy has been guaranteed by the PRC for 50 years. The territory occupies 404 square miles.

Macau has been governed by the Portuguese since 1557 and was for centuries the base of Portuguese trading activities in the Far East and at the same time the base for the introduction of Christianity into China and Japan. Since 1974, it has officially been described as "a territory under Portuguese administration." Though a ceded, not leased, territory, the Portuguese have agreed to let sovereignty revert to China on December 20, 1999, under similar guarantees as those for Hong Kong. The territory consists of a peninsula and two islands; the overall area is only a bit more than six square miles.

Hong Kong and Macau are just forty miles apart, separated by the Pearl River estuary.

Tiny Macau, which is accessible mainly via Hong Kong, actually attracts more visitors (four million annually) than Hong Kong each year, because Hong Kong's Chinese citizens flock to Macau in droves on public holidays to try their luck at the casinos, which are banned in Hong Kong.

The populations of both Hong Kong and Macau are predominantly Chinese, 98 percent and 95 percent respectively. English and Chinese are Hong Kong's official languages, while the most commonly spoken dialect is Cantonese. In Macau, Portuguese remains the official language, but Cantonese is the most widely spoken. However, English is generally used in trade and tourism and it is taught in schools.

There is complete freedom of worship in both places, the principal religions being Buddhism, Taoism, Christianity, and Islam in Hong Kong, and Buddhism and Christianity in Macau.

Hong Kong means "Fragrant Harbour" in Chinese and is pronounced "Heung Gong" in the Cantonese dialect. The word Macau is derived from the name of a Chinese goddess "A-Ma." When Portuguese sailors first landed there and asked the the name of the place, they were told "A-Ma'Gao," or Bay of A-Ma. With time this was shortened to Macau.

1

WHEN TO GO. The weather is best from October through December. Skies are usually blue and temperatures range from 60 degrees to 80 degrees Fahrenheit. January and February are generally dank, with the temperature hovering around 60 degrees but often dipping below 50 degrees and as low as 40 degrees. March and April are unpredictable; an 80-degree sunny day can be followed by a 15-degree drop and a week of rain. The temperature reaches the low 80s by May and stays in the high 80s from June through September. This is the hot, sticky rainy season, in which humidity averages 83 percent but is often well over 90 percent.

Hong Kong is subject to typhoons during the summer months and when Typhoon Signal No. 8 is hoisted, indicating that a typhoon with gale force winds is heading directly for Hong Kong, everything comes to a halt. Transport to and from Macau stops when a typhoon is approaching, and if you are in Macau when the No. 8 signal is raised, you may not get back to Hong Kong for a day or two.

Whenever it rains heavily in Hong Kong, demand for taxis far exceeds supply. It is quicker to rely on public transport or, if you are not pressed for time, to go and have a coffee and wait until the sun comes out again.

WHAT TO TAKE. Whatever the time of year, it is wise to pack a folding umbrella. From May to September, lightweight short-sleeved or sleeveless clothes in cotton or linen are most suitable for the high temperatures and high humidity. Bring some comfortable shoes and loose-fitting cotton shorts for walking. Air-conditioning in hotels and restaurants can be glacial so ladies should bring a wrap or shawl for indoor evening wear. Don't forget your swimsuit and high-protection factor suntan lotion. Several hotels have pools and you may want to spend some time on one of the many beaches. Dress in Hong Kong is fairly informal, but a few hotels and restaurants do insist on a jacket and tie for men in the evenings. It is best to pack a lightweight summer jacket. In most places, the popular safari suit is acceptable for men at any time of day throughout the summer.

In October, November, March, and April, a jacket or sweater should suffice, but during the winter months of December to February, you should bring a raincoat or a light overcoat. It never really gets cold enough to wear furs, yet you will see them worn by fashion-conscious Hong Kong women as soon as the first winter breezes blow.

WHAT WILL IT COST? The average expenditure per head by visitors to Hong Kong in 1986 as calculated by the Hong Kong Tourist Association was HK$4,969 (approximately US$592) for an average length of stay of 3.5 nights. This works out to HK$1,316 (approximately US$169) per day, which covers hotel bills, meals, shopping, day tours, entertainment, and miscellaneous expenditure, but does not, of course, cover the cost of your air fare. Most visitors spend more than half of their spending money on shopping. (Hong Kong is a free-money market. All major currencies and brands of travelers' checks are acceptable.) Take currency fluctuations into account when estimating how much spending money to take with you. At press time the exchange rate is HK$7.80 = US$1.

TOURIST INFORMATION. When planning a trip to Hong Kong and Macau write to the nearest branch of the Hong Kong Tourist Association or the Macau Tourist Information Bureau: Connaught Centre, 35th fl., Box 2597, Hong Kong; (5)244191. Addresses and telephone numbers of some of the Hong Kong Tourist Association's overseas offices are below.

421 Powell St., Suite 200, San Francisco, CA 94102–1568; (415) 781–4582.

548 Fifth Ave., New York, NY 10036; (212) 869–5008/9.

333 N. Michigan Ave., Suite 2323, Chicago, IL 60601; (312) 782–3872.

4th Fl., Toho Twin Tower Bldg., 1–5–2 Yurakucho, Chiyoda-ku, Tokyo 100, Japan; (03) 503–0731.

Hongkong and Shanghai Bank Bldg., 4th fl., 45 Awajima-ohi, 4-chome, Higashi-ku, Osaka 541, Japan; (06) 229–9240.

125 Pall Mall, London SW1Y 5EA, England; 01–930–4775.

National Australia Bank House, 20th Level, 255 George St., Sydney, N.S.W. 2000, Australia; (02)251–2855.

10 Collyer Quay, #13–08, Ocean Bldg., Singapore 0104; 532–3668.

Information about Macau can be obtained from the following Macau Tourist Information Bureau, and from all Portuguese National Tourist Offices:

Travessa do Paiva-Macau, 77218.

Toho Twin Tower Building, fourth floor, 1–5–2 Yurakucho, 1-chome, Chiyoda-ku Tokyo 100, Japan; (03)501–5022.

608 Fifth Ave., New York, NY 10020; (212) 581–7465.

Suite 308, 150 Dundas Street West, Toronto, ON, Canada M5G 1C6; (416) 593–1811.

Portuguese National Tourist Office, 1 New Bond St., London W1Y ONP, England; (01) 493–3873.

Suite 604, 135 Macquarie St., Sydney N.S.W. 2000, Australia; Telex:24667; (02) 241–3334.

3133 Lake Hollywood Dr., Los Angeles, CA 90068; (800)331–7150; (213) 851–3402.

999 Wilder Ave., Honolulu, HI 96822; (808) 536–0719.

457 Main St., Vancouver, BC, Canada V6A 2T7; (604) 687–3316.

#06–03 Afro Asia Bldg., 63 Robinson Rd., Singapore 0106.

Ave. 5 de Outubro 115, 5th fl., 1000 Lisbon, Portugal; 779334.

HOW TO GET THERE. Most visitors reach Hong Kong by air. Hong Kong International Airport (known locally and abroad as Kai Tak) is served by thirty scheduled international carriers and by several charter airlines.

Another way to enter Hong Kong is on a passenger liner. The *Queen Elizabeth II* and the *Canberra* call at Hong Kong on their round-the-world cruises. The *Pearl of Scandinavia,* the *Yao Hua,* and other ships that cruise the China Coast all call at Hong Kong, docking at the Ocean Terminal in the heart of the shopping district of Tsimshatsui, Kowloon.

It is also possible to enter Hong Kong from China and an increasing number of tourists choose to relax in Hong Kong after the rigors of a mainland trip.

Going the other way, you can enter the People's Republic of China from Hong Kong by rail, by air, and by hoverferry, or via Macau. By buying a group tour (see the Tours section in this guide) you can enter China on a group visa obtainable with only forty-eight hours notice. Otherwise, it is advisable to obtain an individual visa before arriving in Hong Kong as obtaining a last-minute visa can be expensive and time consuming.

TIME ZONES. Hong Kong and Macau are both on Hong Kong Standard Time (GMT+8) which is constant year-round. Below are the differences in standard time between some major countries and Hong Kong.

Argentina	−11
Australia	0 (west) to +3 (east)
Canada	−11.5 (east) to −16 (west)
India	−2.5
Indonesia	−1
Japan	+1
Malaysia	0 to .5
New Zealand	+4
Philippines	0
Singapore	0
South Africa	−6
South Korea	+1
Sri Lanka	−2.5
Taiwan	0
Thailand	−1
UK & Ireland	−8
USA	−13 (east) to −16 (west), −18 (Hawaii)

TRAVEL DOCUMENTS. Americans holding valid passports may visit for one month without visas, provided they have onward or return tickets and enough money for their stay. Europeans, South Americans, most Asians, Commonwealth citizens, and nationals of non-Communist countries may visit for one to three months without a visa under the same conditions. Holders of British passports issued in the United Kingdom may visit Hong Kong for six months; no visas required. Extensions are normally granted quite easily.

Visas for longer periods may be obtained from British Consulates, High Commissions, and passport offices throughout the world. Persons who intend to work, study, or live in Hong Kong normally must apply for visas *before* arrival. Only rarely can you switch from a tourist visa to a working visa without first leaving the territory, though some of the paperwork can be completed before departure.

Any questions about visas should be directed to: Department of Immigration, Mirror Tower, 61 Mody Rd., East Tsimshatsui, Hong Kong; (3)733–3111.

Certificates of cholera and yellow fever are *not* required unless you are arriving from an infected area.

To enter the neighboring territory of Macau, visas are not required for nationals of the United States, Philippines, Japan, Australia, Canada, New Zealand, Malaysia, Thailand, Brazil (up to six months' stay), Austria, Belgium, Denmark, Spain, France, Greece, Italy, Norway, the Netherlands, the United Kingdom, West Germany, Switzerland, and Sweden (up to six months stay), or Hong Kong residents. Nationals of countries that do not maintain diplomatic relations with Portugal may not obtain visas on arrival, but must obtain them from Portuguese Consulates overseas. The Portuguese Consulate in Hong Kong is at 1001–2, Tower II, Exchange Square, 8 Connaught Place, Hong Kong, and is open from 9:00 A.M. to 3:00 P.M., Monday through Friday; (5)225789.

 ARRIVAL AT KAI TAK. Efficiency is the word for arrival at Kai Tak. Except for peak periods, you will usually clear customs, immigration and quarantine, locate your baggage and pass through customs in less than forty-five minutes.

There are free baggage carts available in the baggage area that you are allowed to wheel straight through to the exits marked "Groups," "Hotel Cars," and "Greeting Area" and "Transport Terminal" (for taxis and buses into town). There are also airport porters who expect to receive HK$2 per piece of baggage.

The Hong Kong Tourist Association has an Information Counter (inside the buffer hall just outside customs hall) where you can pick up information leaflets and make inquiries. The Hong Kong Hotel Association runs a reservation service there too. The desks open from 8:00 A.M. to 10:30 P.M. There are also banks and currency exchange counters in the buffer hall.

There is often a long queue for taxis, so if you are staying at a hotel, it is best to follow the signs to the area where hotel limousines are waiting. If you do take a taxi, expect to pay about HK$20–25 for a Kowloon destination and up to HK$55 for a destination on Hong Kong Island, inclusive of HK$20 tunnel fee for the Cross Harbour Tunnel, which does not show up on the meter. A fast and efficient way to get to and from the airport is to use the airbus service, which runs on a fixed 15–minute frequency from 7:00 A.M. to 11:00 P.M. Route A1

(HK\$5) runs through the Kowloon tourist area, serving the Ambassador, Empress, Grand, Holiday Inn (Golden Mile), Hong Kong, Hyatt Regency, Imperial, International, Kowloon, Niramar, New World, Park, Peninsula, Regent, Shangri-La, and Sheraton hotels, plus the YMCA, Chungking Mansions, and the Star Ferry. Routes A2 and A3 (KH\$7) go to Hong Kong Island; the former through Wanchai to Central, serving the Furama, Harbour, Harbour View International House, Hilton, Mandarin, New Harbour, and Victoria hotels, while A3 covers the Causeway Bay hotels—Caravelle, Excelsior, Lee Gardens, and Park Lane. Note: Only Hong Kong currency is accepted. Telephone (3) 745–4466 for information.

CUSTOMS. Hong Kong permits the duty-free import of almost everything except liquor, cigarettes, and tobacco. Non-resident visitors are allowed to bring in duty-free 200 cigarettes or 50 cigars or 250g of tobacco, one liter of liquor, 60ml of perfume, and 250ml of toilet water. Hong Kong residents coming into Hong Kong from China or Macau can only bring in one liter of wine (no liquor), plus 100 cigarettes or 25 cigars or 125g of tobacco.

Visitors traveling from Hong Kong to Macau are not usually subjected to customs formalities, but routine checks are sometimes conducted. There are no export duties levied upon departure from either Hong Kong or Macau.

Import of firearms and ammunition is prohibited in both territories, as is any form of drugs or narcotics. The customs search on arrival in Hong Kong, especially for passengers arriving from Southeast Asia, is very thorough, and penalties for drug offenses and carrying arms are severe.

There are no restrictions on currency movements in either Hong Kong or Macau.

CURRENCIES. The Hong Kong currency is the Hong Kong dollar, which is divided into 100 cents. At the time of writing, HK\$7.80 is roughly equivalent to US\$1 but there is always fluctuation. Notes come in denominations of \$1,000 (gold in color), \$500 (brown), \$100 (red), \$50 (blue or purple), \$20 (orange and grey), and \$10 (green), while coins are in denominations of \$5, \$2, \$1, \$.50, \$.20, \$.10, and \$.05. (New banknotes are being distributed so some denominations will have two different-sized notes.)

There are no currency restrictions in Hong Kong and money-changing facilities are available at the airport, in hotels, and in banks, as well as at private money-changers scattered throughout the tourist areas. As the Hong Kong dollar is pegged at HK\$7.80 to US\$1, the rates are never too far off the official peg. However, beware of "commissions," particularly those that advertise "no selling commission" and do not mention the "buying commission," which comes into play when you pass over your foreign currency or travelers' checks for Hong Kong dollars.

The official currency unit in Macau is the pataca, which is divided into 100 avos. Banknotes come in five denominations, 500, 100, 50, 10 and 5 patacas, while coins are 5 and 1 patacas, 50, 20, and 10 avos. The pataca is pegged to the Hong Kong dollar within a few cents. Hong Kong currency circulates freely in Macau but not vice-versa, so remember to change your patacas before your return to Hong Kong.

TIPPING. Hotels and restaurants usually add an automatic 10-percent service charge to all bills. This does not necessarily find its way into the waiters' pockets, so they expect you to leave some loose change behind on the tray.

Taxi drivers, hairdressers, barbers, and waiters are not as unctuous as they are in many other countries, but they certainly appreciate receiving a tip, which should be around 10 percent.

SECURITY. Security is not as serious a problem in Hong Kong as it is in many cities. However, it is wise to take the obvious precautions. Do not carry vast amounts of cash and check your valuables into the hotel safe. It is also advisable not to open your handbag in a public place or to flourish bank notes.

Pickpockets frequent the areas where tourists flock, such as shopping streets and arcades, popular sightseeing places, the racetrack, and wherever else there are vast crowds. If you run into trouble, call the Royal Hong Kong Police's Visitor Hotline at (5)277177; (5)290000 if you are Japanese. The Police Hot Line also will listen to complaints against taxi drivers.

EMERGENCIES. Hong Kong. In a real emergency, dial 999 and ask for the service you require: police, fire brigade, or ambulance.

English-speaking policemen wear a red shoulder tab.

Macau. In a police emergency in Macau, call 999. Other emergency numbers to call are: fire, 572222, and ambulance, 573366.

MEDICAL SERVICES. Western medicine practiced in Hong Kong is up to international standards. Hotels have a list of accredited doctors and can arrange for a doctor to visit you in your hotel room. Otherwise, the Hong Kong Tourist Association recommends visitors to consult the nearest government hospital. Check the Government section of the telephone directory under "Medical and Health Department" for a list of government hospitals and clinics. The main ones are the Queen Mary Hospital, the Queen Elizabeth Hospital, the British Military Hospital, the Tang Shiu Kin Hospital, and the Princess Margaret Hospital. The fee for an office consultation can run from HK$80 to HK$200; ask your hotel to recommend one.

Although Chinese medicine is not officially recognized by the Hong Kong government, many visitors undergo acupuncture or finger pressure treatment while they are in Hong Kong. Chinese herbal medicines are popular with Japanese and overseas Chinese visitors and, in recent years, increasingly so with Westerners.

Herbal medicine shops abound in all the shopping districts and inside the Chinese emporia and China Products stores. Yu Yan Shan at 109 Queen's Road Central (5)443872, has a wide selection of herbal remedies. Even if you do not intend to buy, it's fascinating to see the rows upon rows of bottles and jars of strange-looking medicines.

CONSULATES AND COMMISSIONS. Major consulates and commissions are listed below, along with the hours during which they handle tourist visas. For those not listed, check the "Yellow Pages" under both "Commissions" and "Consulates."

It is always advisable to call up before visiting a consulate, as the opening hours of visa sections often differ from normal office hours. Consulates usually celebrate their country's national holidays and so can be closed on what is a normal working day in Hong Kong. Also, especially in the case of the smaller consulates, these offices are sometimes run by Honorary Consuls who are engaged in their own business activities. It is advisable to telephone first, particularly where smaller countries are concerned, as many are run by Honorary Consuls who are normally businessmen employed in commercial firms.

Australia. Harbour Center, twenty-third/twenty-fourth floors, 25 Harbour Road, Wanchai, Hong Kong; (5) 731881; Monday through Friday, 9:00 A.M. to noon, 1:00 P.M. to 4:00 P.M.

Britain. c/o Overseas Visa Section, Hong Kong Immigration Department, Upper Basement, Mirror Tower, 61 Mody Rd., East Tsimshatsui, Kowloon; (3)7333111; Monday through Friday, 8:45 A.M. to 4:30 P.M.; Saturday, 9:00 A.M. to 11:30 A.M.

Canada. Exchange Square, Tower I, 13th & 14th floors, 8 Connaught Place, Hong Kong; (5)810–4321; Monday through Friday, 8:30 A.M. to 11:00 A.M.

China (People's Republic of). China Travel Building, 77 Queen's Rd., Central, Hong Kong; (5)259121; Monday through Saturday, 9:00 A.M. to 1:00 P.M., 2:00 P.M. to 5:00 P.M. (Or contact the Hong Kong Tourist Association for a list of recommended travel agents dealing in trips and tours to China.)

Hong Kong. Immigration Department, Visitors Section, Third Floor, Mirror Tower, 61 Mody Rd., East Tsimshatsui, Kowloon; (3)733–3111; Monday through Friday, 9:45 A.M. to 4:30 P.M.; Saturday, 9:00 A.M. to 11:30 P.M.

India. Unit D, Sixteenth Floor, United Centre, 95 Queensway, Central, Hong Kong; (5)284029; visa applications, Monday through Friday, 9:30 A.M. to 12:30 P.M.; collection, Monday through Friday, 3:00 P.M. to 4:30 P.M.

Indonesia. 6–8 Keswick St., Causeway Bay, Hong Kong; (5)890–4421; Monday through Friday, 10:00 A.M. to 12:30 P.M., 2:30 P.M. to 4:30 P.M.

Japan. Bank of America Tower, 12 Harbour Rd., Central, Hong Kong; (5) 221184; Monday through Saturday, 9:30 A.M. to noon, 2:00 P.M. to 4:00 P.M. (except Wednesday and Saturday afternoons).

Nepalese Liaison Office. HMS Tamar, Prince of Wales Building, Harcourt Road, Central, Hong Kong; (5)28933255; Monday through Friday, 10:00 A.M. to noon.

Pakistan. Room 307, Asian House, 1 Hennessey Rd., Wanchai, Hong Kong; (5)274622; Monday through Friday, 10:00 A.M. to 1:00 P.M.; Saturday, 10:00 A.M. to 11:30 A.M.

Portugal. Exchange Square, 1001-2, Tower II, 8 Connaught Place, Hong Kong; (5)225789; Monday through Friday, 10:00 A.M. to 3:00 P.M.

Taiwan. c/o Chung Wah Travel, Room 102, Tak Shing House, 20 Des Voeux Rd., Central, Hong Kong; (5)258315; Monday through Friday, 9:00 A.M. to 1:00 P.M.; Saturday, 9:00 A.M. to noon.

Thailand. Eighth floor, Fairmont House, 8 Cotton Tree Drive, Central, Hong Kong; (5)216481; Monday through Friday, 10:00 A.M. to noon, 2:30 P.M. to 5:00 P.M.

United States. 26 Garden Rd., Hong Kong; (5)239011; Monday through Friday (except Wednesday), 8:30 A.M. to noon; Wednesday, 8:30 A.M. to 10:30 A.M.

 PLACES OF WORSHIP. There are many English-speaking churches of every denomination in **Hong Kong;** a few of the more conveniently located churches are listed here.

St. John's Cathedral, Anglican, Garden Road, Hong Kong; *St. Andrew's Church,* Anglican, 138 Nathan Rd., Kowloon; *English Methodist Church,* 271 Queen's Rd. East, Hong Kong; *Kowloon Baptist Church,* 300 Junction Rd.; *Union Church* (Interdenominational), 22A Kennedy Road, Hong Kong; *Tsim Sha Tsui Baptist Church,* 31 Cameron Rd., Kowloon; *St. Joseph's Church* (Roman Catholic), 37 Garden Rd., Hong Kong; *St. Theresa's Church,* (Roman Catholic), 258 Prince Edward Rd., Kowloon; The yellow pages list many more.

Hong Kong's Jewish community worships at the *Ohel Leah Synagogue* at 70 Robinson Rd., Hong Kong.

There are about 30,000 Muslims in Hong Kong. The majority are Chinese while the others originate from Pakistan, India, Malaysia, Indonesia, and the Middle East. The main mosques are the new *Kowloon Mosque* in Kowloon Park, Nathan Road, Kowloon; the *Masjid Ammar* on Oi Kwan Road, Morrison Hill, Hong Kong; and the *Shelley Street Mosque,* just off Robinson Road, Hong Kong.

There is a *Hindu Temple* in Happy Valley, Hong Kong, and a *Sikh Temple* in Wanchai, Hong Kong, at 371 Queen's Rd. East.

The Catholic church has always played an important role in **Macau.** Today there are approximately 23,500 Catholics and masses are said every day in most churches. Schedules are posted on the doors.

The Department of Tourism publishes a leaflet on the churches of Macau, listing the history of seventeen of the most interesting places of worship. The *Cathedral* is in the Largo da Sé.

Services are still held regularly in the small Protestant chapel, known as the Morrison Chapel, in the Old Protestant Cemetery.

 BUSINESS HOURS. Office hours are generally from 9:00 A.M. to 5:00 P.M. in both Hong Kong and Macau. Banks are open from 9:00 A.M. to 3:00 P.M.; money exchangers are open longer.

In Macau, many places of business and all government offices are closed from 1:00 P.M. to 3:00 P.M.

There are no set hours for shops in Hong Kong, but as a general guideline, the usual opening hours in the three main shopping areas are: Central District, Hong Kong, 10:00 A.M. to 6:00 P.M.; Causeway Bay and Wanchai, Hong Kong, 10:00 A.M. to 9:30 P.M.; Tsimshatsui East, Kowloon, 10:00 A.M. to 7:30 P.M.; Tsimshatsui, Yaumatei, and Mongkok, Kowloon, 10:00 A.M. to 9:00 P.M.

Most shops are open on Sundays and public holidays, the exception being the first two or three days of the Chinese New Year.

On Sundays and public holidays, the shopping centers are extremely crowded and it takes a long time to move around and to get served. The same applies to travel on public transport, especially ferries to the outlying islands. Holiday-makers would be well advised to plan their excursions during the week while greater Hong Kong is at work.

Transport between Hong Kong and Macau is almost always fully booked at weekends and on the day before and during public holidays. Tourists are advised to travel midweek when ferry tickets and hotel rooms are more readily available.

In Macau, you will have some difficulty persuading taxi drivers to take you over the Taipa Bridge after dusk, and they will expect a double fare. If you find yourself on Taipa or Coloane islands late at night, you may experience difficulty finding any means of transport at all back to Macau.

 HOLIDAYS. Hong Kong has eighteen annual public holidays. Although banks and offices are closed on these days, almost all the shops are open—except at Chinese New Year, when the place comes to an almost complete standstill. The holidays for 1988 are: New Year's Day, January 1; Chinese New Year holidays, February 17–19; Easter holidays and Ching Ming, April 2–5; the Queen's Birthday holidays, June 11–13; Dragon Boat Festival, June 18; Liberation Day, August 27–29; Mid-Autumn Festival, September 26; Chung Yeung Festival, October 19; Christmas holidays, December 25 and December 26.

Macau has 20 public holidays scheduled for 1988. These are: New Year's Day, January 1; Chinese New Year holidays, February 17–19; Easter holidays and Ching Ming, April 1–4; Anniversary of the Portuguese Revolution, April 25; International Labor Day, May 1; Corpus Christi, June 2; Camões and Portuguese Communities Day, June 10; Dragon Boat Festival, June 18; Feast of St. John the Baptist, June 24; Feast of the Battle of July 13, July 13; Feast of the Assumption of Our Lady, August 15; Mid-Autumn Festival, September 26; Chinese National Day October 1; Republic Day, October 5; Chung Yung,

October 19; All Saints and All Souls' Day, November 1 and November 2; Restoration of Independence Day, December 1; Feast of the Immaculate Conception, December 8; Winter Solstice, December 22; Christmas holidays, December 24 and December 25. (Though not an official holiday, important dates on the Macau calendar are November 28–29, the weekend of the XXXIV Macau Grand Prix.)

WATER AND ELECTRICITY. Although the Hong Kong government declares that the water is quite safe to drink, the local populace tends to boil all drinking water or to stay with bottled distilled or mineral water.

Macau's water supply and much of Hong Kong's is supplied from reservoirs in China and is chlorinated for extra protection. Hotels and restaurants in both places serve chilled distilled drinking water.

Electricity in Hong Kong and in the newer parts of Macau is supplied at 220 volts and 50 cycles. In the old section of Macau the electricity is 110 volts and 50 cycles, so it is wise to check before plugging in an electrical appliance. Shaver adaptors are standard in hotel rooms but hair dryers and heated rollers often require special adaptors.

LAUNDRY. Laundry service in the hotels is available seven days a week. In many cases there is an express charge for same-day service. Laundries and dry-cleaning shops are plentiful in the shopping areas and even inside the Mass Transit Railway concourses. Coin-operated laundries are rare. Check the Yellow Pages under "Launderers-Self Service." An average load costs HK$19, including machine wash, dry, and a measure of detergent.

HAIRDRESSERS/BARBERS. Most of the hotels have ladies' and men's hairdressing salons on the premises, staffed with hairdressers who are used to European hair styles. Cost is around HK$100 to HK$200 for a cut, shampoo, and blow dry for ladies, HK$80 to HK$150 for men. Fashion-conscious locals favor *Le Salon,* on Wyndham Street, Central; *Rêver,* inside the Lane Crawford Department Store in Central, the Holiday Inn Golden Mile, Regal Meridien, Furama, Excelsior, Lee Gardens, and Marco Polo hotels; and the *Rodger Craig Salon,* in the Shangri-la and Peninsula Hotels. Men who want a simple haircut should try *Talianna* in the Hilton Hotel.

MEASUREMENTS. Hong Kong has gone "metric," while Macau, as a Portuguese-governed territory, always has been. A metric conversion table is provided below.

CONVERTING METRIC TO U.S. MEASUREMENTS

Multiply:	by:	to find:
Length		
millimeters (mm)	.039	inches (in)
meters (m)	3.28	feet (ft)
meters	1.09	yards (yd)
kilometers (km)	.62	miles (mi)
Area		
hectare (ha)	2.47	acres
Capacity		
liters (L)	1.06	quarts (qt)
liters	.26	gallons (gal)
liters	2.11	pints (pt)
Weight		
gram (g)	.04	ounce (oz)
kilogram (kg)	2.20	pounds (lb)
metric ton (MT)	.98	tons (t)
Power		
kilowatt (kw)	1.34	horsepower (hp)
Temperature		
degrees Celsius	9/5 (then add 32)	degrees Fahrenheit

CONVERTING U.S. TO METRIC MEASUREMENTS

Multiply:	by:	to find:
Length		
inches (in)	25.40	millimeters (mm)
feet (ft)	.30	meters (m)
yards (yd)	.91	meters
miles (mi)	1.61	kilometers (km)
Area		
acres	.40	hectares (ha)
Capacity		
pints (pt)	.47	liters (L)
quarts (qt)	.95	liters
gallons (gal)	3.79	liters
Weight		
ounces (oz)	28.35	grams (g)
pounds (lb)	.45	kilograms (kg)
tons (t)	1.11	metric tons (MT)
Power		
horsepower (hp)	.75	kilowatts
Temperature		
degrees Fahrenheit	5/9 (after subtracting 32)	degrees Celsius

Traditional Chinese weights, such as the "catty," are used in the food markets. If you are offered a "catty" of vegetables or seafood, you will get about 1.5 pounds or a bit more than half a kilogram's worth. One "tael" equals 1.3 oz or 38 g.

 LETTERS, CABLEGRAMS, AND MAILING PACKAGES. Hong Kong. First-class air-mail letter rates are currently HK$1.30 for the first 10 grams and HK80¢ for each additional 10 grams to countries in Zone 1 (Asian countries from Japan to Pakistan) and HK$1.70 and HK90¢ for Zone 2 (Europe, the Americas, Australia, and countries as far east as Iran). Postcards go at full letter rates.

Aerograms are obtainable at any post office and may be sent to all countries at a uniform rate of HK$1.30. Express delivery service costs an extra HK$4 and registration is HK$5.

Parcels and small packets are subject to certain regulations concerning weight limitations, customs declarations, dispatch notes, and compensation. The weight limit for small packets is 1 kilogram or 500 grams, according to the destination. All goods sent abroad by post must be declared to customs on special forms available at all post offices.

For further information about parcel services ask at any post office or call the Post Office Enquiry Bureau on (5) 231071. A rate sheet is obtainable on request from all post offices.

You can send cables and telexes and make international telephone calls from your hotel. Most hotels are now equipped with international direct-dialing facilities for which they add on a surcharge to the published tariffs. A cheaper alternative is to go to the Cable and Wireless Company offices at Exchange Square, 8 Connaught Place, Hong Kong (across from the General Post Office and Connaught Centre); Hermes House, Middle Road (across from Sheraton); Kai Tak Airport; or the General Post Office.

Macau. Similar rates apply in Macau. It is advisable to arrange postage through the front desk at your hotel as you may experience long waits at the Post Office.

 HONG KONG FOR THE DISABLED. Hong Kong is not the easiest of cities for people in wheelchairs or on crutches. Callously, the city is just not geared to ramps or special accesses because such things cost money and there is no government legislation to force a builder, architect, or developer to be considerate of his fellow man. However, some progress has been made. The Airport, City Hall, and Hong Kong Arts Centre have made a big effort to assist wheelchair users. If you or one of your party is physically handicapped, "A Guide for Physically Handicapped in Hong Kong," available through the Hong Kong Tourist Association, will prove to be invaluable. Not only does it list those rare places that have special facilities for the handicapped, but it also explains the best access to hotels, restaurants, and churches.

AIRLINES. Both on-line and off-line airline ticketing offices for selected airlines are listed below.

   Aer Lingus, 18th fl., Euro Trade Centre, 13–14 Connaught Road Central, Hong Kong; (5)265877.

Air Canada, 1026 Prince's Building, Hong Kong; (5)221001.

Air France, 2114 Alexandria House, Hong Kong; G07 Hotel Regal Meridien, Kowloon; (5)248145.

Air India, 1002 Gloucester Tower, Hong Kong; (5)214321.

Air Lanka, 505 Bank of America Tower, Hong Kong; (5)252171.

Air New Zealand, Swire House, Hong Kong; (5) 884–1488.

Alitalia, 2101 Hutchison House, Hong Kong; (5)237047.

American Airlines, Room 202, Caxton House, Duddell Street; (5)257081.

British Airways, 30th fl., Alexandra House, Hong Kong; 112 Royal Garden Hotel, Kowloon; (5)868–0303.

British Caledonian, BCC House, 15th fl., 10 Queen's Rd., Central, Hong Kong; (5)260062.

Canadian Airlines International, 17th fl., Swire House, Hong Kong; Peninsula Hotel Arcade, Kowloon; (5)227001.

Cathay Pacific Airways, Swire House, Hong Kong; Peninsula Hotel Arcade, Kowloon; Lee Gardens Hotel, Hong Kong; Ocean Centre, Kowloon; (5) 884–1488.

China Airlines, St. George's Building, Hong Kong; G/F Tsimshatsui Centre, Kowloon; (5) 218431.

Civil Aviation Administration of China, Gloucester Tower, Hong Kong; (5)216416.

Continental, 46th fl., Hopewell Centre, 183 Queen's Road East, Hong Kong; (5)299011.

Delta, 18th fl., Euro Trade Centre, 13–14 Connaught Road Central, Hong Kong; (5) 265875.

Eastern Airlines, 201 D'Aguilar Place, 7 D'Aguilar St., Hong Kong; (5) 237065.

Flying Tigers, 223 New Cargo Complex, Kaitak Airport; (3) 769–7564.

Garuda Indonesia Airways, Fu House, 7 Ice House St., Hong Kong; (5) 235181/2.

Japan Air Lines, Gloucester Tower, Hong Kong; Harbour View Holiday Inn Lobby, Kowloon; (5)230081.

Jardine Airways, Alexandra House, Hong Kong; 112 Royal Garden Hotel, Kowloon; (5)868–0303 reservations, (5)868–0768 flight information.

KLM Royal Dutch Airlines, Fu House, 7 Ice House St., Hong Kong; (5) 251255.

Korean Air Lines, Tsimshatsui Centre, Kowloon; St. George's Building, Hong Kong; (5)235177.

Lufthansa German Airlines, 6/F Landmark East, Hong Kong; Empire Centre, E. Tsimshatsui, Kowloon; (5)212311.

Malaysian Airline System, 13/F Prince's Building, Hong Kong; (5)218181.

Northwest, St. George's Building, Ground fl., Hong Kong; (5) 217477.

Pakistan International Airlines, 1104 Houston Centre, Kowloon; (3)664770.

Philippine Airlines, East Ocean Centre, 98 Granville Rd., Kowloon; (3) 694521.

Qantas Airways, Swire House, Hong Kong; Sheraton Hotel Lobby, Kowloon; (5)242101.

Royal Brunei Airlines, 1406 Central Building, Hong Kong; (5)223799.

Royal Nepal Airlines, 1114–6 Star House, Kowloon; (3)699151.

Sabena, 201 D'Aguilar Place, 7 D'Aguilar St., Hong Kong; (5) 237065.

SAS, 2407 Edinburgh Tower, Hong Kong; (5) 265978.

Singapore Airlines, 115 Gloucester Tower, Hong Kong; Wing on Plaza, Tsimshatsui East, Kowloon; (5)202233.

South African Airways, Alexandra House, Hong Kong; 112 Royal Garden Hotel, Kowloon; (5)868–0303.

Swissair, Tower 2, 8th fl., Admiralty Centre, Hong Kong; Peninsula Hotel Kowloon; (5)293670.

Thai Airways International, Shop 122, World-Wide Plaza, Hong Kong; Peninsula Hotel Arcade, Kowloon; (5)295601.

Trans World Airlines, 2205 Yardley Commercial Bldg., Hong Kong; (5) 413117.

United Airlines, 29th fl., Gloucester Tower, Hong Kong; and Empire Centre, Tsimshatsui East, Kowloon; (5) 810–4888.

Western Airlines, 18th fl., Euro Trade Centre, 13–14 Connaught Road Central, Hong Kong; (5)216268

DEPARTING FROM KAI TAK INTERNATIONAL AIRPORT. To get to Kai Tak you can either order a hotel car in advance, take a taxi, or, if you are not encumbered with luggage, take the airport coach or tunnel bus. The cost varies from around HK$90 to HK$155 for a hotel car from Hong Kong (HK$50 to HK$195 from Kowloon) to as little as HK$5–HK$7 for the Airbus service.

The Airbus service has three routes, which pass by most of the major hotels on both sides of the harbor. Route A1 (HK$5) serves the major hotels in Kowloon, while Routes A2 and A3 (HK$7) serve the major hotels in Wanchai and Central (A2) and Causeway Bay (A3). (For the list of hotels, see "Arrival at Kai Tak" in this section.) The frequency of this service is every quarter hour from 7:00 A.M. to 11 P.M. Only Hong Kong currency is accepted. Telephone (3)745–4466 for information.

At Kai Tak the departure tax is HK$120 and HK$60 for children under 12. This is collected at the airline check-in counters, though some travel agents collect it when you pay for your ticket.

At Kai Tak the authorities are particularly strict about the amount of hand baggage you can take on board. If it will not fit into a box measuring *22-by-14-by-9* inches you will have to check it in. A 20-kilo baggage allowance applies on most flights, except those to the United States, where you are allowed to check in a maximum of two pieces of baggage per person, each weighing a maximum of 70 pounds. There is a left-luggage office in the departure hall, charging HK$10 for the first 24 hours, HK$5 per day thereafter.

Overseas phone calls can be made from the Cable and Wireless office in the departure or transit halls. There is also a nursery in the transit lounge.

Kai Tak Airport makes no flight-boarding announcements, so check developments on the arrivals and departures boards.

 CUSTOMS ON RETURN TO THE UNITED STATES AND UNITED KINGDOM. You are allowed to take 200 cigarettes, 50 cigars, or 3 pounds of tobacco, or combinations of these back to the United States, plus one liter of liquor.

If you are a returning **U.S. resident,** you can mail up to US$50 worth of gifts back duty free or carry up to US$400 of gifts. For the next US$1,000 you pay 10 percent; anything over the value of US$1,400 is subject to full duty.

Non-residents can take an extra 200 cigarettes, 100 cigars, and US$100 worth of gifts into the USA free of duty and must pay 10 percent on the next US$600 worth and regular duty on anything over US$700.

When returning to the **United Kingdom,** residents are allowed to take in 200 cigarettes, 100 cigarillos, 50 cigars, or 250 grams of tobacco. You are also allowed to take in 1 liter of alcohol over 38.8 proof, or 2 liters under 38.8 proof, or 2 liters of fortified sparkling table wine. Persons under 17 are not entitled to either allowance. People residing outside Europe can bring double the above quantities of tobacco.

Narcotics are strictly prohibited in Hong Kong and Macau and there are restrictions on the importation of certain plants and animals. Health and innoculation certificates are required for dogs and cats traveling to the United States, while a six-month quarantine periods applies in the United Kingdom for all animals. Regulations for birds are very complicated, and it is advisable to pick up a copy of the U.S. Consulate's booklet "Pets and Wild Life." Fresh food, or meat in any form, cannot be taken into the United States. Food cannot be brought into the United Kingdom.

INTRODUCTION TO HONG KONG AND MACAU

by
RUTH LOR MALLOY

Ruth Lor Malloy, a Canadian of Chinese ancestry and a resident of Hong Kong, is the author of several travel guides.

In Cantonese, Hong Kong means "Fragrant Harbor," a name inspired either by the incense-making factories that once dotted the island or by the profusion of scented pink bauhinias, now the national flower. Hong Kong is a British Crown Colony, one of the few left, though now it is also called a "dependent territory" of Britain. As a major section is leased from China, Hong Kong is also part of China. All these terms are misleading, simplistic though official. Hong Kong is a very complicated lady.

But some things about Hong Kong are straightforward. It is located at the mouth of the mighty, muddy Pearl River on the southeast coast of China, the same latitude as Hawaii and Cuba. It is 2¾ hours by air from Beijing; at least 17 from New York; 12¼ from San Francisco; and 13 from London. It consists of three main parts: Hong Kong Island, which is roughly 32 square miles; Kowloon, 3.5 square miles; and the New Territories, 365 square miles—more or less. Mountains here are frequently blasted apart and made into land-fill. Hong Kong's land area expands daily.

The name "Hong Kong" is confusing too. It refers to the overall territory, as well as to the main, though not the largest, island in the colony. Hong Kong Island, popularly referred to as "Hong Kong-side," is made up of "districts" and "villages." You will probably visit "Central," which is officially named "Victoria" even though nobody calls it that any more. Also located on the island are Wanchai, Causeway Bay, Repulse Bay, Stanley, and Aberdeen.

Kowloon includes Tsimshatsui, East Tsimshatsui, Hung Hom, Mongkok/Yaumatei, and the area north to the aptly named Boundary Street. The New Territories extend from Boundary Street north to the China border and encompass the container port, airport, and most of the major industries plus the outlying islands. If you want to shop, aim for Central and Tsimshatsui. Night life flourishes in Wanchai and especially on Friday evenings in Tsimshatsui.

The weather in Hong Kong is semitropical. Winters rarely get cold enough for frost, but a topcoat is needed for the evenings. The best time to visit is from October through February, when it is mostly sunny and pleasant, although there are exceptions. From March through September, you are likely to encounter first the rainy season then typhoons. Few of these tropical hurricanes actually hit Hong Kong directly, but they might come close enough to pour tons of water on the place, closing stores, offices, and the airport—forcing plane schedules to change. The months of June through August are oppressively hot and muggy, a good time for enjoying air-conditioned amenities, taxis, shopping malls, and hotels.

Hong Kong is overwhelmingly (98 percent) Chinese. Other nationalities include British, Indian, and American. While the official languages are English and Cantonese, Mandarin, Hakka (an early arriving Chinese minority group), Tanka (Chinese boat people), Shanghainese, and Chinglish (a mixture of Cantonese, English and pidgin) are also heard. Don't be surprised if you also hear Filipino languages, especially around the Star Ferry and Statue Square. Approximately 23,000 Filipinas work in Hong Kong as domestics.

The signs of Hong Kong's religions are everywhere: Buddhism, Taoism, ancestor worship, Christianity, animism. Pragmatism and money-making are such a part of the way of life that you can almost call them religions, too. Again, each category is confusing, because Chinese people tend to be eclectic in their beliefs. It is not uncommon for the same Hong Kong citizen to put out food and incense for his departed ancestors at Spring Festival time, invite a Taoist priest to his home to exorcise unhappy ghosts, pray in a Buddhist temple for fertility, take communion in a Christian church, and cheat the government of taxes. All possible roads to success in this world and the next are taken.

Hong Kong is delightful to visit. It has the best shopping in the world if you work at it; great Chinese flavor and food; and mountains, beaches, harbors, and parks; exotic festivals. It also provides a good introduction to China. You can experience first-hand here an economically successful feat of human achievement at its height—5.5 million people on 400 square miles of land with few natural resources other than its deep harbor and China-coast location. You can also get a feel of history in the making, as Hong Kong approaches the end of its New Territories lease.

Hong Kong is a beautiful cluster of 236 islands and a peninsula, from which rise twenty mountain peaks more than 1,000 feet tall, two of them towering some 2,700 feet. Forty percent of Hong Kong's land is green country park; only 9 percent is built-up with the skyscrapers familiar to tourists. Hong Kong is grubby and garbage-strewn in places, but no one can accuse it of being as drab as China. It sparkles in the sun and in the rain. At night, neon lights add to the liveliness of its store-lined streets.

Hong Kong defies simple definitions. It is not entirely "dependent" on Britain. It trades more with China, the United States, and Japan. Britain pays only 25 percent of Hong Kong's defense budget, while the Hong Kong government picks up the rest of the tab. But Britain makes most of the important decisions. Hong Kong also provides jobs for Britain's educated unemployed and gives to the motherland millions of dollars a year in remittances and investments. It is also a captive market for such British products as buses and railway cars. It is Britain's largest Asian market.

Part of Hong Kong's phenomenal success stems from its British government ties, judicial system, expertise, and resulting stability. These attributes have attracted and kept local and foreign capital. The decision to make Hong Kong a free port, a trading center, was British. But the territory has also benefited from Chinese entrepreneurial skills, hard-working Chinese refugee labor, and, of course, the harbor and the other advantages of its location.

Hong Kong is also economically and politically dependent on China for markets, resources, and cooperation. Most of the food—1.8 million squealing pigs a year—the basic necessities, and about half of the water consumed in Hong Kong come from China. The Chinese mainland provides for sale relatively cheap pots, pans, blankets, sweaters, textiles, and beds. Hong Kong is China's fourth largest export market, worth around US$1.6 billion a year, excluding real estate, foreign exchange funds, and banking.

While the paucity of elected citizen representation in government might justify the outdated "colonial" label, British officials do go politely to consult with China about mutual concerns. This is a far cry from Britain's nineteenth-century imperialistic arrogance. Unofficially, China deals directly with many Hong Kong citizens, Britain notwithstanding.

In past years, Hong Kong has also been aptly described as "a pimple on China's ass," and "a gem in China's navel." Depending upon which body part one cares to attribute to the bulge of land on which Hong Kong sits, both descriptions fit—almost. The Communist Chinese have been very embarrassed with its blatantly capitalistic offspring. But China has been earning an estimated 40 percent of its foreign exchange, about US$6 billion to US$8 billion dollars a year, here. Many Hong Kong business people have also invested in China and more particularly China's new Special Economic Zones, the largest of which, Shenzhen, is on Hong Kong's northern border. Financially Hong Kong is worth more to China than it is to Britain. But it is also politically inconsistent.

Hong Kong is shamelessly "capitalistic." But while it is the world's foremost example of laissez-faire free enterprise with a minimum of government interference, it has surprisingly many socialistic infrastructures. Its government is a benevolent facilitator, an oiler of squeaks, a road builder, an organizer. It has no minimum wage laws and no unemployment insurances. But there are compulsory workmen's compensation schemes, minimum working-age regulations, and nine years of compulsory education. About 2.5 million people—almost 50 percent of the population—live in government-subsidized housing. Government hospitals provide almost free medical care. An ambulance ride, X-rays, 14 stitches, overnight stay, and medicines cost less than US$5.

It is far from the classic image of a "colony" or a sweatshop based on cheap labor. It has an infant mortality rate lower than either Britain or the United States, more secondary students per capita than Britain, and one of the highest protein-consumption rates in the world. It had a maximum 5.2 percent unemployment rate during the recent world recession when Britain's was more than twice as high.

Hong Kong has not just survived, it has thrived. It is up there in world-class: third-largest financial center, third-largest diamond and gold trading center, the largest market for 24K gold jewelry, the second-largest container port, the largest manufacturer of toys, textiles, clothing, watches, clocks, and radios, the thirteenth-largest trading entity, and so on.

Major North American, European, and Japanese computer companies compete for customers here, sometimes at prices less than at home because of lower mark-ups, no sales taxes, and no duties. Computers not only keep track of customers and orders in Hong Kong, but they are also used to cut cloth into dresses in the most cost-efficient manner, to design machines, and to do other complicated tasks. Such services as electricity and telecommunications function in Hong Kong.

Of 152 banks, 117 incorporated outside Hong Kong stand ready, along with an additional hundred-plus representative offices of foreign banks, to provide capital or facilitate financial transactions. Publishing houses open in Hong Kong primarily because world copyright and trade marks registry are protected under British law, while costs are low. In addition, the government avoids interfering with editorial content (aside from pornography and libelous material).

Some companies have departed, however, because of the incredibly high rents of the late 1970s and early 1980s—among the highest in the world for commercial and post-war residential property. Relatively new, modest (by American standards), three-bedroom flats have cost as much as HK$25,000 a month, or over US$3,000.

Real estate has not only been a principal money maker for many Hong Kong citizens, it has been the largest single source of revenue for the government. Ever since British Hong Kong began, the government has controlled practically all the land. People can buy buildings only on long-term leased land.

The economy is also based on light industry, manufacturing, old-fashioned trading, and tourism. Hong Kong was founded as an *entrepôt* and remains one.

Hong Kong makes no pretense at being a democracy. It isn't. But it is more sensitive to its citizens than most "democratic" countries in Asia. Only illegal immigrants and criminals need fear the police.

Hong Kong's top political leader is the governor, who represents the British sovereign. In the absence of a "Colonial Office," the British foreign secretary is answerable to Britain's parliament for Hong Kong. Its legal powers stem from Queen Victoria's "Letters Patent" and "Royal Instructions." Next in line to the governor are the chief secretary, financial secretary, and the attorney general. The highest-ranking body is the seventeen-member Executive Council, which combines the functions of a cabinet and top advisory board. Its sessions are held "in camera." Since September 1985, as part of the plan to prepare the territory for self-rule under China in 1997, the Council has included 24 indirectly elected members.

The first semblance of popular government came with elections held in 1952 for seats on the Urban Council, which takes care of beaches, playgrounds, cultural centers, and garbage collection. In 1982, elections were first held for the eighteen newly created District Boards, where elected representatives, government officials, and appointed citizens discuss issues on a level different from public toilets and vermin control. After the District Boards, the partially elected Regional Council, the rural version of the Urban Council, was created.

Citizen participation also takes the form of lively letters to the editors of newspapers or participation on open-line radio talk shows. Questions are usually answered by the government official concerned. District Offices have regular "Meet the Public" schemes for citizens to make criticisms and offer suggestions directly to District Board Members. Some 320 citizen advisory boards and councils give advice. Demonstrations and petitions to the governor take place quite freely. Political stability, however, is a critical factor, as it affects the whole economy.

Hong Kong started from humble beginnings. The earliest visitors, probably boat people of Malaysian-Oceanic origin, left geometric-styled graffiti 5,000 years ago, still visible on rocks in Big Wave Bay (Hong Kong Island), Po Toi Island, and other places. The earliest structure found so far is the 2,000-year-old Han dynasty tomb at Lei Cheng Uk, its tiny kiln-like size indicative of the significance of the area. Over 600 years later the Tang dynasty left an archeological mystery with the next oldest structures: lime kilns full of deep-sea shells, although we have no clues as to what the lime was used for. Some of these kilns can be seen on Lamma Island, though they are not marked.

The oldest land records are from the Sung dynasty, when loyalists fled the invading Mongols with their emperor to south China. Many courtiers settled in Hong Kong. Today, anyone visiting Po Lin Monastery high in the mountains of Lantau Island will pass Shek Pik reservoir, where innumerable Sung coins were found during the reservoir's excavation.

The last of the Sung emperors, a boy, is said to have spent a night in the late 1270s near what is now the airport. One of his men is credited with naming Kowloon, which means the "nine dragons" (eight mountains and one emperor). Because he was the only Chinese emperor believed to have set foot here and because of the highly developed Sung civilization, a reproduction of a Sung village was built here and is worthwhile visiting. It is small, but exudes spirit and charm.

Western traders first appeared in the Hong Kong area in 1513. The Portuguese were soon followed by the Spanish, Dutch, English, and

French. All were bent either on making fortunes trading porcelain, tea, and silk, or saving souls for their respective religions. Until 1757, the Chinese restricted all foreigners to neighboring Macau, the Portuguese territory 40 miles across the Pearl River estuary. After that time, traders—but not their families—were allowed to live just outside Canton for about eight months each year. Canton, now known as Guangzhou, is only 20 minutes away by plane, or three hours away by train or hovercraft.

Trading in Hong Kong was frustrating for the foreigners. It took at least twenty days for messages to be relayed to the emperor, local officials had to be bribed, and Chinese justice seemed unfair. The Chinese confined foreign traders to a small, restricted zone and forbade them to learn Chinese. On top of that, the Chinese wanted nothing from the West except silver, until the foreigners, especially the British, but also the French and Americans, started offering opium.

The spread of the opium habit and the growing outflow of silver alarmed high Chinese officials as early as 1729. They issued edicts forbidding the importation of the drug, but these were not strictly enforced until 1839. Then a heroic and somewhat fanatical Imperial Commissioner, Lin Ze-xu (Lin Tse-hsu), laid seige to the foreign factories in Canton and detained the traders until they surrendered over 20,000 chests of the drug, almost a year's trade. The foreigners also signed bonds promising to desist from dealing with it "forever," upon threat of death. The opium was destroyed.

The traders did not find Lin's inflexible manner the least bit amusing. The resulting tension led to the "Opium Wars" and a succession of "unequal treaties" forced by superior British fire power. A bewildered, angry, and reluctant China had no choice but to open its doors to foreign trade and missionaries. China's present government refuses to recognize the treaties.

Locally, the Treaty of Nanking (1842) gave Hong Kong Island to Britain "in perpetuity"; the Convention of Peking in 1860 ceded the Kowloon peninsula and Stonecutter's Island in the harbor outright to England. The Convention of Peking in 1898 gave Britain the ninety-nine-year lease on the "New Territories."

British Hong Kong flourished from the start because of trade, especially opium. (Opium was not outlawed in Hong Kong until after World War II). The population grew quickly from 4,000 Chinese in 1841 to over 23,000 in 1847 as Hong Kong attracted anyone anxious to make money or just to live without the fetters of feudalism and family.

Each convulsion on the Chinese mainland—the Taiping rebellion in the mid-1800s, the 1911 republican revolution, the warlords of the 1920s, the 1937 Japanese invasion of China—resulted in another group

of refugees here. Then Japan invaded Hong Kong itself. The population, which was 1.4 million just before the Japanese arrived, dropped
to a low of 600,000 by the time of their defeat in 1945. Many Hong
Kong people were forced to flee to Macau and the rural areas of China.
The Japanese period is still remembered with bitterness by many local
residents.

The Japanese captured Hong Kong on Christmas Day 1941 after a
hard seventeen-day fight that took place partly in the now demolished
Repulse Bay Hotel, with a last stand at Stanley Village, where tourists
currently flock to buy cheap designer jeans. Allied military and civilian
prisoners were interned at Stanley's St. Stephen's College, a maximum
security prison, and at the Shamshuipo Barracks. The latter now
houses some of the Vietnamese "boat people."

The largest group of Chinese refugees came as a result of the civil
war in China between the Nationalists and Communists that ended
with a Communist victory in 1949. Many refugees, especially the
Shanghainese, brought capital and business skills. While the population
of Hong Kong was 1.8 million in 1947, by 1961 it stood at 3.7 million.
For twenty-five days in 1962, when food was short in China, Chinese
border guards allowed 70,000 Chinese just to walk into Hong Kong.
However, it is usually very difficult for Chinese citizens to get permission to leave China.

With the anti-landlord, anti-capitalist, and anti-rightist campaigns in
China, and especially with the Cultural Revolution (1967 to 1976),
more and more refugees risked imprisonment and the sharks in Mirs
Bay to reach Hong Kong. Inspired by the leftist fanaticism of the Red
Guards on the mainland, local activists in Hong Kong set off bombs,
organized labor strikes, and demonstrated both against the British
rulers and Hong Kong's Chinese policemen. They taunted the latter
with "Will the British take you when they go?" But the revolutionaries
did not have popular support and the disruptions lasted less than a
year.

A side note: people who bought property then and sold in the early
1980s made a fortune.

In the late 1970s half a million Chinese refugees, disillusioned with
Communism and eager for a better standard of living for themselves
and their families, came to Hong Kong.

Until October 1980, the Hong Kong government had a curious
"touch-base" policy, a critical game of "hide and seek." Any Chinese
who managed to get past the barbed wire, attack dogs, and Gurkha
border patrols to the urban areas was allowed to stay and work—
manpower was needed for local industries then. At first, a similarly
lenient policy was applied to the Vietnamese boat people who arrived
between 1975 and 1982. Over 100,000 of these refugees were allowed

to work in Hong Kong pending transfer to permanent homes abroad, and 14,000 were given permanent resident status. As the number of countries willing to take them has dwindled, Hong Kong has been detaining recently arrived refugees indefinitely in closed camps, much like prisons, in the hope that no more boat people will come. Hong Kong simply doesn't have room for many more people. You will pass one of the detention centers if you take a ferry to Silvermine Bay on Lantau Island.

In 1980, jobs became less plentiful as a result of the worldwide recession. With an ever-increasing population, the standard of services in Hong Kong was deteriorating. After consulting China, the government decreed that everyone had to carry a Hong Kong identification card. No one could get a job, hospital treatment, or even take part in a lottery without one. Police roadblocks and boat checks became common. Illegal Chinese immigrants were sent back to China, and some repeat offenders were jailed.

The future of Hong Kong after the expiration of the New Territories lease on June 30, 1997, was understandably the big question hanging over the colony from the moment Britain's Prime Minister, Margaret Thatcher, set foot in Peking in September of 1982, to start the talks with China's top man, Deng Xiaoping. China stated from the beginning that it wanted to repossess all of Hong Kong. Officially, Britain was only willing to return the New Territories, but no one believed a Hong Kong without them would be economically viable. The New Territories consist of more than 97 percent of the territory in Hong Kong and include most of the manufacturing facilities, the airport, and the container port.

China proposed that Hong Kong become a Special Administrative Region under the Chinese flag, with a Chinese governor. The Chinese added a 50-year guarantee of autonomy, effective July 1, 1997, labeling the deal "one country/two systems."

The negotiations between China and Britain lasted for nearly two years, with China applying pressure by announcing that if a solution was not found by September 1984, it would declare one unilaterally. An agreement was inevitable.

Hong Kong's economy didn't react well to political uncertainty. Land prices fell. The stock market plunged by as much as 50 percent from the end of 1981 to the end of 1983. The Hong Kong dollar careened to almost HK$10 to the US dollar in September 1983, from HK$5.70 at the end of 1981, forcing the government to intervene reluctantly by stabilizing the local unit at HK$7.80 to one US dollar. Emigration reached record levels.

The final agreement, both signatories say, gives Hong Kong as many safeguards and special freedoms as possible (very different from what

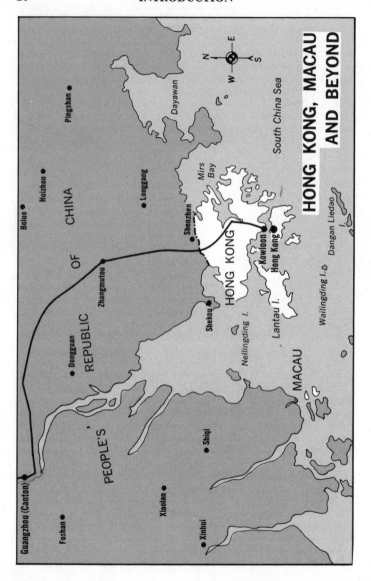

HONG KONG, MACAU AND BEYOND

is practiced and allowed across the border in the People's Republic of China). For the most part, the people of Hong Kong are resigned to a "it could have been worse" philosophy. But Hong Kong's uncertainty about its future as a Special Administrative Region of China continues; no one can know what it will mean. Yet, Hong Kong is still where the action is, where money can be made. So life goes on as usual.

Macau

The Cantonese call Macau "O Mun," or trade gate. The name actually means "Bay of the goddess A-Ma," patroness of seafarers. The territory is across the Pearl River delta from Hong Kong, 45 miles southeast, accessible from there by jetfoil, hydrofoil, hoverferry, jet catamaran, or just plain ferry. The jetfoils take only an hour. The only other way to get there is difficult—by land from China.

Macau, the territory, consists of a peninsula also named Macau (2.1 square miles) and two offshore islands: Taipa (1.4 square miles) and Coloane (2.5 square miles). Taipa is joined to Macau by a 1.6 mile bridge and to Coloane by a 1.5 mile causeway. Most visitor attractions are on the peninsula and can be seen in one day, but are better savored with more time.

Not surprisingly, the weather in Macau is similar to that in Hong Kong, but there is less smog. Macau is what Hong Kong used to be ten years ago, a sleepy little place with lots of charm. It also has legalized gambling. The territory has preserved much more of its old architecture than has Hong Kong: pastel-colored Iberian mansions, baroque churches, and ornate, iron-balconied townhouses. Old Chinese mansions show off ceramic tile trim. A hike up the cobbled roads of at least one of Macau's seven hills is imperative for the view and flavor.

Macau exhibits more apparent history than Hong Kong does, especially on the peninsula, but there has been the inevitable spillover of Hong Kong's prosperity and modern highrises. However, with the Portuguese's relaxed attitude to life, Macau will probably never catch up with Hong Kong, thank goodness. Macau *does* lack several of the advantages of Hong Kong, such as British orderliness and drive, as well as its deep-water harbor. (When Macau's harbor began silting up in the early nineteenth century, traders went on to Hong Kong.)

Macau's population of 400,000, of which 95 percent is Cantonese and 3 percent Portuguese, bases its livelihood on tourism, gambling, trade, textiles, garments, toys, and silk flowers. The official language is Portuguese, but Cantonese is much more common and even English is spoken more frequently than Portuguese.

Macau is a center of Catholicism in Asia. Among its people are also Buddhists, Taoists, ancestor worshippers, animists, and Protestants, and its churches and temples are older by a couple of centuries than Hong Kong's. (One should visit Macau looking for both the flavors of old Europe and old Asia.) Then there's the gambling, the cheaper accommodations, and the less-expensive but superb food—Portuguese, Macanese, and Chinese.

Macau is also a duty-free port. Many Chinese products are cheaper than Hong Kong's because rent and labor in Macau is less expensive. There are Portuguese and Chinese festivals, the annual Grand Prix weekend with motor car and motorcycle races, and the noisy excitement of firecrackers (forbidden in Hong Kong). Macau is a gateway to China, which borders it on two sides. You can easily see the mainland, setting across a narrow stretch of water. Macau is a territory administered by Portugal. Its Portuguese period began with the visit of Chinese merchant ships to the Portuguese colony of Malacca on the Malay peninsula in 1513. Portuguese adventurers, intent on lucrative trading, subsequently reached Canton, upriver from today's Macau. In spite of some discouraging results, the Portuguese tenaciously continued their quest and in 1557 the Chinese allowed them to settle.

This, the only piece of China voluntarily ceded to foreigners, was probably presented in return for Portuguese efforts in ridding the area of Japanese and Chinese pirates. The Portuguese wanted a controllable series of small Catholic enclaves in Asia to support their trading.

Using Macau as a base, the Portuguese began to monopolize trade in Asia, especially between China and Japan: silk, Persian carpets, firearms, and spices to Japan; silver to China. Macau also became an important shipbuilding center, having been settled centuries before by sea-faring Fukienese fishermen blown there by a typhoon. With the Portuguese, Macau developed into one of the busiest ports in Asia.

The impressive front of St. Paul's church, built in 1602 by Christians seeking refuge from religious persecutions in Japan, is indicative of Macau's religious importance. The façade—all that remains—was once part of the largest church building in Asia. Just try to imagine the Church's original size from the façade. A typhoon-related fire in 1835 destroyed the church, which was never rebuilt because of lack of funds.

Government at first was by the founding traders themselves. Beginning in 1623, Portugal appointed a succession of captains-major of Macau, who tried unsuccessfully to impose their authority over merchants used to governing themselves. China also controlled Macau by threatening or actually cutting off food supplies and Chinese labor.

Macau's original glory did not last long. In 1639, Japan closed its gates to all but a handful of foreigners. In the next two years, the Dutch captured Malacca and took control of the sea lanes between China and India. The Dutch attempted to capture Macau but failed, and the city remained the only trade entrance for the west. As such it survived on revenues from European and American merchants. In 1808, British troops actually took over Macau, but they withdrew when China strenuously objected.

In 1846, Governor João Maria Ferreira do Amaral tried to strengthen Portuguese authority; he was assassinated by a group of Chinese. But the support given the Portuguese by American, British, and Spanish gunboats helped discourage Chinese attempts at sovereignty for about a century.

Without much business of its own, Macau survived because of licensed gambling, which was introduced in 1850, and gold smuggling. In 1887, Portugal pressed for a treaty, and China confirmed "the perpetual occupation and government of Macau and its dependencies by Portugal."

Macau was proclaimed a province of Portugal in 1951. In 1966, four days of anti-government riots left eight people dead and 212 injured. Touched off by a minor issue, the riots were probably inspired by the Red Guard rallies, which involved more than a million people, in Beijing. Afterwards, Portugal signed a document accepting responsibility for the riots, paid HK$2.5 million compensation, and offered to return Macau to China. But China did not want Macau back. It is a foreign-exchange earner like Hong Kong, though on a much smaller scale. In addition, anything that China did with Macau would affect Hong Kong.

Like Hong Kong, Macau has also received refugees from China from time to time, and during the Japanese occupation of Hong Kong during World War II, some grateful Hong Kong residents flocked to its neutral shores for sanctuary. The population soared to well over today's half a million.

In 1974, Portugal's new socialist government wanted to get rid of its colonies and withdrew all troops from Macau. China again requested that Portugal remain. Macau then became "a Chinese territory under Portuguese administration."

After the Sino-British Agreement of 1984, China turned her attention across the Pearl River estuary and to the question of Portuguese-run Macau. Though a ceded territory—in fact, the first, and it was as a reward—the Portuguese were quite willing to give up Macau a third time. This time China accepted the territory and, in 1987, Lisbon and Peking signed on the dotted line. Macau's sovereignty reverts to China on December 20, 1999. The Sino-Portuguese Agreement is similar to the Sino-British one, guaranteeing Macau's economic and social systems for a further half-century after the hand-over.

THE HONG KONG
WAY OF LIFE

by
SAUL LOCKHART

Saul Lockhart, an American based in Hong Kong since 1967, is the author or co-author of six guidebooks on Asia. He has written numerous articles over the years for a variety of American, Asian and European publications.

As an accident of nineteenth-century history and a modern-day anachronism—albeit a very successful and well-to-do one—Hong Kong is accustomed to walking an emotional tightrope. Though the majority of the 5.5 million Chinese who call this place home were born within its 400 square miles, the territory still very much reflects the refugee mentality of the previous generations.

The waves of humanity that crossed the Sino-British border after Chairman Mao Tse-tung's victory over Generalissimo Chiang Kai-shek in 1949 were matched by different waves of equally desperate Chinese in 1956 and 1962. A steady stream continued escaping during the decade-long Cultural Revolution (1967-1976), culminating in yet another gigantic wave of more than half-a-million between 1978-1980.

These people and their descendents, whether they started out rich and became richer, as many Shanghai industrialists did, or began life in this colony poor—as was the case with most—and slowly worked their way up to the economically comfortable middle-class plateau, still feel the presence of that colossus of the north, which is at one and the same time their cultural heritage and their greatest fear.

For the uninitiated, the words Hong Kong are spelled M O N E Y. Unabashedly, the China-Coast Traders of the 1840s forced this place on a reluctant Lord Palmerston, Queen Victoria's Foreign Secretary, because of its superb and protected anchorages in a large natural harbor that could replace Macau's silted-up one. (His Lordship has carved his own niche in Hong Kong's short history. Upon learning of Her Majesty's latest acquisition, he scornfully described it as "a barren rock with nary a house upon it.")

The gunboat diplomacy of the Opium Wars (and it was this substance on which Hong Kong was founded and its early wealth built) against the weak and hopelessly corrupt Ching Dynasty eventually added more land to the colony and secured Britain's hold.

Through disease and famine, world wars and enemy occupation, corruption and overcrowding, through a high-tension lifestyle which occasionally over the years has erupted into rioting—to say nothing of the eternal political problems which could tear this place asunder—this tiny capitalistic dot has managed to claw its way into the top twenty of the world's trading nations by sheer hard work and business acumen. Aside from that famous harbor, its only "natural" resource is its resourceful people.

Many call this place an "urban beehive," referring to the crowded living conditions and the fast-paced workers in this land-scarce territory. (The Mongkok section in Kowloon has the densest population on earth: 165,000 per square kilometer.) Others refer to it as "an enormous pressure cooker" just waiting to explode. There are those who explain Hong Kong's existence and success as a "combination of British arrogance and Chinese apathy."

A "capitalist pimple on China's communist ass" is probably the most popular epithet, even though this has recently been modified to the more polite "a benign tumor on the underbelly of China." Novelist Han

Su-Yin aptly described Hong Kong in a 1959 article for *Life* with the words "Borrowed Place–Borrowed Time," a phrase which was ignored until used a decade later as the title of a book by the late Australian journalist Richard Hughes about Hong Kong's own Red Guard riots of 1966 and 1967.

All these descriptions are true to a greater or lesser extent. However, the key factor in understanding Hong Kong's collective psyche is that the local population realizes how little control they have, and have had, over their lives and futures. This accidental state of affairs is more apparent in business than in government, for in spite of being a "non-democratic" colony, Hong Kong is one of the freest places in Asia, and the non-elected government takes great care to consult the population before initiating legislation. Like many well-meaning governments, though most times they get it right, every so often they get it wrong and the great cry of public opinion wells up.

The Chinese who live in Hong Kong by choice have abrogated their pure one-man/one-vote type of western democracy in favor of a very stable British-run administration, with a separate executive and judiciary. (And in the Chinese milieu in Asia, where can you find such a democratic institution outside of Singapore?)

The stability afforded Hong Kong by its strict and fair rule of law (à la the West) is, of course, in direct contrast to the instability and cyclical upheavals in China during the same period. Life is by no means perfect in Hong Kong, but life is certainly good and stable enough for formerly desperate people to feel secure enough to settle down, get a job or start a business, and either inch up or leap up the economic ladder to success.

So successful has this process been that Hong Kong, unlike any other colony in history, is financially independent and virtually self-ruling, including participating in and, at times, actually negotiating international treaties. Hong Kong pays 75 percent of the tab for the privilege of keeping British troops in Hong Kong to show the flag. It also built five ships for the Royal Navy on the promise they would be used in Hong Kong waters replacing the three World-War-II minesweepers—which now constitute the British naval presence in Asia—on permanent station in Hong Kong. When in history has a colony voluntarily paid for the colonial troops to be stationed in it and helped outfit the colonial power's navy?

It is in business, though, where Hong Kong's dependence on outside forces beyond its control is paramount. Hong Kong is an export-based economy. If a major market like the United States (the territory's largest) sneezes, it is Hong Kong that gets sick. The reverse is true too, of course. A boom in the U.S. means a large economic spurt in Hong Kong. The imposition of a small trade barrier in the U.S. (perhaps put on for political reasons in an election year) can have drastic consequences here. On the other hand, the removal of a onerous blockage to trade somewhere abroad can bring vast fortunes. The fact that their prosperity or failure may be decided in another country's parliament or congress is fatalistically accepted by businessmen here.

Existing in Hong Kong in complex and at times uncontrollable economic conditions means focusing on the immediate and almost ignoring the future. "A journey of 10,000 miles begins with but one step" is the overriding philosophy.

This attitude carries over directly into business. In London or New York or Tokyo investors talk of getting their return over decades. In Hong Kong, a businessman with that philosophy would not have a chance. He would be stripped to the bone in seconds as if gorged upon by piranha fish. The Hong Kong businessman concentrates on getting his investment capital and profit back in an unbelievable one or two years.

The "long term" does not exist in Hong Kong. Hong Kong is a "now" society and everyone is in a rush. The Territory is almost a perpetual-motion machine. What with the time zones between the financial and stock markets in London and New York, trading—the colony's lifeblood—goes on twenty-four hours a day, pausing only for a public or bank holiday *in the West*. If it is a holiday here but not in the West, trading continues unabated, with the sole exception of a couple days off at Chinese New Year. Visitors need only pause in the crowded and bustling streets to savor the motion and pace of this vibrant, and perhaps vibrating, place.

While an economically successful "perpetual motion" money-making machine, Hong Kong is, nevertheless, constantly forced back upon its own wits and resources because it suffers from a form of isolation much greater than the traditional longing a refugee naturally feels for his homeland and culture. The Chinese in Southeast Asia are actually feared in many countries. Whether they have brought this upon themselves with their superb economic wheeling and dealing, which has upset the ruling Malays, Indonesians, Filipinos, and Thais, is a moot point. But the fact remains that while Hong Kong Chinese are welcome to spend their money on holiday and to invest in many Asian countries, the host countries really do not want them, and have laws restricting their activities and rights.

Singaporeans, for example, can fall back on the natural pride of their nationality. Hong Kongians cannot, because Britain has made it abundantly clear with progressively restrictive immigration laws beginning in the 1960s that Hong Kong Chinese are only tolerated in small, restricted numbers.

Such total lack of control over life and a fatalistic dependence on *joss* (luck) takes its toll. The fates (gods) and *joss* rule their lives and the life of the colony as a whole, so most Hong Kong Chinese do not waste time thinking of the pros and cons of the latest problem or restriction. They adjust and buckle down to make money, that being one of the few unifying threads in the Middle Kingdom's turbulent millennia that has given these uprooted millions a semblence of stability.

But even a tightly focused society like Hong Kong feels strain and perhaps is in danger of being overwound.

Hong Kong's frenetic but comfortably familiar assumptions of life were thrown completely topsy turvy in September 1982 when the populace woke up to find British Prime Minister Margaret Thatcher (fresh from her victory over Argentina preserving Britain's sovereignty in the Falklands) in Peking negotiating Hong Kong's future with China's paramount leader, Deng Xiaoping.

All of a sudden the long-hidden future jumped to the fore. The time bomb that was always there could be heard ticking. The future became the present, and negotiations over what happens after the expiration of Britain's lease on the New Territory (90 per cent of the colony) in June, 1997, was being not only discussed, but negotiated.

Though history will of course have the final say, Mrs. Thatcher began by reaffirming Britain's sovereignty over Hong Kong Island and the miniscule Kowloon Peninsula, which combined are an economically unviable one-tenth of the territory. (Of course she never mentioned anything about defending Hong Kong against the Chinese who can regain the territory by force with a phone call if they wanted an economic wreck of a city and 5.5 million more mouths to feed.)

China reacted sharply and bitterly. Successive Chinese governments have always rejected the three nineteenth-century treaties (two of which ceded Hong Kong Island and the Kowloon Peninsula to Britain in perpetuity, while the third leased the New Territories for 99 years) as "unequal." Furthermore, the Chinese have always stated publicly that the question of Hong Kong (and, for that matter, its colonial neighbor Macau) was an internal one and would be solved when it suits China.

No Chinese leader wants to go down in history as giving Hong Kong away a second time by ceding British sovereignty over treaties which had been questioned ever since they were signed in the 1840s. If it ever came down to a choice between national pride (sovereignty) and logic (the desperately needed foreign exchange earned through Hong Kong), there is no doubt China would choose the former.

It is said Mrs. Thatcher ignored the Foreign Office advice in this matter and declared her stand for sovereignty, effectively eliminating at the very beginning any chance of the quick "Macau" solution. (In

1974, after a coup back in Portugal, China refused to take Macau back. So Macau was changed from a "colony" to a "Chinese territory under Portuguese administration," complete with a Portuguese governor and flag.)

As the Year of the Pig began in 1983, Hong Kong hunkered down for a battle of the giants. China unleashed a bombardment of propaganda, "consulting" with various Hong Kong organizations and people who traveled north in a steady stream. Britain kept a stiff upper lip and remained silent. About mid-year, China, evidently fed up with the British position, tightened the thumbscrews by announcing that if an agreement was not reached by September, 1984 (in the Year of the Rat, "a year of re-building and revitalization," according to the fortune tellers), China would announce its own unilateral solution to the problem, effectively fulfilling a Year of the Pig prophecy: "A time to make those long-considered moves at home or at work."

"Stability and prosperity," the key words used in all joint communiqués illustrating the aims of both sides, was renamed by local wags the "S & P Syndrome" to illustrate the near panic which hit Hong Kong.

The fall in Hong Kong's property market (which began a year earlier) was exacerbated. The stock market fell as a result. Investment and re-investment levels slid, in spite of a record growth in 1983 of 25 percent in exports (which in any other year would have been cause for celebration). The Hong Kong dollar came under severe attack, falling to a record HK $9.50 to the US$1, from around HK $5.60 before Mrs. Thatcher's visit, before the government intervened pegging it at its current rate of HK $7.80. The Hong Kong budget (1983/84), for the first time in a decade, went into deficit spending, something very familiar in the United States, but unheard of in Hong Kong, which believes in surpluses.

Record long lines formed at the various commissions and consulates as the diplomats reported an astronomical number of requests for immigration papers. No one knows precisely how much money flowed out of Hong Kong, but it was probably in the billions. So much was flowing out that neighbors like the Philippines, Thailand, and Malaysia actually set up programs to attract and entice this Hong Kong panic money.

Through it all, "1997" became the buzzword of 1983 and 1984. Even those who had no hope of leaving, whose main concern was filling their rice bowl daily, were drawn into the frenzy. Fear, as only a refugee can express it, slowly surfaced as the talks dragged on with no results.

British MPs came and went, each adding a bit to the fire. Questions in the House of Commons were raised and were answered. The National People's Congress gave its guarantees. The Hong Kong governor divided his time between Hong Kong, Peking, and London, often taking a group of Executive Council (the highest body) members with him to Number 10 for face-to-face meetings with the Prime Minister.

China toned down its earlier threats, presumably as Britain, in the secret negotiations, refined its demands on sovereignty, probably a polite way of saying it would give up its claims. China announced that Hong Kong would become a special administrative region with its own currency and laws, ruled by Hong Kong people. In early 1984, China's Prime Minister Zhao Ziyang, on tour in the U.S., stated that the capitalist system would be guaranteed in Hong Kong for 50 years after 1997. Foreigners and foreign investment would be welcome.

There are hundreds of questions to be answered when Hong Kong's current status will alter. What about such international treaties as the General Agreement on Trade and Tariffs, the basis for Hong Kong's trade and quotas with the West? Aviation treaties? Shipping Conference treaties? Free-port status? Interpol? The reserves (currently put at HK$18 billion)? Its position in the Asian Development Bank and the International Monetary Fund? What happens to Hong Kong's excellent international credit ratings? The effect on current government-backed long-term borrowings by the Mass Transit Railway? The booming money and stock markets? What about Hong Kong's fair and separate judiciary, with its appeals system and democratic checks on strong government? Even the mundane must be decided: What side of the street should Hong Kong vehicles drive on?

From the sidelines, watching Hong Kong's future with as much interest as Hong Kong, London, and Peking, is Macau. Technically, there are no problems for Macau. Its political status has already been decided. But in reality Macau's future will be affected by whatever is decided about Hong Kong.

On September 26, 1984, China and Britain finally initialed their agreement, one which is to allow capitalism to flourish in Hong Kong. But China's political instability leaves Hong Kong uneasy about the validity of the agreement. Will an agreement—any agreement—reached with a circa 1984 Chinese government be binding or mean anything to a circa 1997 Chinese government? It is China's historical instability compared with Hong Kong's stability that has Hong Kong on edge. An agreement that allowed the pursuit of capitalism to flourish whilst in the bosom of the Middle Kingdom would probably be most Hong Kongers definition of nirvana, since they have always felt a bit uneasy about the necessity of making their pile under auspices of a foreign flag.

Whatever the eventual outcome, it is hard to imagine Hong Kong without its lifeblood: business. And as long as there is business, there will be visitors, so come and enjoy yourself in this mad hothouse.

FOOD AND DRINK IN HONG KONG AND MACAU

by
BARRY GIRLING

If you are coming to Hong Kong for the first time, there are certain misconceptions that you must leave at home. First off, Hong Kong doesn't just have some of the better Chinese food in the world; *it has the best.*

Such a statement may not find immediate recognition in Taiwan or the People's Republic of China, but the proof of the pudding is in the eating, as they say in the barbarian West: A lot of Taiwanese and mainland Chinese come to Hong Kong to eat. It is historical fact that the past Imperial Chinese dynasties brought their Southern Chinese cook-subjects up from Canton to Peking to serve in the emperors' kitchens. For many centuries the Cantonese (the people from what is now Hong Kong's adjacent Chinese province of Guangdong) were acknowledged as the Middle Kingdom's finest cooks.

There is an old Chinese maxim that tells listeners where to find the prettiest girls, where to get married, where to die, and so forth—the "where to eat" is Canton (now called Guangzhou in the approved official romanization of Chinese names).

Hong Kong's 5.5 million-plus population is 98 percent Chinese. The vast majority of that percentage is Cantonese (they include the significant group of Chiu Chow people, whose families originated around the port city of Swatow). It sometimes seems that *every* Cantonese is a natural cook. Food is a subject of overriding importance, and most Cantonese are skilled judges of a roast chicken, snake soup, black-bean sauce, steamed fish, barbecued pig, vegetable soup, double-boiled duck, *dimsum* daytime snack, or the 400 or more "classic" standard dishes on a Cantonese restaurant's menu.

Indeed it is often rightly claimed that the Cantonese "live to eat" (as do the French) rather than "eat to live." Find out how true that statement is on a culinary tour of Hong Kong. Then take a side excursion to Macau, the Portuguese-administered enclave 40 miles and an hour's jetfoil away. There you will discover a few facts that restore a little "face" to the non-Chinese food lover.

You must also lose some other misconceptions. There's *no* such thing as a fortune cookie in a Hong Kong restaurant. Being great marketing minds, the "overseas" Chinese came up with that business-attracting novelty. The Cantonese also invented "chop suey" overseas. The origin is disputed: some people say the Californian goldfield canteens produced the last-minute hotchpotch of chop suey, some give the credit (or blame) to the Australian goldfields.

Whoever is responsible, chop suey is a symbol of the Cantonese skill of making a silk's purse out of a sow's ear, in culinary terms. The standard Cantonese menu illustrates a kitchen's and a people's imagination. Every part of an animal or fish or vegetable is made edible, deliciously so. In the bad old days, when southern China was an economically depressed, far-from-fertile agricultural region, such abilities to create feasts out of anything at hand were crucial. But the Cantonese made an art out of a necessity. Their cooking is their claim to immortality.

Some of the dishes on a typical Hong Kong menu may sound strange, even unappetizing. Don't choke when you read the names of certain ingredients. Try goose webs, cockerels' testicles, cows' innards, snakes (in season), pig's shanks, and other things that may not be served at McDonalds. After all, the thrill of foreign travel *is* the taste of new experiences. Who scorns the French for eating snails and frogs, or the Japanese for eating raw fish, or the Scots for stuffing mince in a sheep's stomach lining? A visit to a fine haven of top-class Cantonese cooking, such as *King Bun, Sun Tung Lok,* or *Unicorn,* is an eye-opener. It shows how an amazing variety of ingredients are turned by culinary magic into food with flair, sauces of distinction, long-simmered double-boiled elixirs of goodness, quick-sautéed taste sensations of freshness that truly tickles the palate.

Then visit a daytime *dimsum* palace. Served up from before dawn to around 5:00 or 6:00 P.M., the Cantonese daytime snacks of *dimsum* are miniature works of art. There are about 2,000 types in the Cantonese repertoire. Most *dimsum* restaurants prepare 100 varieties daily. Generally served in bamboo baskets, steaming mildly, the trios of Cantonese-style buns, rissoles, crêpes, and cakes are a parade of the world's finest hors d'oeuvres. Many are works of culinary engineering expertise—such as a soup with prawns served in a translucent rice pastry shell, or a thousand-layered cake, or the ubiquitous spring roll that *has* to be tasted in Hong Kong.

There are hundreds of *dimsum* restaurants. The Hong Kong Tourist Association publishes a comprehensive listing of some of the better ones that welcome tourists. The publication also provides color illustrations of the main *dimsum* favorites. Try them out on the *Jumbo* floating restaurant in Aberdeen harbour, at Ocean Centre's *Ocean Palace,* the New World Centre's *Ocean City,* the *Blue Heaven* on Queen's Road, Central, or *King Bun.* Or, preferably in the company of Cantonese colleagues, visit the hallowed culinary shrine of the *Luk Yu Teahouse* in Central.

A word about the Luk Yu. Luk Yu is more than a restaurant. It is a rare historical monument in Hong Kong. It's fitting that a restaurant should be an unofficially preserved monument in this culinary capital of the world. First operated early in the twentieth century as a wood-beamed, black-fanned, brass-edged spot for Chinese gentlemen to partake of tea, *dimsum,* and gossip, the Luk Yu was lovingly relocated over a decade ago. Everything was kept intact—marble-backed chairs, floor spitoons and kettle-warmers, brass coat hooks, lock-up liquor cabinets for regular patrons, and a Sikh doorman. Despite the modernity of air-conditioning, the fans still decorate a plain ceiling that looks down on elaborately framed scrolls, carved wood booth partitions, and colored glass panels. The ancient wooden staircase still creaks upwards to the upper floors, where Hong Kong's gentlemen gather quietly to run the territory's government and business.

Modernity has brought English-language fluency, bilingual menus (but not for the individually served *dimsum* items), and some good manners to Luk Yu. The adventurous tourist will seek out daytime *dim sum* palaces where such modern affectations do not exist—as in the authentic teahouses of Mongkok, where local customers still "walk the bird" at dawn (taking one's pet caged bird out for a morning gossip with its friends is thought to be a very masculine old-fashioned Chinese concept that lives on in Hong Kong).

Birds are also to be eaten, of course. As far as the Cantonese are concerned, anything that "keeps its back to Heaven" is fit for cooking. Only cannibals won't be satisfied in Hong Kong. Bird-tasting experiences in Hong Kong should include a feast of quails, smooth salted chicken, sweet roasted chicken in lemon sauce, or minced pigeon served in lettuce leaf "bowls" (that are rolled up with a plum sauce "adhesive"). Pigeons in dozens of different forms can best be enjoyed in the New Territories, around the new city of Shatin.

Fish can be relished anywhere. Hong Kong is a major port and collection of fishing communities—something easily forgotten once the sophisticated metropolitan urbanity surrounds the city-centered visitor. Go to the islands, to Lamma especially, for fine seafood feasts. Or take the bus and ferry trip way out to Lyemun, a village of stilted restaurants at the far east of the harbor. Out there one wanders along roofed-over gangplanks to pick fresh fish from the massive fish tanks, haggle over its price, and take it into any restaurant for cooking into a feast of an almost-instant seafood *al fresco* occasion.

At Causeway Bay, a small fleet of sampans turns dining out into a memorably different experience. Your private floating restaurant table bobs past other craft selling shellfish, fresh fruit and vegetables, beer and spirits. There is even a floating Cantonese Opera mini-troupe that can be hired to serenade your open-air floating meal.

The floating experience is of course the *Jumbo* restaurant at Aberdeen. It is moored to another couple of Disneylandish floating homes of seafood and gaudy *chinoiserie*. Their multi-colored carvings and murals are a sight worth seeing. The *Jumbo*, a 2,000-seat three-decker, is a marvel of outrageous ostentatiousness. It has a smaller sister ship out at Shatin, moored near the Royal Hong Kong Jockey Club's new racetrack.

It's time to note that there is no such thing as "Chinese" cooking here in China. Every good "Chinese" cook has his (or sometimes her) own repertoire that will reflect his family clan's origin. Most of Hong Kong's restaurants are Cantonese. Others concentrate on Pekingese or northern styles, Shanghainese specialties, or the other regional styles of Sichuan (*a.k.a.* Szechuan) or Chiu Chow cooking. There are a few spots that offer Hakka-style food, some Mongolian specialty restaurants (featuring hot pots), and even a Taiwanese café on Food Street.

Food Street, in Causeway Bay, is a good place for a first-timer to start discovering the variety of food available in Hong Kong. There are now two covered, fountained arcades of relatively well-managed restaurants to suit most tastes and budgets. All around them, in an area that's generally named after the "Daimaru" department store, are literally hundreds of other cafés and restaurants.

Other favored concentrations of eating places are found in old Wanchai, once the fictional home for Suzie Wong and now a struggling night life area that's run out of sailors. Restaurants have appeared instead, alongside the topless bars, hostess-filled nightclubs, and dance halls that are expensive ways to get a drink in Hong Kong (and should be avoided by any serious drinker).

In "old" Tsimshatsui, to both sides of Nathan Road from the Peninsula Hotel up to the Jordan Road junction, there is another batch of good long-established restaurants. And Tsimshatsui East has skyscraper podiums bursting with a wide variety of eating spots—from grand Cantonese diners to cheerful little cafés. There, as everywhere, you'll find not just Cantonese fare, but Korean barbecues, Singaporean satays, Peking ducks, Shanghainese breads and eel dishes, fine Western cuisine—and junk food, of course.

Deciding what and where to eat can therefore be a headache in Hong Kong. There *is* an embarrassment of riches. This guidebook's restaurant listings will help. Once in Hong Kong, buy the Hong Kong Tourist Association's "Visitor's Guide To Chinese Food In Hong Kong" from the H.K.T.A. offices. It costs HK$10 and is a useful introduction to Chinese regional cuisines, chopstick wielding, *dimsum* selecting, and other topics that can terrify a novice.

It helps to think of China as a Europe with a difference. As in Europe there are obvious culinary variations between the cold-wintered northern regions (the Pekingese/Mongolian cuisine) and the temperate or semitropical southern climes (where Sichuan's chilied spiciness seems natural). The "difference" is that the various Chinese regions have been practicing cooking as a fine art for quite a few centuries longer than their European counterparts.

In simple terms, the Northern or Peking cuisine is designed to fill and warm—noodles, dumplings, and breads of various types are more evident than rice. Mongolian or Manchurian hot pots (a sort of fondue-cum-barbecue) are specialities, and firm flavors (garlic, ginger, leek, etc.) are popular. Desserts, of little interest to Cantonese, are heavy and sweet. Feasts have long been favored in the north, and not just by emperors composing week-long banquets with elaborate centerpieces such as Peking Duck (a three-course marvel of skin slices, sautéed meat, a rich soup of duck bones, and Tien Tsin cabbage). Beggar's Chicken, about which you'll hear varying legendary origins, is another culinary ceremony, in which a stuffed seasoned lotus–leaf-wrapped, clay-baked bird releases heavenly aromas when its clay is cracked open.

Farther south, the Shanghai region (including Hangzhou) developed tastes similar to Peking's, but with an oilier, sweeter style that favored preserved meats, fish, and vegetables. In Hong Kong, the Shanghainese cafés are generally just that—unostentatious cafés with massive "buffet" displays of preserved or fresh snacks that are popular with late-nighters.

The territory's Chiu Chow restaurants also come alive late at night—especially in the Chiu Chow-populated areas of the Western District (on Hong Kong Island) or in parts of western Kowloon. As with Shanghainese and Cantonese cuisine, the Chiu Chow repertoire emphasizes its homeland's marine traditions, especially for shellfish. The exotic-sounding "bird's nest" is the great Chiu Chow delicacy. Although it is actually the refined congealed saliva "glue" of nest-building swallows (mainly gathered from Gulf of Siam cliff-face nests) and may therefore sound terrible, its is often exquisitely flavored. The dish is also deemed to be aphrodisiacal, as are many of China's most expensive luxury food items. That's why a visit to a Chinese department store should include a shocked glance at the "medicine" counters' natural foods. The prices of top-grade bird's nest, shark's fins, deer horns, ginseng roots, and other time-tested fortifications are staggering. The laws of supply and demand are very apparent on the price tags—the demand for aphrodisiacs did not die out in 1949.

The roughest, simplest fare can appear to be that of the Sichuan (or Szechuan) region. At first tasting, the chilied, spicy fieriness of pepper-corned dishes, akin to both Thai and Indian cuisines, can seem tongue-searingly overwhelming. After a while, when the taste buds have blossomed again, the subtleties of Sichuan spicing will be apparent—particularly in the classic Smoked Duck specialty, where camphor wood chips and red tea leaves add magical tinges to a finely seasoned, day–long-marinated duck.

Other regional variations (such as those of Hunan or the Hakka people) are not as distinctive as the major regional cuisines and are rarely found in Hong Kong. But there are a host of alternates for any visitor who wants a taste of adventure.

Chinese-influenced Asian cuisines are well represented. Even before the exodus of ethnic Chinese from Vietnam, that nation's exciting blend of native, French, and Chinese cooking styles was popular in Hong Kong. Now there are many cafés and a few smart restaurants specializing in prawns on sugarcane, mint-leaved meals, Vietnamese-style (labeled "VN") salamis, omelettes, and fondues.

The most ubiquitous Asian culture is the multi-ethnic "Malaysian," a budget diner's culinary United Nations that includes native Malay, Indian, and Straits Chinese dishes, as well as "European" meals and the Sino-Malay culinary cross-culture of the *nonya* cooking, which Malay wives developed to satisfy Chinese spouses.

"Indian" restaurants are also popular, and not just with Hong Kong's significant long-resident population of immigrants from the subcontinent. Usually the Indian kitchens concentrate on the northern Moghul styles of cooking, with reliable tandoori dishes. Vegetarians also find pleasures at Indian cafés. Thailand has not been forgotten, and the territory sports more than a half a dozen spicy Thai restaurants.

Northeast Asia is also well represented. Some observers claim that Hong Kong has some of the world's finest Japanese restaurants, which thrive on local seafood catches and still tempt big spenders with their imports of the highly prized Kobe or Matsukaya beef (marbled slices of fine flavor produced by beer-massaged and pampered steers). Smaller spenders welcome the many local Korean cafés, whose inexpensive barbecues (bulgogi) provide that country's distinctive garlicked, marinated meats and the mini-buffet of preserved *kimchee* selections.

Then there's Indonesia, which has given Hong Kong another host of cheap nourishing cafés. And then there's Europe, and a culinary wonderland of fine French restaurants (mostly in the top hotels), British pubs, Germanic wining-and-dining havens, deli delights, and a sprinkling of delightful offbeat eating experiences—from Dutch-Flemish to plate-smashing Graeco-Levantine.

Does it all sound too good to be true? Well, there are a few caveats to note before you enter what Hongkongers feel is the culinary capital of Asia.

Although the Cantonese are the world's finest cooks, they make some of the impolitest service staff in the world. The Cantonese are proud, some say arrogant, and their dialect has a belligerent tone and abruptness that translates poorly in English. Don't expect smiles, gushing servitude, and obsequiousness: Hong Kong isn't Bangkok or Manila. It's friendly, in its own abrupt way, and it's certainly efficient. If you meet smiles as well, count yourself lucky. And give the extra percentage on the tip that the pleasant waiter deserves.

Don't tip at local corner cafés or the few remaining roadside *dai pai dong* food stalls; it's not expected. And wherever you eat, at the top or lower ends of the culinary scale, *always* check prices beforehand, especially for fresh fish, which is now a luxury in Hong Kong. "Seasonal" prices apply to many dishes, and can be steep. And do note that there are various categories of prized Chinese delicacies on menus—"superlative" shark's fin, abalone, bird's nest, and bamboo fungus, for example, can cost an emperor's ransom. Although few Hong Kong restaurants set out to rip off tourists (certainly not those that are sign-bearing members of the Hong Kong Tourist Association), waiters will of course try to "sell up."

Also, don't settle for the safe standbys for tourists. Sweet and sour pork, chop suey, and fried rice *can* be marvelous in Hong Kong. But the best dishes are off the menu, on tablecards written only in Chinese advertising seasonal specialties. Ask for translations, ask for interesting recommendations, try new items—show that you are adventurous, and the captains will respond, giving you the respect and fine tastes you deserve.

Hong Kong's great food requires little lubrication. Although beer is quaffed happily by the younger generation, drinking is not a favorite occupation for Hong Kong's workoholics. Sobriety is—with exceptions, which nearly all take place at celebratory occasions. A visitor soon understands why Hong Kong is the largest per capita export market for French brandy producers. Toasts are proposed with every course at a banquet, along with convivial phrases of alcoholic exhortation for each guest to drink his or her neighbor under the table. Each toast is a tumblerful of neat brandy. A visitor will not be expected to keep up with the toasting, which brings flushes of embarrassed joy to Chinese cheeks. Visitors should certainly not attempt to keep up if the toasting is being conducted with Chinese rice wines of lethal potency, such as the *mao tai* with which former President Richard Nixon celebrated the resumption of Sino-American diplomatic relations with Chairman Mao Tse-tung.

Some Chinese wines are a connoisseur's delight. Several, when warmed, have the full-bodied flavor of a good sherry. Most are rotgut potions, though, and guided sampling is wise. In the past few years China has started to mass-produce its own grape wines, with French supervision. The results aren't bad, and a bottle of *Great Wall* or *Dynasty* white wine is a pleasant companion for Cantonese food, if there is nothing else available.

Budget tax increases since 1983 have made drinking more expensive than it used to be in the free port of Hong Kong. However, most of the top Western restaurants in the major hotels laid down fine cellars some years back. Bargains can be found, and there are excellent vintage products from Europe, California, and Australia.

Macau

For good, cheap, and cheerful wines that have traveled wonderfully well, go to the nearby Portuguese enclave of Macau, 40 miles across the Pearl River estuary. Red and white table wines and sparkling *vino verde*—the young green wine—can be drunk with happy abandon on sunlit terraces facing the blue open sea that laps against harborside promenades, in this magical Mediterranean-style retreat for Hong-kongers.

Despite its recent attempts to catch up with Hong Kong's modernity, the four-century-old Portuguese territory is still a place where time stopped in the middle of the nineteenth century. Food is one of Macau's finest charms. Few visitors appreciate that there is a special Macanese cuisine. It reflects the sea-going Portuguese colonists' catholic culinary tastes. They took the appetizing influences of the Mediterranean, Brazil, Africa (Angola and Mozambique), India (Goa), and all Asia, brought them to Macau, absorbed the traditions and ingredients of South China, and cooked up a culinary storm of excitements.

Codfish *(bacalhau)* is a staple fish dish, in various forms. So is the Macau sole that rivals Dover's for flavor. Local prawns are jumbo joys when spiced in African style, peppered and chilied in a *piri-piri* fashion. And the "simple" chicken is just a bouquet of spices when it becomes the famous African chicken. The homeland favorite of Portuguese sardines is supplemented by local Pearl delta stocks. For meat dishes the Macanese take the ox and create oxtail magic. Or they catch local rabbits to make hunter's stews. Pork goes into Brazilian-style stews *(feijoadas)* packed with beans, vegetables, and pungent Portuguese sausages.

With most dishes the early Macanese housewife added her Portuguese Empire's spices, and heavy traces of garlic, and lots of oil. Who cared if the climate didn't really recommend them; potatoes and crisp bread rolls (always served warm) were essential companions. Then the Macanese met Chinese quails and ducks, ginger and soy, and the resulting feast of textures and tastes gave Macau a glory that may last longer than its countless churches, bewitching banyan trees, and sleepy fortresses.

The cheapness of Macau's bistros (a breed of casual diner Hong Kong cannot afford to supply) is just good luck for Hongkongers. However, it must be admitted that most Hong Kong Chinese go to Macau to gamble, and no one goes there for its Cantonese restaurants.

Culinary adventurers go to Macau for the romance. There are various ways to eat in Macau. In the open air—on terraces overlooking the harbor or Coloane's beaches; in Mediterranean-style houses with white-washed or pink-speckled walls, gnarled wood staircases, sunlight-filtering shutters, and quarry tile-flooring complementing pretty hand-painted Portuguese ceramic wall tiles; in farm cottages, converted Macanese homes, or even (at lunchtimes only) on a balcony overlooking a supermarket.

Above all else, one eats slowly, savouring the food and the moment. That can be done in Hong Kong, but only in top-flight restaurants at great expense. In Macau the residents cannot imagine rushing a meal, diluting wine with ice, or getting upset if a waiter gets orders completely confused.

Take time out in Macau to remember what food and drinks are meant to be—leisurely necessities of life that should also be life-enhancing. Find a balcony or terrace, sip your happy humble wine or powerful Portuguese brandy, watch Chinese junks and sampans chug slowly through the green-and-blue South China Sea islands, and past rusty Portuguese cannons, chew thoughtfully on an African chicken, pause, and enjoy life. Or gather with friends and babble as animatedly as the Macanese do, using a meal for the inconsequential conversation that is part of the splendid enclave's lifestyle.

There's nothing much wrong with Hong Kong's dining-out scene. It *is* one of the world's finest. It's just that there's so much right about Macau's laid-back style. Gourmets may scoff, but true travelers will taste the difference.

 SIGHTSEEING CHECKLIST. Nobody can see or do everything during a brief stay in Hong Kong. What with all the shopping—and *that* after all is the territory's main claim to fame—there is rarely enough time to attend all the fittings at your tailor and tuck in a few grand Chinese repasts. The following attractions and experiences are "musts" on anyone's list of things to do.

Two tips, though: If you are having clothes made here, get on with that laborious task the moment you arrive—which will allow you more time for fittings, even if the tailor insists you do not need them. The second tip is: Do yourself a favor and and get out of the hotel and try some real Chinese cuisine. Just because it's different from the Chinese food you're accustomed to back home, doesn't mean it's bad.

HONG KONG

Aw Boon Haw Gardens. Since these are commonly known as the Tiger Balm Gardens, we are referring to them as such in this book. See "Tiger Balm Gardens."

Cat Street. Once the center for Hong Kong's dens of iniquity and a Thieves' Market, Cat Street is now one of Hong Kong's famed shopping alleys and ladder streets. Most of the street stalls have been replaced by buildings with real shops, but it is still worth a trip. The real name of Cat Street is Upper and Lower Lascar roads.

Cityplaza I & II. If you have kids with you and want to keep them occupied while you hunt, this place—one of Hong Kong's largest shopping centers—has ice skating and roller skating, plus tons of shopping.

Cloth Alley. This is the local term for the alleys that sell clothes and cloth. The real cloth alley—which only sells cloth—is called Wing On Street and is located in Central District. The two other clothing alleys in Central District—Li Yuen Street East and Li Yuen Street West, which run between Queen's Road

Central and Des Veoux Road Central—are also often referred to collectively as "cloth alley."

Causeway Bay. A fine shopping area with big Japanese and Chinese department stores, street hawkers, and lots of little shops. Prices are cheaper than they are in Central. If you travel by tram, tell the driver you want to get off at Daimaru (the name of the first Japanese department store in the area). From Kowloon or Central, use Mass Transit Railway. There is good eating in this area, too.

Deep Water Bay Beach. A lovely place to while away your holiday.

Food Street. Hong Kong's answer to one-stop eating, this is a street full of restaurants in Causeway Bay—everything from Cantonese *dimsum* to Japanese "sushi," and Western food, too.

Floating Restaurants (Aberdeen). The three floating eateries are so world famous they must be included in any sightseeing recommendations. However, these three are not the best places to sample Cantonese cuisine, nor are they known for their courtesy. Read the in-depth report in the "Dining Out" section of this guide.

Floating Sampan Restaurants (Causeway Bay Typhoon Shelter). Not to be confused with Aberdeen's famous eateries, these are *sampans* with tables and chairs sculled into the shelter. Like fish attracted to a beacon, the floating kitchens, floating bars, even a floating orchestra, pull up alongside for your pleasure. (Open only from April–October.)

Happy Valley Racetrack. Of interest only to those who follow the Sport of Kings. See "Gambling" and "Spectator Sports" sections of this guide to find out how a visitor can partake of the action.

Hollywood Road (between Arbuthnot Road and its junction with Lyndhurst Terrace). Antique row. Shop after shop selling high-quality Chinese and Asian antiques. For the older antique shops, keep walking down Hollywood Road in a westerly direction (away from town).

Landmark. One of the territory's best shopping centers with a beautiful atrium. The fountain in the middle becomes a stage through some deft maneuvering and there is free entertainment daily, as well as a weekly Chinese cultural presentation sponsored by the Hong Kong Tourist Association. Home of some of the classiest boutiques in town.

Ocean Park. A 170-acre marineland on the south side of Hong Kong Island. Performing dolphins and a killer whale, whale-feeding area, kiddie's zoo, seal shows, bird shows, seals, penguins, and many other creatures of the sea living *au naturel* in a wave cove (with overwater and underwater viewing) and an aquarium that is home to more than 5,000 saltwater fish, including sharks. Ocean Park also has a walk-through aviary and a water-world type of amusement park, complete with roller coaster and other rides.

The Peak, Peak Tower, Peak Tram. The top of the colony, not only in geography but in prestige if you live there. Take the venerable (almost 100-years-old) Peak Tram (which is actually a funicular railway) up to the futuristic-looking Peak Tower for one of the most spectacular views in the world. (Free bus service from Star Ferry, Hong Kong.)

Poor Man's Nightclub. An open-air night market near the China Ferry Terminal, Hong Kong Island. Well worth a wander through for the occasional good buy and, of course, the ubiquitous local color.

Repulse Bay Beach. The territory's most popular beach, easily reachable by public bus (and taxi and mini-bus) from Central. Very crowded on weekends and public holidays.

Stanley Village. The once sleepy fishing village has now become one of the territory's largest street markets for over-run designer fashions and other sturdy, but non-designer, clothes: parkas, sweaters, jeans of all types, etc. Easily reachable by bus from Central.

Star Ferry. For less than a U.S. dime or U.K.7p, the seven-minute first-class excursion across Hong Kong's bustling and beautiful harbor aboard the famous Star Ferry can't be beat.

Aw Boon Haw Gardens. Home of some of the most garish and zany statues you could ever imagine, plus Chinese pagodas and grottos. A Chinese view of the Chinese netherworld of spirits.

Tram. Slowly clankity-clanking down Hong Kong Island's north shore is definitely the way to see the real Hong Kong. The tram is much better than any tourist bus. Shutterbugs should sit on the top deck. A bit crowded during rush hour.

Wanchai. Home of the mythical (and now quite venerable) Suzie Wong. The Wanch (as the area is known to aficionados) is still home to many a bar and brothel, and you will still find the streets crowded with the latest generation of sailors when the fleet's in. But, excellent restaurants—to which you will feel quite comfortable taking your wife or your mom—have sprung up these past few years, as have some non-girlie pubs.

Water World. A 65-acre aquatic fun park with giant water slides, a wave cove, rapids, and artificial beaches. Open May–Oct.

KOWLOON

Jade Market. From 10 A.M. daily on Kansu St., here is the place to buy anything jade, from a tiny trinket for a few bucks to raw jade or carved statues. It is particularly fun to watch the jade merchants bidding secretly for the rocks and to haggle with the street hawkers. Don't spend much money, though, if you don't know much about jade.

Kaiser Estate, Hung Hom. Home to many of the small factory shops selling designer bargains and over-runs. Check the back page of the *South China Morning Post* classifieds daily or see the "Shopping" section of this guide.

Kowloon City Market. The largest market in the territory has everything from clothes to chinaware.

Lei Cheng Uk Tomb. On Tonkin Street in the housing estate of the same name lies this Han Dynasty (206 B.C.–A.D. 221) tomb, which was discovered in 1955 when the land was being cleared for the estate. It dates to around A.D. 100.

Leiyumun. A bit difficult to reach (see "Dining Out" section of this guide), this is one of the markets where you choose your fresh "jumping" (i.e., live) fish from the fishmongers and take it to a restaurant to be cooked.

Nathan Road-The Golden Mile. That strip of Nathan Road (plus the numerous side streets) where many of the major hotels (The Peninsula, Sheraton, Hyatt-Regency, Holiday Inn-Golden Mile, and several smaller ones) are located. Shops, restaurants, bars—everything cheek-by-jowl.

Ocean Terminal-Ocean Centre-Harbour City-Hong Kong Hotel Complex. Stretching from the Star Ferry Concourse right along Canton Road, miles of air-conditioned shopping on several levels. The largest shopping center in Asia, and who knows, maybe the world.

Peninsula Hotel Lobby. Give yourself a break and have 4 o'clock tea off a real silver service in the famed lobby and watch the world go by. *The* famed crossroads (Times Square or Clapham Junction, depending on your point of view) of Hong Kong.

Regent Hotel Lobby. With four-story-high, see-through glass walls, you can have a drink and watch the fascinating movements in the harbor. One of Hong Kong's newest meeting places and an up-and-coming crossroads.

Space Museum. A combination planetarium and space museum, just the thing you would never expect to find in Hong Kong.

Sung Dynasty Village. Step back into a traditional Chinese village in ancient (A.D. 960 to A.D. 1279) China. The scene is an authentic reproduction of that time long ago, complete with processions, street acrobats, magnificent costumes, and a wax museum depicting characters in Chinese history. (Tours available.)

Temple Street. The mile-long outdoor street market, open only from dusk to midnight, has just about everything under the sun.

Tsimshatsui East-Mody Road. A shopping/tourist district with five deluxe hotels, a dozen massive shopping arcades, hundreds of stores, plus bars, discos, and nightclubs.

Wong Tai Sin Temple. The temple that is most popular with Hong Kong's population, and since it is right on the M.T.R. (underground or tube or subway or metro, depending on what language you speak), an easy one to visit. If you only have one chance to see a genuine Chinese temple, and perhaps to have your fortune told at the same time, this is the place.

NEW TERRITORIES

Kam Tin Walled Village. Built in the seventeenth century, this is one of the best examples of the traditional walled villages that used to dot the landscape in ancient China. The inhabitants are a wee bit rude hereabouts and demand a Hong Kong dollar or two to be photographed. Admission to the village itself is HK$.50.

Lau Fau Shan. Hong Kong's oyster capital. This is another of the fish markets where you buy your fish and take it to a restaurant to be cooked. Oyster capital, notwithstanding, do not eat the oysters raw as Hong Kong's are grown in polluted waters. The rest of the seafood is caught at sea and is quite safe.

Lok Ma Chau. A vantage point to look across the Shenzhen River into China, and before that country opened up to tourism in 1978, about as close as any ordinary mortal was going to get. Still, it is a beautiful pastoral view across the rice paddies and the Shenzhen River. Be warned: some of the rugged peasant faces sitting on those benches charge for photographs.

Shatin Racetrack. Only a passing interest to those not intending to have a go at the nags (see "Gambling" or "Spectator Sports" sections of the guide to see how you can go to the races), but probably one of the few tracks in the world with air-conditioned stables. It also has the second-largest video screen in the world (the biggest is across the harbor in Happy Valley) so the back-stretch is always in view.

Temple of Ten Thousand Buddhas. In Shatin, atop some 500 steps, is one of the world's greatest collections of Buddhas—some 13,000 in all, despite the name.

ISLANDS

Cheung Chau. A Mediterranean-looking harbor, this is supposedly the territory's artist's colony. Nice beaches, restaurants, one resort hotel, friendly residents, and no cars. A nice place to get away to.

Lamma. Famed for its seafood restaurants along the quai.

Lantau. Larger than Hong Kong Island, Lantau has everything: beaches, monasteries, hiking trails, restaurants, and small hotels. A great place to get away from it all.

MACAU

Unlike Hong Kong, the Portuguese territory of Macau thrives on its history. In Hong Kong, the destruction of what physical history there was has continued uninterrupted in the name of progress and land development (spelled M-O-N-E-Y). Except for the last few years when Hong Kong's property boom spread to Macau (but unlike in Hong Kong was reined by a concerned government before too much damage was done), Macau has allowed its 400-year-old history to remain standing just where it was built. The result is that from a European point of view, Macau is a Latin Orient, a slice of the Iberian peninsula complete with old churches and pastel-colored buildings.

A-Ma Temple. A section of this temple, located at the base of Barra Hill, is Macau's oldest edifice, dating back to the Ming Dynasty reign of Emperor Wan Li (1573–1621). Other sections date from a major renovation during the nineteenth-century rule of Emperor Tao Kuang (1824–1856). It is dedicated to A Ma (from whence Macau got its name), who is known as Tin Hau in Hong Kong and Matsu in Taiwan), the goddess of the fisherfolk and by extension swimmers, lifeguards, sailors, etc.

Avenida de Almeida Ribeiro. Known in Cantonese as *Sanmalo,* this is Macau's main shopping street, which runs through the center of town. The more adventurous might care to wander off into the markets in the side streets.

Bela Vista Hotel. This century-old hostelry is completely overshadowed by the modern hotels in Macau. But it is still a lovely old place, if a bit rundown, and a favorite of old China- , Hong Kong- , and Macau-hands. When you are a bit tired and need to put your feet up, pull up a chair on the lovely verandah overlooking the entrance to the Inner Harbour, whet your whistle with a cold *vinho verde* (a young white wine), and watch life sail by slowly.

Bishop's Palace. Though the present building only dates back to the 1930s, it was from here on Penha Hill that the Portuguese Catholic priests directed Roman Catholic church matters in a diocese that included all of China and reached as far west as India. There has been a chapel on this site since the seventeenth century. The Palace is closed today—and no bishop has been in residence for decades—but it is still a good place to get an overview of the city.

Camoes Museum and Gardens. Named for Luis Vaz de Camoes (1524–1580), whose epic poem *O Lusiadas* has made him Portugal's most famous bard. The nineteenth-century building was once the residence of the president of the select committee of the all-powerful East India Company.

Casinos. That's what Macau is most famous for: its incessant, no-frills casino gambling. Forget the fancy shows and girls of Las Vegas and the posh sophistication of old-world Monte Carlo. In Macau, coolies in sweaty shirts mix with millionaires and either considers himself lucky if he gets so much as a free glass of clear Chinese tea, so intent is everyone on the business of gambling.

Coloane Island. One of the two outer islands that make up the territory of Macau. Connected to its neighbor Taipa Island by a causeway, the island is famous for its Chapel of St. Francis of Xavier (with a relic from the saint), Cheoc Van beach (white sand) and Hac Sa beach (black sand)—the former is overlooked by a lovely Portuguese inn called the Pousada de Coloane. If you have the time, the island is well worth a visit.

Gambling. The reason most people come to this tiny Portuguese territory. In addition to the casinos, you have your choice of Jai-Alai, the greyhounds, and the trotters.

Kun Iam Temple. For trivia lovers, the very first Sino-American Treaty was signed in the garden on July 4, 1844, by one Caleb Cushing, representing President John Tyler, and by the Viceroy of Canton, Ki Ying. The temple is dedicated to the goddess of mercy, Kun Iam (Kuan Yin in Hong Kong), and some buildings in the complex date back to the seventeenth century. It is also a favorite place to get your fortune told.

Leal Senado. This beautiful eighteenth-century building was restored in the 1930s. It is located in Largo do Senado (Senate Square), right at the beginning of the main street, Avenida de Almeida Ribeiro. Take the time to go inside to see the beautiful wrought iron work and old wall tiles. The Senate library and council chamber are also quite beautiful.

Macanese food. Do yourself a favor and try some. It is a delicious mix of Portuguese, Cantonese, Malaysian, and African cuisines. (See the "Dining Out" section of this guide for more details.)

Monte Fort. Overlooking the ruined façade of St. Paul's, this seventeenth-century fort was originally part of a complex that included the church and a seminary. The Dutch attack in 1622 was repulsed from the half-completed fortress. A good sight for taking photos of the façade, as well as good vantage point from which to see the city.

Portas do Cerco. Anyone entering China from Macau will pass through the beautiful and ornate portals of this nineteenth-century border gate. And it is still worth a photograph, even if you are not going in.

Pousada de Sao Tiago. This new, small, luxury inn is built in the Barrier Fortress (or the Fortress of St. James), which dates back to 1629. The open-air patio overlooking the approaches to the Inner Harbor is a lovely place to have breakfast. Be sure and see the old chapel just by the patio.

Praia Grande. This beautiful, windy road leads from near the town center to the Inner Harbor. Lovely, centuries-old banyan trees drooping over the road protect strollers from the fierce sunlight. Be romantic and take a walk, particularly a moonlight one. You can also rent a bike or, if that is too much, try a pedicab.

Restoration Row. The name given to a group of restored homes on Avenida do Conselheiro Ferreira de Almeida.

Ruins of St. Paul's. The first church on this site was destroyed by fire in 1601. A new church stood until 1835, when it, too, was consumed by fire—along with the finest Western library in Asia. The façade stands at the top of a granite staircase and is the best known, and probably the finest, Christian monument in the Orient.

Taipa Island. This is the island at the other end of the bridge that arches up over the harbor. It is quite a large island and there are plans for a deep-water port and possibly an airport on reclaimed land off it. The trotting track is on Taipa, as is the luxury Hyatt-Regency Hotel and a super, little, easy-to-find restaurant called Pinnochio's. It is quite pleasant to walk through the village of Taipa, particularly along the "little" Praia Grande, lined with banyan trees and ancient, colonnaded, pastel-colored houses.

DOING BUSINESS IN
HONG KONG

Made in Hong Kong. That familiar phrase—seen on everything from designer fashions and computers to toys, radios, and the proverbial left-handed widget—is the clue to the territory's export-oriented, manufacturing economy. The spirit of Hong Kong is the spirit of entrepreneurship; with people as its only natural resource, this tiny island is the world's 13th largest trading entity outside OPEC and COMECON.

Kong Kong is one of the rare places on earth that play the free-trade game according to the classical rules, with only one or two peculiarities arising out of its colonial past. It is a free port—that is, there are no import duties or export levies, although there are domestic excises on alcohol (therefore on alcoholic beverages and perfumes), tobacco and tobacco products, petroleum products, and soft drinks. Some articles, such as firearms, ammunition, certain toxic drugs and, of course, narcotics, are controlled. There are limited controls on banking and finance, and on stock, futures, and commodities exchanges. But, by and large, these are minimal and usually implemented only after some calamitous, often illegal, happening. The territory's bankers practice confidentiality, though it is not codified, as in Switzerland. The Independent Commission Against Corruption has the power to force banks to disclose all accounts and transactions.

With a few historical exceptions, you cannot own land in Hong Kong; it all belongs to the Crown (the government), but long- and short-term leases are auctioned off to all comers. With the signing of the 1984 Sino-British Agreement, which will return sovereignty to the People's Republic of China at the end of June 1997, land leases and mortgages are to extend past the magic 1997 mark as if it were not there. Otherwise, there are no business ownership limitations. A national of any country may do business or set up business, although nationals of countries that for the time being are not politically friendly with either Great Britain or China may be refused entry, working visas, or residence permits—most particularly those from the Eastern bloc who were not here before the Sino-Russian split. (See sections on *Working Visas* below.)

The Law

Until midnight, June 30, 1997, Hong Kong will closely follow English Common Law, with modifications for Hong Kong's unique circumstances. Barristers and solicitors make up a two-tiered legal system. The judiciary is separate and independent from the rest of government and the governor appoints all judges and magistrates, who, unlike their counterparts in Britain, are part of the civil service. Ultimate appeal is to the Judicial Committee of the Privy Council in London. As in Britain, the defendant is assumed innocent until proven guilty, except in cases of corruption, pornography, and dissemination of false news, in which the onus of proof rests with the defendant.

Hong Kong's rule of law has always been a great attraction to the international business community. Since 1841, with few exceptions Hong Kong has offered full redress in its civil and criminal courts. The government is held in check by the very people whose salary it pays.

Part of Hong Kong's attraction as an international business center is its proximity to the People's Republic of China. Hong Kong's China-watching role naturally decreased once China opened up, but because of the hassles of living, working, negotiating, and doing day-to-day business in the PRC, Hong Kong's overall role in the worldwide China trade has increased. Hong Kong also shares a border with the Shenzhen

Special Economic Zone, the most successful of the SEZs China has created to funnel in foreign investment. In short, Hong Kong is still China's foreign-exchange window and a very good place to position yourself if you are interested in trade with China, or just learning what business in Asia is all about.

The Future After 1997

As we go to press, the Basic Law Drafting Committee of the People's Republic of China is toiling away at the territory's post-1997 miniconstitution, putting in writing the guarantees set down in the 1984 Sino-British Agreement, and ratified by both parties in May 1985. Many prominent Hong Kong natives sit on these committes to insure Hong Kong's input.

Although there is considerable uncertainty in Hong Kong about life after 1997, Chinese premier Deng Xiaoping has given Hong Kong a half-century guarantee from July 1, 1997. This promise will allow the territory to exist as a Special Administrative Region (SAR) of the People's Republic, with separate laws and a high degree of autonomy in domestic affairs. The SAR will be vested with executive, legislative, and independent judicial powers, including the authority of final adjudication. The laws currently in force will remain basically unchanged.

Rights and freedoms, including those of person, speech, press, assembly, association, travel, movement, correspondence, strike, occupation, inheritance, and religion, will be ensured, as will the right of academic research. Private property and foreign investment will be protected. Hong Kong will retain its status as a free port with its own shipping registry, a separate customs authority, and an international financial center. Foregin exchange, gold, securities, and futures markets will continue. The Hong Kong dollar will continue to circulate as a separate, freely convertible currency, distinct from the *renminbi;* there will be no exchange controls. Hong Kong will manage its own finances and China will not levy any taxes on the SAR.

Hong Kong will be allowed to maintain and develop independent economic and cultural relations and to conclude agreements with foreign countries and trade organizations, such as the GATT and MFA, and air and tax agreements.

China will hold sway over foreign and defense matters, and Chinese troops will replace the British garrison. A Chinese-appointed governor, who may or may not be Hong Kong Chinese, will be responsible to Peking, much as the current governor is responsible to London. Whether he'll be as independent as Hong Kong's British governors have traditionally been is a moot point. A special tripartite Joint Liaison Group, with members from Hong Kong, Britain, and China, meets regularly to hammer out the fine points necessary for a smooth hand-over. The Basic Law is due to be published in 1990.

For its part, the Hong Kong government is reviewing the way things are run with a view to instituting changes to prepare this huge populace for the future. In November 1984, it issued a White Paper (statement of policy) called *The Future Development of Representative Government in Hong Kong,* followed in May 1987 by a Green Paper (nonbinding suggestions on policy meant for public debate) called *The 1987 Review of Developments in Representative Government.* Behind both papers is the desire that Hong Kong citizens have a greater say in government before 1997, so that everything will be in situ come the changeover. Briefly, the idea of one man-one vote is anathema to the PRC and also to powerful sectors of the Hong Kong business community. A White Paper due on the issue in 1988 and is expected to "converge" (a PRC term) with the Basic Law.

Economy

Economist Milton Friedman called Hong Kong's the "last *laissez faire* economy," which must have been music to the ears of the local government. Hong Kong is living proof that Rudyard Kipling's state-ment about East and West—"ne'er the twain shall meet"—was wrong. Not only do East and West meet in Hong Kong, but each side also generally makes a profit on the relationship.

Profit making starts at the top. Only in the most adverse of times has the Hong Kong government's budget gone into the red. Annual sur-pluses are planned and expected; deficit spending is anathema. In fact, an intentional game is played each year at budget time, when the economic performance for that year is always underestimated; 5.6 percent was the growth-rate prediction for 1986, while at the year end, the figure stood at 8.7 percent.

This mercantile community has a light-industrial and manufactur-ing-based economy. It is the world's largest exporter of clothing, furs, toys and games, watches and clocks, imitation jewelry, metal watch-bands, electrical hair-dressing apparatus, artificial flowers, flashlights, and electric lamps. On-shore and off-shore financial and business ser-vices fill out the rest of the economic equation.

To support this thriving export manufacturing economy, Hong Kong imports—to the tune of US$35.4 billion in 1986, making it the world's 15th largest importer. With the exception of narcotics and firearms—which are illegal—and duty on liquor, perfumes, petroleum products, and soft drinks, any and all goods can be brought into the colony without hindrance. That is why Hong Kong cries "foul" when it is thrown into the same basket—particularly by the U.S. and the EEC—as Japan, Korea, and Taiwan, countries going to great lengths to block the importation of foreign goods.

With little land and no natural resources, Hong Kong's heavy industry is negligible. The territory's greatest asset is a hard-working and entrepreneurial people, who share with Singaporeans the highest living standard in Asia outside Japan.

Recent arrivals are stunned by the pace of Hong Kong, and staggered by cocktail chitchat from perfect strangers who want to know, after a two-minute acquaintance, how much rent you pay, how much you make, how much your car costs, etc. Natives are direct in situations in which Westerners are more circumspect. But that is because everyone in Hong Kong is in a rush to make his or her pile. The mentality is probably due to the historical uncertainty of Hong Kong's status—everyone knew that one day China would deal in her own way and in her own time with what she always considered an internal matter. Which is precisely what happened, much to the chagrin of Prime Minister Thatcher, who had her own ideas about Britain staying on to run the place when she initiated the September 1982 negotiations that led to the Agreement two years later.

Novelist Han Suyin summed it all up in a 1959 *Life* magazine article. Hong Kong, she said, "works splendidly on borrowed time in a borrowed place." Add to the mixture a bit of the refuge syndrome—more than half of the 5.5 million people have fled the Middle Kingdom, the Motherland, at one time or another since 1949—the Hong Kong's business (and social) pace is more understandable.

Finance

Hong Kong is the world's third largest financial center, after New York and London, and the third leg of the 24-hour trading triangle. Hong Kong has a three-tier banking system—154 licensed, full-service banks are followed by 38 *licensed* and 254 *registered* deposit-taking companies (DTCs). Different regulations govern issued share capital and paid-up capital for each type of DTC. Interest rates for both are unrestricted and very competitive. Interest rates for the licensed banks, by contrast, are set up by the Hong Kong Association of Banks, to which all licensed banks must belong.

Registered DTCs, with a minimum deposit of HK$100,000, are smaller operations, specializing in mortgages, hire purchase, and stock-market financing. Licensed DTCs, most often affiliated with foreign banks, have a minimum deposit of HK$500,000, and tend to go for project finance, syndicated loans, underwriting, corporate advice, investment, and related financial services.

There is no central bank in Hong Kong, though many believe the Bank of China may take over that role after 1997. Supervisory functions and management of the foreign exchange reserves are shared by various government departments—including the Commissioner of Banking, the Commissioner of Securities and Commodities Trading, and the Secretary for Monetary Affairs—and private institutions, particularly the Hongkong and Shanghai Banking Corporation (HKSBC), the government's banker. The HKSBC and its neighbor, the Chartered Bank, are the two note-issuing banks, although it is assumed the Bank of China will issue currency after 1997.

Currency

The Hong Kong dollar is freely convertible. There are no restrictions whatsoever on the movement of currency in or out of the colony. Since October 15, 1983, the Hong Kong dollar has been pegged to the U.S. dollar at US$1:HK$7.80. The Hong Kong Exchange Fund, the territory's reserve fund, issues and redeems Certificates of Indebtedness to the two note-issuing banks, the Hongkong and Shanghai Banking Corporation and the Chartered Bank. For their part, the two institutions buy and sell banknotes to other licensed banks, in effect acting as agents for the fund.

The government has not made the HK$7.80 conversion facility available to the nonbanking public, and has given no guarantee of the foreign-currency price of deposits or cash held by the public, who are free to trade at market rates. The spread between the official and the free-market rates is where the industry makes its profit or takes its loss.

But for the trading public—and that includes business—the stable rate has given an impetus to Hong Kong's economy by allowing the United States a steady position as the territory's largest trading partner besides China. When the greenback is high, the Hong Kong dollar is high against other currencies, and vice-versa, tending to be more competitive vis-à-vis other currencies when the U.S. dollar is low.

The Markets

The Hong Kong Stock Exchange, which opened trading on April 2, 1986, is one of the most modern and sophisticated in the world. Its vast trading floor holds 800 booths and has room for more. At the end of 1986, 253 public companies were listed, with a total capitalization of HK$419 billion. The Exchange had 151 corporate members and 708 individual members at the end of 1986. The Hang Seng Index, calculated every quarter hour, measures performance.

The Hong Kong Futures Exchange offers contracts in five markets: cotton (though no trading has taken place in recent years), sugar, soybeans, gold, and the Hang Seng Futures Index. The last of these, which began on May 6, 1986, allows investors to hedge their share portfolios against adverse price fluctuations, and is now the most active stock-futures index market outside the U.S. By the end of 1986, the Futures Exchange had 106 members.

There are two gold markets. The Chinese Gold & Silver Exchange Society operates a gold bullion market, one of the most active in the world. The gold is of 99 percent fineness and traded in *taels,* traditional Chinese measurement equal to about 1.2 troy ounces. The 193-member firms closely follow the markets in London, Zurich, and New York. The other gold market is called "loco-London" and its participants are, in the main, the major gold-trading companies. Dealings take place in U.S. dollars per troy ounce of 99.5 percent fineness, with deliveries in London.

Foreign Investment

Hong Kong's political stability, hard-working labor force, easy immigration laws, pleasant environment, and proximity to China (particularly the biggest of the Special Economic Zones, Shenzhen), make the territory very attractive to foreign investors. At the end of 1986, the United States was the largest overseas investor, at 36.4 percent of total investment, with Japan (21.1 percent) and China (18.4 percent) following. To no one's surprise, the electronics industry, excluding toys, watches, and clocks, receives the largest share of the foreign investment pie.

The Industry Department runs a "One-Stop Unit," which helps cut through red tape, at Ocean Centre, 14th Fl., 5 Canton Road, Tsimshatsui, Kowloon; (3) 722–2434. They maintain offices in New York, San Francisco, London, Stuttgart, and Tokyo. The Hong Kong government does not offer tax holidays as some countries do, but factory space is available at reasonable prices through the Hong Kong Industrial Estates Corporation, which runs two estates in the New Territories, Tai Po and Yuen Long.

Setting up a Business

To set up a sole proprietorship, partnership, or unlimited company with a Hong Kong address, you must obtain a Business Registration Certificate from the Business Registration Office of the Inland Revenue Department, Windsor House, 311 Gloucester Road, Causeway Bay,

Hong Kong; (5) 894–3149. The annual fee is HK$650. The process generally takes only a couple of days.

Formation of a limited liability company is scarcely less simple: a lawyer will get you a "shelf" (ready-made) company for about HK$5,000, including the statutory books and a smart little seal-press. If you want a specially named company you must propose a name, with one or two alternatives, to the Registrar of Companies before going ahead with the simple legal paperwork. This will cost about HK$5,000 –$10,000. The minimum number of shareholders is two, with one share each.

Forming a publicly quoted company is a much bigger chore, with the need to satisfy the listing procedures of the stock exchange authorities, issue a prospectus, etc. At the end of 1986, 164,224 local limited companies were registered, including 2,238 foreign firms with establishments in the territory, 551 of them American and 267 Japanese. A copy of the Companies Ordinance can be purchased at the Government Publications Centre, in the General Post Office, Connaught Pl. (next to Star Ferry), Hong Kong.

The number of publicly quoted companies in Hong Kong is quite small, although many loom very large in the economy. The overwhelming majority of businesses are private, family-group, sole trader, partnership, and independent concerns, engaged in an incredible range of activities. Among the manufacturing industries, nine in 10 have fewer than 50 employees. In "white-collar" activities, there are myriad concerns, some working out of living rooms with tiny staffs and others sprawling over marble floors in palatial high-rises.

Hong Kong boasts that you can find *any* supplies and *any* services for a wide range of costs at short notice. It is a frenetic, energetic, and sometimes apoplectic shopping complex—not only for the retail goods so visible to the tourist, but also for the factory, wholesale and service industries. You can buy and sell and live like a millionaire in Hong Kong, buy and sell and live like a penny-pinching street-hawker, or find any gradation in between.

The rules of business in Hong Kong are few. Whether you are a visiting businessperson or a potential entrepreneur, you will not go far wrong if you remember this: You are in a free country. If you succeed, you can take all the credit; if you fail, you must take all the blame. The authorities give no subsidies, tax reliefs, or featherbeds, but neither will they hinder you.

Taxation and Government

Taxes are moderate. A salaried person can pay up to a maximum 16.5 percent on assessable income which includes any wages, salaries, leave pay, fees, commissions, bonuses, gratuities, perquisites, or allowances. Three other types of benefits are specifically included: lump sums from unapproved pension schemes controlled or managed in Hong Kong, any gain realized upon the exercise or release of stock-option rights granted to an employee by virtue of his employment in Hong Kong, and the personal benefit derived from occupying a subsidized or rent-free accommodation provided by the employer. This latter category is taxed at 10 percent of the employee's assessable income. Persons holding a directorship of a corporation with its central management and control in the colony are liable to Salaries Tax, even if the director does not reside in or ever visit Hong Kong. If during a financial year—which in Hong Kong runs from April 1 to March 31—an employee is outside the colony on business for a period of more than 60 days, his remuneration will be automatically time-apportioned.

Unlimited businesses, including sole proprietorships or partnerships, are taxed at the Salaries Tax rate of 16.5 percent. Limited companies and corporations pay 18 percent Profits Tax. Dividends are not taxed a second time when received by the shareholder, and there is no capital-gains tax. On royalities, there may be a withholding tax of 1.85 percent or 1.7 percent.

Other taxes include: property tax (16.5 percent on 80 percent of the rent received, less rates, by noncorporate owners of land and buildings); interest tax (16.5 percent withholding tax for income sources in Hong Kong, excluding interest on deposits with financial insitutions in Hong Kong); estate duty (from 6 percent to 18 percent on a sliding scale on inheritances over HK$2 million); stamp duty (2.75 percent on land transfers over HK$508,998, less for smaller sums, and 0.6 percent on share transfers, half payable by the purchaser, half by the seller); and capital duty (0.6 percent on authorized capital).

A few minor taxes complete the list: a HK$120 departure tax at the airport and a HK$15 departure tax at the Macau Ferry Terminal; a 5 percent hotel accommodation tax; excise taxes on petroleum products, cosmetics, tobacco, perfumes, liquor, and soft drinks; entertainment duties on horse racing, cinema tickets, and the lottery.

The Hong Kong salaries tax return consists of a single sheet folded into four pages, which can often be completed in 30 minutes. There are few allowances, and when a taxpayer reaches a certain (relatively low) level of income, all allowances are abolished and a straight 16.5 percent is payable on any amount. There is no income-tax withholding or PAYE, although you can buy interest-bearing tax reserve certificates from the Inland Revenue Department if you want to save tax money that way.

The government's intervention in business affairs is minimal. Apart from an annual return of income or profits, there are only a few other forms to complete each year: the business names renewal, the corporate return of shares and directors, and a form to be sent to the tax people every time you engage or lose an employee who is paid over the minimum taxable level. If you deal in excisable goods such as drinks or cigarettes, or run a restaurant, there are a few more forms. And that's all.

But the government departments and a number of government-allied institutions render a great deal of assistance, information, and advice. Grouped in a small area, they are honest, efficient, and easy to reach. The government helps business in this manner, because business is what Hong Kong lives by.

Cost of Living

Though Hong Kong is not the most expensive place in Asia (that honor belongs to Tokyo), it is very close. Rents—commercial, industrial, and residential—are high when compared to those in New York or London, as are outright values of premises and land. To chart your way through the ups and downs, there are three Consumer Price indices published monthly. The average increase in the cost of living in 1986 was 2.8 percent.

Labor

Labor costs vary widely, with a steep climb from unskilled manual labor up to top executive level. In recent times, there has been sharp competition for skilled labor, and the general level of pay has risen. Unemployment has for many years been at the "full employment" rate, despite the influx of new workers from the mainland. Training institutions and higher education have been expanded and improved in recent years, but there are still many areas where on-the-job training is vital.

The workers in Hong Kong are ambitious. That's the good news. The bad news is that they are also mobile. If you can't pay them what they think they can get, they leave. Labor unions are few and small and very politicized, but engage in little strike action. There are some 870,000 workers in the labor force, working in 49,000 factories. Nearly half the factories are small establishments with under 100 employees. For advice, contact the Labour Relations Division, Labour Department, Harbour Bldg., 38 Pier St., Hong Kong, (5) 852–3511.

Family loyalties are strong, and, even now, Chinese family businesses are usually close-knit and tend to be authoritarian, whatever their size. Executives of these kinds of firms tend to be immobile. The virtue of this family-group structure, however, is that if you become a good supplier or good buyer, your own personal relationships will assure that they will be most cooperative and mutually supportive. So make friends. Hong Kong is *not* an impersonal place.

The Layout of The Territory

Hong Kong Island is where the big-time commerce is: the bank HQs, the big company HQs, the lawyers, accountants, p.r. and advertising people, etc. Central District, as the name implies, is where the giants live.

Kowloon is where the industry is, and also the main tourist activity. In any case, you can get to and from the Island and Kowloon by road (through an undersea tunnel) in about twenty to thirty minutes, or by passenger ferry (the famous Star Ferry) in ten minutes, except at the rush hours.

In the New Territories there are *seven* new towns being built, with new factories, offices, dwellings, schools, hospitals, hotels and other facilities. Finally, a number of the outlying islands are also developing fast, with new incomes and market possibilities. Visit at least one (and also Macau which, after many decades of sleepy stagnation, is also busting out all over in development; you can get there in forty-five minutes by jetfoil).

Premises

There is a wide range of premises and rents, from the marble-faced palaces of the Central District to modest offices only a few blocks away. Through the late 1970s, until rents soared in Hong Kong, the property-developing industry overbuilt, and the boom collapsed during 1982. Beginning in late 1986, rents—industrial, commercial and domestic—began to rise again, buoyed by the booming economy. According to a survey published in mid-1987, Hong Kong's office rentals are now the sixth most expensive in the world at US$571 a square metre. (Tokyo takes first place of course.)

The supply of premises gives the businessperson a wide choice of costs. If you simply must put on a show of great wealth, for your business and your executives, there are millionaire-style offices and dwellings; if you judge that hard work and no frills is your style, then you can find well serviced, well placed premises at only a few Hong Kong dollars a square meter in rent. There are fine dwellings and expensive on the sunny south side of Hong Kong Island. (Repulse Bay, Deep Water Bay, Stanley); or on The Peak, also on Hong Kong Island; or in Kowloon, in the Kowloon City/Beacon Hill area. Farther from the main business areas in Sai Kung and Clearwater Bay, both in the

New Territories, rents are usually less expensive. They are cheaper still on the outlying islands, which have frequent ferries for commuters.

Businesspersons will find dozens of letting agencies listed in the classified section of the *South China Morning Post.* Also available are fully furnished and maintained service apartments—usually one- or two-bedroom studios. The *New World Apartments,* next to New World and Regent Hotels in Tsimshatsui, Kowloon, and the Victoria Apartments, next to the Victoria Hotel, 200 Connaught Road, Central, are at the top of the line, while *Goshen Mansions,* 175–180 Gloucester Road, Causeway Bay, Hong Kong, are priced more moderately.

Business Centers

Most of the major hotels have business centers, which provide secretarial, translation, courier, and printing services—even private word processors. Charges vary from hotel to hotel, but secretaries run HK$50–HK$75 per hour, typing HK$25–HK$30 per page, and word processing about HK$30 per page. Each hotel has a business-center tariff, so check before you act.

In a mercantile community like Hong Kong, you'd expect business centers outside the hosteleries, and there are many. Some are considerably cheaper than those in hotels. Others cost about the same but offer private desks (from HK$500 weekly, private offices (from HK$1,000 weekly), and meeting facilities.

Other amenities include a private address and personal answering and forwarding services. Many service centers are tied in with accountants and lawyers for those who want to register a company quickly. Some will even process visas and wrap gifts for you.

One hotel business center equipped like those normally found outside the hosteleries is the *China Traders Centre* in the Regal Meridien Airport Hotel. A short walk across a footbridge from the passenger terminal, it has offices and conference rooms. It is popular with transient businesspersons who need only the daylight hours to transact business before winging their way out again. Their club, the China Traders Circle, which has free membership, offers discounts on offices, which can be rented by the hour, day, week, or month.

The *American Chamber of Commerce* not only offers short-term rental of office and conference space, but also has a splendid and succinct Business Briefing Program (US$75 members /$150 nonmembers, plus breakfast costs for the six to eight volunteer businessmen willing to impart their expertise). The chamber also has a library and a *China Trade Services* section. 1030 Swire House, Central, Hong Kong; (5) 260165. Telex: 83664 AMCC HX. Fax: 5–8101289. Cable: AMCHAM.

Other organizations of note:

Hong Kong Business Centre, Bank of Canton Building, 6th Fl., 6 Des Voeux Rd. Central, Hong Kong; (5) 212511. Telex: 65779 HKBC HX. Fax: 852-5-8100235. Cable: HKBZCTR.

Margaret Sullivan Secretarial Services, 13 Duddell St., Central, Hong Kong; (5) 265946. Telex: 63210 ALAYE HX. Fax: 852-5-845-0989. Also runs the Business Centre at the Garden Hotel in Canton.

Pacific Centre, Bank of America Building, 10th Fl., 1 Kowloon Park Dr., Tsimshatsui, Kowloon; (3) 721-0880. Telex: 56443 WATC HX.

Riggs Business Centres, 702-3 Ocean Centre, Canton Road, Tsimshatsui, Kowloon; (3) 696607. Telex: 49601 RGOC HX. Fax: 3-694226.

Trademark, Design Registration, Patents, and Copyright

Hong Kong has its own Trademark legislation that closely follows the U.K. legislation. Trademarks are registrable in the territory. The protection of Registered Designs in Hong Kong is governed by U.K. legislation. Patents are not granted in Hong Kong, although its Patents Registry accepts certain patents that have been granted elsewhere, conferring the same privileges and rights as those granted in the U.K. to patents with an extension to Hong Kong.

Copyright law in Hong Kong is also based on U.K. and Hong Kong legislation. Hong Kong is a member of both the Universal Copyright Convention and the Berne Copyright Union. Literary, artistic, and publishing copyrights are strictly enforced (and long gone are the days when you could pick up pirated audio tapes on any street corner).

What happens after July 1st, 1997 is a moot point. At this writing, China is not part of any international agreement on trademarks, patents, or copyright, though it does have its own laws. There have been complaints by Hong Kong manufacturers of infringements from across the border. As so much of Hong Kong's protections stems from U.K. legislation, Hong Kong or China will have to write its own legislation to guarantee the necessary protection in the Special Administrative Region.

Many law firms specialize in this type of law. The *Trademarks and Patent Registry* is in the Queensway Government Offices, 15th Fl., Central, Hong Kong; (5) 862-2628. The Trade Controls Section of the *Customs and Excise Department* assists in the investigation and settlement of commercial disputes on behalf of overseas firms. The Investigation Branch is on the 9th Fl., Rumsey St. Car Park Building, Connaught Road, Central, Hong Kong; (5) 456182. The Operations Branch is located in the main offices, on the 8th Fl., Harbour Building, 38 Pier Rd., Central, Hong Kong; (5) 852-3306.

Product Testing

Laboratory product verification to international standards acceptable to the United States or the EEC, for example, is available from the *Hong Kong Standards & Testing Centre,* 10 Dai Wang St., Taipo Industrial Estate, Taipo, New Territories; (0) 653–0021.

Product Design

The *Hong Kong Design Innovation Company* was established with government assistance in 1986. The firm specializes in bringing new ideas to fruition or devising ways to improve existing products. It specializes in mass-produced, domestic, office, and light-industrial items. 1007 Tsimshatsui Centre, Tsimshatsui East, Kowloon; (3) 739–1122.

Product Sourcing

How would you go about finding the widget maker of your choice out of the tens of thousands of Hong Kong factories? The answer is to head to the Trade Enquiries Section of the *Hong Kong Trade Development Council,* Great Eagle Centre, 31st Fl., 23 Harbour Rd., Wanchai, Hong Kong; (5) 833–4333. The TDC has some 25,000 companies in its computer listed by category. It also has offices in 24 overseas cities, including four in the U.S.: New York, Chicago, Dallas, Los Angeles; and London in Britain.

Product or Company Research

The *Hong Kong Trade Development Council* has a superb general library to help you with your research (Great Eagle Centre, 31st. Fl., 23 Harbour Rd., Wanchai, Hong Kong; [5] 833–4333), as well as a specialized fashion library for those in the rag trade (Room 1304, 13th Fl., Block "B," Watson's Estate, Watson's Rd., North Point, Hong Kong; [5] 701606).

Language

Hong Kong, it should be realized, is a Chinese city, not an English city. The great bulk of the population speaks Cantonese, though Pou-tongua (Mandarin) is becoming more widely spoken. Even the taxi drivers often have little English. But the international communications, the hotels, and the Western-style entertainments are conducted multilingually, and it is possible to do business for years without knowing more than a few politesses in Chinese and a snatch of taxi-driver's lingo. But, in an office, you must have at least one good bilingual secretary.

Translations and Translators

There may come a time when you need an official translator or an official translation of a document. The hotel business centers can be of assistance as can those outside the hotels. See *Business Centers* above. For specialist work in all languages, try *Translanguage Center*, 1604 Tung Wah Mansion, 199 Hennessy Rd., Wanchai, Hong Kong; (5) 732728 or *Polyglot Translations*, 601–B Great China House, 14 Queen's Rd., Central, Hong Kong; (5) 215689.

Style

Business in Hong Kong is cosmopolitan and formal. Despite the summer heat, a suit is necessary when calling on people. When you have become a familiar face, then more casual attire is suitable for daytime factory visits. Meetings with Chinese businesspersons can become very formal and very alcoholic. Be sure to have bilingual business cards printed—hundreds of them. Many in the West may laugh at the Asian penchant for whipping out their cards, but it is the preferred way of keeping track of people in Hong Kong.

Transport

Hong Kong has many modes of transport that have grown up in an unplanned manner. The harbor, one of the largest deep-water ports in the world, is served by every kind of vessel, from the ancient Chinese junk to the superbulker. At first, the port looks chaotic: most vessels moor on buoys in mid-harbor, and the goods are craned off into lighters, which then plough their way to any of forty jetties and piers around the perimenter and even further afield along the coast. But it is better and quicker to transfer these goods by open water than to congest roads on land.

The exception is the centralized container port, at Kwai Chung, just outside Kowloon. This is the second-largest port in the world, behind Rotterdam, in terms of through-put of TEUs (twenty-foot equivalent units, the standard measure of container activity). The containers, however, are handled with high-speed, state-of-the-art machinery, and operations are mostly computerized.

Hong Kong International Airport—known so widely as "Kai Tak," the name of the previous owners of the land, that if you gave the official title to a taxi driver he would not know where to go—is one of the major hubs in Southeast Asia, in terms both of its 10 million annual passengers and its air cargo, which carries 28 percent of Hong Kong's exports. Hong Kong is served by 30 airlines, operating about 1,100 flights weekly between Hong Kong and 70 cities throughout the world. And the best part of Kai Tak is the beautiful landing, over either Kowloon or the harbor. Even hardened pilots enjoy "turning left at the Hitachi sign and right when you spot Mrs. Wong's bloomers drying on a bamboo pole stuck out her twentieth-floor window."

Road traffic conditions are Hong Kong's perpetual problem. The government barely keeps up with needs, even though new roads are being built day and night. So if you are in a business requiring lots of transport, study your logistical situations with care.

Public transportation is excellent and offers a wide choice; swaying double-decker buses and minibuses are the most prevalent. Hong Kong Island also sports ancient trams rattling across the northern shore and an equally ancient funicular (the Peak Tram). The colony is inundated with taxis, except when you want one. A superb Mass Transit Railway (subway, tube, metro, U-Bahn, depending on your language) covers 38.6 air-conditioned kilometers with 37 stations connecting Hong Kong Island with Kowloon and the New Territories, and interchanging with the Kowloon Canton Railway, a commuter train running from Hung Hom in Kowloon to the Chinese border. The Star Ferry, of course, is Hong Kong's most famous mode of transport, but there are many smaller ferries—*walla-wallas*—to take you across the harbor if you can't find a taxi to take you through the cross-harbor tunnel when the Star Ferry closes.

One word of warning: Hong Kong is not the place to pick up a car at the airport and drive off. You can hire self-drive cars, from Avis, National and many local agencies, and all you need is an International Driving License, but you'd have to be plum loco to try it. Hong Kong's traffic is lethal and parking is irritating. It takes a while to get accustomed to Hong Kong drivers' terrible habits and lack of courtesy, and surely no businessperson would travel all this way to upset both mind and body on the road.

The answer is to hire a car *with* a driver and leave the problems to him. All the major hotels offer such a service. Avis and National charge HK$450 and HK$400 respectively for the three-hour minimum, then HK$150 and HK$120 respectively for each additional hour. Daily and weekly rates are available; local companies are somewhat cheaper. Fung Hing Hire Car Company, for example, charges HK$66 per hour (two-hour minimum) for a car seating five, while their stretch Mercedes

Benz, which seats seven, goes for HK$90 per hour. *Mutual Transport & Trading Co.* charges HK$65 per hour (two-hour minimum) for a small car. You get the idea.

Avis, 50 Po Loi St., Zung Fu Car Park, Hung Hom, Kowloon; (3) 346007.

National Car Rental, Intercontinental Plaza, 94 Granville St., Tsimshatsui East, Kowloon; (3) 671047.

Fung Hing Hire Car Co., 4 Tsui Man St., Happy Valley, Hong Kong; (5) 720333.

Mutual Transport & Trading Co., 39 Tak Wan Shopping Arcade, 1st. Fl., 12 Pak Kung St., Hung Hom, Kowloon; (3) 636939.

All in all, there are 20 varieties of transport in Hong Kong, from a few old rickshaws and trams to helicopters and jetfoils. Transport will get even more crowded as time goes by, because the Chinese economy next door is opening up rapidly to trade, commerce, and finance, and most of that will be through Hong Kong. Already an additional transit point has been developed over the border; a multilane highway is being built from Hong Kong through to Canton and Macau. But that is another story—the whole new business ballgame with China, which requires another book for itself.

Meeting Places

At the end of 1987 there were some 21,000 hotel rooms available in 60 hotels, ranging from world-class establishments like the Peninsula, Mandarin, and Regent and those belonging to the major chains (Hilton, Sheraton, Holiday Inn, Hyatt Regency, Inter-Continental, Marriott, Ramada, Regal Meridien, and Nikko) to more modest hostelries. By the end of 1988, there should be an additional 3,000 rooms in six new hotels. Many have ballrooms and most have smaller function/ meeting rooms. For an overview of Hong Kong meeting, convention, and incentive facilities, contact the Convention and Incentive Department, *Hong Kong Tourist Association,* 35th Fl., Connaught Centre, Central, Hong Kong; (5) 244191.

The end of 1988 will see the opening of the Hong Kong Convention and Exhibition Centre, a purpose-built, state-of-the-art, completely integrated, 4.4 million-square-foot complex on the Wanchai waterfront. There will be two exhibition halls of 97,000 square feet each, with a main convention hall capable of seating 2,600. The complex will house two hotels, a Grand Hyatt and a New World, a serviced apartment block, and a trade-mart/commercial office building. *Hong Kong Convention and Exhibition Centre,* 2008 New World Tower 16–18 Queen's Rd., Central, Hong Kong; (5) 844–3427.

Social and Health Clubs

Hong Kong is very much a club town and visitors quite often feel left out, particularly at lunchtime or on weekends. Quite obviously, you will not be able to join a social or sporting club just for your few days here, but there still may be a way to partake by checking on your own memberships before you depart. Most of Hong Kong's private social and sporting clubs have reciprocal arrangements with clubs overseas. For example, membership in the Club Corporation of America, with its more than 200 clubs in the U.S., can gain you entrance to the Pacific Club in Central, the Tower Club in Kowloon, or the Marina Club in Aberdeen on the south side of the island for a bit of weekend recreation. The American Club has reciprocal rights with other American Clubs in Asia, the World Trade Centre Club has sister clubs in the U.S., and Foreign Correspondents' Club members can use about two dozen press clubs around the world. Many country clubs, private clubs, eating clubs, and cricket, golf, and sailing clubs have reciprocal rights. A little forethought before you depart could make the difference between a lonely and an enjoyable trip. Have your club write ahead and be sure to bring an introductory letter. Here is a list of major clubs with reciprocal facilities: *Royal Hong Kong Jockey Club:* free entry to the members enclosure during racing season, no use of the recreational facilities. *Royal Hong Kong Golf Club:* free greens fees 14 times a year. Other clubs: *Royal Hong Kong Yacht Club, Hong Kong Cricket Club, Kowloon Cricket Club, Hong Kong Football Club, Hong Kong Country Club, Kowloon Club, Hong Kong Club.*

Health Clubs are another matter. With the exception of the *Tom Turk Fitness Clubs* (King's Theatre Building, 30 Queen's Rd., Central, Hong Kong; [5] 268881 and Albion Plaza, 2 Granville Rd., Tsimshatsui, Kowloon; [3] 680022—HK$100 day, you must be a member. Guests of the Mandarin and Excelsior can use the facilities of the *Spa on the Square* in Exchange Square.

You may also want to refer to the "Restaurant" section in this book for further advice on dining out.

Hotels

More than four million people visited Hong Kong in 1987, a healthy percentage of whom were conducting business of one sort or another. The hotels in Hong Kong realize this and, like the airlines with Business Class, many have created a business oasis within their establishments to pamper their business guests, and most have some sort of "guest recognition program." The *Hyatt-Regency,* for example, has its

Regency Club floors while the *Hilton* has special Executive Floors. Recognition at the *Sheraton* is through its Sheraton Club International, at the *Furama Inter-Continental* through its Six Continents Club, and at the *Holiday Inns* through their Insider Club. Have your travel agent or company make it known in advance you are a businessperson; in Hong Kong, which thrives on commerce, that makes you a VIP.

Visas, Residence Permits, and ID Cards

Those wishing to settle here, with or without their families, need work visas for themselves and residence permits for their families. This includes Britons, after an initial six-month stay, and Commonwealth members. As in most countries, you will have to prove your job cannot be filled by a local and, in most cases, a letter from your company is sufficient. Unlike most countries, Hong Kong welcomes new members to its overseas business community, provided they can pay their way. Entrepreneurs, even without the backing of large corporations, are welcome, though they may have to talk a little bit faster since they do not have a big-name letterhead to back them up. All the above must be accomplished *outside* the colony at any British Embassy or Consulate—it takes time—though much of the preparation can be done in Hong Kong on a temporary visa, the type given out to visiting tourists. Lengths of stay vary, so see the *Visa* section in the front of the book. Extensions to visas are readily granted.

Anyone here for over three months needs an identity card, issued by the *Registry of Persons Office,* Provident Centre, 9th Fl., 21–53 Wharf St., North Point, Hong Kong; (5) 642374, which is to be carried on your person at all times. Your passport will suffice to prove your identity. This card does not bestow landing and residence privileges, which are the sole bailiwick of the *Immigration Department* (Mirror Tower, 61 Mody Rd., Tsimshatsui East, Kowloon; (3) 733–3111). You cannot run a business, be hired or hire, fill in a government form, pick up an insured package at the Post Office, or do almost anything without an ID. It sounds drastic, but it really isn't, even though there are spot checks on roads and pedestrian areas. The reason for this is to prevent illegal immigrants, mostly from the PRC but also from Vietnam and other countries, from blending into the population, which, as you will find out when you arrive, is bursting at the seams with legal residents.

Timing

Busiest business seasons are January through May and October through early November; October is the top foreign-buying and commercial-show season. But much business works round the clock, except for Chinese New Year. Most banks are open 10:00 A.M. to 4:00 P.M., but some open in the evening and even on Sundays for special purposes; there is 24-hour automated banking in many branches. Office hours are more or less the same as in the West, 9:00 A.M. to 5:00 or 6:00 P.M., but the shops usually open about 10:00 A.M. and stay open until late at night, especially in the tourist and residential areas.

Trade Information

Hong Kong Trade Development Council, Great Eagle Centre, 31st Fl., 23 Harbour Rd., Hong Kong; (5) 833–4333. Telex: 73595 CONHK HX; Cable: CONOTRAD HONGKONG. (The TDC has twenty-three overseas offices, including four in the United States and one in the United Kingdom.)

Trade Department, Ocean Centre, ground, first, 13th, 14th, and 15th floors, 5 Canton Rd., Kowloon, Hong Kong; (3) 722–2333. Telex: 75126 HX.

Industry Department, Ocean Centre, 14th Fl., 5 Canton Rd., Kowloon, Hong Kong; (3) 722–2573.

Chambers of Commerce. *Hong Kong General Chamber of Commerce,* United Centre, 22nd Fl., Queensway, Hong Kong; (5) 299229. Telex: 83535 HX; Cable: CHAMBERCOM HONGKONG.

American Chamber of Commerce in Hong Kong, 1030 Swire House, Connaught Road, Hong Kong; (5) 260165. Telex: 83664 HX; Cable: AMCHAM HONGKONG.

Federation of H.K. Industries, 408 Hankow Centre, 5–15 Hankow Rd., Kowloon, Hong Kong; (3) 723–0181. Telex: 84652 HKIND HX; Cable: FEDINDUSTR HONGKONG.

Chinese Manufacturers Association, Chinese Manufacturers Association Building, 64–66 Connaught Rd., Hong Kong; (5) 456166. Telex: 63526 HX; Cable: MAFTS HONGKONG.

Hong Kong Productivity Council, World Commerce Centre, 12th and 13th Fl., 11 Canton Rd., Kowloon, Hong Kong; (3) 723–5656. Telex: 32842 HX; Cable: PROCENTRE HONGKONG.

The Indian Chamber of Commerce Hong Kong, Hoseinee House, 2nd Fl., 69 Wyndham St., Hong Kong; (5) 233877. Telex: 64993 HX; Cable: INDCHAMBER HONGKONG.

The Hong Kong Japanese Chamber of Commerce and Industry, Hennessy Centre, 38th floor, 500 Hennessy Rd., Hong Kong; (5) 776129. *British Chamber of Commerce,* 6th Fl., 8 Queen's Rd., Central, Hong Kong; (5) 810–8118. *Swedish Chamber of Commerce,* 3607 Gloucester Tower, Pedder St., Central, Hong Kong; (5) 250349. Telex: 85946.

Travel Information

Hong Kong Tourist Association (H.K.T.A.), Connaught Centre, 35th Fl., Hong Kong; (5)244191. Telex: 74720 HX: Cable: LUYU HONG-KONG (eleven overseas offices, including three in the United States and one in the United Kingdom).

Area Travel

Hong Kong is a hub for travel in the area. In fact, it takes longer to drive to Kai Tak Airport and proceed through the facilities than it does to fly to Manila and Taipei. Most Asian countries have a National Tourist Office here. The cost of tickets or holiday packages is cheaper in Asia than in the U.S. or Europe, and Hong Kong is no exception to the rule. See the classified ads in the *South China Morning Post* for up-to-date listings. The most crowded times to travel in and out of the colony are Chinese New Year, the Easter/Ching Ming holidays, especially when they fall together (see *Public Holidays* in the front of the book), and the year-end. "Crowded" takes on meanings in Hong Kong you would never contemplate. Picture 25–30 percent of the colony on the move to China or Macau, and you will get the picture.

Useful Tips

Publications. Hong Kong is the international publishing center of Asia, not only because of its excellent business environment, but because, with the exception of libel and pornographic regulations, publishers are free to print what they like whether or not the Hong Kong or Chinese governments, or any other government, likes it. In other words, even though Hong Kong is a colony, there is more freedom of the press here than in most independent countries.

Aside from the myriad of guidebooks and picture books on Hong Kong, there are many specialist publications available. Most of the banks, and major realty companies for example, publish economic newsletters for their customers. The Hong Kong Trade Development Council publishes eight product magazines that are on sale in Hong Kong or free to qualified companies. The Asian Sources series has 11 product magazines and one newsletter. Business International has newsletters and studies on China and Asia. Asia Letter also has a series of newsletters on Asia and specific countries. The American Chamber of Commerce publishes books on Hong Kong and China, including *Living in Hong Kong, Doing Business in Hong Kong, Establishing an Office in Hong Kong,* which are available to members and nonmembers. The *Far Eastern Economic Review Yearbook* and the Hong Kong Government *Yearbook* are required reference books; the *Monthly Digest* from the government's Census & Statistics Department may also be useful. *Hong Kong Tax Planning,* as the name implies, is a useful book to cut through all the legalese of Hong Kong's tax codes. The China Phone Book Co. publishes a slew of useful publications on China in addition to their telephone and telex directories.

Newspapers and magazines from all over the world are readily available in Hong Kong. Both the *Asian Wall Street Journal* and the *International Herald Tribune* print international editions in Hong Kong to supplement the two excellent English-language daily newspapers, *The South China Morning Post* and the *Hong Kong Standard,* both of which carry a great deal of international news. The *Far Eastern Economic Review* leads the pack in business publications. *Time* and *Newsweek* both print in Hong Kong and the newsweekly *Asiaweek* is also here.

With satellite feeds on both radio and television, you will never be starved for information during your stay in Hong Kong.

Accountants. It should be little surprise to find that all the big accounting firms—*Arthur Anderson; Arthur Young; Coopers and Lybrand, Deloitte, Haskings & Sells; Ernst & Whinney; Peak Marwick Mitchell; Price Waterhouse,* etc.—have offices here.

Stockbrokers. Because of Hong Kong's geographical location, you can play the market 24 hours a day. All the big stockbrokers from all countries are represented in Hong Kong.

Couriers. The Post Office runs a *Speedpost* service akin to the overnight express service run by the U.S. Postal Service. Big international couriers, like *DHL, Federal Express, TNT Skypak,* and *Purolator,* all have large operations here.

Medical services. You have your choice, Western or Chinese—scalpels or needles—in modern hospitals or small acupuncture clinics. Everything exists side-by-side. Ambulance service is free.

Education. The nonprofit English Schools Foundation runs four secondary schools and eight primary schools, all based on the British system, culminating in the British exams: the GCSEs (formerly "O" levels) and "A" levels. *The Hong Kong International School* (the American school) runs from kindergarten through 12th grade. SATs and other college entrance exams are administered here. There is a *French International School,* a *German-Swiss International School,* and a *Japanese School.* There are extramural programs for adults run by the *Hong Kong University, Hong Kong Polytechnic,* and some of the secondary schools.

Maids. Maids, or domestic helpers, are available, but don't count on the traditional Chinese *amah,* beloved of the *New York Times* crossword—they're scarce. So scarce in fact that there are more than 30,000 Filipinas and a sprinkling of Thais and Sri Lankans working in Hong Kong as maids. If you hire a foreign maid, you are completely responsible for her while she is in your employ, which includes, in addition to room and board, medical coverage, minimum wage, state holidays, mandatory home leave, and passages. Contact the *Labour Department,* Harbour Building, 38 Pier St., Hong Kong; (5) 852–3537.

Shopping. If you can't manage to search out all the goodies in the "Shopping Section" due to pressing business engagements, try *Riggs Shopping Service,* Ocean Terminal, Tsimshatsui, Kowloon; (3) 696607.

Hotel "home delivery." Call the *Beverley Hills Deli* (3) 698695 or (5) 265809 for hotel delivery.

Florists. Use the ones in major hotels. It's easier and they all deliver. Hosts and hostesses here appreciate flowers as gifts, as do their counterparts around the world.

Chocolates. Hong Kong natives have a sweet tooth, too. *See's Candies,* flown fresh from California daily, are available in their outlets in Landmark (Central District), Ocean Terminal (Kowloon), and Cityplaza (Quarry Bay, Hong Kong Island) seven days a week. *Peninsula Chocolates,* from the hotel of the same name, are also sold in the Lucullus outlets and have an excellent reputation.

HONG KONG

by
**SAUL LOCKHART, HARRY ROLNICK, ROGER
BOSCHMAN, and BARRY GIRLING**

Saul Lockhart is the Area Editor for Fodor's Hong Kong. *Harry Rolnick, who has lived in Asia since 1965, has written over ten books, including the first restaurant guide to China and a definitive history of Macau. Roger Boschman is the author of* Hong Kong by Night *and is Hong Kong correspondent for many American and British magazines. Barry Girling is a food, travel, and entertainment columnist who has lived in Hong Kong since 1977.*

Chances are that on your first trip to Hong Kong, you'll be run so ragged shopping or keeping up with your various business appointments that you will probably not get to see much of this place.

Too bad, because in spite of the first impressions of a cold, concrete jungle, there are lots of things to see and do and experience in Hong Kong besides dashing to and fro between tailors and curio shops, business appointments and restaurants. (If you fit the above description, have faith: the Hong Kong Tourist Association reports that statistically, slightly more than half the visitors return.)

The feeling of Hong Kong—what it is and why it still exists in this modern age—can best be discovered in the harbor. That body of water, chosen so long ago by those anonymous Tanka boat people as a perfect shelter from the raging *tai foos* (the "big winds"—the origin of the English word "typhoon"—that occasionally ravage the South China Sea) is still the territory's centerpiece, even in this heavenly age of jet planes and satellite communications. The astute European China traders in the 1840s, after using the Portuguese colony of Macau for nearly 250 years, moved across those forty miles of Pearl River estuary water after Macau's harbor silted up, discovering the attractions of the same harbor the Chinese fishermen had founded hundreds of years previously. Those big China clippers would have a deep draft port and protection from the weather in Hong Kong's large natural harbor.

Local wags point out you can always tell the visitors from the residents on the Star Ferry because the latter are always buried in a newspaper or a racing sheet. The former, of course, are agog at one of the most magnificent sights in the world—Hong Kong's ever bustling harbor. (And you can't beat the price either. The Star Ferry must be the cheapest seven-minute harbour tour anywhere.)

Hongkongers, whether they be native Chinese or foreign residents, are historically very insular in their thinking. Literally. Hong Kong islanders think Hong Kong. Kowlooners think Kowloon. The NTers (those in the New Territories) think their territories. And then there are the other islanders: Lantauians, Cheung Chauians, and Lammaians, who in addition to good naturedly disdaining all other Hongkongers, feel quite separate from those who do not live on their islands.

Lest you think this has a racial bias, the reasons for the insularity are purely historical, even though these days there is a great deal of commuting between the areas, especially along the routes of the Mass Transit Railway (the subway or underground, if you prefer).

After all, it was not until the middle 1970s that the cross harbor tunnel road linked Hong Kong Island, the financial, banking, government, and business center of the colony, with the mainland section. And the Mass Transit Railway (M.T.R.), which has done so much to unite the far-flung parts of the territory, only opened in late 1980. Before that, the populace depended on passengers and vehicular ferries, the latter being slow with great lineups at either end, to cross the harbor. Furthermore, Hong Kong was run as a dual economy, with

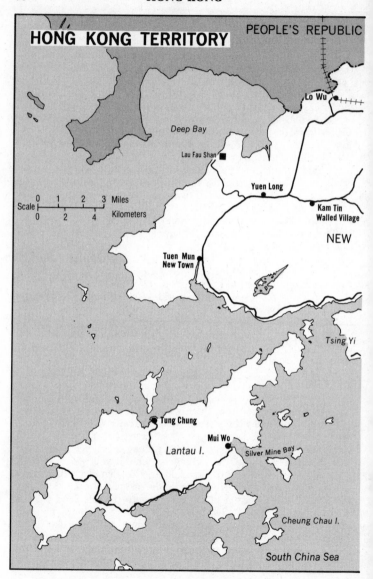

HONG KONG TERRITORY

PEOPLE'S REPUBLIC

Lo Wu

Deep Bay

Lau Fau Shan

Yuen Long

Kam Tin
Walled Village

Scale 0 1 2 3 Miles
0 2 4 Kilometers

NEW

Tuen Mun
New Town

Tsing Yi

Tung Chung

Mui Wo

Lantau I.

Silver Mine Bay

Cheung Chau I.

South China Sea

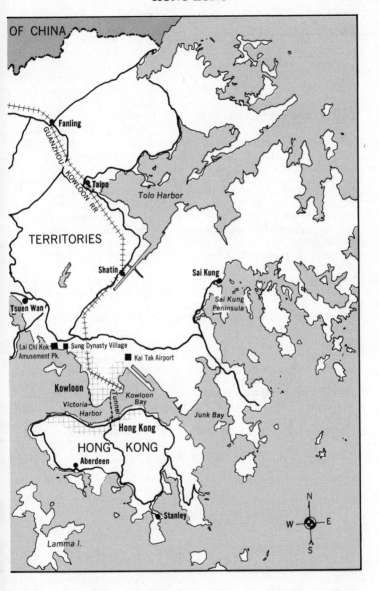

branches of offices, delivery fleets, and other businesses on one side of the harbor duplicating the facilities of the other. There were even separate laws and charges covering buses, taxis, and electricity.

The historical separation still sticks mentally, even though it now only takes a few minutes to drive through the tunnel (excluding the long waiting times on either side to get into the tunnel) or less than 30 minutes to get from Hong Kong Central to the farthest point of the territory on M.T.R., and the Hong Kong business world has long ago given up the dual economy system and rationalized their operations.

"Let's have dinner in Kowloon," says a Kowloon-side resident to his Hong Kong mate and the first thought passing through the Hongkong-ers mind is "all the way to Kowloon!" The reverse is also true. Invite your colleague to dinner at your home on the south side of the island in Repulse Bay or Shouson Hill and, in spite of the Aberdeen Tunnel that cuts traveling time to that side to mere minutes, the first mental response is likely to be "so far!." And for Hongkongers or Kowlooners to venture to the New Territories . . . and for mainlanders to the islands.

New residents from countries where the population is accustomed to hopping into a car and driving for hundreds of miles—America, Cana-da, Australia, New Zealand, and the Western Europe—are often aston-ished at the insularity. After all, their daily commute in London or Los Angeles might be three or four times the distance from Hong Kong to Kowloon or the New Territories. But, they too eventually fall into the local mentality.

Visitors, of course, are not plagued by this mentality and think nothing of shopping in Stanley Village in the morning just prior to heading out to the New Territories, all the way up to the border. So the visiting tourists to Hong Kong have two distinct advantages over those of us who live here. Firstly, they invariably look at this vibrant world crossroads with a fresh eye and pick out details that are often missed by the bored and perhaps jaded eye of the resident. Secondly, tourists do not fall prey to the false insularity that is prevalent among residents.

Read on and discover Hong Kong's hidden and not-so-hidden de-lights. And with any luck you will get to see some of them on your first trip and all of them when you return.

HONG KONG ISLAND

Until 1841, the thirty-square-mile South Seas island that is now modern Hong Kong was home to a few fishing families. Hong Kong didn't have a single natural water source, its mountainous center was foreboding, its vegetation sparse. Except for the harbor, all the geographical, historical, and demographic factors should have guaranteed that Hong Kong remain forever obscure and remote.

Even after it was officially ceded to Great Britain in 1841, Hong Kong was less a prize of war than a parish of the victors. The British military acknowledged its usefulness as a berth or trans-shipping port, but was riled that it wasn't offered a port on the mainland. The British Foreign Office laughed at what the Foreign Minister called "that barren island," and Queen Victoria's consort, Prince Albert, publicly giggled at this inconsequential diadem in the British Crown.

Even the official treaty described Hong Kong in less-than-glowing terms. Article 3 cites the possession of Hong Kong "so the British Subjects should have some Port whereat they may careen and refit their Ships when required and keep stores for that purpose."

Hardly an auspicious start for the island that author Han Su-Yin described a century later as "the deep roaring bustling eternal market . . . which life and love and souls and blood and all things made and grown under the sun are bought and sold and smuggled and squandered."

Yet this is the impression one gets when arriving on the island for the first time by Star Ferry. (One of the great regrets of progress is that most visitors now get their initial picture of Hong Kong from the cavernous Cross-Harbor Tunnel or the steps of the Mass Transit Railway, rather than from the legendary Star Ferry.

It was only blocks away from the Star Ferry that Captain Charles Elliot of Britain's Royal Navy first set foot on "this barren rock." That which was barren land then is today some of the world's most expensive real estate—today the skyline from the harbor to Central looks nothing less than futuristic.

Central Hong Kong is officially named Victoria City, but nobody ever calls it this. Central is like a cemetery erected by Fabergé, the buildings ornate tombstones with the most incredible designs. They gleam in gold and silver and ivory and ebony, reflecting a jewellike iridescence from the harbor to the land. True, the Chinese like to give scurrilous nicknames to the buildings—"The Amah's Tooth" for a gold-curtained Far East Finance Centre or "The House Of A Thousand Derrieres" for Connaught Centre with its endless rows of circular windows. But no one can fail to be overwhelmed by the first view of Hong Kong from the harbor.

The British who set up their little warehouses here were mainly of Scots ancestry, but they were among the most nationalistic (or homesick) in the Victorian world. Almost everything of importance was named after their Monarch. The Central section was Victoria City. The mountain was Victoria Peak. The military barracks at the eastern end of Victoria City was Victoria Barracks. The prison was Victoria Prison. And later Hong Kong would have a Victoria College and Victoria Park, where the statue of the Monarch would be moved from her spot directly in the center of Victoria City, in Statue Square.

Hong Kong Island almost immediately achieved an importance far out of proportion to its size and location. By 1846, the handful of dwellers had increased to 24,000. And while only 600 of them were British, they established their identity immediately.

Most of the Chinese had been living on the southwestern side of the island to be near the sea. The British first erected its settlement in the Central section toward the west. Disease struck quickly, and blaming the small farms, which they felt to be unsanitary, the British banned farming everywhere on the island (a rule that has never been repealed) and moved farther back from the sea to a section they called, with optimistic prescience, "Happy Valley."

The Hong Kong Club was built by the sea in Central. (Land reclamation later pushed that point three blocks on.) The race course was erected in Happy Valley (the original site is still used). And within 30 years of Hong Kong's founding, a guidebook referred to the "magnificent public buildings and hotels" on the island.

To orient oneself to Hong Kong Island, Central (the original Victoria City) is still the core around which everything lies. Yet just because Hong Kong is relatively small (the truly energetic could walk around it in about a day), the various areas are neatly perceivable.

Central lies smack in the center of the north side of the island. The extreme western end is Western district (of course). To the east of Central lie Wanchai, famed at one time for its night life, then Causeway Bay, which was once middle-class Chinese but is now more tourist-oriented, thanks to the Cross-Harbor Tunnel.

Going farther east, one reaches Quarry Bay, once just a factory and tenement section, now a middle-class housing area too. Shaukiwan and Chaiwan are at the eastern end. Originally very poor, they are now undergoing revolutionary urban development.

One of the great tourist trips of the world starts at Shaukiwan and ends in Western District (or vice versa, of course) on the Hong Kong tram, the old narrow-gauge, double-decker electric contraption.

Onto the middle of Hong Kong Island. Going across the island, on the middle-levels of the Peak, is the aptly named Mid-Levels area, which is almost entirely residential. Mid-Levels includes some of the few remaining examples of Victorian apartment architecture, Hong Kong University, the Botanical Gardens, and greenery in the most unlikely places.

High above Mid-Levels is Victoria Peak, 1,809 feet above sea level. The residents here take a special pride in the positions to which they have, quite literally, risen.

The southern side of the island was inhabited originally by Chinese. They would sail from what is now Stanley and Aberdeen to fertile fishing grounds or take shelter in pirate coves.

Aberdeen, with its vast array of fishing boats, is now changing as the harbor is filled in. Moving east, you come to progress of sorts. First to Wong Chuk Hang, the factory section of Aberdeen, then into a modern highway cloverleaf system, the interchange for the Aberdeen Tunnel, which slices through the mountains to come out in Happy Valley. (This is in front of Ocean Park and Water World.) Beyond that is scenic Deep Water Bay. Farther along, you come to one of Hong Kong's most prestigious residential areas and most popular beach, Repulse Bay.

Still following the winding road, there is the tiny village of Stanley, with its open-air market. Then Big Wave Bay, home to the territory's few surfers, and the pleasant village of Shek-O, another old settlement that today is a mix of old village houses and baronial mansions.

More than 1.5 million people live on this small island. The kaleidoscopic lifestyles, peoples, and—let's be frank—tensions are many. Central's architecture may be futuristic, but the nervousness that accompanies success is evident everywhere, from the nasty temper of your average sales clerk to the quiet panic at lunchtimes when crowds surge around the Stock Exchange foreign exchange and gold listings. Everything in Hong Kong is geared to the sweet and occasionally acrid smell of success.

Central

The successful aroma is sensed at its best and worst in Central. By New York standards, the skyscrapers are paltry, the tallest merely 54 floors. But to see all those great monoliths in one group, set against the harbor (from the Peak) or against the Peak (from the Ferry), is awe-inspiring.

Virtually all Central was created by ambitious men, from the ground up. The original seashore was roughly where Queen's Road Central runs today. All the rest has been reclaimed from the sea. Buildings over a decade old are considered anachronisms in this fast-paced, business-mad territory. And the new structures are phenomenal. From the Star Ferry through the pedestrian passage to Statue Square and the heart of Central, the steel, glass, concrete structures hum with money-making activity.

Enter the Landmark with its 20,000-square-foot atrium and hundreds of shops . . . so large that it becomes a stage for free entertain-

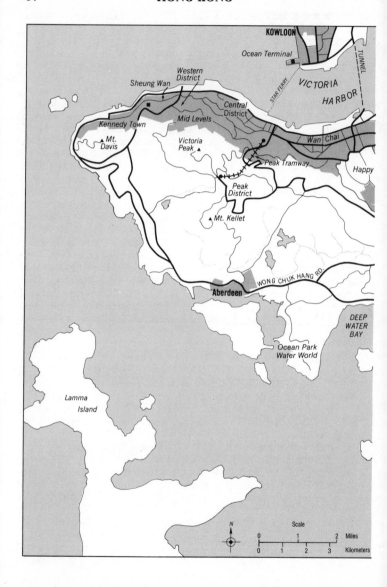

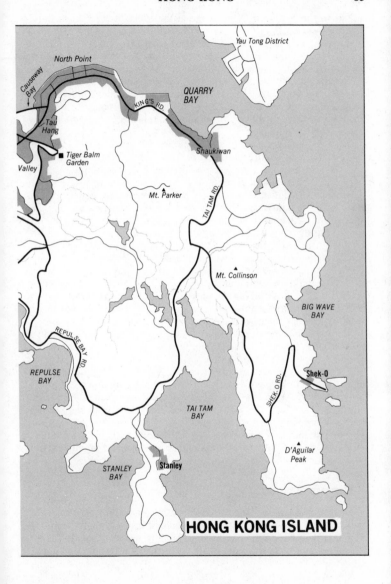

Yau Tong District

North Point

Causeway Bay

QUARRY BAY

KING'S RD.

Tau Hang

Shaukiwan

Valley

■ Tiger Balm Garden

Mt. Parker

TAI TAM RD.

Mt. Collinson

BIG WAVE BAY

REPULSE BAY RD.

REPULSE BAY

Shek-O

SHEK-O RD.

TAI TAM BAY

STANLEY BAY

Stanley

D'Aguilar Peak

HONG KONG ISLAND

ment. In the Mandarin Hotel—one of the 1960s-built "ancient buildings"—local businessmen make million-dollar deals in the Chinnery
Bar, toasting their success with silver tankards. If you get an invitation
to the Hong Kong Club, you can see the tycoons of Hong Kong, one
eye on the Stock Exchange, another on the fine menu.

But there is another side to Central. When people think of "prosper-
ous" Hong Kong, they think of the buildings around Statue Square:
banks, stock exchanges, massive complexes with Escherlike stairway
mazes linking them above ground and symbolically linking their financial entanglements.

True, on the ferry side of Statue Square is City Hall, with its libraries
and art museum, auditoriums and recital halls. But this "culture" and
the seasonal festivals, impressive as they may be, are simply outcrops
of the main business of Hong Kong, which is business.

Modern as Central may be, another face comes into view when you
walk up Wyndham Street to Hollywood Road, with its mass of antique
shops, and walk west to Peele Street, one of the famed "ladder" streets,
made entirely of steps heading up the mountain. Literally five minutes
from Central megoliths, Peele Street is China of the eighteenth century
(or, to some people, like Lower East Side New York of 1900). Walk
up these old ladder streets and thousands of ideographs from each side
of the street almost shout out their wares: flags and pennants, open-air
stalls, butcher shops selling the most incredible innards, paper-makers
with their toy cars for funerals, gownmakers with their toy gowns for
weddings, shops filled with the most unlikely merchandise.

The signs become wordless decoration, a kind of artistry that does
exactly what the suit-and-tie computerized modern offices of Central
are doing: selling, selling, selling.

If the walk up Peele Street is tiring, simply stay on Hollywood Road
until you reach the great Man Mo Temple, then walk down Cat Street
to the harbor. Again, the side streets virtually shout out their wares.
Near Central Market is Wing On Street, selling only cloth. Farther
west is Wing Kut Street, selling mainly baby clothing. Farther east are
Li Yuen streets East and West with their ubiquitous clothing stalls.

This, then, is Central with many faces: modern and ambitious, old
and traditional.

Western District

Most tourists make their way to Wanchai from Central. But to see
the really old Hong Kong, take a long walk or tram through the mazes
of Western district. One can become happily lost here, ready for an
adventure in streets that seem to have been built for an Alan Ladd
movie.

Western is an area in which to run across the unexpected. After all, this was one of the oldest settlements and is still the major market for wholesale foodstuffs. The lanes always lead to something new. There are dozens of routes, each with surprises. A long walk on Connaught Road West along the waterfront takes you to shops selling different grades of rice, vegetables, and teas. The lighters put up almost at the shore, the longshoremen take the goods straight to the wholesalers who sit outside their open-front shops waiting for buyers.

Or you can cut across to Des Voeux Road West to the interesting side streets. Tung Loi Lane sells only sharkfin and birds' nest. Mercier Street sells only fishing tackle and tropical fish, yet smack in the middle is the frenetic Chinese Gold and Silver Exchange. At Centre and Eastern streets are incredible Chinese markets. Farther on is Tai Ping Shan, the residents of which were once followers of a famous Chinese pirate. The old tenements are reminders of nineteenth-century village China. There are three temples in Tai Ping Shan, all crowded with joss sticks, tablets in memory of the dead, and fortune tellers.

Kennedy Town Praya, one of the older settlements, is all the way at the end of Western district. The name praya is Portuguese—from the nineteenth century when Hong Kong was simply a poor cousin to booming Macau—and the town still has an easy-going Mediterranean atmosphere. The architecture, of abattoirs and squatter huts, is fairly depressing. But the views to Macau and Green Island are always interesting.

Chances are that you'll want to take the tram (or a mini-bus) back to Central from Kennedy Town. But should you have the time, this is an interesting approach to Mid-Levels.

To reach the University of Hong Kong at the western reaches of Mid-Levels, travel up Smithfield Road to Pokfield Road. The University opened in 1911, but a few of the buildings predate this, though they are rapidly being demolished. Visit the Campus Museum for some good examples of pottery and porcelain.

To get back to Central, you can take the direct route down Robinson Road or Bonham Road. Bonham Road has some of the more interesting old buildings, and runs into Ladder Street, the old street that runs directly into Hollywood Road. Robinson Road takes you past the old Ohel Leah Synagogue, which dates back to the late nineteenth century. It also passes Ladder Street, zigzagging over to Hollywood Road. It is said that this 200-feet-long street was built for the bearers of sedan chair to carry passengers from Central to residential Caine Road. The corner of Ladder Street and Hollywood Road is officially known as Upper and Lower Lascar Roads, after the East Indian sailors who crewed the merchantmen and lived there when ashore. They were a tough lot, and the area was a den of thieves and whoremongers. So

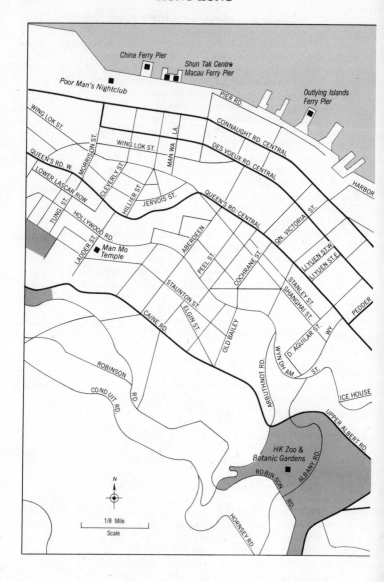

China Ferry Pier

Shun Tak Centre
Macau Ferry Pier

Poor Man's Nightclub

Outlying Islands
Ferry Pier

PIER RD.

CONNAUGHT RD. CENTRAL

WING LOK ST.

MORRISON ST.

WING LOK ST.

MAN WA LA.

DES VOEUX RD. CENTRAL

QUEEN'S RD. W.

LOWER LASCAR ROW

CLEVERLY ST.

HILLIER ST.

JERVOIS ST.

QUEEN'S RD. CENTRAL

HARBOR

TUNG ST.

HOLLYWOOD RD.

LADDER ST.

Man Mo
Temple

ABERDEEN

QN. VICTORIA ST.

PEEL ST.

COCHRANE ST.

LI YUEN ST. W.

LI YUEN ST. E.

STAUNTON ST.

CAINE RD.

ELGIN ST.

OLD BAILEY

STANLEY ST.

SHANGHAI ST.

WY.

PEDDER

D. AGUILAR ST.

WYNDHAM ST.

ARBUTHNOT RD.

ST.

ICE HOUSE

ROBINSON RD.

CONDUIT RD.

UPPER ALBERT RD.

HK Zoo &
Botanic Gardens

ROBINSON RD.

ALBANY RD.

HORNSEY RD.

N

1/8 Mile
Scale

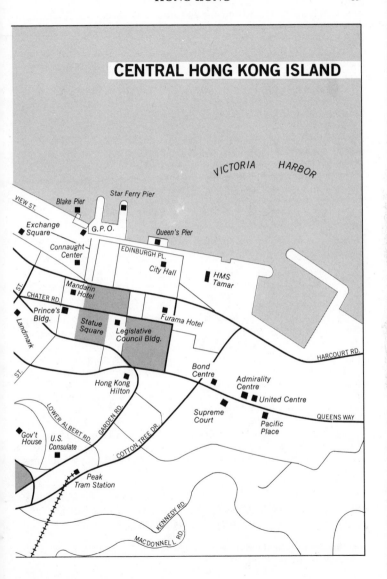

CENTRAL HONG KONG ISLAND

VICTORIA HARBOR

VIEW ST

Blake Pier

Star Ferry Pier

Exchange
Square

G.P.O.

Queen's Pier

Connaught
Center

EDINBURGH PL.

City Hall

HMS
Tamar

CHATER RD.

Mandarin
Hotel

ST.

Prince's
Bldg.

Landmark

Statue
Square

Legislative
Council Bldg.

Furama Hotel

HARCOURT RD.

ST.

Hong Kong
Hilton

Bond
Centre

Admirality
Centre

United Centre

Supreme
Court

Pacific
Place

QUEENS WAY

LOWER ALBERT RD.

GARDEN RD.

Gov't
House

U.S.
Consulate

COTTON TREE DR.

Peak
Tram Station

KENNEDY RD.

MACDONNELL RD.

today the street is known to one and all as Cat Street. Why? Some say it's because they were cat burglars, others that the brothels or "cat houses" were in the area.

When you reach Hollywood Road, you may want to detour to Lan Kwai Fong, a tiny street off Wyndham Street lined with trendy restaurants and discotheques.

The area between Central and Wanchai is rather uninteresting now, but it was the original home for the military. Where the Hilton Hotel stands now was the parade grounds of an earlier time. When Queen's Road Central fronted the sea, this was where the few delicate British ladies of the colony, dressed in crinoline, would march with their smart military beaux, admiring the sunset. Today, you can visit the original Victoria Barracks, where one of the buildings has been transformed into a Museum of Tea. Take the Peak Tram from this area for one of the most entrancing views in Asia.

The Peak

Victoria Peak was a forbidding (if beautiful) spot during the first thirty years of the colony. In the 1870s, the Governor would spend the humid summers there. He was followed by other influential citizens hoisted up by sedan chair. (In fact, the old sedan chair transport is re-enacted each year for charity races, with proceeds going to Matilda's Hospital on the Peak.)

By 1888, the Peak Tram, a funicular railway, was built. Something is offered at all the stops on the tram's route. You might, for example, stop at Bowen Road and see the Botanical Gardens. Once on the Peak, the view is overwhelming. It's *de rigueur* to walk around the Peak, along Harlech Road and Lugard Road. On a clear day you can see all the way to China and Macau. For the less energetic, the Peak Tower Restaurant is a good place to rest weary feet and have a meal. Peak Tower also has some interesting book and souvenir shops.

But why restrict yourself to the common views? Every street has a lovely old house. You can walk down Mount Austin Road to the gardens of the old summer residence of Hong Kong governors. At the end of the road, 1,805 feet above sea level, you can watch an astonishing sunset over the astonishing island.

It is possible to walk down from the Peak (a lot less strenuous than walking up, though this, too, is enjoyable) or take the Number 15 bus from the Peak down to Central. The ride is a hair-raising, hair-breadth, 30-minute experience, but never has there been an accident or a second of boredom.

Once on the "lowlands," take a tram or taxi through Queensway, to the land of Suzie Wong, Wanchai.

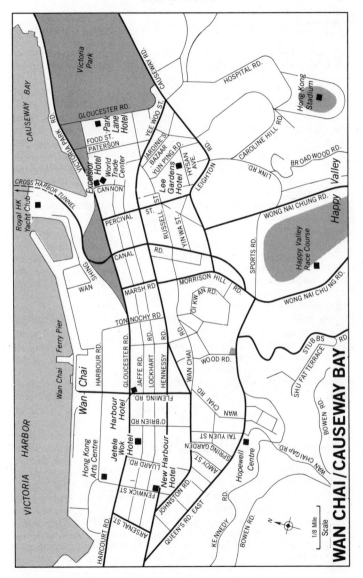

WAN CHAI/CAUSEWAY BAY

Wanchai

Those who expect the raunchy, exciting, scurrilous, loud and bustling world of Wanchai may be disappointed. Wanchai still has its nocturnal charms (which are discussed in the "Night Life" section of this guide) but the "Wanch" of Richard Mason's fine novel, *The World of Suzie Wong,* seems a bit faded now.

Wanchai was always something of a magnet for seamen on holiday, but during the 1960s and 1970s it boomed, thanks to the rest-and-recreation leaves of Vietnam War military men. Today, it's a bit more jaded and expensive, but you can still find topless bars, seamen of all nations, the occasional fight. MP's still patrol the street when the fleet's in town, reviving some of the old traditional atmosphere of Wanchai.

The legendary Suzie Wong Hotel, the Luk Kwok, is now gone, but you can still wander about Lockhart Road and environs and see the girlie bars, almost cheek by jowl, interspersed with the occasional British pub or Chinese tailor.

During the day, Wanchai does what the rest of Hong Kong does: business. Wanchai was once one of the five *wan* or areas that the British set aside for Chinese residence. Of course it's totally integrated now: office buildings, a few good restaurants, some apartment buildings. Culturally, Wanchai has the Hong Kong Arts Centre and the Academy of Performing Arts.

On Queen's Road East (parallel with the main Hennessey Road that runs through the district), you might pop into the Colony's tallest building, the 66-story Hopewell Centre, and view the sites from the Revolving 66 Restaurant. Nearly adjacent are Hung Shing Temple, with its good pottery, and Sui Pak Temple, a.k.a Chai Kung Woot Fat Temple, with its lucky mirrors left by those who had been cured of illness. You might also visit Wanchai Market, and the side streets off Queen's Road East sell a myriad of wares, from birds, crickets, and snakes to paper offerings to the dead.

Happy Valley and Causeway Bay

Queen's Road East runs into Happy Valley and the famous Happy Valley Race Course. The course is less than a mile long, but it attracts thousands of racegoers from September through May, on weekends and Wednesday evenings.

Happy Valley also has five cemeteries, each a respectful distance from the other: the Muslim Cemetery, the Catholic Cemetery, the Colonial Cemetery, the Parsee Cemetery, and the Jewish Cemetery, all of them built within 20 years of each other, between 1846 and 1879.

The Aw Boon Haw Gardens, 150,000 square feet of the most garish, awful, colorful, zany statues, pagodas, grottos, scenes of torture, religion, love, and everything else, are also in Causeway Bay. One does not think of taste—good or bad—at the gardens, they are simply a phenomenon.

Toward the harbor is Causeway Bay, known for its marvelous restaurants of every description, its good hotels (Excelsior, Park Lane, and Lee Gardens) and the famed noonday gun. Once a "suburb" of Central, Causeway Bay, most of its land reclaimed from the sea, it is now a huge shopping mart, crowded, somewhat chaotic, and a lovely place to eat and spend an evening.

While much of the sea has been turned into land, the bay itself houses the Royal Hong Kong Yacht Club and the Typhoon Anchorage. The latter, opposite the Excelsior Hotel, is the place to pick up a "floating restaurant" sampan (a sampan with tables and chairs seating eight to ten people). You can spend a few hours weaving through the sea lanes of the typhoon basin, enjoy a meal bought from a "kitchen" sampan that instantly materializes, enjoy drinks from the bar sampan, even hear some music by a live-band sampan. A song list is passed, but the combo is universally considered to be the worst in all of Asia. The cost per tune is about HK$30. Your notes are worth a lot more than the raucous—and entertaining—notes that come from the guitars.

Victoria Park, the home for go-carting, tennis, jogging, soccer, and, in the morning, *tai chi* exercises, is on the outskirts of Causeway Bay. Nearby is Food Street, with dozens of different restaurants of varying quality.

North Point, Quarry Bay, and Shaukiwan

The area east of Victoria Park offers very little for the one-time traveler. True, North Point and Quarry Bay are both undeniably the "real" Hong Kong. But this means tenements and factories.

Shaukiwan has two noteworthy sights. One is the ferry service to Kowloon's Lei Yue Mun Village, with its fishing restaurants. The other is Taikooshing, a massive city-within-a-city. Some years ago this was barren reclaimed land. Today, it's a middle-class housing estate. The shopping center, Cityplaza, has an ice-skating rink, gardens, restaurants, and hundreds of shops. The village is virtually self-suficient in everything except home-grown food.

The South Coast of the Island

The southern side of Hong Kong is old, picturesque, and filled with surprises. You can begin in Aberdeen (named after an English lord, not the Scottish town), which has a series of histories.

Aberdeen got its start as a pirate town (fishing and piracy were intermingled about 200 years ago). After the Second World War, Aberdeen became fairly touristy, mainly because of the Tanka "boat people." They lived in the anchorage on their houseboats and were as picturesque to the occasional visitor as their economic conditions were depressing. Some myopic visitors regret the fact that boat people are turning to factory work on land. Drab as that work may be, it's a definite improvement over their old way of life. The government, wisely, offers the younger people schools geared to the needs of a fishing community.

You can still see much of traditional Aberdeen, such as the Aberdeen Cemetery, with its enormous gravestones (and a glorious view of hill and water, the most auspicious place to be buried). Along Aberdeen's side streets, you can still find outdoor barbers and a myriad *dim sum* restaurants. Out in the harbor, along with the floating restaurants, you have 3,000-odd junks and sampans and you will undoubtedly be asked to come on one for a ride through the harbor.

The Tin Hau Temple is rather shabby, but this shrine to the goddess of the sea—appropriately the most popular deity in Hong Kong—is especially colorful during April and May's Tin Hau Festival, when hundreds of boats converge along the shore.

Aberdeen's most interesting section is Aplichau Island, which can be reached by bridge or sampan. The island has a boat-building yard that constructs mainly junks, but yachts, sampans, and sloops as well. Almost all are the boats here are built without formal plans.

From the bridge you can get a superb overview of the harbor and its myriad junks. (You'll have to walk back to take a picture, since vehicles cannot stop on the bridge.)

Near Aberdeen is Ocean Park and Water World, owned and managed by the Royal Hong Kong Jockey Club. Ocean Park is situated on 170 acres of land overlooking the sea. It is one of the world's largest oceanariums, its two sections attracting thousands of visitors.

On the "lowland" site are gardens, parks, and a children's zoo. A cable car, providing spectacular views of the entire south coast, takes you to the "headland" side and Ocean Theatre, the largest marine mammal theater in the world, with seats for 4,000 people. One of the world's largest roller-coasters and various other rides are also up top.

The adjacent, 65-acre Water World, an aquatic fun park, has slides, rapids, pools, and a wave cove.

To the east is Deep Water Bay, the site of the film *Love Is a Many-Splendored Thing*. Its beauty and deep covers are still many-splendored.

The best-known beach in the territory is Repulse Bay, named after the British warship *H.M.S. Repulse* (not, as some wags say, from the pollution of the water). The famed Repulse Bay Hotel was demolished in 1982, spawning a replica of the hotel's famed verandah restaurant and adjacent Bamboo Bar on Christmas Day, 1986. This new establishment is called the Repulse Bay Verandah Restaurant and is run by the same folk who ran, and then demolished, the original hotel. The hills behind the restaurant were used by the Japanese, who clambered over them in December 1941 to come into the Repulse Bay Hotel gardens, then the British headquarters. After a brief battle, they took the British captives.

Another remnant of World War II is Stanley, notorious as the home of the largest Hong Kong P.O.W. camp run by the Japanese. Fortunately, you would never notice anything malevolent there today. Known for its street market, Stanley also has superb beaches. Even Stanley Prison (set apart from the village) has a good beach, though it's now restricted to prison personnel.

You can still see old one-story village houses in Stanley, side by side with modern apartment buildings. The Tin Hau Temple is noted for its tiger skin (supposedly shot by the Japanese) and an ancient bell and drum still used to open and close the temple.

An intriguing market, where designer fashions are sold at virtually wholesale prices, is in Stanley. Today, Hong Kong has dozens of shops dispensing these bargains, but it's more fun shopping for them around Stanley. You can also find rattan, fresh food, ceramics, paintings, hardware, even second-hand books. Not really a flea market, the roundabout market street curving through the town gives the impression of something countrified and spontaneous.

Shek-O, the easternmost village on the south, has old village houses, millionaire mansions, a few plain restaurants, a pretty beach, and fine views of the south. Leave the little town square and take the curving path through the town across a little footbridge. This is the island of Tai Tau Chau. Now walk across the great rock to a lookout position to espy far into the South China Sea.

Little more than a century ago, this open water was ruled by pirates. Today, it stands as the southernmost area of that phenomenal "barren island" called Hong Kong.

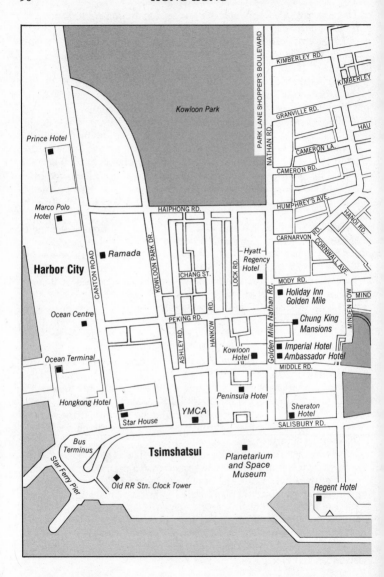

Kowloon Park

KIMBERLEY RD.

KIMBERLEY

PARK LANE SHOPPER'S BOULEVARD

NATHAN RD.

GRANVILLE RD.

HAU

CAMERON LA.

CAMERON RD.

HUMPHREY'S AVE.

HANOI RD.

Prince Hotel

Marco Polo Hotel

HAIPHONG RD.

Harbor City

Ramada

CANTON ROAD

KOWLOON PARK DR.

ICHANG ST.

LOCK RD.

CARNARVON RD.

CORNWALL AVE.

Hyatt Regency Hotel

MODY RD.

Holiday Inn Golden Mile

Chung King Mansions

MINDEN ROW

MIND

Ocean Centre

PEKING RD.

ASHLEY RD.

HANKOW RD.

Golden Mile Nathan Rd.

Imperial Hotel
Ambassador Hotel

Ocean Terminal

Kowloon Hotel

MIDDLE RD.

Hongkong Hotel

Peninsula Hotel

Sheraton Hotel

Star House

YMCA

SALISBURY RD.

Bus Terminus

Star Ferry Pier

Tsimshatsui

Old RR Stn. Clock Tower

Planetarium and Space Museum

Regent Hotel

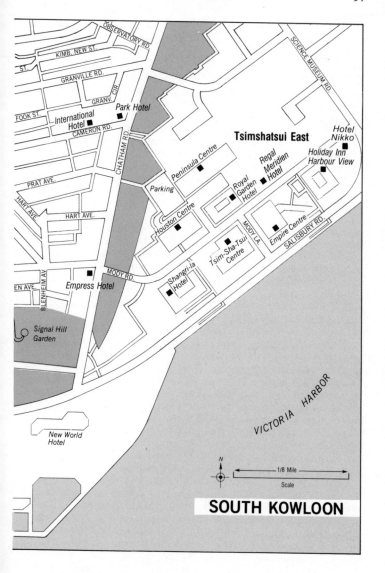

Tsimshatsui East

SOUTH KOWLOON

KOWLOON

A comedian visited Kowloon some years ago, saw how crowded it was, and quipped: "There are no cows in Kowloon—they wouldn't have room to moo!"

Kowloon, a peninsula that is just across Victoria Harbour from Central, *is* crowded, but the name has nothing to do with cows. Back in the Sung Dynasty, when the boy emperor fled here, he counted eight hills on the peninsula and called them the Eight Dragons. A servant reminded him that an emperor is also said to be a dragon, so there were a total of nine dragons present. In Chinese this is *gau-lung* and is written in English as *kow-loon.*

Years ago the much-fabled *Star Ferry* was like a spinal cord running from the body of Kowloon and the New Territories into the administrative head on Hong Kong Island. The Kowloon-Canton Railway terminal stood next to the Star Ferry. People used to come on the ferry from Hong Kong, stay overnight at that famous railway hotel, The Peninsula, then climb aboard the train en route to Peking, Moscow, Calais, and London.

Now, you can take a taxi via the Cross Harbour Tunnel from Kowloon to Causeway Bay or Central District. On the Mass Transit Railway you can go to Central District in the time it took to find the benches where you sat to wait for the next Star Ferry to arrive. But the ferry that Suzy Wong rode to meet novelist Richard Mason still plies the route across the harbor from Hong Kong Island.

Kowloon is where most of Hong Kong's hotels are, in the old Tsimshatsui and new East Tsimshatsui districts. The old Tsimshatsui is now represented by the remaining clock tower of the Kowloon-Canton Railway station, the Y.M.C.A., the Peninsula Hotel, and the bustling Nathan Road area. The new Tsimshatsui is The Regent Hotel, the New World Hotel and shopping center, the Space Museum, and the waterfront esplanade running through to the newer East Tsimshatsui, with its glittering new hotels, office buildings, and shopping centers.

Ocean Terminal has been partially eclipsed by the Ocean Centre shops and offices and now the enormous Harbour City commercial and residential complex. Visitors arriving by ship or foot flow through these interconnected shopping centers (some three miles of air-conditioned shopping) and then over to the Golden Mile on Nathan Road, and on down such side streets as Carnarvon and Mody Roads, perhaps ending up in Tsimshatsui East.

Hotels are the gathering points in Tsimshatsui, not only as group tour accommodation, but as eating and entertainment spots. The largest concentration is on lower Nathan Road, dominated by the Holiday Inn Golden Mile, Hyatt Regency, Ambassador, Sheraton, Imperial and of course the Peninsula. The venerable Pen retains the atmosphere of the British colony that once was and East still meets West (or perhaps a neighbor) in the colonnaded lobby for tea.

On Canton Road, the Hong Kong Hotel's shops are attached to the Ocean Terminal, blending well with the shopping centers. The Marco Polo and Prince Hotels in the Harbour City complex anchor the other side of this giant shopper's labyrinth. Across Canton Road, the giant Silvercord shopping complex beckons.

What has changed the face of the Kowloon peninsula is the East Tsimshatsui development. The Regent Hotel has probably the best harbor view in Hong Kong, from its see-through lobby and mezzanine. Its neighbor, the New World Hotel, is set in one of the largest shopping arcades in the territory.

Just along the waterfront walkway is a whole brace of deluxe hotels —the Shangri-La, Holiday Inn Harbour View, Royal Garden, Regal Meridien, and Nikko. As you will see in the Night Life section of this guide, these are not merely additions to the shopping and accommodation facilities.

The tip of the Kowloon peninsula, from Harbour City to Tsimshatsui East, contains shopping and night life. Many visitors never get any farther. They shop, eat, shop, drink, shop, and occasionally sleep in that area without seeing the rest of Kowloon. But there is much, much more to Kowloon than this shopper's paradise.

Exploring Kowloon

Along the waterfront, just beyond the Harbour City shopping center on the west side of the peninsula, is the Yaumatei District, with its colorful floating community in the typhoon shelter. This is one of the headquarters for a traditional junk fishing fleet. Many families still live on board, dropping off their catch in Kowloon, loading supplies, and heading back out to sea again.

The famous "mile long" night market on Temple Street, where things really brighten up when the sun goes down, is near the typhoon shelter. For visitors it is more of a spectacle than a shopping spot, an exotic Far East bazaar. The bargains here are really geared for sale to the locals, but that does not mean a visitor cannot find something.

Not far away at the junction of Kansu and Reclamation Streets is the famous jade market, which still operates in much the traditional way. Traders bid for uncut jade rocks, using secret signs, their hands hidden under handkerchiefs or newspapers. The items sold range from blocks of raw jade to tiny amulets and modern jewelry. This is a daily activity, starting around 10 o'clock. The fever fades around 4:00 P.M.

Nearby a multi-story carpark is the 1980s version of the traditional letter-writer's craft. For a price, the scribe will set down the thoughts of the illiterate in delicate Chinese script. For many a hesitant bumpkin, the scribes find the terms to describe the romantic feelings of the sender, perhaps to be understood by a receiver many thousands of miles away in another culture. Among the traditional scribes are those who merrily pound out letters on typewriters.

Something entirely new in the last couple of years is the Golden Shopping Centre in nearby Shamshuipo, where visitors flock to buy cut-rate computers, word-processors, and peripheral equipment, many of which are made in Japan but are not marketed in the West. Here the visitor may purchase hardware, and software, at a quarter of the price to be paid in the U.S. or Europe.

Nearby, in the middle of a housing estate, is the Lei Cheng Uk Tomb, built in the Han Dynasty. It is a new attraction, as it was only discovered in 1955 during excavations for the estate.

Farther along the waterfront is the Mei Foo Sun Chuen housing estate and the nearby Lai Chi Kok Amusement Park. In addition to the usual Ferris wheel and games of skill and chance, there is a Chinese opera theater and a wax museum that gives a glimpse of the history of 5,000 years of civilization in China.

For a glimpse of traditional daily life in China 1,000 years ago, there is the Sung Dynasty Village, a part of the amusement park but operated separately. Groups are conducted around a typical Chinese town, re-created with great care from paintings of an actual town of that time. The builder imported much of the material and most of the workers, especially carpenters, from China for the project. The tiny wooden flowers that adorn the eaves of buildings in the "ancient" town were carved by hand, much as they would have been so long ago. Everything has been made exactly as it was in olden times, from the wine shop to the bank (where the first paper money in the world was used). Special performances for visitors include a traditional wedding ceremony with old-style costumes (the bride and groom are carried in a sedan chair for part of the way) and have kung-fu demonstrations. The restaurant serves food prepared as it would have been centuries ago. The wine is made traditionally and served in bottles especially made for this restaurant in the old Sung Dynasty style.

Going the other way from the tip of the peninsula, just beyond Tsimshatsui East in the Hung Hom area, is the new Kowloon-Canton Railway terminal, where you can board a train for Canton or Peking, and via the Trans-Siberian railway, Moscow, Calais, and London. The

Colisseum, a new sports arena seating 12,000 designed to stage athletic events and concerts, is next door.

The Kaiser Estate, where the best of the factory-outlet shopping in Hong Kong is to be found, is also near the station. Farther along the harbor, in nearby Kowloon Bay, is Telford Gardens, a huge new housing estate. The recreation center in the estate includes a roller-skating rink and bowling lanes.

Next is Kai Tak Airport, where a plane lands or takes off, on average, every three minutes. The Kowloon Walled City is just a few hundred yards from Kai Tak Airport. From earliest times, Kong Kong police hesitated to pursue criminals into the Walled City for fear of upsetting the Peking government. So the area, just a few city blocks, became a no-man's-land with no authority governing it.

Now you can stroll past the Walled City and wonder at the rows of dentist and doctor practices. These medical people are unregistered in Kong Kong and many of them have no real qualifications. Others are qualified in Chinese medicine but are not recognized by British and Hong Kong authorities. Whatever their background, these practitioners' fees are definitely attractive to the local populace.

There have been several attempts to clean up the Walled City. Religious groups have done wonders in rehabilitating drug addicts. But still the Walled City is no place for tourists, though you can get quite a thrill just walking past and peering into the tiny staircases that disappear into the dark, wet gloom of this no-man's-land. By the way, don't look for the walls around the Walled City—it hasn't got any. The walls were torn down by the Japanese during the World War II and the stone was used to extend the runway at Kai Tak Airport.

Near the airport is Kowloon City, best known for its bargain-center market where goods, mostly low-quality clothing, are sold in open-air stalls.

Nearby is Kowloon Tong, a residential area boasting some short-time motels, known as "blue motels," where a trysting couple can drive in and get a room at hourly rates while an attendant places a signboard to cover the number on their license plates. These establishments also serve a more noble purpose. In a city where newlyweds may live in crowded tenements, and where good downtown hotels would be far too expensive for their honeymoon, this may be the only way a young couple can escape from family, friends, and reality for one night of privacy.

Strolling up Nathan Road you will see a large new mosque set in what is left of Kowloon Park. Farther up Nathan Road you find Yue Hwa stores. They are devoted to Chinese products, featuring bolt cloth and magnificent carpets.

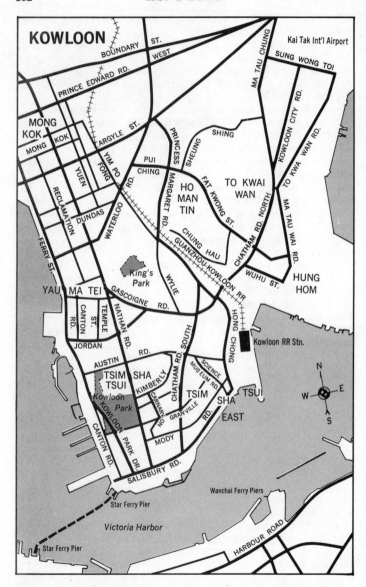

Going farther up Nathan Road you may stroll into the Mongkok District, where prices will be lower in inverse ration to the ability of the shopkeepers to speak English.

After looking around the shops you may take a stroll to nearby King's Park, not far from the junction of Nathan and Jordan roads. You will find tennis and squash courts, plus other outdoor recreation.

Mongkok is the most densely populated area on earth. The last census estimated 165,000 people per square kilometer there. This is apparent in the evenings when most residents seem to be thronged in Nathan Road and Argyle Street.

The name, Mongkok, is a mystery even to local people. It doesn't make sense in Chinese or English. The best guess is that it was named Wong's Corner, which would be *Wong-kok* in Cantonese. But the sign-painter flipped the W and made it an M instead, and the name stuck: Mong-kok. Or so the story goes.

One of Kowloon's best attractions, easily reached by Mass Transit Railway, is the Wong Tai Sin temple. It is a community center and for much of its life was not open to visitors. Only economics forced administrators to allow tourists in to ogle the sacred rites. Built in 1921, the temple was strictly a religious preserve until 1956, when an admission charge of HK$.10 was introduced. Since then about HK$4 million has been raised from admissions. But visitors were also generous in donations to the collection boxes, and these earnings went to rebuild the temple completely. What you see was completed and opened in 1973. There is no admission charge, but a donation is expected.

At the temple, you will see hundreds of incense sticks and paper money being burned in honor of the gods. People interested in their future can be seen shaking a cup of numbered sticks until one falls on the floor. The numbered stick is presented to an attendant who looks up the corresponding fortune and reads it out to the worshipper.

The Sanpokong District, although north of Boundary Street (the legal demarcation between Kowloon and the New Territories) is administered as part of Kowloon. It is a factory area but attracts many visitors with its factory outlet shops.

Past Kai Tak Airport is Kwun Tong, a big manufacturing area with huge housing estates and enough population to warrant a special line of the Mass Transit Railway.

Nearby is the fishing village of Leiyumun, right at the entrance to the harbor and across from Shaukiwan on Hong Kong Island. Leiyumun has become a dining attraction for visitors and local people. In the past few years it has blossomed, and the restaurants themselves are quite well-appointed. The real attraction, though, is that you pick out your dinner on the way to the restaurant. On either side of the path from the pier are glass tanks of prawns, garoupa, lobster, clams, and other seafood, all fresh-caught and still alive. You make your choice, then go to the restaurant, sit down, have a drink, and minutes later your choice arrives—cooked—on the table.

NEW TERRITORIES

The adventurous visitor who has taken the trouble to explore Hong Kong and Kowloon, and possibly even the outlying islands, deserves to go one step farther and spend at least a day in the New Territories. There are 350 square miles to explore, with ancient temples, forested mountainsides, and views of mainland China across the border.

The best way way to see the New Territories is to take a circle tour from Tsimshatsui via Tuen Mun, Fanling, and back through Taipo and Shatin. As you cross into the New Territories you pass the Lai Chi Kok Amusement Park and Sung Dynasty Village (see Kowloon section). The modern highway runs past Kwai Chung Container Terminal, one of the biggest in the Far East, and through the built-up industrial area of Tsuen Wan.

Then, suddenly, you are out in the country, with paddy fields and maybe a tired-looking water buffalo pulling a plow. On the left, all the way to Tuen Mun along Castle Peak Road, the old seashore road, are swimming beaches (see "Beaches" section in this guide).

You will pass the camp of Gurkhas Regiment, the world-famous Nepalese fighters who have for so many years supported the armed forces of the British Commonwealth.

A regular visitor attraction is the Ching Chung Koon Temple, in Tuen Mun. It is a huge temple, with room after room of altars. Sticks of incense burn in bronze holders outside each room, giving the whole place a strange sense of mystery. On one side of the main entrance is a huge cast bell about five feet around. This is typical of all the big monasteries in ancient China. The idea was to ring it at daybreak to wake up the monks and nuns. They would go out into the rice fields and work all day. On the other side of the entrance is a huge drum that was used to call the workers back to the temple in the evening.

You will see rooms with walls of small pictures of people who have died. Their relatives pay the temple to have these photos displayed, and forever after the living can visit to pray for the departed.

The temple also includes an old-folks home, built from donations and providing a quiet and serene atmosphere for the elderly. The grounds are beautiful, with plants and flowers, hundreds of dwarf shrubs, ornamental fishponds, and pagodas.

Commuters skip all this by taking the Tuen Mun Highway, a regular turnpike that slices through the hills farther away from the coastline.

Tuen Mun, with a population of 200,000, is one of Hong Kong's "new towns," independent small cities created to take the spillover of population from the crowded urban areas of Kowloon and Hong Kong Island, and providing both industrial areas and accommodation for the workers. Other new towns are Tsuen Wan, Yuen Long, Shatin, Taipo, Fanling, and Junk Bay. By 1990 the seven towns are expected to house three million people, or 41 percent of Hong Kong's projected population of 7.3 million.

Farther on is Yuen Long, also completely redeveloped as an industrial and residential complex, then you come to Lau Fau Shan. Basically it is a huge fish market, but it has become a visitor attraction. A narrow street, closed to vehicles, takes you past dozens of restaurants, both small, open-air affairs and the larger, smart, air-conditioned places. There are sellers of dried fish, salt fish, live shrimp, prawns, and larger fish. The idea is that you look around at the live fish, pick out what you want, pay for it, and take it to one of the restaurants to have it cooked. This is the oyster capital of Hong Kong, but don't eat them uncooked.

Kam Tin Walled Village is a regular stop on most tours. Built in the 1600s, it is a fortified village, belonging to the Tang clan. The walls are intact, with guardhouses on the four corners and arrow slits for fighting off attackers. The image of antiquity is somewhat spoiled now by the few modern homes and the television antennae peeping over the ancient fortifications. Directly inside the main gate you find a narrow street of souvenirs and mass-produced oil paintings. At the gateway, the only entrance, note the massive wrought-iron gates, which do not match. Donations are accepted as you enter (HK$1).

There are also several human museum pieces, middle-aged ladies whose sole occupation is posing for tourist pictures. First you pay (HK$1 should do) and then you snap. They get angry and spit if you do not pay.

The next stop is Lok Ma Chau, where the big attraction is the view. You stand on a hill and look down on a lot of fields and the Shenzhen River winding through them. On the other side of the river, barely half a mile away, is The People's Republic of China. Unless you plan a tour to China, this is as close as you will ever get. Elderly models here demand HK$1 before you take pictures of them.

Fanling town has the serene atmosphere of the Royal Hong Kong Golf Club, as well as the chaos of rapid redevelopment. The nearby Luen Wo Market is a traditional Chinese market and one worth visiting.

"Taipo" means shopping place in Chinese, and as every visitor discovers, it lives up to its name. Located in the heart of the New Territories' breadbasket, this bustling town has long been a trading and meeting place for local farmers and fishermen. It is now being redeveloped, with housing estates and highways everywhere you look.

South of Taipo the Chinese University looms large. Across the road is the Yucca de Lac restaurant with outdoor facilities overlooking the entire scene. Also nearby is the jumping-off point for a ferry tour of Tolo Harbour and the Sai Kung Peninsula.

Whether you enter the town of Shatin by road or rail, there is little doubt you will be amazed to find this bustling metropolis in the middle of the New Territories. It is another of the "new towns" (with a resultant population jump to almost a quarter of a million, from 30,000, in less than a decade) and home of Hong Kong's second racecourse, complete with air-conditioned stables. Nearby is the huge Jubilee Sports Centre, a vast complex of tracks and training fields designed to give Hong Kong's athletes rare space to train under professional, full-time coaches. (Unbeknownst to most visitors, this little territory regularly sends teams to compete in the Olympics, the Commonwealth Games, the Asian Games, the Davis Cup, and many other international competitions. The sports center is one of the best training facilities in all of Asia.)

Nestled among the town's foothills is the Temple of Ten Thousand Buddhas, visible from the railway station. A path leads up some 500 steps to the temple. It's worth every step. Inside the main temple are nearly 13,000 almost-identical Buddha statues. The gilt-painted clay statues were made by Shanghai craftsmen and donated by worshippers. In addition to the main temple there is a pagoda and some smaller temples. The exhumed body of the temple's founder, Yuet Kai, is housed in the Amitabha Temple near the main temple.

From this lofty perch you can see the Shatin Racecourse. You can also see the famous Amah Rock, which looks like a woman with a child on her back, and is part of a Chinese folktale. Women worship at the rock.

Shatin is also home of the most extensive shopping complexes in the New Territories. New Town Plaza provides approximately one million square feet of offices and shops in the middle of Shatin.

There is one section of the New Territories that is not overwhelmed by development—the Sai Kung peninsula, which is mostly country parkland.

Past Kai Tak Airport, Clearwater Bay Road takes you up into the mountains and down into the partially developed area of forest-clad mountains and Spanish-style villas overlooking the emerald sea and islands.

In the middle of this is Shaw's Movie Town, the Far East equivalent of Hollywood. Here many of the kung-fu and sword dramas have been made.

Clearwater Bay Road goes on down to a large park with views of Hong Kong Island in the distance and the Clearwater Bay Golf and Country Club nearby.

A side trip is down Hiram's Highway past the new Marina Cove resort, a super-luxury private club dedicated to the top-level senior executive lifestyle. There are more yacht clubs and a marina, and finally the town of Sai Kung itself, which is now being developed.

Beyond that the road divides. The left fork goes over hills and dales with little traffic or habitation—hard to believe you are in Hong Kong —and ends at a ferry pier where you can catch a boat to Shatin.

The other road goes further to a barrier that stops all private cars. Buses go on into the country park, an unspoiled land of trees, sea-vistas, beaches and rocky headlands.

THE ISLANDS

Looking out of the airplane window on the approach to Kai Tak Airport on a fine day, you will see clusters of bright green islands dotting the South China Sea. Fishing fleets trawl slowly through the blue waters. Tiny specks of sampans scamper from one outcrop to another, ignoring the junks, liners, and cargo ships steaming in and out of the fabled Hong Kong harbor. Look closer and you will see sandy coves, long strands of fine yellow sand massaged by gentle surfs, and countless tiny village settlements clinging to rocky bays and small sandbars.

These outer islands are the "Other Hong Kong," that unspoilt natural beauty which is as much a part of Hong Kong as Kowloon's crowded tenements or Hong Kong Island's concrete canyons. But most visitors miss the opportunity to see the different side of this famous territory. Hong Kong is definitely much more than just a shopper's paradise and banker's mecca.

The Hong Kong and Yaumati Ferry Company's extensive fleet of air-conditioned triple-decker ferries connects the four major outlying islands with Central Hong Kong from dawn to late at night. These islands are all less than an hour away from the skyscrapers. Unless you visit them on a Sunday or public holiday during the summer months, when thousands of Hongkongers flee urban claustrophobia, the ferry rides are quite peaceful.

The four major islands, apart from Lantau, are traffic-free. They are Hong Kong's green lungs—for walkers, swimmers, slow-paced sightseers, visitors seeking a sun-blessed retreat from metropolitan mayhem. Tour companies offer guided tours to Cheung Chau and Lantau Islands. There are many other islands to visit, too, primarily up in Tolo Harbour or Mirs Bay or south of Hong Kong Island. Scheduled ferry, or *kaido,* service to these places is very limited however. Check out the Hong Kong Tourist Association offices for fuller details, including their excellent brochure "Outlying Islands." Whatever you do, give yourself at least one extra day in Hong Kong just to see the islands. They are Hong Kong's magical plus factor.

Lantau

The biggest of all the islands is Lantau, at 55 square miles almost twice the size of Hong Kong Island. The population is less than 17,000, compared with Hong Kong Island's 1.5 million. Lantau is well worth a couple of day trips; there is much to discover.

Safe sandy beaches, such as Cheung Sha, stretch along southern Lantau's shoreline. The island's private bus services link the main ferry town, Silvermine Bay's Mui Wo, with a Sung Dynasty fort at Tung Chung and the far-off "capital" of Lantau, Tai O, which has a rope-drawn ferry raft connecting the two parts of the ancient fishing village.

In the mountainous interior of the island, where sunrise and sunset scenes flash kaleidoscopic tones across green foothills and barren cloud-decked trekking trails, you will find a tea plantation with horse-riding camp and exuberantly commercial Buddhist monastery. The almost gaudy Precious Lotus Monastery near Ngong Ping is a dazzling destination on the slopes of 3,000-foot-high Lantau Peak. It is famed for its vegetarian meals served in a temple refectory.

The visitor with historical or archaeological interests will find many surprises on Lantau. At Mui Wo there are derelict silver mines from the Qing Dynasty era, when a Portuguese-Japanese joint project tapped a vein at the Village of White Silver. At that time Imperial Chinese officials were stationed at Tung Chung, their old fort, trying to defend the islands from notorious bands of pirates.

The Imperial hold on the South China Sea islands was tenuous, but at one time Lantau had become the temporary home for an Emperor. That was in 1277, when ten-year-old Emperor Ti Cheng and his small retinue set up camp just behind modern Silvermine Bay's pleasure beaches while fleeing the Mongol forces of Kublai Khan. The young emperor died on Lantau. The Sung Dynasty was finally crushed the following year, and there are no traces of the island's brief moment of imperial glory.

There are extensive traces of earlier settlements, though: Neolithic sites have been identified on various sandbars. Sung Dynasty communities, including their kilns and burial grounds, have also been excavated. When you stroll away from the well-beaten paths you will find it easy to imagine an age of isolated Southern Chinese communities battling the seas and tilling small fertile valleys.

Visit the wonderfully subdued Trappist Monastery on Eastern Lantau, where you will find a full dairy herd. At the top of a steep embankment, where pine trees and birds sing in the clear ocean breezes, the monks (sworn to a life of silence or whispers) run a haven—overnight accommodation is available, with advance reservations. Although the monastery can be reached from Silvermine Bay, over hill passes, it's best to travel via Peng Chau Island, a small community en route to Silvermine Bay. (See Peng Chau Island.)

It is possible to stay overnight at the tea plantation, the Precious Lotus Monastery, and sometimes at the Trappist Monastery. There are also several smaller hostelries utilized by Hongkongers taking a brief respite from city life. And at the 78-room Silvermine Beach Hotel is the island's first "resort." The Hong Kong Tourist Association has an information sheet on all the accommodation available on Lantau.

Lamma

For a gentle two-hour dip into rural China, wander across Lamma Island, which faces the major fishing port of Aberdeen on Hong Kong Island's south side. Hakka farmers, shielded from the sun by black-fringed firm straw hats, grow vegetables as their ancestors always did. Hoklo fisherfolk gather shellfish. Ignore the power station and cement factory, and seek out the small bays along narrow paths that present new aspects of Hong Kong Island's hills or the ocean's beauty.

Do allow time to stop awhile for a meal at either of Lamma's ferry villages, Sok Kwu Wan and Yung Shue Wan. Lines of friendly open-air harborside restaurants, some with amazingly diverse wine selections, offer feasts of freshness, their fish and vegetables tasting a thousand times better than they would in urban Hong Kong.

Cheung Chau

Dining out, literally, is a major joy on Cheung Chau Island, which lies to the south of Lantau. Almost every Western visitor's favorite Hong Kong island, it has a score of good open-air cafés on either side of its crowded sandbar township—on the waterfront Praya promenade and overlooking the main public beach of Tung Wan.

Hong Kong's most crowded outlying island, with 30,000 or more people who mostly live on the sandbar that connects the dumbbell-shaped island's two hilly tips, Cheung Chau has a Mediterranean mood that has attracted an expatriate artist's community of painters and writers. The entry into Cheung Chau's harbor, through lines of gaily bannered fishing boats, is an exhilarating experience, comparable to the first sighting of a bustling Aegean Sea island.

There is history on Cheung Chau, too—pirate caves, ancient rock carvings, and a 200-year-old temple built to protect the islanders from the twin dangers of plagues and pirates. The annual springtime Bun Festival is one of Hong Kong's most colorful community galas. Throughout the year local ferry services (by sampans called *kaidos*) can take you away from the madding crowds to virtually deserted beaches with clear water. Or else you can climb a trail past scores of varieties of wild fern and over cliffs where village children fly magic kites to meet a couple of lonely lowing cows.

With the opening of the Cheung Chau Warwick Hotel, the island's first hotel and one of the few resort hotels in the territory, on Tung Wan Beach, it is now possible to stay on the island in first-class comfort.

Peng Chau

The tiniest of Hong Kong's four major islands, Peng Chau was once home for a few farmers, fishermen, and a fireworks factory. Now the factory is closed and the villagers have built three-storied weekend retreats for Hong Kong's city folk, but the community feeling remains.

Stand on the Peng Chau ferry quay. Watch the *kaido* for Lantau's Trappist monastery splutter off toward dark green hills. Choose your fresh shellfish from the baskets held aloft by local fishermen bobbing in boats below the quay and take it back to a harborside café to be cooked. And breathe in that stirring ambience of Hong Kong's islands —salt air, shrimp paste, dried fish, local pride, and a sense of independence that has been lost or never found in urban Hong Kong.

PRACTICAL INFORMATION FOR HONG KONG

TELEPHONES. The area code for Hong Kong Island is 5, for Kowloon, 3, and for the New Territories, 0. The Outlying Islands all share the common prefix 5, followed by their individual area codes: 981 for Cheung Chau, 982 for Lamma, and 984 and 987 for Lantau. You need not dial the area code if you are dialing within an area.

For international operator-assisted calls outside your hotel (person-to-person or station-to-station), dial 010. For collect calls, dial 011. (Neither of these require any payment if you are at a call box.) For International Direct Dialing assistance, dial 013.

Local calls are free and therefore most shops, restaurants, and businesses allow you to use their telephones. Hotels, however, do not; they have pay phones that take HK$1 coins, the cost of a local paid call, as do the pay phones in the street kiosks, which are few and far between.

To place a long-distance call outside your hotel, head for the nearest Cable and Wireless office. The main, 24-hour telephone offices (plus cables and telexes) are in New Mercury House, Fenwick Street, Wanchai; Exchange Square, near the General Post Office and Connaught Centre; and in Hermes House, Middle Road, Tsimshatsui, Kowloon. Smaller offices are located in the Lee Gardens Hotel arcade (Hysan Avenue, Causeway Bay) and in the General Post Office (next to the Star Ferry), both in Hong Kong. In Kowloon, Cable and Wireless has offices in both the Departure and Transit Lounges at the airport. (There are also offices in the industrial areas of Kwun Tong, Tsuen Wan, Tuen Mun, and Mongkok.)

Direct-dial calls, known as international direct dial in Hong Kong, can also be made at the Cable and Wireless offices. Calls to the United States cost HK$63 per three-minute call (minimum charge time) and calls to Great Britain cost HK$60. Calls to many countries are charged at a rate per six seconds.

Calls to Macau are also included in international calls and cost HK$10.80 per three-minute period minimum period from 8:00 A.M. to 8:00 P.M., HK$7.20 or HK$4.80 during off-peak hours. For emergencies, dial 999 and ask for Police, Fire or Ambulence.

HOTELS. Until the early sixties Hong Kong didn't have one international hotel. Indeed the little-developed colony, still showing signs of Pacific War damage, wasn't much of a tourist attraction. International tourists preferred to sail into the famous harbor on cruise liners, berth at the newly erected Ocean Terminal, and stay afloat in luxury. There was the Peninsula, of course, and its associate Repulse Bay Hotel, and a couple of other now-demolished colonial havens in Central. But Hong Kong was a backwater.

Then a fortuitous combination of political and economic factors put Hong Kong firmly on the world's map, initially for business travelers. The fledgling Hong Kong Tourist Association drummed up overseas-agency interest. Inexpensive charter flights, the boom in group travel (particularly from North America) and Hong Kong's airport's open-skies policy started to produce tourist business on a scale that warranted the appearance of Hyatt International (taking over the old President Hotel on Nathan Road in Kowloon) and Hilton International (building a skyscraper on a site that then overlooked the Hong Kong Cricket's Club's priceless Central field). Hong Kong's major property owner, Hong Kong Land, decided to built itself a hotel, The Mandarin, giving the city and its visiting businessmen their first taste of modern luxury and somewhat proper British management styles.

There are now around 22,000 hotel rooms available in a city that comfortably welcomes more than 4 million visitors annually. That total room count only includes those hotels that belong to the Hong Kong Tourist Association. There are some others that limit their market appeal to regional visitors from Taiwan, the People's Republic of China, and Southeast Asia. Such hotels have not been included in our listings. We only list hotels that are Tourist Association or Hong Kong Hotels Association members.

However, as the price ranges indicate, Hong Kong isn't a budget traveler's paradise. It doesn't set out to be. Land is still very expensive, rentals are steep in a small territory where almost every piece of land is a "good" location in one way or another, and labor costs aren't low any more.

The vast majority of Hong Kong's hotel rooms are in the high-priced categories of First Class or above. Individual visitors not on group packages must expect to pay around HK$550 and more for a hotel room of normal international standards. For that price the visitor probably won't get a harbor view. But the visitor will get very reliable facilities—*en suite* bathrooms with unfailing hot and cold water supplies, color TV and radio (and a channel of in-house movies in most luxury hotels), same-day laundry and valet service, 24-hour room service, telephones that always work, and an evening turn-down service by ever present room attendants (generally room "boys" in Hong Kong). Air-conditioning is everywhere.

Due to the limited price ranges available for even halfway decent accommodation, economy-minded visitors are recommended to take advantage of tour-group bookings. A group member can take the room and the MAP meals, and then branch out on solo explorations of a fascinating territory, possibly finding out how to get hotel bargains on an individual basis.

Although room rate discounts are frowned on by the Hong Kong Hotels Association, and your local travel agents, they are frequently available during the "low" season—generally taken as June through August. Most years the weather isn't bad enough to discourage summer visitors. Typhoons are rare, even if the humidity level is usually high. Another quiet period when hotels seek discounted business is the weeks on either side of Chinese New Year, a moveable feast that usually occurs in January or February. However, as a large proportion of Hong Kong's population leaves town during that period, and most businesses and restaurants close for a very long annual holiday, Hong Kong can seem boringly quiet then. Christmas and New Year (the Western one) are better "quiet" times when hotel rates can be "negotiated."

At such lean periods the visitor can shop around and negotiate directly with the reception staffs of hotels. However, it's always wisest to have your travel agent conduct the negotiation in advance, to ensure that you have a guaranteed room waiting for you. For when Hong Kong is full, it's very full. Until the late 1970s the super-peak periods coincided with the biannual Canton Trade Fairs (April and May and October and November). Visitors without advance reservations could find themselves sleeping way out in the New Territories or even on the airport floor.

Luckily for Hong Kong's image in the world tourism stakes, the rash of new hotels and the Canton authorities' dispersal of their Trade Fair calendar took the pressure off receptionists selling rooms to the highest bidder. Nevertheless, the spring and fall months are still the city's busy periods, and advance reservations are wise for March through June and September through early December. Hong Kong's climate is most comfortable during these months.

The Hong Kong Tourist Association (H.K.T.A.) publishes a list of hotel members in a brochure called "Hotels" that provides full details of facilities and rates (N.B.: the twice-yearly brochure's rates are usually at least one price rise behind the current situation). The H.K.T.A. does not arrange hotel reservations. The Hong Kong Hotels Association does, but only via its Kai Tak International Airport reservations office, located immediately beyond the Customs area, and is only intended for visitors arriving by air without advance reservations. It does not arrange discounted accommodation and, understandably, will only accept reservations for Hotels Association members.

Following the reconstruction of Kai Tak Airport, hotel hawkers are no longer allowed access to it. Hotels Association members have been allowed to keep "airport representatives" on the pavement outside the arrivals hall (follow the arrows that point to "hotel transport"). The legitimate representatives of the hotels are there to greet guests with reservations and call up the hotel limousines or mini-buses (provided at a slightly higher rate than the public taxi or limousine services).

Journey times from the airport to hotels vary, depending on rush-hour traffic conditions. Be warned that the Harbour Tunnel connecting Kowloon and Hong Kong Island reaches saturation point at the usual commuter rush hours, is worst (from Hong Kong to Kowloon) on Friday afternoons from 4:00 to 7:00 P.M., and can create ulcers for departing visitors. Always consult your hotel front office for advice about check-out times if flight connections are crucial.

Choosing where to stay in Hong Kong depends on a visitor's business needs or tourist ideals. With the opening of both the Harbour Tunnel and the M.T.R. (Mass Transit Railway) subway system, it no longer matters so much whether one stays on "Hong Kong-side" or "Kowloon-side." The journey under the harbor only takes 4.5 minutes.

Central is preferred by businessmen needing to be near the city's financial hub. As busy as Manhattan during the daylight hours, Central is quiet at night and on weekends. Central as it is on the north shore of Hong Kong Island, the area contains major government offices, top stores and boutiques, most bank head offices, and the City Hall complex. Central has only three hotels—the Hilton, Furama Inter-Continental, and Mandarin—and all are expensive.

Wanchai, to the east of Central, was once a sailor's dream of Suzie Wongs and booze-ups. It is still one of the city's more entertaining nightlife areas. Reclamation work has given it a harbor-fronting new area of skyscrapers. Wanchai's few hotels will soon be supplemented by a luxurious Grand Hyatt Hotel and a deluxe New World Hotel, both part of the Hong Kong Convention and Exhibition Centre.

Causeway Bay, farther east on the Island, has three major international-style hotels—Lee Gardens, Excelsior and Park Lane—and a couple of moderate-rate hotels. Ideal for tourists on shopping trips or eating-out fanatics, Causeway Bay has become rather sophisticated. The extension of the M.T.R. Island Line through Central to the far east of Hong Kong Island makes Causeway Bay an even more popular area in which to stay. One further advantage of the Causeway Bay area is its proximity to the Island end of the Harbour Tunnel.

Tsimshatsui, the name of the harbor-facing promontory at the end of mainland Kowloon, can now be divided into three areas as far as its hotel and shopping facilities are concerned:

"Old" Tsimshatsui lies on and off the fabled shopping "Golden Mile" of Nathan Road. Warrens of back streets are filled with restaurants, boutiques, stores, and old-style hotels. Large modern international hotels are to be found at the harbor end of Nathan Road, a short walk from the Star Ferry or the Tsimshatsui M.T.R. station. This is home to the Peninsula, Sheraton, Holiday Inn Golden Mile, Hyatt-Regency, Ambassador, Kowloon, and Park hotels.

Tsimshatsui East is the newly developed mini-Miami of Hong Kong. Built on land that was partially reclaimed and partially former British Army compounds, the grid of office blocks and luxury hotels is not a cheap place to stay, but "old" Tsimshatsui is just across the Chatham Road. Two of Tsimshatsui East's four new hotels—the Shangri-La and Holiday Inn Harbour View—face the harbor with uninterrupted views. The other two—The Regal Meridien and Royal Garden—have interrupted harbor views. The nearby New World Centre, home for the New World and Regent Hotels, is closer to old Tsimshatsui's action.

Harbour City, on the western side of Tsimshatsui promontory's tip, is the preserve of the Peninsula Group, whose owners are associated with the development of the City, Asia's biggest integrated air-conditioned shopping and commercial complex, along with the Hong Kong, Prince, and Marco Polo hotels.

Kowloon, generally spoken of as beginning north of Jordan Road (and the Jordan M.T.R. station), contains a lot of moderate-rate smaller older hotels. Most still are on Nathan Road, within the magic "Golden Mile," and are generally the best bets for economy-minded visitors. Excellent bus services and the M.T.R. ensure that Kowloon and North Kowloon are not far, in time, from Tsimshatsui's thick of things.

Our indicated *hotel rates* show published price ranges for a *double room for two people* as at the time of writing. As in all tourist destinations, there will be few rooms at the lower end of the range. It should also be noted now that few of the major hotels have specially designed single rooms and that the price difference between single and double rates is usually minimal (just a few dollars). All rates are subject to a 10-percent service charge and 5-percent Government tax (which is used to fund the activities of the Hong Kong Tourist Association, so don't feel too badly about it).

Our hotel categories are arbitrary; Hong Kong has no official or unofficial hotel rating or starring system. Our *Deluxe* hotels are the few that are genuine world beaters, recognized as such by the *Institutional Investor's* annual survey, pools of travel agents, and such hotel critics as Rene Lecler. *Deluxe* room prices range from HK$900 to HK$1,750. *Luxury* hotels are generally chain-associated international hotels with amenities and facilities that rival those of the Deluxe hotels. For one reason or another—smallish rooms, less-polished staff, over-obvious group usage, etc.—they have failed to enter the *Deluxe* category. But not for want of trying; they are all good hotels by any standard. Hotels considered to be in the *Luxury* category range from HK$600–HK$990.

First-Class hotels are humbler, but have often undertaken renovation plans that make them very recommendable. The competitive spirit of Hong Kong has been very obvious in the hotel industry. Room revamping, restaurant upgrading, and, inevitably, price hikes have given the city a top-heavy concentration of good-quality and fairly expensive accommodation. Lodgings listed in the *First Class* category range from HK$300–HK$600. A few of the *Moderate* hotels fill the gap, but most are only interested in attracting regional business. *Moderate* rooms range from HK$180–HK$330.

Inexpensive accommodation is difficult to find. The best bargains are the YMCA's and YWCA's. The most popular is the YMCA on Salisbury Road, Kowloon, (3) 692211—no doubt because of its location and pool. On Hong Kong Island, the YWCA Headquarter Hotel at 1 Macdonnell Road, Central, Hong Kong, (5) 223101, is quite popular. The YMCA on Hong Kong Island is at 4 Harbour Road, Wanchai, (5) 201111. The other YMCA in Kowloon is at 23 Waterloo Road, (3) 319111. The YWCA is at 5 Man Fuk Road, Waterloo Hill, (3) 713–9211. Right on Nathan Road, between the Sheraton and the Holiday Inn Golden Mile, Chung King Mansions contains other small hostel-style operations, with shared rooms or dormitories. If the noise and the smells (from the block's many Indo-Pakistani cafés) can be borne, backpackers will find the prices and central location to be the best they can get in Hong Kong.

On the *Outlying Islands,* accommodation is very limited. Cheung Chau has a Warwick Hotel. Lantau Island, Hong Kong's biggest island, now has a vaca-tion-hotel operation, The Silvermine Bay Beach Hotel, and various cheap ram-shackle local cottage colonies behind the beach. For something different, consider staying at a monastery, such as the beautifully hushed Trappist Monas-tery on the hills of Lantau facing Peng Chau Island. Such retreats require advance reservations for their Spartan rooms, vegetarian meals, and the closest thing to solitude one can get in Hong Kong. The H.K.T.A. offices can advise where to write. Backpackers can always locate rooms for rent on the islands; just ask at the ferry pier cafés and an English-speaking student will soon advise which shophouse or farm cottage to try.

The *New Territories*, north of Kowloon, are also very limited for staying visitors. Apart from the three hotels included in our listing, there is the Shatin Heights hotel near Shatin and the Rose Garden near Yuen Long. New Territories hotels don't necessarily expect overseas visitors, but they'll make you feel welcome—and there is nothing better than a meal of locally bred pigeon and locally made bean curd eaten on an open terrace.

As one might expect in the world's third most important financial center, Hong Kong is a businessman's paradise. Every hotel in the Deluxe or Luxury categories has some form of *Businessman's Center,* providing secretarial services, translators, easy access to telex machines, and libraries of local publications. Each hotel in the top two categories has front-desk personnel who attend promptly to businessmen's needs. Similarly, most of the listed First-Class hotels can arrange secretarial services quickly.

With every hotel indulging in renovation and modernization plans, we regret that this guide's listing will soon be outdated. But one thing won't be changing: good service is the name of the hotel game in Hong Kong, and the city's top fifteen or so hotels probably provide the best all-round hotel services of any city in the world. The fact that they contain some of Asia's finest restaurants is a major plus.

The prices provided for hotels on the following pages are for a double room, double occupancy.

DELUXE

Hong Kong

Mandarin. 5 Connaught Rd., Central; (5)220111. Right in the center of Central, the two-decade-old hotel combines British rectitude and Oriental reserve. It's the flagship of the Hong Kong-based Mandarin Hotels Group, and the 540-roomer has been judged the best hotel in the world by an *Institutional Investor* survey. Two sides of the hotel's square block face the harbor; double-glazing on balcony windows keep out the roar of the waterfront road traffic. Some 60 of the units—most of them on corners—are suites. The British element is obvious in the clubbish *Chinnery Bar,* named after a nineteenth-century South China Coast painter whose portrait smiles down on a lunchtime roast beef wagon and silver tankards. Off the lobby, the popular cocktail lounge, the *Captain's Bar,* has a luncheon roast wagon, too, and a band at night (when gentlemen wear a coat and tie after 9:00 P.M.). Seafood, and roasts of course, are the smartly businesslike *Mandarin Grill's* specialties. Up on the twenty-fifth-floor rooftop the *nouvelle cuisine* of *Pierrot* has established it as one of Hong Kong's better and most expensive restaurants. Similar stylishness graces the adjacent *Man Wah* Chinese restaurant, which shares a harbor-gazing *Harlequin*

Bar with *Pierrot.* The Californian-influenced groundfloor *Coffee Shop* (a Greco-English indoor garden) and the all-day open-plan snacking snobbery of the mezzanine's tiered *Clipper Lounge* are the best of their kind in town. Rooftop *health club* facilities, including a Greco-Roman columned pool and a business center, are good.

Kowloon

The Peninsula. Salisbury Road, Kowloon; (3)666251. The grand old lady of Hong Kong hotels, "The Pen" was built in 1928, in an age when the world traveler took many weeks, and trunks, to travel by train from London's Victoria Station to Tsimshatsui's now-relocated terminus in front of the Peninsula. Almost a British colonial institution, with a baroque lobby reminiscent of Europe's great railway station lounges, the hotel was actually built by a Shanghai-based company (which fled to Hong Kong in 1949) and has long been managed by traditionalist Swiss hoteliers. Her New Wing having been demolished, the hotel is now back to her former glory as a 220-room low-rise living museum of good taste. That's met first in the ornate-columned and gilt-corniced lobby, the place to see and be seen eating scones and cucumber sandwiches. (The "in" side is on the right as you pass the diminutive white-clad pageboys holding open the etched glass doors that face a fountained driveway filled with the hotel's fleet of Rolls-Royces). *Gaddi's,* arguably Hong Kong's most distinguished gourmet restaurant, has its own elevator, famed Squire Lunches, and very formal evening dining. The chalet-like Swiss *Chesa* restaurant serves glorious fondues. The club-like atmosphere of the *Verandah Bar and Restaurant* is available to 2:00 A.M. There is now a Japanese restaurant, *Inagiku,* and a Chinese (Cantonese) one, *Spring Moon.* Now the flagship for a group of Hong Kong and regional hotels, The Peninsula's old-world style (large, high-ceilinged bedrooms, attentive room valets) isn't outdated and has consistently put the hotel among the top ten in opinion surveys of the world's best hotels.

The Regent. Salisbury Road, Tsimshatsui; (3)721–1211. Flagship for the Regent International Hotels group, this 1980-built, 600-room elegantly modern hotel has become a symbol of the new Hong Kong. Mirror-like polished granite flooring in the 40-foot-high glass-walled open lobby is a trend-setter's setting as a tea lounge and bar. Deliberately exclusive *Plume,* a deluxe dinner-only restaurant, also overlooks the harbor. Plume's affectations succeed discreetly—glass elevators, antiques, open-to-view 10,000-bottle wine "cellar," tandoori oven (for the only house bread), and fine French cuisine. The very American-style *Steakhouse* has a splendid fresh salad and berry bar. There's a luxurious *health center* (private rooms), open-air pool (Hong Kong's largest), a Carrara marble ballroom staircase, well-equipped marbled guestroom bathrooms (baths and shower units and separate toilets), and a good business center.

The Shangri-La. 64 Moody Rd., Tsimshatsui East; (3)721–2111. Owned by the family that gave Singapore its Shangri-La, this 719-room property is managed by Westin Hotels. On the best side of the new Tsimshatsui East's main street, Mody Road, it overlooks the harbor-front road and pedestrian promenade. The lobby, also a tea lounge, contains two massive, almost garish "Chinese" paintings (by a Western artist). A bank of escalators links the cavernous lobby, with its discreet reception off to one side, to the various restaurants—a tip-top Japanese *Nadaman* branch, a richly red Imperial *Shang Palace* Chinese restaurant, the comfortably formal French *Margaux* dining salon, and a graciously spacious *Coffee Garden* (with a *Steak Place*). Fine health center facilities include a small indoor pool. There are minibars in the large smart guestrooms, where TV sets run a 24-hour information service (in addition to movies) for the business traveler who needs to keep abreast of world affairs while away.

LUXURY

Hong Kong

The Excelsior. Gloucester Road, Causeway Bay, Hong Kong; (5)767365. The city's second-largest hotel, with 950 rooms, this harbor-fronting skyscraper overlooks the Royal Hong Kong Yacht Club marina and the flight path into Kowloon's Kai Tak airport. Ideally located for shopping trips into Causeway Bay, the hotel isn't that far from Wanchai's night life or Central's banks—there's a shuttle bus service to Central. Tennis courts (pro on call) and golf practice area are special features. Good dining in *Excelsior Grill,* which has the jolly *Noon Gun Bar* adjacent. Managed by the Mandarin Oriental Hotels Group, it houses one of Hong Kong's most popular watering holes, *The Dickens Bar.* It has a business center as well.

Furama Inter-Continental. Connaught Road, Central, Hong Kong; (5)255111. Overlooking City Hall from the front and Chater Gardens at the back, the Furama, part of the Inter-Continental chain, has the advantage of being in the quiet side of Central. Rooms tend to be small but are much favored by business travelers. The thirty-first-floor rooftop revolving restaurant, *La Ronda,* offers seventy-five-minute panoramic trips (and buffet feasts) and the *Rotisserie* is a lunchtime favorite. There are fine new businessmen's office-bedrooms (convertible pulldown beds) on the sixth floor and two fine Japanese restaurants in the basement shopping arcade.

Hongkong Hilton. Queen's Road, Central, Hong Kong; (5)233111. Recent revamping of its bedrooms has given the long-established hotel, one of Hong Kong's first international hostelries, fresh favor with Central business visitors. The second-floor lobby, up two flights of escalators, has a popular *Dragon Boat Bar,* a good old-fashioned *Grill,* and the *Jade Lotus Restaurant.* The rooftop Chinese restaurant, the *Eagle's Nest,* has great food, views, and evening ambience. In the basement *Den,* magnificent Mediterranean-style buffets are served day and night. A heated open-air swimming pool and the adjacent health club relax tired business bodies; minds can be stretched by the hotel's business center; and a private brigantine cruises around the harbor and beyond.

Lee Gardens. Hysan Avenue, Causeway Bay, Hong Kong; (5)895–3311. Popular with British and Australian groups, this 820-roomer is neatly placed for shopping on an "inland" site surrounded by good inexpensive boutiques and restaurants. The rooftop Chinese *Rainbow Room* is justifiably famed for *dim-sum* and Peking duck, while a fine Japanese restaurant is in the basement.

HOTELS

Park Lane. 311 Gloucester Rd., Causeway Bay, Hong Kong; (5) 8903355. This 840-room hotel, right in the heart of the Causeway Bay Shopping Area and adjacent to Victoria Park, has been completely renovated. Its *Park 27* is a casually elegant place serving Continental cuisine with one of the best panoramic views to be seen, while the *Gallery Bar and Lounge* has live entertainment nightly. Business Center.

Victoria Hotel. Shun Tak Centre, 200 Connaught Road Central, Hong Kong; (5)407228. The 540 luxury guest rooms occupy the top 15 floors of this 40-story building. The *Victoria Club* for business travelers occupies two floors. Restaurants include *Bocarino's Grill* with its mesquite charcoal specialties, *Dynasty* with its superb and original Cantonese food, and the *Cafe Terrace* coffee shop. Swimming pool, sun deck, tennis, health and business centers.

Kowloon

Holiday Inn Golden Mile. 46 Nathan Rd., Tsimshatsui, Kowloon; (3)693111. Right in the thick of "old" Tsimshatsui's action, this 600-roomer is relatively inexpensive, having encouraged its business guests and higher-rate groups to move to the new Inn over in Tsimshatsui East. The popular and crowded lobby bar, coffee shop, and good Germanic *Baron's Table* restaurant still attract a loyal local custom. You'll also find a pleasant rooftop pool and this superb *Delicatessen Corner* (all smoked items from hotel's own kitchens).

Holiday Inn Harbour View. 70 Mody Rd., Tsimshatsui East, Kowloon; (3)7215161. At the "far" end of the new Tsimshatsui East belt of hotels (and that's not far from anywhere), this Inn indicates how different the Asia-Pacific Holiday Inns are to their North American counterparts. Good harbor views from 60 percent of the rooms, which are handsomely decorated. A fine collection of eating places includes an above-average coffee shop, an interesting Mediterranean specialty bistro, a top Japanese francbise, and a rooftop-pool snack bar. An Executive Club floor is devoted solely to business travelers, and includes a business center.

Hongkong. 3 Canton Rd., Tsimshatsui, Kowloon; (3)676011. A HK$30-million facelift has given this 800-room Peninsula Group favorite more of an up-market image. It always held the city's occupancy records, primarily because of its location as an integral part of the Ocean Centre-Ocean City shopping arcade complex. A visiting shopper need never go into the open air. But the Star Ferry and bus terminals are just outside; Old Tsimshatsui is a short walk away. The enormous range of restaurants in the hotel and shopping complex include the fine Asian-food *Spice Market* and the cosy *Tai Pan Grill.* Open-air swimming pool.

Hyatt Regency. 67 Nathan Rd., Tsimshatsui, Kowloon; (3)662321. A huge facelift has given a new image to this fine hotel, though *haute cuisine* is still the specialty of *Hugo's* gourmet restaurant, one of Hong Kong's finest. Added to this is *Nathan's,* a bright place open all day for eating and meeting, an adjacent Chinese restaurant, and the trendy *Café.* The *Regency Club* appeals to business-people, as does the business center. All visitors welcome tbe proximity to Tsimshatsui's shops, restaurants, transportation, and nightlife. Locals reciprocate by making the *Chin Chin Bar* one of Kowloon's most popular drinking spots.

Kowloon. 19–21 Nathan Road, Tsimshatsui; (3)698698. The Peninsula Group's new "business hotel" has two good restaurants—the *Pizzeria*, renowned for its pasta buffet, and the *Chinese*, for its economical food. But the accent is on business travelers, who enjoy the location and the relatively moderate prices. Harbor-view rooms are a bit more expensive but worthwile for any entertaining.

Marco Polo. Harbour City, Canton Road, Tsimshatsui, Kowloon; (3)7215111. The flagship of Marco Polo International, the 440-room Marco Polo has small functional rooms and a price range that suits economy-minded business travelers. The most distinguished feature is the *auberge*-like *Brasserie*, one of Hong Kong's most relaxing French restaurants. Guests are allowed to use the Hongkong Hotel's swimming pool.

Miramar. 134 Nathan Rd., Tsimshatsui, Kowloon; (3)681111. Over 1,100 rooms, with huge restaurant complex, shopping arcade, extra security with electronic cards, swimming pool.

New World. New World Centre, 22 Salisbury Rd., Tsimshatsui, Kowloon; (3)694111. This 740-room hotel is smack in the middle of a huge shopping complex, so you'd never guess they'd have a 40,000-square-foot landscaped garden with pool and terraces. The *Park Lane* is a Continental gourmet restaurant, while *Panorama* has a splendid harbor view and good luncheon buffets. *Faces* is one of Hong Kong's top discos. Good business center.

Nikko. 72 Mody Road, Tsimshatsui East, Kowloon; (3)739–1111. Part of the Japanese Nikko chain; 461 rooms with French, Japanese, and Chinese restaurants, swimming pool, health and business centers. Nikko has special floors for VIPs and business executives. Opening early 1988.

Prince. Harbour City, Canton Road, Tsimshatsui, Kowloon; (3)723–7788. Marco Polo International's "economy" hotel in the middle of a large shopping complex, with restaurants, use of *Hongkong Hotel* swimming pool and conference facilities.

Regal Meridien. 71 Mody Road, Tsimshatsui East, Kowloon; (3)7221818. Chic and *petite*. Functionally stylish low-ceilinged rooms (some with harbor views) are well-designed. There is fine dining at the *Restaurant De France*, and the French culinary accent is augmented by a first-floor *Brasserie*. The basement levels hosts one of Kong Kong's top discos, the *Hollywood East*.

Regal Meridien Hong Kong Airport. Sa Po Road, Kowloon; (3)7180333. Connected to Kai Tak Airport's Passenger Terminal by an air-conditioned walkway (with a moving luggage conveyor belt) this 380-room hotel is ideal for brief transit visitors or any businessman with business in north Kowloon. The rooms are excellently sound-proofed and comfortable. The fine rootfop *Five Continents* French restaurant overlooks the airport and harbor. The *China Coast Pub* is a comfortable place to bend an elbow, whether you a are waiting for a plane or not. The *China Trader's* (business) *Centre* is well equipped and used by those who have short stays in the territory.

Royal Garden. Mody Road, Tsimshatsui East, Kowloon; (3)7215215. Hong Kong's only atrium hotel. If you like exquisite *bijou-cum*-Disneylandish atrium effects, you'll love the Royal Garden's—glass elevators, fairy lights, trailing greenery, a grand white piano fit for Liberace, and trickling pools. The third-floor atrium leads to the fine *Lalique* French restaurant and open-plan coffee shop and terraces. The lower atrium contains "lakeside" *Flower Lounge* Cantonese restaurant. *Falcon* is an English-style pub during the day and a disco at night. Business center.

Sheraton. 20 Nathan Rd., Tsimshatsui, Kowloon; (3)691111. Ideally located on the corner of the "golden mile" of Nathan Road and the harbor-edging Salisbury Road, the 922-room Sheraton has renovated its rooms and facilities, offering upgraded competition for the newer hotels. The *Someplace Else* American-style duplex pub-diner has good Texan and Mexican fare. The Rooftop *Pink Giraffe* supper club and the long bar have good city views and are reached by Hong Kong's first set of glass-walled external elevators. The Osaka-based *Unkai* Japanese restaurant is top class. Good business center.

New Territories

Riverside Plaza. Ta Chung Kiu Rd., Shatin, New Territories; (0)649–7878. The first deluxe hotel in the N.T., it is situated on the river. Free shuttle bus service to Tsimshatsui. *Asian Delights* restaurant features food from Thailand, Indonesia, Malaysia, Singapore, and Japan, while *Bottania Cafe* serves Continental food. *Regal Restaurant* specializes in Chinese seafood. Disco, business, and health centers.

FIRST CLASS

Hong Kong

Caravelle. 84 Morrison Hill Rd., Happy Valley, Hong Kong; (5)7544455. Overlooking the Royal Hong Kong Jockey Club's Happy Valley racecourse, near the Queen Elizabeth Stadium, this 94-roomer has a brightly decorated, cheerful coffee shop, a grill room, and a bar. Causeway Bay shops and Wanchai nightspots are only a short walk away.

Cathay. 17 Tung Lo Wan Rd., Causeway Bay, Hong Kong; (5)778211. At the quiet end of Causeway Bay, facing Victoria Park, near the major China Products department store, the Cathay is favored by economy-minded groups and by Southeast Asian visitors (who find an Indonesian and Spanish slant to the cozy coffee shop's menu).

Emerald. 152 Connaught Road West, Hong Kong; (5) 4681111. 324 rooms in the territory's first hotel in the Western District. Cantonese, Chiu Chow, and Taiwanese food.

Harbour. 116–122 Gloucester Rd., Wanchai, Hong Kong; (5)748211. Renovated and taken over by Chinese interests, it is favored by budget travelers and delegations from the PRC. Good *dimsum* and Cantonese food.

Harbour View International House. 4 Harbour Rd., Wanchai, Hong Kong; (5)201111. Part of the YMCA group. Next to the Arts Centre and Academy for Performing Arts, and a short stroll from the heart of Wanchai.

New Harbour. 41–49 Hennessy Rd., Wanchai, Hong Kong; (5)861–1166. Old budget travelers to Hong Kong will remember this place as the Singapore

Hotel. Taken over by Chinese interests, it is now a favorite of visitors from the mainland.

Ramada Inn. 51–73 Lockhart Rd., Wanchai, Hong Kong; 861–1000. This 284-room inn is aimed at the budget traveler. It has only two outlets, *Abe's,* the coffee shop, which serves western food, and its watering hole, the *Captain's Bar.*

Kowloon

Ambassador. 4 Middle Rd., Tsimshatsui, Kowloon; (3)666321. Actually fronting on Nathan Road's "golden mile," facing the Sheraton, the 300-room Ambassador is a reliable business and group hotel. Its rates reflect the central value of its location. The expansive lobby lounge and reasonable coffee shop now add a touch of middle class to the recently renovated hotel.

Empress. Chatham Road South, Tsimshatsui, Kowloon; (3)660211. Formerly part of the Peninsula group, this 190-room balconied hotel is now a member of a small local hotel group. Higher-floor rooms have good views across the undeveloped spaces of Tsimshatsui East, which lies to the east across Chatham Road. The Empress is close to both "old" Tsimshatsui's shops and restaurants and to "new" Tsimshatsui's office blocks and shopping complexes.

Grand. 14 Carnarvon Rd., Tsimshatsui, Kowloon; (3)669331. One of the older Tsimshatsui hotels that tries to offer international qualities, the 200-room Grand has a pleasant grill room (good value buffets), a casual coffee shop, and a pub-like bar.

Hotel Fortuna and Fortuna Court, 351 Nathan Rd, Kowloon; (3)851011. A fair way up Nathan Road, the Fortuna and its nearby 80-room annex are favored by groups for above-average service and their feeling of being right in the heart of a Hong Kong shopping scene that's geared more to locals than to tourists. All beds are queen-sized. The *Loong Tan Kok* Chinese restaurant is run by the Unicorn group of restaurants. The annex is in a quieter area than the 200-room main hotel building, which fronts on Nathan Road.

Imperial. 32 Nathan Rd., Tsimshatsui, Kowloon; (3)662201. Located centrally between the Sheraton and the Golden Mile Holiday Inn, the refurbished Imperial is now a cosily comfortable small (220-room) hotel. An above-average, spacious coffee shop, the *Gardena,* and the lively basement *Hideaway* music bar, are attractions. Aimed at commercial visitors, the hotel has automatic tea boilers and vending machines on each floor (both are still rarities in Hong Kong).

International. 33 Cameron Rd., Tsimshatsui, Kowloon; (3)663381. Quietly unostentatious, the International's restaurant menu indicates its chosen market —it offers French (i.e., "Continental") food and Swatow Chinese dishes, appealing to both Western travelers and Northeast Asians. This 95-roomer is one of several smallish hotels in the heart of old Tsimshatsui.

Nathan. 378 Nathan Rd., Kowloon; (3)885141. At the far end of Nathan Road's "golden mile" of shopping, the 120-roomed Nathan has refrigerators in all rooms, serves both Western and Chinese cuisine, and isn't far from Tsimshatsui's action now that the M.T.R. subway system has opened up the farther reaches of Nathan Road.

Park. 61 Chatham Rd. South, Tsimshatsui, Kowloon; (3)661371. Tsimshatsui's biggest independent hotel, the 450-room Park has been extensively renovated. It now offers stronger competition with its guestroom facilities—modernized bathrooms, TVs, and refrigerators. The top-floor Western restaurant and bar is pleasant.

MODERATE

Kowloon

Bangkok. 2 Pilkem St., Kowloon; (3)679181. Tucked into a back street behind the London theater, near the Jordan M.T.R. station, the Bangkok has one of Hong Kong's four Thai restaurants. Its lobby, coffee shop, and rooms are cozily scruffy, but the atmosphere is friendly.

Chung Hing. 380 Nathan Rd., Kowloon; (3)887001. Plain and simple, this 90-room old-timer has some spacious rooms that look rather Spartan, even if they are clean.

First. 206 Portland St., Kowloon; (3)305211. Way out, in Hong Kong terms, this local-style 50-roomer is adjacent to the Argyle M.T.R. subway station. It's convenient if you have business in Mongkok. Only some rooms have TV.

Galaxie. 30 Pak Hoi St., Kowloon; (3)307211. North of the Jordan M.T.R. subway station, just off Nathan Road, this 50-room five-floor economy hotel has a distinctive red-and-yellow striped façade. Fair-sized rooms and an okay Western-style café make this a conveniently located stop for regional business travelers on a budget.

Grand Tower, 624–641 Nathan Rd., Kowloon; (3)910468. For budget travelers who want the real Hong Kong. Right by the Mass Transit Railway with Chiu Chow, Japanese, and "all-purpose" Asian restaurants, the real attractions are the teeming side streets.

Guangdong Hotel. 18 Prat Ave., Kowloon; (3)739–3311. Appeals to many overseas Chinese visitors. Special Chinese-section business center. Japanese and Chinese restaurants.

King's. 473 Nathan Rd., Kowloon; (3)301282. Up near Waterloo M.T.R. subway station, this 72-room small hotel is best known for its six-tabled, air-conditioned Thai restaurant. Visitors from other lands enjoy the food. Bedrooms have usual amenities.

Ritz. 122 Austin Rd., Kowloon; (3)672191. With fifty inexpensive rooms just north of the main Tsimshatsui area, close to the Jordan M.T.R. subway station, the Ritz may not live up to its name, but it's a relative bargain for anyone just looking for somewhere to rest his or her head between shopping and dining experiences.

Shamrock. 223 Nathan Rd., Kowloon; (3)662271. Near a Jordan M.T.R. subway station exit, this brightly and comfortably decorated 150-room hotel is the pick of the "Moderate" bunch of northern Nathan Road hotels. A restaurant and lounge are on the tenth floor; the lobby is garish and Oriental-styled.

OUTLYING AREAS AND ISLANDS

Carlton Hotel. 4½ Miles, Tai Po Rd., Kowloon (North Kowloon); (3)866222. Virtually in the New Territories, off the Tai Po Road that snakes through the range of hills leading out to Tai Po (a fast-developing country town near the Chinese University campus), the old Carlton holds nostalgic memories for local old-timers. The three-storied, 60-room retreat had (and still has) an open pool and dining terrace. Dinner at the Carlton once inspired Ian Fleming to write that it "unfolds one of the world's most memorable panoramas, the jewelled lights of Kowloon, the harbor and the island." Visitors with a lot of time to spare for an exploratory Hong Kong visit might consider booking one of the Carlton's ten suites. But be warned that neither the hotel nor its setting are as romantic as the sadly missed, demolished Repulse Bay Hotel.

Discovery Bay Village Resort. Lantau Island; (5) 987–6080. In addition to various water sports, squash, and tennis, there is also a golf course.

Pearl Island. 17½ Miles, Castle Peak Road, New Territories, Hong Kong; (0)808119. In Castle Peak harbor, facing the new town developments of Tuen Mun across the waters, the Pearl Island has a private beach and two restaurants for Continental and Chinese cuisine. Its 35 rooms are still favored by locals seeking a night or weekend away from it all, either with their families or their temporary secretaries.

Surf. Tai Mong Tsai Road, Sai Kung, Kowloon; (3)2814411. Not a member of either the H.K.T.A. or the H.K.H.A., the 32-room Surf is a popular weekend retreat for Hongkongers getting out to the unspoilt eastern side of Kowloon peninsula. On the beach near the old fishing community of Sai Kung (now an up-market residential area), the hotel is right on Sha Ha beach, where you can go windsurfing or rent rowboats, and has good pools, and an all-weather tennis court, serves up fair Western and Chinese cuisine, and claims to be only twenty minutes by car from Tsimshatsui (outside the rush hours, of course).

Warwick. East Bay (Tung Wan), Cheung Chau Island; (5)9810081. Soaring above the popular public beach of Tung Wan, facing across miles of water to Hong Kong Island, the Warwick is the Outlying Island's first first-class hotel. Features include a swimming pool with sunken bar, a disco, two restaurants with bars, a squash court, and a private pier. Part of the Hong Kong-based Warwick International Hotels group (which has operations in North America, Europe, and Jamaica), the eight-floor, balconied vacation hotel is Hong Kong's first semi-deluxe seaside hotel. The crowded Mediterranean-style island of Cheung Chau *is* worth visiting (and Hong Kong is only an hour away by frequent ferry) but the hotel will probably be most popular with local families.

Silvermine Beach Hotel. Silvermine Bay, Mui Wo, Lantau Island; (5)984–8295. This 78-room "Moorish-Iberian" looking hotel is Lantau's first resort establishment. It is built right on Lantau's most accessible beach at Silvermine Bay, not far from the ferry pier. The hotel has two pools, the smaller one being for children, a children's playground, and barbecue facilities, emphasizing the fact that it will be catering to local families intent on getting away from it all, as well as to overseas visitors. The modest restaurant serves both Chinese and European fare.

 HOW TO GET AROUND. There are probably more kinds of transport in Hong Kong than anywhere else in the world. Hong Kong is a series of interlinked islands, plus a chunk of the Chinese mainland. Ferries, a subway system, and road tunnels connect Hong Kong Island with the Kowloon peninsula and the Outer Islands. There are also excellent bus services throughout Hong Kong Island, Kowloon and the New Territories, and a number of routes link the two sides of the harbor. On Hong Kong Island there are two kinds of trams—a street level tram running across the north shore of the island and the Peak Tram, which is a funicular railway traveling up Victoria Peak, the mountain that dominates the central part of the island.

Airport. Coming from or going to Kai Tak Airport, the visitor can take the Airbus or a taxi. The Airbus serves the major hotels on both sides of the harbor: Route A1 (H$5) goes to the hotels in the Tsimshatsui, Kowloon area; Route A2 (HK$7) goes to the Wanchai and Central districts on Hong Kong Island; A3 (HK$7) goes to Causeway Bay, also on the island. The service has a fixed 15-minute frequency between 7:00 A.M. and 11:00 P.M. daily. (For route details, see "Arrival at Kai Tak" in the Facts at Your Fingertips section.) For information, call (3)745–4466.

Taxi fares to Tsimshatsui on Kowloon run roughly from HK$20 to HK$25 from the airport, to Causeway Bay about HK$50 (including the cross-harbor tunnel fee of HK$20, which is added on to the meter) and to Central about HK$55 (including tunnel fee).

By subway. This underground railway system is known in Hong Kong as the Mass Transit Railway, or M.T.R. It is a splendid air-conditioned railway that links Hong Kong Island to the shopping area of Tsimshatsui and outwards to parts of the New Territories. Trains are frequent, safe, convenient, and easy to use.

Station entrances are marked with a simple line symbol resembling a man with his arms and legs outstretched, and with a tail. There are clearly marked ticket machines inside the station, taking exact denomination coinage. You can get change in the station at the HK$1 and HK$2 change machines and at Hang Seng Bank counters. Ticket machines issue plastic tickets with a magnetic strip through them. Tickets are the size of credit cards and give you access to the system through an electronic gate. Fares range from HK$2 to HK$5.50 and there is a special "Tourist Ticket" for HK$15, which will save you money if you are really on the go.

It is not easy to get lost on the M.T.R. as there are only three routes. One route ends up at Tsuen Wan new town in the west, with Laichikok and its Sung Dynasty village en route, while the other runs east to Kwun Tong (via Wong Tai Sin where you can get off at Hong Kong's favorite temple and have your fortune told). Change trains at Argyle if you want to go on to Kwun Tong. To get to the Island Line from Kowloon, change at Admiralty. This line puts the central business district, the bars and restaurants of Wanchai, and the shops of Causeway Bay and Cityplaza, plus Chaiwan in the East and the Macau and China Ferry Terminals in the Western side of Central, just minutes away from the main hotels. (The changeover to the Kowloon–Canton Railway for travel out towards Shatin and the border is at the Kowloon Tong Station.)

Be warned: there are no toilets on the M.T.R. system; you are not allowed to eat, drink, or smoke on the trains; and you must not flick your ticket—it damages the electronic tickets and ticket-flickers pay fines up to HK$1,000.

Trains run from 6:00 A.M. to 1:00 A.M.

Buses. Double-decker buses run on both sides of the harbor. In Kowloon they are the red and cream Kowloon Motor Bus vehicles; on Hong Kong Island they are the blue and cream China Motor Bus vehicles. Buses sometimes cross the tunnel routes. (All the cross-harbor buses have red destination signs with white lettering.)

The best place to catch a bus in Kowloon is at the Star Ferry or Jordan Road ferry terminus; in Hong Kong the best places are near the Connaught Centre by the Star Ferry and at Admiralty M.T.R. Station. Fares on the different routes run from HK$1 to HK$7. Information on major routes for visitors is contained in a leaflet issued by the Hong Kong Tourist Association and available at any tourist office. Further bus information can be had from the information services of the two major bus companies: China Motor Bus, (5)658556 and Kowloon Motor Bus, (3) 745-4466.

It is worthwhile to take at least one good trip on the top of a bus. Many visitors like to take the 260 or 262 bus on the Hong Kong Island from the main terminus by Connaught Centre along a scenic route to Repulse Bay Beach or to the little fishing village of Stanley, with its excellent market.

Taxis. Taxis are easy to spot in Hong Kong because they are usually red and have a roof-sign saying "TAXI" that is lit up when the taxi is available for hire. They are obliged by law to have working meters. Fares in the urban areas start at HK$5.50 and go up by $.70 per 0.25 kilometer. There is a surcharge of HK$2 per large piece of baggage and a HK$20 surcharge for crossing the harbor through the Cross-Harbour Tunnel. The Aberdeen and Lion Rock Tunnels carry surcharges of HK$3. None of these surcharges are shown on the meter but they are enumerated on a small sign on the dashboard. Most people give a small tip, either by leaving the odd change or from HK$.50 to HK$1 for a large fare. Taxis are usually reliable in Hong Kong, but if you do have a complaint—about overcharging, for example—there is a special hot-line, (5)-277177. Be sure you have the taxi license number, which is usually displayed somewhere on the dashboard.

It is difficult to find taxis from 4:00 P.M. to 7:00 P.M., as this is rush hour. Apart from these times, except on rainy days, there is seldom a shortage of taxis. If a taxi does not stop for you, check to see if you are in a non-stopping zone. Most taxi-drivers speak some English, but to avoid problems, get someone at your hotel to write out your destination in Chinese.

Outside the urban area, in the New Territories, taxis are mainly green and gray. They cost less than urban red taxis, fares starting at HK$4.50 for the first two kilometers (1.2 miles), then $.90 per 400 meters (roughly, one-fifth of a mile). The boundary areas dividing urban taxi limits from rural taxis come around the junction of Hiram's Highway with Clearwater Bay Road, Sekkong, north of the Chinese University, Shum Cheng, and the ten-mile-stone on Castle Peak Road. Urban taxis can travel from their permitted limits outward, but rural taxis must not cross limits. There are no interchange facilities for these taxis, so you are advised not to try to reach the urban area using a green taxi. Urban taxis are, however, allowed to go through the Lion Rock Tunnel.

Many taxis are radio-controlled. Usually you pay for the whole journey, including the pick-up run.

Minibuses. Also known as Public Light Buses, these fourteen-seater yellow vehicles with single red stripes rush round all over Hong Kong. They are quicker and slightly more expensive then ordinary big buses, stop almost anywhere at your request, and are frequently used by Hong Kong people to get about speedily and efficiently. Their destination is written on the front, but the English-language characters are very small. You wave the minibus down when you see what you want and pay the fare marked in front. Notice the fare as you get in. Since fares are adjusted throughout the journey, you could pay as little as HK$1 or as much as HK$5 according to time and place. Visitors who want to travel from Central to Causeway Bay for shopping should look for the minibus marked "DAIMARU," the name of a big store in Causeway Bay.

Maxi-cabs are curiously named, since they are the same as minibuses but have single green stripes. From beside the car park at the Star Ferry, Hong Kong side, they go to Mid-levels and Ocean Park, and from *HMS Tamar* (just beyond City Hall at Star Ferry) they run to the Peak. Fares vary from HK$3 upwards.

Trams. All visitors should take a street tram, even if only once. It is a very rare form of transportation and a tourist's delight, allowing plenty of time to see everything. Take your long lens and head for the upper deck. The trams run along Hong Kong Island's north shore from the Kennedy Town in the west all the way through Central, Wanchai, Causeway Bay, North Point, and Quarry Bay, ending in the former fishing village of Shaukiwan. There is also a branch line that turns off in Wanchai toward Happy Valley, where horse races are held during the season. The destination is marked on the front and the fare is only HK$.60 for adults (HK$.20 for children). Avoid rush hours, but otherwise this is a very enjoyable way to see Hong Kong.

Peak tram. This is another visitor's must. This funicular railway dates back to 1888 and rises from ground level to Victoria Peak (1,305 feet), giving a wonderful panoramic view of Hong Kong and its islands, all the way out to the distant hills of Kowloon. There are five stations, and both residents and tourists use the tram, paying flat fares of HK$5 (round trip ticket HK$9). Stop to eat in one of the cafés or restaurants at the top; while enjoying Hong Kong's best view. The tram runs from 7:00 A.M. to midnight, making runs every ten to fifteen minutes. There is a free shuttle in a double-decker bus to and from the Star Ferry.

Rickshaw. This humiliating and exploitive form of transport exists only as a tourist gimmick now. No more rickshaw licenses are issued and the few old men left wait for tourists to take their pictures (for which they charge heavily) and to go for a token ride (for which they charge even more heavily). The scale of charges is supposed to be around HK$50 for a five-minute ride, but the rickshaw men are merciless and practical dealers. A posed snap costs from HK$10 to HK$20, but make sure the price is fixed *before* you take the shot—otherwise unpleasant scenes may follow. Frankly, the rickshaw men are best avoided.

By train. The Kowloon-Canton Railway is a small (only 10 stops) electrified commuter line which serves both Kowloon and the New Territories, right up to the Chinese border. There is a change-over station to the Mass Transit Railway at Kowloon Tong. Prices range from HK$2.70 to $10.40. Telephone (0)606–9606 for information. The interchange with the Mass Transit Railway (subway) is at the Kowloon Tong Station.

Hire-car limousine. Most of the best hotels have their own limousines. (The Mandarin and The Peninsula have chauffeur-driven Rolls-Royces for hire). It is an expensive way to travel, but guarantees comfort, reliability, and easy travel to your destination. You can also get rental cars from Avis (the only agency in the airport), Hertz, and Budget. But beware! Only masochists rent cars in Hong Kong. Cars with drivers can be arranged through your hotel.

If you must drive in Hong Kong, you will need an international-driver's license—and don't forget to drive on the left-hand side of the road.

Helicopters. Hong Kong's only helicopter service offers tours (See Tours section) and limited sky taxi service. They fly to Sekkong Airstrip in the New Territories and a few other places in the area. They also have two helicopter pads in Lantau, one a Ngong Ping by the Po Lin Monastery, and the other by the popular beach of Cheung Sha. Fees for the air taxi service vary from HK$400 to $3,375 (contact Heliservices, (5) 202200). The helipad is on Harcourt Road, Hong Kong.

Ferries. Among the greatest attractions of Hong Kong—and a must for tourists—are its numerous ferries. The best-known of course is the Star Ferry, made famous by the film *Love Is A Many Splendored Thing*. This is one of the most spectacular and cheapest ferry rides in the world. A trip across the harbor costs HK$.50 water-level, second-class, and HK$.70 upper-deck, first class (children, HK$.40). By the way, there is no real difference in the standards in the classes and many people think that second class is more fun. Very frequent service (every five to ten minutes) runs from 6:30 A.M. to 11:30 P.M., although the late-night service can be very slow.

The Hong Kong and Yaumatei ferries (H.Y.F.) go to Hong Kong's beautiful outer islands. These are two- and three-decker ferries (three-decker boats have a first-class, deluxe, air-conditioned section on the top deck. with access to the top deck outside, from which views are best) going regularly to Lantau, Lamma, Cheung Chau, and Peng Chau, the main attraction for visitors. The H.Y.F. ferries leave from the Outlying Islands Pier, about a half-mile walk west of the Star Ferry Pier on Hong Kong Island.

For exact time-table, call (5)423081 or get ferry schedules from the Hong Kong Tourist Association. Fares vary from HK$4 to HK$11. Most journeys take about an hour and are very scenic. Try to avoid trips on weekends, when the ferries are very crowded and noisy.

If you have to go to the more distant parts of Hong Kong, you may find there is a linking ferry service that will enable you to beat the traffic. For example, there are high-speed hoverferries from Central to Tsuen Wan, and North Point. The fares are a flat rate HK$5. These trips take about twenty minutes per section, much quicker than going by road.

You can also take the ferry from Star Ferry Pier to Hung Hom, which is quick and cheap—$.70 for adults, $.40 for children.

On foot. If you are not defeated by the heat, it is pleasant to stroll around parts of Hong Kong. On Hong Kong Island, for example, you may enjoy a walk through the very traditional western district, where life has not changed much in a hundred years. If you are a very keen walker, you can go for a long walk in the New Territories or on Lantau Island. Contact the Hong Kong Tourist Association for more information.

 TOURIST INFORMATION. The Hong Kong Tourist Association (H.K.T.A.) operates four Information & Gift Centres staffed with multilingual information officers who speak English, French, Spanish, German, and Japanese, and several Chinese dialects. They can tell you how to get around on public transport, fill you in on what to see and where to shop, and tell you of events during your stay. They can also supply information on religious services and medical treatment.

The H.K.T.A. information centers are in the Buffer Hall (after customs, before exiting) at Kai Tak Airport; on the Star Ferry Concourse, and Shop G8, ground floor, Empire Centre, 68 Mody Road, Tsimshatsui East, both in Kowloon; and in the foyer of the H.K.T.A.'s main office on the 35th floor of the Connaught Centre, Central District, Hong Kong.

An excellent series of information leaflets called Fact Sheets (in-depth survey plus map of one particular geographic area) and a shopping guide are obtainable free of charge from these centers. An H.K.T.A. official guidebook is published monthly and available free in the hotels or for HK$10 at the K.H.T.A. offices. If you are pressed for time you can call the H.K.T.A.'s Telephone Enquiry Service at (3) 722–5555. Japanese visitors can obtain information in Japanese by calling (5)233996. For cultural events, call the Hong Kong Tourist Association or consult the English language daily newspapers, the *South China Morning Post* and the *Hong Kong Standard,* and the comprehensive "Out and About" section in the weekly *TV & Entertainment Times.* For concerts and other performances, call (or preferably visit) City Hall, (5)229511 close to the Star Ferry on Hong Kong Island, or the Arts Centre at 2 Harbour Road, along the Wanchai waterfront, (5)823–0230.

For details of free afternoon performances in the Landmark Atrium (Central District) pick up a monthly program from H.K.T.A. information centers or at the Landmark.

Hong Kong, a newspaper for the tourist, is published weekly. It describes topical events and festivals while giving insight into local customs. It also offers shopping, eating, and sightseeing tips. *Hong Kong* is distributed free in the hotels, airlines, some shops, and, of course, the Hong Kong Tourist Association Centres.

For directory enquiries, call 108 or consult the Yellow Pages of the telephone directory.

The Royal Hong Kong Police runs a hotline for tourists in distress. Specially trained English, Cantonese, and Japanese-speaking police personnel will assist you on (5)290000. Policeman who speak English wear red shoulder tabs.

For Post Office inquiries, dial (5) 231071. For the time and weather forecast, dial 1152 for information in English and 1151 for information in Chinese.

Macau. A series of leaflets, a map, and helpful advice can be obtained from the Macau Tourist Information Bureau (M.T.I.B.) in Hong Kong, located at 305 Sun Tak Centre (which is the Macau Ferry Pier), 200 Connaught Road Central, Hong Kong; (5)408180. There is also an office in Macau at the ferry pier. The Macau Department of Tourism is at Travessa do Paiva, Macau, 77218. All offices stock leaflets, maps, and copies of the M.T.I.B.'s monthly newspaper, *Macau Travel Talk.*

 SEASONAL EVENTS. In Hong Kong, people live by two calendars: the Gregorian calendar, in official use everywhere, and the Chinese lunar calendar, by which most festivals are set. This means the date of most Chinese festivals varies each year on the Western calendar, because they are fixed according to the lunar timetable, which has 12 30-day months per year. To complicate matters further, two of the major Chinese festivals are solar celebrations, set at spring and autumn solstice: Ching Ming and Chung Yeung. (Note: if the public holiday falls on a Sunday, the Monday or the preceding Saturday becomes the holiday.)

January. First. *New Year's Day* (Western calendar), a public holiday. *Hong Kong Arts Festival* takes place every January and February and is an opportunity for Hong Kong people to get a taste of some of the best in Western culture. Internationally known artists come to Hong Kong to give concerts, plays, and performances of all kinds; it has become one of the best festivals of its kind in Asia. Telephone the Arts Festival Office at (5)295555 for information. The 42-km Hong Kong International Marathon is run this month, as is the entertaining annual charity run, The Rickshaw Derby.

February. Continuation of *Arts Festival. Chinese New Year* is the most important festival in the Chinese calendar, rather like Christmas, New Year's, and the summer holidays all rolled into one. The date varies according to the moon, and Chinese New Year can fall as early as mid-January or as late as early March. This is family time supreme. The actual festivities take at least three days, and the preparation and the aftermath makes it difficult for visitors to get anything done in Hong Kong. Shopping, too, is limited, with most of the shops closing (for the only time in the year). *Lantern Festival* (Yuen Siu) marks the official end of Chinese New Year. Elaborately decorative lanterns beautify homes, temples, and restaurants. The *Hong Kong Open Golf Championship* is held during this month.

March. *International Seven-a-Side Rugby Championships,* sponsored by Cathay Pacific and the Hong Kong and Shanghai Bank, have become a big sporting attraction and draw rugby fans from all over the world. Early booking for rooms is necessary as fans fill the colony. Buy tickets from Cathay Pacific or the Hong Kong Bank.

April. *Ching Ming Festival* is the time families visit ancestral graves to make offerings and perform traditional rites of worship. It is also a time of great road congestion on the routes leading to the major cemeteries. *Birthday of Tin Hau,* the festival of the Goddess of the Sea so beloved of the fishing people. The fishing boats, covered with gaily colored flags and pennants come streaming into Hong Kong on their way to the Tin Hau temples in the territory. A special festival with traditional rites goes on at the Joss House Bay temple and includes a dragon dance and procession taking place in Yuen Long in the New Territories. It is an extraordinary sight and a delight for photographers. Tour operators run special trips to Joss House Bay. *International Film Festival* is a once-a-year binge for film freaks. Films from Asia, Europe, and America are shown to packed houses morning, noon, and night for a two-week period. Tickets are hard to come by, but try the box office at (5)229928. The *South China Sea Race* series, an internationally certified, biennial yacht race from Hong Kong to Manila, takes place under the sponsorship of the Royal Hong Kong Yacht Club and the Manila Yacht Club. In the alternate year, the R.H.K.Y.C. organizes the Hong Kong-to-San Fernando (in the Philippines) race.

May. *Lord Buddha's Birthday.* Buddhism is deeply imbued in Chinese culture and the celebration of Buddha's birthday is a big temple event. It is therefore a good time for visitors to go to Buddhist temples (where they are most welcome) and watch the ceremonies, which include the bathing of the Buddha's statue. The Po Lin monastery on Lantau Island is visited by many people at this time and special ferry services are laid on. *Tam Kung* is the day when fishing people celebrate their patron saint. There is a special devotional rite held at the Shaukeiwan Tam Kung Temple on Hong Kong Island. *Cheung Chau Bun Festival* is a week-long Buddhist/Taoist rite during which Cheung Chau people are not supposed to eat any meat. The week climaxes in a colorful procession and a ceremony of scrambling for lucky buns, cooked especially for the occasion. Operas and other entertainments are performed in the narrow lanes of Cheung Chau all week, but the last day of the festival is the best for spectacle. It is said the festival originated as a way of exorcizing the ghosts of those people murdered by pirates.

June. *Dragon Boat Festival* is another chance to enjoy a colorful and noisy Chinese spectacle. The dragon boats are long and many-oared and are rowed to the beat of an insistent drum. The Festival is probably a remnant of ancient fertility and rain rites, but local legend ties it to the story of an honest official who drowned himself in despair at the corruption of his time. The boats, say the legends, are those of the fishermen who rowed in vain to save the man. Races take place in fishing communities all over Hong Kong, and are followed by the International Dragon Boat Day reaces, attended by contestants from all over the world. The best places to see the races are at Stanley on Hong Kong Island and the various typhoon shelters.

July. *Birthday of Lu Pan.* This is an important local festival for builders and construction workers, as Lo Pan is their patron god. However, it is not a high-visibility event.

August. *Hungry Ghost Festival—Yue Lan* is perhaps the most powerful of Hong Kong's festivals. Legend has it that the dead are allowed out of hell to wander the earth for one month and that to placate them, people make offerings at the sides of the roads. Burning special paper money and giving food is said to ease the hunger of the wandering spirits, or Hungry Ghosts. (A hungry ghost is a person who has died without family or a proper grave and is comdemned to wander homeless forever.)

September. *Mid-Autumn Festival.* On the days before this festival, the shops are full of lanterns and traditional moon cakes, which are hard with a sweet stuffing. On the night of the festival, Hong Kongers head for parks, beaches, and other open spaces. All green areas, including the Peak, are filled with families carrying lanterns. People picnic and gaze at the full moon, recalling the legends of the Moon Goddess. *Birthday of Confucius. Horse-Racing Season* starts this month and continues through May, with racing at Happy Valley and Shatin. Tourists who are not staying more than 21 days in Hong Kong can take their passports to the Badge Enquiry Office in the Members' Enclosure of either racetrack on racing day to receive, for HK$50, temporary membership for the day. (Hong Kong Tourist Association racing tours are available. See "Tours" on following page.) *Soccer Season* also starts this month, but aficionados from other countries will probably be disappointed in the level of professional soccer in Hong Kong. But top-rank visiting teams do come for exhibition matches.

October. *Chung Yeung* is said to have originated when in ancient times a family was told by a fortune teller to go to a high place to avoid disaster. In the family's absence, everyone in the village was killed by a plague. In Hong Kong, it has become a pleasant picnic time, as well as a time to visit family graves and pay respect to the dead. *Asian Arts Festival* runs for two or three weeks in October and November. It is a biennial bonanza of Asian performers, with many indoor and outdoor performances all over the colony. You may well be able to get tickets, as they are seldom sold out completely. Try the box office at (5)-229928. The *Hong Kong Tennis Classic* is a big-match draw with top international players.

November. The *Macau Grand Prix.* Macau, 40 miles away, is Hong Kong's gambling playground, with casinos, greyhound racing, trotting, and jai alai. The Grand Prix weekend is a two-day event, for cars and motocycles. Like the Monaco Grand Prix, it is run along winding public roads. Hotels are booked months ahead, so if you want to see this, you must reserve very early. Some 50,000 racing fans invade the Portuguese territory from Hong Kong for the weekend. The *Hong Kong International Kart Grand Prix* is the week after the Macau Grand Prix. The Open Windsurfing Championships also take place this month as does the San Miguel Far East Match Racing (Impala Class One boats) Series.

December. *Christmas Day* (December 25) is celebrated only mildly in Hong Kong. Following British custom, the day after Christmas is *Boxing Day*, also a public holiday.

 TOURS. It is possible to travel the length and breadth of Hong Kong Island, Kowloon, the New Territories, and the Outlying Islands using a combination of the cheap and varied methods of public transport and perhaps a taxi or two. The island of Macau can be tackled on bicycle, in taxis, or on foot. Public buses operate to the two islands of Taipa and Coloane.

Information leaflets provided by the Hong Kong Tourist Association and the Macau Tourist Information Bureau are comprehensive and will help you work out your routes.

But for those whose time is limited or who prefer to relax and leave the organization to the professionals, there is a wide variety of tours available. Unless stated otherwise, the tours listed here can be booked at the major hotels. Costs are for adults; children's rates are usually lower.

Hong Kong Island Tour. The tour lasts three to four hours and departs from all the major hotels daily in the morning and in the afternoon. Cost by coach is HK$80, by private car with a maximum of four passengers, HK$400 to $450. Routes vary, but the following spots are generally covered: Victoria Peak, Wanchai, Aw Boon Haw Gardens, Repulse Bay and Deep Water Bay, Aberdeen, the University of Hong Kong, and Western and Central districts.

Horseracing Tour. The Hong Kong Tourist Association runs this special tour—complete with hotel pick-ups and a meal—to each of the 65 race meetings at both tracks. You must bring your passport. Call (5)244191 for information and bookings. Around HK$200.

Star Ferry Photographic Cruises. One-hour juants up and down the harbor: Noon Day Gun Cruise, 11:00 A.M. to 12:15 P.M., adults HK$30/children HK$20, free drinks; Afternoon Tea Cruise, 3:00 to 4:00 P.M., HK$50/HK$35, including high tea; Harbour-lights Cruise, 9:15 to 10:15 P.M., HK$30/HK$20, free drinks. Call (3)669878 for information.

Tram Tour. This combination tour features an hour's clanking on one of Hong Kong Island's private trams—and a marvelous way to see the city—daily each evening from 7:00 P.M. The tour also includes a stop at the Poor Man's Nightclub (street market) and a grand dinner cruise or dinner in a leading hotel of your choice (HK$265–335). Hotel pick-ups from the Sheraton, Royal Garden, Furana, and Excelsior. Call Travel Entertainment (3)674143 for information and bookings. Incidentally, among the most popular cocktail parties in Hong Kong are those thrown on trams . . . ordinary ones, or a 1920s antique tram complete with open balconies. From HK$700 to HK$1,000 for two hours. Call Tram Tours (5)891–8765 for information.

Kowloon and New Territories Tour. With morning and afternoon departures from all the major hotels, the tour lasts three to four hours and costs HK$80 by coach and HK$400–$450 by private car. Routes vary but usually take in Kwai Chung Container Terminal, Castle Peak fishing village, a Taoist temple, the town of Yuen Long, the Chinese border at Lokmachau, the Royal Hong Kong Golf Club at Fanling, Plover Cove and Shatin, and past Chinese University and Amah Rock.

Sung Dynasty Village. This three-hour tour takes in lunch, dinner, or a snack. Prices range from HK$105 to HK$155, and departures are staggered between 10:00 A.M. and 5:30 P.M. The Sung Dynasty Village is a recreation of a 1,000-year-old southern Chinese village. Wander through traditional shops to sample the wares, witness a traditional Chinese wedding ceremony, and have your fortune told.

Ocean Park. To visit this marineland, amusement park, and aviary, tours range from HK$145 to $160, (children HK$125) which includes all rides. Alternatively, you can purchase a City Bus tour from any Mass Transit Railway Station for HK$87 (children HK$43). The ticket includes round-trip open topped, double-decker bus transportation from the Admiralty M.T.R. Station. The highlight of the marineland section is the spectacular dolphins and killer-whale show. Other attractions include an aquarium (called the Atoll Reef) with thousands of fish, including sharks, a wave cove, where marine mammals live and cavort on a rocky seashore. Adjacent to the Ocean Park is Water World, which is not included in the tour. Open between May and October.

Land and Water Tours. Water Tours of Hong Kong Ltd. and the Seaview Harbour Tour Co. Ltd. operate a variety of tours by junks and cruisers within the harbor and to some of Hong Kong's 235 outlying islands including Lamma, Lantau, and Cheung Chau. Some of the tours offer a land-and-sea combination. The variety of tours are too numerous to list, but they vary from a two-hour Harbour Afternoon Tour (HK$90) to an 8.5-hour Grand Combined Tour by junk, cruiser, and coach (HK$305). The Sunset cruise lasts four hours and costs HK$175. Water tram and tour combinations available.

Sports & Recreation Tour. Run by the Hong Kong Tourist Association, this tour provides hotel pick-ups, a Western meal, and admission to the Clearwater Bay Golf & Country Club, where you can play golf or squash or tennis, and enjoy saunas and jacuzzis. Various prices depending on the activity. Call (5) 244191 for information and bookings.

Wan Fu. The Hilton Hotel operates pleasure cruises on its brigantine, the *Wan Fu,* which can also be hired privately. Cruise costs vary from HK$110 to $340 (BBQ dinner) per person. The entire boat costs HK$700 to HK$950 per hour for a minimum of four hours. For full information call the Hilton at (5)233111.

The Land Between Tour. This variation on the more traditional New Territories tours lasts six hours and costs HK$180 (adult)/HK$140 (child). It offers a glimpse at rural Hong Kong and takes in Tai Mo Shan, Hong Kong's tallest mountain, the fish breeding ponds and chicken farms of the New Territories, the Luen Wo Market in Fanling, and the Chinese border at Luk Keng. The return route passes Plover Cove Reservoir, Tolo Harbour (where you'll eat lunch on a terrace), and back to Kowloon past the splendid new racetrack at Shatin.

Night Life Tours. Most of the nighttime tours take you out on the water for a glimpse of reflected neon. They include the Hong Kong Night Tour, which offers a choice of Chinese or Western dinner (HK$240–300)—at the famous Jumbo floating restaurant in Aberdeenor the Peak Tower Restaurant, which offers a panoramic view of the harbor from high atop Victoria Peak. Dinner is followed by a visit to a famous Chinese nightclub. Among the other tours available are the Peak and Harbour by Night Tour (HK$310; five hours); the Tour with Dinner (HK$300; five hours); the Open Top Bus Cocktail Tour with Dinner (HK$300; 5½ hours); cheaper prices for children on most tours.

The Hong Kong Tourist Association runs its own "Yum Sing"—Night on the Town Tour. This do-it-yourself-on-your-own-time tour features many of the territories' top pubs, bars, discos, hostess clubs, and nightclubs. Payment at the establishments is by coupon. Deluxe (HK$270) includes one pub/bar/nightclub coupon good for one or two drinks and one hostess club coupon good for two drinks, a bowl of fruit, and an hour with the lovely of your choice. Grand Tour (HK$150) offers two pub/bar/nightclub coupons for one or two drinks each plus one disco coupon good for entry and one standard drink. Call (5)244191 for information.

And if you are not satisfied with the run of the mill bus, boat, tram, walking tours, Heliservices Hong Kong Limited offers a choice of three "standard" flightpaths during the daylight hours. The cheapest is a 15-minute spin around Hong Kong Island for HK$1,485. Then there's a 30-minute flight to Lantau Island, costing HK$2,970, and a 45-minute grand tour to the New Territories and the border, costing HK$4455. There is also an air-sea combination with water tours. The chopper is a four-seater Bell 206B Jetranger and the heliport is on Harcourt Road, Central. (See How To Get Around section.) Contact Heliservices (Hong Kong) Ltd, St. George's Bldg. 22nd Fl., Hong Kong.; (5) 202200. (All prices are based on a full complement of four passengers.)

MACAU TOURS

Macau Tours that are booked in Hong Kong include jetfoil or hydrofoil transportation, while those booked after arrival in Macau cover land transport only.

Day Tours from Hong Kong last six to eight hours and cost from HK$306 to $450. Visa fees, embarkation tax, transportation, sightseeing by air-conditioned bus, and lunch are included.

Overnight Stay Tours include all of the above, plus the cost of accommodation and all appropriate meals and run from HK$640 to $690.

For help in booking Macau tours in Hong Kong, contact the Macau Tourist Information Bureau, 305 Shun Tak Centre, 3rd Fl., 200 Connaught Road, Central, (5)408180, or ask at the information desk at your hotel. Macau tour operators with offices in Hong Kong are: *Able,* 8–14 Connaught Rd. West, 21st

Fl., Central, Hong Kong; (5)445656; *Estoril,* 3rd Fl., Shun Tak Centre, Connaught Road, Central, Hong Kong; (5)591028; *Hi-No-De and Caravela,* Flat "C" Kiu Yip Building, 5th Fl., 18 Granville Rd., Kowloon; (3)686181; *International,* 2nd Fl., Burfield Building, 143 Connaught Rd., Central, Hong Kong; (5) 412011/3; *Macau,* Champion Building, 9th Fl., 287 Des Voeux Rd., Central, Hong Kong; (5)422338; *Sintra Tours,* 3rd Fl., 331 Shun Tak Centre; (5) 408028; *STDM,* 3rd Fl., 312 Shun Tak Centre; (5)408028; and *T.K.W.,* Room 602, Rise Commercial Building, 5–11 Granville Circuit, Tsimshatsui, Kowloon; (3)723–7771.

Tours bookable in Macau are the *City Tour,* which lasts 3 to 3.5 hours and includes Barrier Gate, Kun Iam Temple, the ruins of St. Paul's Cathedral, Dr. Sun Yat Sen's Memorial Home, the Guia Circuit, the Lou Lim Leoc Garden, the Camoes Museum, Penha Church, the Leal Senado (Municipal Council), the Floating Casino, and the Jai-Alai Stadium. The cost varies from 62 to 67 patacas, according to the number of passengers. The same tour is available by limousine at 150 patacas for one person and 100 each for two.

The Island Tour takes you on a two-hour jaunt over the bridge to Taipa Island to visit the Trotting Club, the Temple of Goddess Kun Iam, and a junk-building village, then over the causeway to the town of Coloane, relics of St. Francis Xavier, Tam Kong Temple, Cheoc Van Resort, and Hac Sa Village and Beach. By coach, the cost per person is 15 patacas, while a guided tour for four passengers or fewer costs 80 patacas an hour.

These tours can be booked through the following tour operators: *Able,* 5–9, Travessa do Pe, Narciso; 89798; *China Travel Service,* 63 Rua da Praia Grande; 88812, 88922; *Estoril,* Hotel Lisboa, ground floor; 73614; *Hi-No-De Caravela,* 6A-4C Rua de Sacadura Cabral; 566622; *H. Nolasco,* 20 Avenida Almeida Ribeiro; 76463; *International,* 9B, Travessa do Padre Narciso; 86522; *Lotus,* Edificio Fong Meng, ground floor; 81765; *Macau,* 9 Avenida da Amizade; 85555; *Macau Zhuhai,* 16 Rua Dr. Pedro José Lobo; 75460; *MBC,* 7–9 Rua de Santa Clara, ground floor, Loja D; 86462; *Sintra,* Hotel Sintra, Avenida de D. João IV; 86394; *STDM,* Hotel Sintra; 85878; *South China,* 15 Avenida Dr. Rodrigo Rodrigues, 1st Fl. A-B; 87211, 87219; and *T.K.W.,* 27–31 Rua Formosa, 4th Fl.; 76200.

Sintra Tours (86394) also offers Budget Tours—using a tape-recorded commentary—that departs from the Hotel Sintra at 10:00 A.M. daily, lasts 2.5 hours, and costs 22 patacas. The same tour is available in the afternoon if demand warrants it. The itinerary includes Penha Church and the Bishop's Residence, A-Ma Temple, Border Gate, Kun Iam Temple, Dr. Sun Yat Sen's Memorial House, and the ruins of St. Paul's Cathedral.

DAY TRIPS TO CHINA

Since 1979, short trips into China have become available. The most popular are the day trips over the Hong Kong border to Shenzhen and via Macau to Zhongshan. The tours need to be booked before noon of the preceding day and passports must be presented at the time of booking. The cost varies from

HK$450 to HK$520. Tours last approximately 10 hours. The Shenzhen tour includes a visit to the reservoir, a nearby art gallery, a Cantonese lunch, a city tour, shopping, and a visit to a kindergarten. The Zhongshan tour includes a visit to the former residence of Dr. Sun Yat Sen, and the Memorial Hall in Zhongshan. A Cantonese lunch is served in Shiqi, Chungshan, or Zhuhai, followed by a visit to either a kindergarten or a people's commune.

Most tour operators and travel agents now handle day trips to China. Overnight stays in China or *en route* in Macau can also be arranged. Contact your hotel tour desk, a travel agent (they advertise in the local press), or China Travel Service (HK) Ltd., Room 2025, 134 Nathan Rd., Kowloon; (3)667201; and China Travel Building, 77 Queen's Rd., Central, Hong Kong; (5)259121. For details on a wide variety of tours to China via Macau see "Side Trips to China" in the Macau section of this book.

 CHINESE CUSTOMS. The observant visitor does not allow all the electronics, the computer and video marvels, or the designer-label fashions to fool him into thinking that Hong Kong is a modern place with no tradition. There is in fact, plenty of tradition in Hong Kong and you will see it everywhere.

Notice the singing birds in beautifully carved cages that hang in shops and even over street stalls; the Chinese have been keeping singing birds for hundreds of years. Look in the temples. There are people burning incense, shaking out lucky sticks to find the answers to their problems, leaving an offering of oranges and rice for the gods. Look in the window of the herbal medicine shops, where most people like to go when they are sick, taking home herbs and roots and even animal products, boiling them carefully as instructed for several hours, and drinking the resulting bitter brew, confident in its power to cure. As to those little hexagonal mirrors with eight-sided diagrams drawn on them that hang in the windows of modern office buildings, they are *fung shui* mirrors, called *bhat gwa*, hung there to deflect any disharmonious elements that might otherwise come inside and disrupt the lives within.

The people who pay attention to these things work to keep the modern and urban metropolis of Hong Kong running.

Those people who say that Hong Kongers are not religious do not know of all the fortune-telling that goes on in the colony—the tortoise-shell and three-coins divination, the psychic bird that picks out your fortune on a card, the fortune sticks you shake out and have read in the temple, the automatic writing done by spirits, the messages to and from the dead, all of this is religion. What other people call chance is the way in which the gods speak to humans in Hong Kong.

The best place in the colony to have your fortune told, as every Chinese will tell you, is Wong Tai Sin Temple. Wong Tai Sin—the Great Sage Wong—can cure illness, grant good health, bring you good fortune and even a win at the races and, best of all perhaps, remove your worries about the future.

The temple complex, built in 1921, is in the center of the Wong Tai Sin housing estate. There are several colorful traditional buildings and, leading up to them, a riot of stalls selling the trappings that go with a place of worship—fruit for offerings, incense, paper money to be burned and sent to the dead. In this predominantly Taoist, but somewhat mixed Buddhist-animist temple typical of Hong Kong's strangely assorted worship, the most important form of divination is to use the fortune sticks. You keep your question in your mind, shake the bamboo holder of the sticks until one falls out, and take it to be interpreted by a medium. Visitors can do this, but if you don't speak Cantonese, take a friend who does.

As with any popular temple, fortune-tellers have set up all around and you can have your fortune told in any way you choose—by your face, on your hand, by paying a little bird to pick a fortune card, by shaking out three coins.

While walking around the streets, you may well come across someone burning paper money at the pavement's edge. This is an offering to appease the spirits (incense and food are also burned) and such a ceremony frequently follows a fatal accident or in connection with a death in the family. In the month of August, such fires are usually part of the Yue Lan, or Hungry Ghost, Festival.

You may hear a great deal about *fung shui* while you are in Hong Kong, but it is difficult to get a clear idea of what it is about. The words *fung shui* mean "wind and water," and this is an extremely complex philosophical system that is an attempt to harmonize the environment. Any action such as building, digging, or excavating can bring about disharmony, and where there is disharmony there is bad luck, illness, or at worst, death. When, for example, the M.T.R. subway system was started, Taoist priests were called in to carry out a ceremony to appease the spirits who would be affronted by the digging of the tunnels.

Conversely, all bad luck and sickness is blamed on bad *fung shui,* and an expert may be called in to check out what exactly is causing bad *fung shui* and bringing misfortune. He might recommend a change of color in the decoration of the place, an exorcism, or that you place a hexagonal *fung shui* mirror to drive back the bad influences. It may also be the *fung shui* expert's recommendation that the furniture, or even the doors and windows, be moved to prevent other evil elements from bringing misfortune.

You may think this sounds primitive, but even the largest and most modern businesses in Hong Kong pay attention to such matters. The government has called in the *fung shui* man on occasion. The Hong Kong and Shanghai Bank, when it moved its famous lions during the construction work on its new headquarters, called in a *fung shui* expert to pick a day and time to move them and a place to put them. The Regent Hotel allegedly built its huge glass atrium for *fung shui* purposes, to allow the flow of harmonies through the hotel's glass wall and into the harbor.

PARKS AND COUNTRY PARKS. Some 40 percent of Hong Kong's tiny land mass is given over to twenty-one country parks found on Lantau Island, Hong Kong Island, and in the New Territories.

These areas have become major getaways for Hongkong people, especially on weekends and holidays. So, if you want to visit them—and you should—try to make it a weekday. If you do go, you will be delighted by the range and variety of the flora and fauna of Hong Kong, as well as the beauty of the scenery.

New Territories. The *MacLehose Trail,* named after a former governor, links eight of the most beautiful parks and stretches for 100 kilometers (60 miles). The walks start at Pak Tam Chung in the Saikung peninsula, New Territories, and are split into ten sections, ranging from five to sixteen kilometers, each graded according to difficulty. Most parts of the trail can easily be reached by public transport.

Hong Kong has a great deal of woodland and a modest range of wildlife, including barking deer, civet cats, porcupines, and long-tailed macaque monkeys. There are a full range of local publications (available at the Government Publications Office in the General Post Office building, by the Star Ferry, Hong Kong-side) that detail the wildlife, flowers, insects, geography, and geology of Hong Kong. You can also buy maps there. You can take the Mass Transit Railway to Tsuen Wan; change to a 32M bus, which will take you to the Cheung Shan Housing Estate; from here you can walk to the Shing Mun Reservoir.

It is easy to get to some of the country parks. The trail crosses the main road and from there you can follow the pleasant and easy track for the few kilometers up to the reservoir. You might want to follow the example of the people of Hong Kong and take a picnic with you. Most people continue around the reservoir and catch the number 32B bus back to Tsuen Wan Ferry Pier and the take the HK$5-hoverferry back to Central. Remember that public transport in Hong Kong is well marked and frequent.

If you fancy a dramatic coastline and sweeping landscapes, you should try the other end of the trail. Take a number 5 bus from Star Ferry to Choi Hung, and change there to the 92, which takes you to Sai Kung. From there pick up a 94 to Pak Tam Chung and take the first section of the trail of Long Ke. When you complete the 11 kilometers to Long Ke, you must either circle and return, which amounts to some 18 kilometers, or continue along the coast until you come to Pak Tam Au—24 kilometers of hard walking. But the scenery is magnificent and you can see the coast of China.

You could also stay on the 94 bus, go past Pak Tam Chung to Pak Tam Au, and from there start on the trail to Kei Ling Ha. This is a short but tough 6.5-kilometer walk. It also allows you a breathtaking view of the entire Sai Kung peninsula. The path goes upwards from the start, through a forest and past some beautiful tree nurseries, then hard uphill until you achieve a stunning glimpse of the whole peninsula, High Island, and the 702–meter-high (2,100 feet) Ma On Shan mountain. The walk down will bring you to the Kei Ling Ha road where a 99 bus will take you to Saikung, an easy trip away from there to Tsimshatsui.

Hong Kong. *Tai Tam Country Park* spreads around the magnificent Tai Tam reservoir. There are several ways to get there, but the most scenic involves taking a number 2 or 20 bus from Central, either at the terminus west of the Star Ferry or outside City Hall, to the Shaukiwan terminus. From there, walk to the main road (two minutes away) and catch bus number 14, which takes you up and down some lovely hills and then right across the Tai Tam Reservoir. There you get off and wander as you please. You could also take the number 6 or 260 buses via Republic Bay to Stanley and then take a number 14.

Up Garden Road, just off Queen's Road Central beside the Hilton Hotel, you will find the *Zoological & Botanical Gardens.* These are small but beautifully laid out and boast some very fine animals and birds.

Victoria Park is easily reached on the tram from Central (get off just beyond Causeway Bay) or by Mass Transit Railway. Check with the Hong Kong Tourist Association to discover if anything worth seeing is being staged in the park. (At Chinese New Year and Mid-Autumn festival colorful fairs are held in the park.)

For the country parks and walks on **Lantau Island,** see the "Islands" section of this guide and the Hong Kong Tourist Association's brochure, "Outlying Islands." The Hong Kong Government Publications Centre in the General Post Office has additional information on country walks in Hong Kong.

BEACHES. Few tourists think of Hong Kong as a place for swimming and lying on a beach. Yet, Hong Kong has hundreds of beaches, mostly unused, and most with clear water lapping on golden sand.

Only thirty-odd of the many beaches are "gazetted," which means they are officially recognized by government as public beaches—which also means they are cleaned and maintained by the government and services, including lifeguards, swimming floats and swimming-zone safety markers, are provided.

Almost all beaches on Hong Kong Island, Kowloon, and the New Territories can be reached by public transport, but it is difficult for visitors to know how to catch the right bus and when to get off. Most bus drivers have neither the time nor ability to give instructions to passengers in English. If you want to try the double-decker buses, call the Hong Kong Tourist Association and ask for the bus route number for a certain beach. Otherwise, use the Mass Transit Railway and then a taxi, or take a taxi all the way. Beaches on outlying islands are reached by ferry and, often, a short walk.

If the red flag—usually indicating pollution or an approaching storm—is hoisted at any beach, stay out of the water. This often happens at Big Wave Bay, so check first with the tourist association or listen to the announcements on radio or TV before heading out there. As we went to press, some of the beaches on Castle Peak Road were temporarily closed due to possible pollution. The situation was to be improved imminently.

ON HONG KONG ISLAND

Repulse Bay. This is Hong Kong's answer to Coney Island. Changing rooms and showers, toilets, bathing sheds, swimming rafts, swimming-safety zone markers, and playgrounds are provided. There are also several Chinese restaurants, and light-refreshment kiosks. The building at the end of the beach that looks like a Chinese temple, with large statues of Tin Hau (the goddess of the sea, and by extension fishermen, swimmers, and lifeguards), belongs to the Lifeguard's Association. Small rowboats are available for hire at the beach. Take bus number 6, 61, 260, or 262 from Central. All drivers on this route speak English and can tell you when to get off. Fare is HK$5 or less.

Deep Water Bay. The action here starts at dawn every morning, winter and summer, when members of the "Polar Bear Club" go for a dip. The beach is packed daytimes in summer, when there are lifeguards, swimming rafts, safety-zone markers, and a police reporting center. Barbecue pits, toilets, and showers are open year-round. The beach is 20 minutes from Central by taxi, or take the number 7 bus to Aberdeen and change for the 73, which passes by the beach en route to Stanley.

Middle Bay. About a mile from Repulse Bay, the beach has few amenities. It is very quiet and rarely crowded, except on Sundays, when it is a popular haven for pleasure boats. Take a Repulse Bay bus, get off one stop after Repulse Bay beach, then walk down South Bay Road for a mile or so. Or take a taxi from Central District or Repulse Bay.

South Bay. A bigger edition of Middle Bay beach. Far from the noise and traffic of the main beaches, it is quiet and rarely crowded, except on Sundays. There are light refreshments, barbecue pits, changing rooms, showers, toilets, and swimming rafts. Take a bus to Repulse Bay and get off one stop past the beach. Then walk down South Bay Road past Middle Bay for a mile and a half. Or take a taxi from Central District or Repulse Bay.

Chung Hom Kok. A short but nice beach between towering cliffs. There are light refreshments, barbecue pits, changing rooms, showers, toilets, and swimming rafts. The easiest way to get there is by taxi or the number 262 bus from Central District. The fare is HK$5.

Stanley Main. This wide sweep of beach, popular with the Hobie Cat crowd, has a Kent Windsurfing Center where you can rent equipment or take lessons. Refreshment kiosk, barbecue pits, changing rooms, showers, toilets, bathing sheds, and a swimming raft. Quite crowded in summer weekends. Take a taxi from Central District or the number 6 or 260 bus; fare is HK$5 or less.

St. Stephen's. About a mile from Stanley Village, the beach has lifeguards, a refreshment kiosk, barbecue pits, changing rooms, showers, toilets, and a swimming raft. Take a taxi from Central District, via Stanley Village or take the buses for Stanley Main Beach, then walk or take a taxi.

Turtle Cove. Isolated, but picturesque, this beach has lifeguards and rafts in summer, plus barbecue pits, toilets, showers, changing rooms, and a kiosk. Take a taxi from Central District or a bus to Stanley Main Beach, then the number 14 bus, or a taxi from Stanley.

Shek O. Almost Mediterranean in aspect, this is a fine, wide beach with nearby shops and restaurants. It has kiosks, barbecue pits, changing rooms, showers, toilets, tents for hire, lifeguard, rafts, and playgrounds. This is one of the few beaches directly accessible by bus—a number 2 from Central District to the end of the line in Shaukiwan, then a number 9 to the end of the line for less than HK$3. Or take a taxi from Central District.

Big Wave Bay. Hong Kong's only surfing beach, the beach is often closed for swimming because of strong waves. Kiosk, barbecue pits, changing rooms, showers, toilets, tents for hire, and a playground. When the red flag—signalling dangerous waves—goes up, get out of the water. Take a taxi from Central District. By bus, take the numbers 2 or 20 from Central to Shaukiwan, which is the end of the line, then a number 9 to the end of the line at Shek O, then walk for about 20 minutes. The combined fares come to less than HK$5.

ON CASTLE PEAK ROAD

Note: To reach these beaches by public transport, take the Mass Transit Railway to Tsuen Wan, then catch bus number 34B, 52, or 53 which pass all of the beaches. Otherwise, take a taxi from Tsuen Wan.

Lido. Popular with school children for outings, this is a fine beach with few rocks. It has rafts, tents for hire, toilets, showers, changing rooms, barbecue pits, and a kiosk.

Hoi Mei. This is a gem of a beach, with sparkling sand and gently lapping waves, ideal for wading. Popular with *amahs,* the often elderly maids. It has most of the amenities, but no swimming rafts, no playgrounds, and no tents for hire.

New Cafeteria. No cafeteria here, but a pretty good beach. There is a kiosk for light refreshments, as well as barbecue pits, changing rooms, showers, toilets, and tents for hire. There is also a Kent Windsurfing Centre, where you can rent equipment or take lessons.

Old Cafeteria. No cafeteria here either, but all the amenities: kiosk, barbecue pits, changing rooms, showers, toilets, tents, rafts.

Kadoorie. This is a tiny beach, but it has most of the amenities, except toilets and swimming rafts. The little sandy strip is "guarded" by two ancient cannons.

SAI KUNG PENINSULA

Silverstrand. The most popular beach, always crowded on summer weekends. A little rocky in spots, but some good, soft sand and all amenities, including new changing rooms, toilets, and showers. Take the Mass Transit Railway to Choi Hung, then a taxi or bus number 91.

Tai Au Mun. There are two beaches on the edge of Clear Water Bay. Both are reached on footpaths from Tai Au Mun village. They have all the amenities. Take the Mass Transit Railway to Choi Hung, then a taxi, or take bus number 91 and ride to the end of the line.

NEAR SAI KUNG

Camper's. Nice, but can only be reached by walking from Clear Water Bay Road or by sampan from Pak Sha Wan village on Hiram's Highway. Take Mass Transit Railway to Choi Hung, then bus number 92 to Pak Sha Wan, then a sampan. Easier-to-reach beaches are just as good.

Kiu Tsui and **Hap Mun.** These beaches are on an island that can be reached only by small boat or sampan from Sai Kung Town. Both beaches have most of the amenities. Take the Mass Transit Railway to Choi Hung, then the number 92 bus to Sai Kung, then walk to the waterfront to pick up a boat.

Pak Sha Chau. A gem of a beach, with brilliant golden sand on a grassy island near Sai Kung Town. Can only be reached by sampan, after the trip by Mass Transit Railway to Choi Hung and the number 92 bus to Sai Kung. Has most of the amenities, but no showers and no swimming rafts.

Sha Ha. The water is sometimes dirty, but remains shallow quite far out and is ideal for beginning windsurfers. You can take lessons or hire a board at the Kent Windsurfing Centre. Take the Mass Transit Railway to Choi Hung, then bus number 92 to the end of the line at Sai Kung, then a taxi for one mile. Refreshments, coffee shop, and Chinese restaurant in the adjacent Surf Hotel.

LAMMA ISLAND

Hung Shing Yeh. Suffering from a nearby construction site, the beach is still popular with local young people. No swimming rafts, but tents for hire, toilets, showers, changing rooms, barbecue pits, and a kiosk. Take the ferry from Central District to Yung Shue Wan and then walk over a low hill.

Lo So Shing. A good beach with all amenities but quite a hike over the hills or along the rocky shore from Yung Shue Wan. Has kiosk, barbecue pits, changing rooms, showers, toilets and swimming rafts.

LANTAU ISLAND

Silvermine Bay. A wide sweep of sand, very popular with local youth in summer. Many restaurants, including an Australian-style pub and a hotel (the Silvermine Beach Hotel). Kiosks, barbecue pits, changing rooms, showers, toilets, and tents for hire, but no swimming rafts. Take the ferry to Lantau, then walk a few hundred yards.

Pui O. A tiny but popular beach just around the headland from the Silvermine Bay ferry pier. Kiosk, barbecue pits, changing rooms, showers, and toilets, but no swimming rafts.

Cheung Sha. This very popular beach is a short taxi or bus ride from Silvermine Bay ferry pier. All of the amenities, except swimming rafts. Buses run every half-hour weekdays. On Sundays and public holidays, buses pull out whenever they are full.

CHEUNG CHAU ISLAND

Tung Wan. This is the main beach, reached by walking five minutes through the village from the ferry landing. The wide sweep of golden sand is hardly visible on weekends, as it is covered by bodies. A modern hotel, the Warwick, is at one end of the beach. Older-style seafood restaurants provide refreshments and shade. Amenities include swimming rafts.

Kwun Yam Wan. Not far from the main beach, but a half-hour hike over the hills along narrow footpaths. This is a popular spot and is crammed with young people on summer weekends. Has all the amenities except showers.

CHILDREN'S ACTIVITIES. Since most visitors to Hong Kong seem hell bent on accomplishing as much shopping or business as they can during their brief stay (the average is about three and a half days), activities for children are usually ignored.

However, about half of the colony's population is under 21, which means there are quite a few youngsters to entertain. So if you end up in Hong Kong with the children, it does not mean you will be forced to leave them in the hotel or drag them along on all the shopping treks. Believe it or not, even in this seemingly concrete jungle, there is a lot you can do *with* or especially *for* your children.

For example, if you are going to shop in the Ocean Terminal-Ocean Centre-Harbour City complex (Tsimshatsui, Kowloon), you might time your trek with the free *cultural shows* performed in the New World Centre under the auspices of the Hong Kong Tourist Association (H.K.T.A.) in Central District. In addition, the Landmark has its own schedule of daily events. If you happen to take your tykes with you to Cityplaza in Taikoo Shing (Hong Kong), you will find roller-skating and ice-skating rinks, in addition to more free shows, to keep them occupied. Schedules of all of these events are available at the H.K.T.A. (For more details on the skating, see the "Sports" section of this guide.)

The *Sung Dynasty Village Tour* is worthwhile. (For full details, see "Exploring Kowloon" section. Specific tour details are available at the H.K.T.A.) Even if the kids are a bit young to appreciate the full meaning of the village, they'll still be captivated by the street acrobats and jugglers. The *Laichikok Amusement Park* is next door. It is not as fancy as the theme parks in the United States, but still it can be a pleasant diversion. The park has a small zoo, but there is a much better one at the *Botanical and Zoological Gardens* in Mid-Levels (Hong Kong). This is a lovely place to take the kids for a run.

Some places cater particularly to children. For example, the McDonald's in Star House, by the Ocean Terminal and the Star Ferry Kowloon-side, has bumper cars, while the Chuck and Cheese in East Tsimshatsui has a game room especially for little ones and has a video games parlor for older kids. The museums—especially the Space Museum in Kowloon—may also appeal to children. (See the Museum Section.) Also in Kowloon is "Crazy Golf," a miniature golf course played through a Chinese environment—pagodas, temples, lakes, etc. Located in Kowloon Tsai—which also has swimming and tennis—it is open from 8 A.M. to 4 P.M. and costs HK$3 for 45 minutes of play. Call (3)367878 for information.

The most obvious place to take children is the *Ocean Park* (and *Water World*) (south side of Hong Kong Island). The upper section—reached by an exciting cable-car ride—has the Ocean Theatre, where performing dolphins and a killer whale hold forth, and a wave cove, where you can watch (from under or over water) seals, sea lions, penguins and other assorted marine animals frolic in and out of their own man-made coastline. And in the Atoll Reef—a giant aquarium—hundreds of fish, including sharks, while away the hours as visitors make their way around the giant tank. The amusement part of the park is also on the headland and includes the "Dragon," one of the longest and most spectacular roller coaster rides in the world. The bottom section of the park has a children's petting zoo, a marvelous children's playground, a dolphin- and whale-feeding pool, lots of park in which to run, and trained bird and animal shows. There is also a huge, walk-through aviary. Admission is HK$80 adults/ HK$40 children for a full day, all rides included. The park and Citybus offer direct transport from Admiralty M.T.R. Station for HK$87 adults/HK$43 children. Call (5) 550947 for information. Open 9:00 A.M. to 6:00 P.M. daily. Adjacent to the park is Water World, a water play park (pools, slides, etc.). The separate admission ranges between HK$15–HK$40, depending on the time of the year and day. Tel. (5) 556055 for information. Opening and closing times vary.

While you are on the south side of the island, you might want to include a trip to the nearby beaches of Deep Water Bay or Repulse Bay (see Beaches section of this guide) or to the nearby Aberdeen Floating Restaurants (see Dining Out section). If the kids are old enough, you might also head for Stanley Village where they can go windsurfing (which is very big in Hong Kong; see Sports section) while you partake of the village's famous street market.

Tennis, golf, squash, scuba diving, boating, water skiing, and many other sports are available in Hong Kong. If you have the money and time and very sporting children, you might consider the Sports and Recreation Tour offered by the *Clearwater Golf and Country Club* (see the "Tours" section of this guide).

As a special treat, you might want to take the kids horseback riding. The *Royal Hong Kong Jockey Club* has riding facilities for children and adults (all levels of instruction) at its Pokfulam Riding School, 75 Pokfulam Reservoir Rd., Hong Kong. The cost is HK$140 for horses and HK$100 for ponies per 45 minutes; telephone, (5)501359. A few Borneo mountain ponies and horses are available at the *Lantau Tea Gardens,* a perfect culmination to a family outing or hike on beautiful Lantau Island. These animals are not for beginners, by the way, so you will first have to prove your equestrian skills; telephone, (5)985–8161.

SPORTS. *Junking,* which consists of picnicking on the water aboard large Chinese fishing junks that have been converted to pleasure craft, is one sport that is unique to Hong Kong. This type of leisure has become so entrenched in the colony that there is now a fairly large pleasure-junk building industry that produces highly varnished, upholstered, and air-conditioned craft that are up to 80 feet long.

These floating rumpus rooms do serve a purpose, especially for citizens living on Hong Kong Island who suffer "rock fever" and need to escape by spending a day on the water. Junking replaces the old-fashioned American tradition of the Sunday drive. Because so much drinking takes place aboard these craft, they are also known as "gin-junks," commanded by "weekend admirals." Above all, they serve as swimming platforms, and focal points for waterskiers, snorkelers, and other water sportsmen. So if anyone so much as breathes an invitation for a boating trip, grab it. To rent a junk, call the Boating Centre, (5)223527.

Most *waterskiing* in Hong Kong is done in conjunction with pleasure junks or motor launches. Usually, a large craft will tow a speedboat rigged for skiing as a tender. Thus you have a bay-full of large boats loaded with audiences—willing and unwilling—watching speedboats and skiers slash the water to a frenzy. Boats and skis can be rented from several outlets; check at your hotel front desk.

One sport certainly not unique to Hong Kong is *windsurfing.* Like most coastline-endowed countries in temperate climates, Hong Kong has welcomed boardsailing with open arms. A company called Kent operates five Windsurfing Centres throughout the territory, offering lessons and renting boards. The cost for lessons is approximately HK$250 for four hours (spread over two days). The four centers are listed below (call for weather information and bookings):

Stanley Beach; (5)660320 or (5)660425. A popular watersports and picnic spot, sheltered, with few rocks along the shoreline. Instruction is given from 9:00 A.M. to 6:00 P.M. From Central, take a number 6 or number 260 bus or take a taxi.

Cheung Chau Island, Tung Wan beach, (5)981–8316. Lessons are from 10:00 A.M. to 5:30 P.M. Take the ferry from the Outlying Islands Ferry Pier in the Central District.

Tolo Harbour, near Taipo; (0)658–2888. A choice of sheltered trail runs or some more sporty stuff farther out. Teaching hours are from 10:00 A.M. to 5:30 P.M., except Mondays and Fridays. Visitors should take a taxi from Kowloon or the Mass Transit Railway and the Kowloon-Canton Railway to Taipo and then a taxi (phone first for instructions on this trip).

Sha Ha beach in front of the Surf Hotel; (3)281–5605, Saturday and Sunday only. Shallow water, refreshments, lessons on weekends only, from 2:00 P.M. to 6:00 P.M. on Saturdays and all day on Sundays. Take a taxi from Kowloon or take the Mass Transit Railway to Choi Hung station and a taxi from there.

Swimming is extremely popular with the local people, which means that most beaches in Hong Kong are packed on summer weekends and public holidays.

The more popular beaches, such as Repulse Bay, are busy day and night throughout the summer (see the Beaches section of this guide).

Shortly after the Mid-Autumn Festival in September, local people stop using the beaches, and there are a few weeks of warm weather when stretches of beautiful sand are empty. Public swimming pools in Hong Kong are either so packed with humanity in summer that the water is barely visible or are closed for the winter. Most visitors wisely prefer to enjoy the pools in their hotels.

Sailing is popular, although you must belong to a yacht club at home that has reciprocal rights with one in Hong Kong to enjoy it.

Scuba diving is also popular in Hong Kong. A number of underwater clubs conduct outings almost year-round, but it is normally difficult for the visitor to join a club outing unless introduced by a friend. However, Bunn's Diving Equipment Corp., 188 Wanchai Rd., Hong Kong, (5)891–2113, offers Sunday outings at HK$90 for non-members. Equipment rental will probably cost around another HK$300.

Jogging is an increasingly popular pastime in Hong Kong. Visitors can join members of the well-known Hong Kong Running Clinic (a Far East chapter of the Honolulu Marathon Clinic) every Sunday morning at 7:30 A.M. at the Adventist Hospital, 40 Stubbs Rd., Hong Kong Island. Non-runners making their first attempt are especially welcomed and looked after. Faster beginners have a separate group that covers about four miles, very slowly. People who run regularly are welcomed at the Wanchai Gap playground off Stubbs Road, also at 7:30 A.M. on Sundays, for a slow hour on level ground or a 90-minute run around The Peak that includes a few gentle hills. These runs are in the Hawaiian tradition of conversation-speed jogging—if you can't talk to your neighbor, you must be running too fast. The Running Clinic also has evening runs on Tuesdays and Thursdays, starting from the Adventist Hospital at 6:30 P.M. For more information, call (5)746211, extension 888, and ask for the director of health services.

There is an official jogging track in Victoria Park, Causeway Bay, across from the Park Lane Hotel. The major races include a series of reservoir runs every winter, plus the annual Hong Kong Marathon. Drop in at a central sports shop for applications for all of these and other runs, or pick up the forms at the Hong Kong Running Clinic.

There are two first-class *roller-skating* rinks in Hong Kong—one at Cityplaza on Hong Kong Island; (5)670400; and the other at Telford Gardens in Kowloon (3)757–2211. Call first to get times for different types of skating (disco, beginners, family, free, etc.). The cost is about HK$20 to HK$30 for non-members, but there are frequent family specials. There is an ice skating rink in town too. The best by far is at the Cityplaza II on Hong Kong Island; (5)675388. Call before you go, as there are different sessions (disco, beginners, free, etc.) during a day. The cost is about HK$15 to HK$25 for non-members.

TENNIS AND SQUASH. Both tennis and squash are popular in Hong Kong, although you will probably have to make arrangements with a private club to play. There are also a limited number of public tennis courts, but they are heavily booked at the preferred times of year and day. To book any public tennis courts, you will need identification such as a passport. The rates are HK$17 per hour from 6:30 A.M. to 7:00 P.M., and HK$33 per hour after 7:00 P.M. The booking numbers are as follows: Victoria Park, (5)790–5824; Bowen Road, (5)282983; Wongneichong Gap, (5)749122; Kowloon Tsai Park, (3)367878.

There are table-tennis tables in Victoria Park in Causeway Bay, Southern Playground in Wanchai, and in Kowloon Tsai Park in North Kowloon.

Squash, like tennis, is very much a club activity in Hong Kong. For visitors, there are public courts at the Hong Kong Squash Centre on Hong Kong Island. To book a court, call (5)706186 to find out availability, then go there, passport in hand, to make the booking; the rate is HK$16 per hour. Squash courts are also available at the Harbour Road Indoor Games Hall (Hong Kong Island) at HK$14 per half hour and HK$28 per hour.

GOLF. Golf is popular in Hong Kong, but space is limited and only three clubs welcome visitors who do not have reciprocal rights from a club at home. The Royal Hong Kong Golf Club allows visitors to play on its 9-hole course at Deep Water Bay, Hong Kong Island, or on its two 18-hole courses at Fanling in the New Territories, Monday through Friday only. The green fees in Fanling are HK$360 for a single round of 18 holes or HK$480 for the day, as many rounds as you like. Club rentals are HK$100 per round. Telephone (0)901211 for information and bookings or the Pro Shop (0)900647 for club rental. At Deep Water Bay, green fees for a single 9-hole round are HK$100; club rental is HK$5. Telephone (5)812–0334.

The Clearwater Bay Golf and Country Club charges HK$300 in green fees, HK$120 for cart hire (two people), and between HK$60 and HK$100 for golf-club rental per 18 holes. Note: This club and the H.K.T.A. run a Sports and Recreation Tour (see "Tours") with special green fees. In addition to golf, the club has tennis, squash, badminton, table tennis, and swimming, plus jacuzzi and sauna. The tour costs HK$190 for adults and HK$150 for children under 12.

The Discovery Bay Golf Club is open to visitors seven days a week. To get there take the hoverferry from Blake Pier in Central. Call (5) 987–7271 for information.

POOL. For those who cannot do without a bout in their friendly neighborhood poolroom, you'll be pleased to hear of the American Pool Leisure Centres, (5)264825, which offer games at HK$10 per half hour from 10:00 A.M. to 10:00 P.M. in their three centers. For visitors staying in Hong Kong, the closest is at

21 Old Bailey Street in Central. In Kowloon, there is one center; 13 Man Tai Street in Hung Hom.

HORSERACING. Horseracing is the nearest thing Hong Kong has to a "national" sport. It is a multimillion-dollar business employing thousands of people and drawing crowds that are almost suicidal in their eagerness to get rid of their hard-earned money during the September through May season.

A day at the races in Hong Kong, either at the modern Shatin track or at the more traditional Happy Valley track on Hong Kong Island, is an absolute must. For the non-punter, just watching the hordes is entertainment enough.

An overseas visitor can go to the Badge Enquiry Office at either the Shatin or Happy Valley tracks on the day of the race meeting, show his or her passport, pay HK$50 for a badge, then go into the Members' Stand to enjoy an afternoon or evening of gambling. Call the Royal Hong Kong Jockey Club at 1817 for information (see the "Gambling" section of this guide). The H.K.T.A. runs a horseracing tour (see "Tours").

Dragon Boat Races: See the Seasonal Events section, June.

GAMBLING. In a place where gambling has developed into a mania, it may come as a surprise to learn that most forms of gambling are forbidden in Hong Kong. Excluding the stock market—which is by far the territory's biggest single gambling event—the only legalized forms of gambling are horseracing and the Mark Six Lottery. Nearby Macau is another story, and you can get you fill of casino gambling there (see the Macau section of this guide).

Of course, you will find a great deal of gambling wherever you happen to hear the clickity-click of the mah jong tiles, particularly if that game happens to be in a mah jong school. (If you are from the United States, substitute poker schools for mah jong schools and you'll soon get the idea.) But presumably mah jong gambling does not count.

There is also another form of gambling, the ancient Chinese sport of cricket fighting (that's cricket as in insect, not as in the sport), but it is so well hidden—particularly from Europeans, who could be mistaken for overzealous gendarmes—that we can skip it. Suffice it to say if you see someone wandering around a market carrying a wash tub and softly calling *"tau chi choot,"* follow him.

The most popular form of gambling in which a visitor can partake is horseracing. The Sport of Kings is run under a royal monopoly by the Royal Hong Kong Jockey Club, one of the most politically powerful entities in the territory. Profits go to charity and such community-benefiting organizations as the Ocean Park and the Jubilee Sports Centre. The season runs from September or October through May and has some 65 races spread over two racecourses—Happy Valley on Hong Kong Island and Shatin in the New Territories. The latter, incidentally, is only a few years old and is one of the most modern in the world. (Would you believe air-conditioned stables?) Both courses have huge video screens at the finish line so that gamblers can see what is happening each and every step of the way.

During the season, races are run every Wednesday night at one track and on one day on the weekend at both tracks. (If it is a particularly rainy season and weather forces the cancellation of races, the Royal Hong Kong Jockey Club runs races on both days of the weekend to catch up.) See also the Horseracing (Sports) section of this guide.

Listed below are the types of bets played in Hong Kong, some of which can be placed at the myriad Royal Hong Kong Jockey Club's Off Course Betting Centres scattered around the colony. (Just ask at the reception desk of your hotel; they'll steer you to the closest one.)

Quinella: The first and second horse in any order in one race.

Double Quinella: Pick the first two horses in two specific races in any order.

Six Up: Choosing one of the first two horses (any order) in six races.

Tierce: Pick three horses in order in any race.

Quartet: First four horses in any order.

Daily Double: Winners of two designated races.

The other form of legalized gambling, The Mark Six Lottery, is also run by the Royal Hong Kong Jockey Club and tickets are sold for the twice-weekly draws (every Tuesday and Friday evening) at the Off Course Betting Centres. The idea is to guess six out of the seven numbers drawn out of total of 40; i.e. 1 to 40. There are many variations and aficionados should ask for the free instruction brochure at the betting centers. The lowest bet is HK$2 per entry, and there are multiple entries per card. Winnings, of course, snowball until the entire colony is talking about the prize. Check with your friendly bellboy or desk clerk; they'll probably have extra forms.

 MUSEUMS AND LIBRARIES. Most museums in Hong Kong specialize in the art of China, but a few collections stress the colony's past and its cultural traditions.

MUSEUMS

Hong Kong Museum of History, Haiphong Road, Kowloon Park, Tsimshatsui, Kowloon; (3)671124. The most comprehensive museum in Hong Kong, with permanent and temporary displays on local history, archeology, arts, crafts, and traditions. There is also a large photographic collection. Open 10:00 A.M. to 6:00 P.M. daily, 1:00 P.M. to 6:00 P.M. Sunday and public holidays; Closed Friday. Admission free.

Hong Kong Museum of Art, 10th and 11th floors, City Hall High Block; (5)224127. Excellent Chinese art and antiquities, including fine ceramics, good displays of paintings, drawings, and a pictorial record of Sino-British relations. Interesting temporary exhibitions change monthly. Open 10:00 A.M. to 6:00 P.M. daily, 1:00 P.M. to 6:00 P.M. Sunday and public holidays; closed Thursday and

Christmas, Boxing Day (December 26), New Year's Day, and first three days of Lunar (Chinese) New Year. Admission free.

Fung Ping Shan Museum, University of Hong Kong, 94 Bonham Rd., Mid-Levels; (5)859–2114. This university-run museum is somewhat out of the way in Hong Kong's Western District, but it has the world's largest collection of Nestorian crosses of the Yuan Dynasty (A.D. 1279 to 1644). It also has superb pieces from pre-Christian periods: ritual vessels, decorative mirrors, and painted pottery. A must for lovers of Chinese art.

Open 9:30 A.M. to 6:00 P.M. Monday to Saturday; 2:00 P.M.–6:00 P.M. Sundays; closed Thursdays, Sundays, and on public holidays, and March 16 (Founding Day for the university). Admission free.

Art Gallery, Institute of Chinese Studies, Chinese University, Shatin, New Territories; (0)695–2218. Artists from the last 300 years in Canton are featured, along with bronze seals, pre-Christian rubbings of stone inscriptions, jade flower carvings. Temporary exhibitions of special themes are also featured. Open 9:30 A.M. to 4:30 P.M. daily, 12:30 P.M. to 4:30 P.M. Sunday and some public holidays. Admission free.

Lei Cheung Uk Museum, Tonkin Street, Lei Cheng Uk Resettlement Estate, Shamshuipo. This museum is actually a burial vault from the Late Han Dynasty (A.D. 25 to 220), discovered in 1955. The four barrel-vaulted brick chambers form a cross around a domed vault. The funerary objects are typical of these tombs. English-speaking guides provide explanations. Off the beaten track, but cynical observers point out a bonus in the area, the *modern* tombs of the Sham Shui Po Housing Estate. Open 10:00 A.M. to 1:00 P.M., 2:00 P.M. to 6:00 P.M. daily, 1:00 P.M. to 6:00 P.M. Sunday and public holidays; closed on Thursdays. Admission charge.

Hong Kong Space Museum, Salisbury Road, Tsimshatsui, Kowloon (opposite The Peninsula Hotel); (3)7212361. The Space Museum forms part of a planetarium. The main exhibition hall has more than 30 exhibits, including the Aurora 7 space capsule, in which Scott Carpenter made three orbits around the earth in 1962. The Hall of Solar Sciences has a solar telescope, which gives a close look at the sun. Many audio-visual devices and microcomputers. The Exhibition Hall opens from 2:00 P.M. to 10:00 P.M. daily, except Tuesday, and 10:30 A.M. to 10:00 P.M. on Sundays and public holidays. Telephone (3)721–2361 for the times of the planetarium shows. There is a simultaneous translation service (through headphones attached to special seats) in English or Japanese if you end up in a Cantonese-language presentation. It is also wise to get there early to be assured of one of the better seats. Admission HK$15.

Sung Dynasty Wax Museum, Sung Dynasty Village, 11 Kau Wa Heng, Laichikok, Kowloon; (3)741–5111. Part of the guided tour of the Sung Dynasty Village, the museum depicts life in the Sung Dynasty (A.D. 960 to 1279), the ancient Greece of China's history. The museum extends the history to include 5,000 years in China. Group tours daily at 10:00 A.M., 12:30 P.M. and 5:30 P.M., and on weekends at 10:00 A.M. The general public can tour on weekends and public holidays between 12:30 P.M. and 5:00 P.M.

Jade Museum, Aw Boon Haw Gardens, Tin Hang Road, Causeway Bay, Hong Kong; (5)616211 (ask for Miss Au). One of the world's greatest collections of jade. Open 10:00 A.M. to 4:00 P.M. Admission free, but must be arranged in advance.

Museum of Tea, Flagstaff House, Victoria Barracks, Queensway; (5)299390. Opened in 1984, this two-story museum has displays of Yi Xing teaware, the most famous tea sets from Jiangsu Province, China. There are also slide shows and exhibitions on tea planting, harvesting, etc. Run by the Hong Kong Museum of Art. Open 10:00 A.M. to 5:00 P.M., except Wednesdays and public holidays. Admission free.

Museum of Chinese Historical Relics, Causeway Centre, 28 Harbour Road, Wanchai, Hong Kong; (5) 832–0411. Exhibitions of ancient Chinese relics. Open daily 10:00 A.M. to 6:00 P.M. (Closed on January 1st, October 1st, and Chinese New Year.)

LIBRARIES

City Hall Libraries, City Hall High Block, near Star Ferry, Hong Kong; (5)246617. Three libraries of general interest. The fifth-floor Reference Library has over 400,000 volumes, half in English, half Chinese, plus microfilm collection of rare books from the Peking National Library and back-dated Hong Kong newspapers. Bring your passport, since the library is meticulous about checking identification. Xeroxing facilities available. The Children's Library is on the fourth floor. The General Reading Library—good for browsing, but only residents are allowed to check out books—is on the third floor. Open 9:00 A.M. to 8:00 P.M. weekdays, 9:00 A.M. to 5:00 P.M. Saturday, 9:00 A.M. to 1:00 P.M. Sunday; closed on Thursday.

United States Information Service Library, first floor, United Center, Queensway, adjacent to Admiralty Center MTR, Hong Kong; (5)299661. Good collection of current and back-dated American magazines, books, and telephone directories from major American cities. Microfilmed editions of the *New York Times* and other documents. Only residents can check out material. Open 10:00 A.M. to 6:00 P.M. weekdays.

For more information, see the Hong Kong Tourist Association's free brochure "Arts and Crafts and Museums."

 HISTORICAL AND OTHER SITES. The British have regarded Hong Kong mainly as an entrepôt. The Chinese have looked on Hong Kong as a way station to home. Hong Kong's history has been of minor importance to both groups, and they have felt that there's little in the colony worth saving except money. However, tourists who can restrain their shopping sprees may find some interesting historical sites and some fairly exotic modern attractions.

Hong Kong is a walking city, so the following sites are listed by areas in which you can stroll easily.

CENTRAL

From the Star Ferry, you can take a basically circular route. First go south, then east, west, and north, then back to the harbor.

Star Ferry. The terminus for one of the world's most famous cross-harbor rides, which takes seven to ten minutes. The Star Ferry was created about a century ago by an Indian businessman and has had only one serious accident. The boats were commandeered by the Japanese to bring goods to Canton during the Second World War, and the Americans bombed them. The fleet consists of ten vessels (all with the names of celestial bodies), which can each accommodate 580 passengers and a ten-man crew.

Connaught Centre. Next to the Star Ferry Concourse, this building is something of a landmark. The mezzanine floor leads to covered, elevated walkways that take you north into the heart of the Central district or west toward the other ferry piers. Home of H. K. Tourist Association.

City Hall. On the opposite side of the Star Ferry from Connaught Centre, the Low Block of City Hall has two auditoriums for the arts. The High Block, adjacent to the Low Block through a little garden, has libraries and an art gallery, as well as Urban Council offices. The Marriage Registry is on the second floor, and happy couples pose in the garden after the ceremonies.

St. John's Cathedral. Completed in 1849, this is the official Anglican church and reflects early Victorian-Gothic elegance. Open 10:00 A.M. to 8:00 P.M. daily, services on Sunday.

Hollywood Road. The most important street for antiques and flea-market merchandise. Nearby are some of the "ladder streets," each step filled with hawkers. Also on Hollywood Road is the Man Mo Temple, Hong Kong's oldest temple, dating back to the 1840s. The temple is dedicated to learning and war and is a favorite of both police and criminals. If the ornate temple looks familiar, this is because much of *The World of Suzie Wong* was filmed here.

Possession Point. From Hollywood Road, turn down to the sea. Unfortunately, the point where the British took possession of Hong Kong in 1841 isn't visible. That was simply a quay, and land reclamation has destroyed whatever historical value there was; nothing marks the spot. But the adjacent streets have some interesting markets and shops.

Poor Man's Nightclub. Just by Macau Ferry Pier, this is one of the two best night markets. Countless restaurants, cheap clothes wagons, fortune tellers, etc. Opens around 6:30 P.M. and closes around 1:00 A.M.

Mandarin Hotel. Frequently mentioned as one of the world's finest hotels, the Mandarin, at the end of the Star Ferry pedestrian underpass, is splendid for people-watching. Try the Captain's Bar off the lobby to see multibillion-dollar deals being negotiated over a brandy or the mezzanine-floor restaurant overlooking the lobby to see the Rolls-Royces pull up.

Statue Square. This is the expanse of grass and concrete bisected by Chater Road, just east of the Mandarin Hotel. Once a statue of Queen Victoria, under whose reign Hong Kong was founded, graced the park, only to be replaced with a statue honoring the Hong Kong and Shanghai Banking Corporation's first manager, which gives you an idea of Hong Kong's priorities. One attraction is the cenotaph honoring the dead of two wars. Large crowds gather in the area on Sundays and holidays, particularly the Filipino community.

Legislative Council (formerly Supreme Court). Chater Road at Jackson. One of the few historic buildings in Central that is still standing (though the vibrations of the drills during the construction of the M.T.R. subway system almost brought about its collapse). Built in 1910, the Italianate architecture is more impressive than the inside decoration.

Landmark. This beautiful edifice on the corner of Pedder Street and Des Voeux Road Central is noteworthy for its 20,000-foot, four-story atrium with more than 100 shops and two shopping basements. Entertainment is held in the atrium weekday afternoons and Sundays.

Hong Kong and Shanghai Banking Corporation Building. The headquarters of Hong Kong's largest bank (on Des Voeux Central, fronting Statue Square) is housed in perhaps the world's most expensive building: over HK$5 billion at last count. The high-technology is revolutionary: a glass-and-steel phenomenon with a cluster of towers, extended modular walls, and electronic gadgetry known nowhere else.

Peak Tram. The Peak Tram terminus, near the Hilton Hotel on Garden Road, was built in 1888 and is the start and finish of the 1,805-foot trip to the top of Victoria Peak. The ride presents Hong Kong's most astonishing panoramic views.

Flagstaff House. Victoria Barracks, Queensway. This building was once the home of the Commander of the Armed Forces, built in 1845. The handsome tree-shaded building was closed to the public until 1984, when the Urban Council reopened it as the Museum of Tea (see Museums section of this guide).

WANCHAI/CAUSEWAY BAY

To begin the Wanchai tour, return to the Peak Tram and cross to the east of Victoria Barracks. Then walk down to Queensway and take the tram about two stops to where Queensway becomes known as Hennessy Road. Alternatively walk up Queensway, past the Admiralty Center M.T.R. stop to Asian House, where the street changes names. This tour goes basically east along Hennessy Road and it ends at Victoria Park on the easternmost end of Wanchai.

Hong Kong Academy for the Performing Arts. This HK$400 million edifice, sponsored by the Royal Hong Kong Jockey Club and the government, houses four major schools in music, dance, drama, and technical service for both Chinese and Western art forms (see Performing Arts section of this guide).

Hong Kong Arts Centre. Across the street from the Academy for the Performing Arts, the Hong Kong Arts Centre has 15 floors of rehearsal rooms, meeting rooms, auditoriums, restaurants, and a good arts bookshop. Cultural events are listed in the lobby. Open from 9:00 A.M. to 10:00 P.M.

Queen's Road East. An interesting street running parallel to Hennessy Road, with bamboo-workers, a few furniture shops, and fine old street markets. Excellent for strolling, but the only tourist sight is the Kwan Ti Temple, filled with magic mirrors left by people who have prayed for cures.

Queen Elizabeth Stadium. The huge stadium sports cultural and sporting events. Open 10:00 A.M. to 8:00 P.M. (See under Performing Arts.)

Noonday Gun. Opposite the Excelsior Hotel, you will find the gun celebrated in Noel Coward's lyric: "In Hong Kong, they strike a gong and fire a noonday gun, to reprimand each inmate who's in late." The recoil-mounting, 3-pounder Hotchkiss cannon, built in Portsmouth, England, in 1901, is still fired each noon, and you can stand discreetly nearby to listen.

World Trade Centre. A 42-story building with plush offices and restaurants. The Center's Palace Theatre is the colony's most modern cinema.

Food Street. Over 80,000 square feet of space, with some three-dozen restaurants that serve up everything from abalone to zabaglione.

Typhoon Anchorage. The Causeway Bay Typhoon Shelter, as well as the svelte Royal Hong Kong Yacht Club, is across the street from World Trade Centre and Excelsior Hotel. Thousands of boats moor here, not only for typhoons (which can be ferocious) but for convenience as well. Tourists can enjoy an evening ride and dinner on the sampans. Simply stand in the area at sunset and a woman will approach you to offer a nighttime outing. (April through October only.)

Victoria Park. This great park has been built entirely from land reclaimed from the sea. Used 24 hours a day for *tai-chi* exercises at dawn, tennis, jogging, softball and soccer during the day, and more exercising and strolling at night. During the Mid-Autumn Festival, the park contains a plethora of lanterns. The Government promotes rallies here (anti-smoking, anti-crime), which are raucous, questionable in desired effect, and enjoyable to watch.

North Point, Quarry Bay, Shaukiwan. East of Victoria Park is little of interest for the casual visitor. Older tenements, a few factories, a large funeral home and, to the south, some hills which the Japanese invaded in 1941—just a century after the British conquered Hong Kong. Near Shaukiwan, though, is the enormous housing estate of Taikooshing, a city in itself. The shopping center, City Plaza, has entertainment, atriums, gardens, roller skating, even an ice-skating rink. This is on the north side of King's Road (the name which Hennessy Road takes east of Victoria Park). On the south side are hillside squatter huts.

HAPPY VALLEY

Happy Valley, the second oldest British settlement in Hong Kong, is south of Causeway Bay. Only two items are of interest to the tourist.

Tiger Balm (Aw Boon Haw) Gardens. A veritable Disneyland of Chinese mythology spread over eight acres. The gardens include an excellent jade museum, open to the public with permission (see the Museums section of this guide). The gardens are open from 10:00 A.M. to 4:00 P.M. Admission is free.

Happy Valley Race Course. One of two race tracks in Hong Kong, this was built in 1841 but is constantly modernized. An up-to-date totalizer board and a huge outdoor video display system shows the race close-up, slow-motion replays, freeze-frames, and information about jockeys and winners. The one-mile course attracts about 50,000 racegoers a session, from September through May. Newspapers give exact days and times of meets.

MID-LEVELS, WESTERN DISTRICT, PEAK

Botanical Gardens. Opened in 1871, the Hong Kong Zoological and Botanical Gardens have a superb aviary, a fair zoo, excellent breeding facilities (where jaguars, cranes, and orangutans multiply faster than an abacus), and, of course, fine trees and flowers. In the morning, the 5.35-hectare (12.5-acre) site is filled with *tai-chi* exercisers. Open from 6:00 A.M. to 7:00 P.M. Admission free.

The Peak. Take the tram from the Botanical Gardens to Victoria Peak. The Peak Tower has a fine viewing platform. Excellent walks, the major one along Harlech Road and Lugard Road around the Peak.

Ohel Leah Synagogue. 70 Robinson Rd., (5)594821. An exceptional example of nineteenth-century Sephardic architecture, unfortunately slated for demolition. The Jewish Recreation Club is adjacent, open all day. Members are happy to take visitors across the lawn to find the *shamus* who has the keys to the synagogue.

Hong Kong University. Pokfulam Road; (5)859-2111. Many of the buildings here are a century old, good examples of Victorian-Colonial architecture. The museum and library are both excellent. Open from 9:30 A.M. to 6:00 P.M., excluding Sundays.

SOUTH SIDE

No road goes along the rocky south side of Hong Kong Island, so these attractions must be visited with detours to the central part of the island. The first attraction is near the university, and you continue east from there.

Aberdeen. One of the two oldest settlements on Hong Kong Island. Still a spectacular waterfront, with up to 20,000 boat people living in sampans and fishing boats on the waterfront. Although Aberdeen is becoming more industrialized, it still presents a colorful sight. The famous floating restaurants are open from 8:00 A.M. to midnight.

Ocean Park and Water World. Wong Chuk Hang Road near Aberdeen; (5) 550947 and (5)556055. One of the most popular family outing places in Hong Kong, this 170-acre park is split into a lowland and headland area linked by cable car. The lowland area has parks, children's zoo, and playgrounds. The headland area has the Ocean Theatre with performing dolphins and a killer whale, a wave cove and aquarium, plus an amusement park (with a wild roller coaster ride) and a walk-through aviary. The adjacent, 65-acre Water World is an aquatic fun park with slides, rapids, and various pools. To get there, take a taxi through Aberdeen Tunnel (entrance to park is opposite tunnel exit). The most convenient way to reach the park is by the special buses from Admiralty M.T.R. Station.

Repulse Bay. Once the home of glamorous Repulse Bay Hotel, which is today literally a hole in the ground. The beach is the colony's most popular and is packed to capacity on the summer weekends.

Stanley. This was the largest town on the island in 1841, when the British came, but the pirate-fisherman population didn't expand much until recently. Now, this is a fairly posh residential town. The Tin Hau Temple is very old and has some beautiful designs around the ledges. A tiger-skin here comes from an animal apparently shot by Japanese soldiers during World War II, when Stanley was a major prison camp holding the British. The market, which actually curves through the town, has fabulous bargains in rattan, garments (mainly export clothes), porcelain, and bric-a-brac.

Shek O. An interesting old town with a path leading to Hong Kong's easternmost point. A few vegetable farms, Cantonese restaurants, a pleasant beach, and millionaire mansions adjacent to peasant huts.

KOWLOON: TSIMSHATSUI

Hong Kong Island was originally the settlement while Kowloon was used mainly for warehousing and as the terminus from China. As a result, Kowloon wasn't developed until after the Second World War. Today, it is primarily known for its shopping and fine hotels. We begin at the Star Ferry, work over to a momentary sojourn in East Tsimshatsui, and then continue north up Nathan Road to a more "Chinese" Kowloon.

Ocean Centre/Ocean Terminal/Harbor City. Even in this city of shopping centers, the two "Oceans" and their "Harbor" are the biggest. You can buy everything from emerald-laden abacuses to gold-encrusted zircons through miles of air-conditioned comfort. A luxury liner may be parked right by the second floor of Ocean Terminal. Take a stroll along the verandah for some unparalleled views across the harbor.

Peninsula Hotel. Once rated by the *Wall Street Journal* as one of the "ten most-exciting hotel lobbies in Asia," this huge colonnaded lobby still has charm, grandeur, celebrities (though with the opening of the Regent Hotel, no longer a monopoly on them), string quartets playing music, and a British "high tea." Rest your shopping feet in style.

Space Museum. Just opposite The Peninsula, the Space Museum has a fine planetarium, a hall of Solar Sciences, and good exhibitions. (See Museums section of this guide).

Tsimshatsui Cultural Centre. Includes a 2,280-seat concert hall, 1,930-seat lyric theater, and a 400-seat drama theater. Museums and libraries are also scheduled.

New World Centre. Another monstrous shopping center, adjacent to New World and Regent Hotels. Seemingly a baffling maze, you can find everything you want, from bookshops to a kosher delicatessen to the unique Bar City—two bars and a disco.

Tsimshatsui East. Five years ago, East Tsimshatsui was just a few wharves, empty lots, even a quarry or two. Today, the area houses four first-class hotels, a dozen shopping centers, and restaurants. The latter run the gamut from pizzas to Peking duck.

Nathan Road. The so-called "Golden Mile," running up through Kowloon to Boundary Street and the New Territories. While the shopping is excellent on the main road, the best specialty shops are in the streets and alleys running at right angles to the main thoroughfare.

YAUMATEI AND NORTHERN KOWLOON

North of Tsimshatsui, off Nathan Road, Yaumatei is not tourist-oriented but provides a number of fascinating sights, walks, and hours.

Shanghai Street. All of the streets in this area are fascinating, day and night. During the daytime, search around Shanghai Street, Temple Street, and Public Square Street for old wine shops, market items, fruits, and street barbers. On Battery Street, you see nothing but paper-making shops, selling paper for everything from kites to the paper symbols given to the dead. Public Square Street has little lanes filled with fortune tellers. The Tin Hau Temple is old and dazzling.

At night, the Night Market (from 7:00 P.M. to midnight) is a mile long, with just about everything made under the sun (or moon) for sale. On Sundays, you may see Chinese opera performed on the side streets.

Kansu and Reclamation Streets. The famous jade market, where the curbs and pavement are covered with jade bangles, pendants, stones. Most of it is exceptionally cheap (after a lot of bargaining) and some of it is fake. But the colors, every shade of green you can imagine, are magnificent. The earlier you arrive, the better the buys to be had. Market open from 10:00 A.M. to 4:00 P.M. daily.

Kowloon City. One of the colony's more fascinating anomalies is the "Walled City," so called because it was built with walls surrounding it (the Japanese later used the walls to build part of Kai Tak Airport's runway). Legally, Kowloon City belongs to China through a complicated diplomatic loophole. But the Hong Kong Government does make efforts to improve lighting, sanitation, etc. Squalor is the order of the day, and picture-taking is definitely frowned upon by residents.

Wong Tai Sin Temple. A new temple dedicated to the god Wong Tai Sin, who does everything from curing illness to forecasting the races. The spacious temple, with hundreds of fortune tellers in its alleys, is just opposite a gigantic housing estate.

Sung Dynasty Village. (M.T.R. stop at Mei Foo Station, then walk for 15 minutes; or take number 6A bus from Star Ferry Kowloon or number 105 from Hong Kong). A miniature village recreating life in the Sung Dynasty (A.D. 960 to 1279). Interesting architecture, costumes (the people who work in the village dress in Sung fashions), restaurants, street performances, and a wax museum (see "Tours").

Bird Market, Hong Lok Street. Here are teahouses and shops filled with all kinds of birds, singing, playing on tables, even being taken for walks. Take the M.T.R. to Mongkok Station and walk two blocks west to Hong Lok Street.

Lei Yue Mun. An old fishing village, once the haunt of pirates, at the eastern end of Kowloon. Marvelous dining, with dozens of restaurants. You choose your fare (live fish) from the markets and the restaurants cook it for a nominal price. The most picturesque way to get here is from Shaukiwan Ferry in eastern Hong Kong near Taikooshing. Alternatively, take the M.T.R. to Kwung Tong and then a taxi to the village. It is difficult to get a taxi back, but a moonlight ferry ride (actually two rides, one by sampan, the other by ferry) after a good meal is much more romantic anyway.

THE NEW TERRITORIES

This area, which makes up nine-tenths of the territory, used to be farmland dotted with old walled villages. Once the "Emperor's rice bowl," today the ports of New Territories are heavily urbanized with factory cities, shipyards, a futuristic race course, auditoriums, and even a few hotels. Still, some of the historic sites are worth a day trip. One should avoid Sundays and holidays, when traffic jams are unavoidable.

Monastery of 10,000 Buddhas. (Take K.C.R. train to Shatin and walk to temple steps, then up the 428 stone steps to "Man Fat Temple." There are *more* than 10,000 Buddhas in this old temple (12,800 exactly, though nobody has counted for many years). They guard not only the main temple, an Indian pagoda, and a temple where the builder is enshrined in gold leaf. He died in 1967, 17 years after the temple was built.

Shatin Racecourse and Jubilee Sports Centre. Opened in 1978 on 250 acres of reclaimed land, this race course has a park, three tracks, air-conditioned stables, and stands for 37,000 punters. The sports center has first-class training facilities for track, tennis, soccer, jogging, hockey, basketball, volleyball, squash, baseball and softball, and dance.

Chinese University. Actually a series of different colleges, once run by missionaries of various sects. The different buildings have some excellent facilities and front right on the road north to Taipo and scenic Tolo Harbor. Students will help you get the morning ferry which goes to the fishing villages on the Saikung Peninsula and Tap Mun Island in the harbor. Telephone (0)695–2111 to arrange a tour of the university.

Sai Kung Country Park. Probably the best preserved flora in the territories. Some beautiful walks and drives. Try part of the 610-mile MacLehose Trail (see Country Parks section in this guide).

Tsang Tai Uk Walled Village. Most tourists go to Kam Tin Walled Village, but this is far more interesting. It is less commercial and gives a good picture of old village life, with a fine community hall and old fields. To get there, drive through Lion Rock Tunnel, turn right before the first right, park, and walk across the fields.

Tai Po. Once a lovely little village, today Tai Po is becoming more industrialized. The most enchanting place is the Tai Ping Carpet Factory, open all day for visits, inspection, and, of course, purchases. Telephone (0)656–5161 for an appointment. Alternatively, visit the retail showroom at Hutchison House, Central; (5)227138

Lok Ma Chau Police Station/Shenzhen. When the People's Republic of China was closed to visitors, Hong Kong tourists would always rush for this border post to stare down at the Shenzhen River and catch a glimpse of the mainland. Even now, when it's easier to get into China, this is still a popular spot.

Kam Tin Walled Villages. On the Western side of New Territories. Kat Hing Wai, Wing Lung Wai and Shui Tau, 500-years-old and known collectively as the Kam Tin Walled Villages, are all interesting, though the first is more than a little tourist-oriented. Pay a dollar to take a picture or those nice venerable weather-beaten faces turn nasty. See the Ancestral Halls and Hung Shing Temple in Shui Tau Village.

Ching Chung Koon Temple. The library holds more than 3,800 books covering 4,000 years of Taoist history. Its jade seal is reputedly more than 1,000 years old and its 200-year-old lanterns hung in the Imperial Palace. Off Castle Park Road near Tuen Mun.

Lau Fau Shan. The "oyster village," a bit difficult to get to (take a taxi from Yuen Long town, which can be reached by mini-bus). Here are dozens of restaurants on Deep Bay, serving delicious cooked oysters (never eat them raw) and other seafood bought in the market. The bay is worth seeing, as many of the fishermen come over from China to sell their seafood.

Kadoorie Farm. A large experimental farm founded in the early 1950s to teach farming methods to the hundreds of thousands of refugees flooding into the colony. Now the farm is inhabited by Gurkhas who are returning to Nepal. Near Yuen Long, the farm is open to the public for recreational walks. Interesting guided tours can be arranged by telephoning (0)981317.

OUTER ISLANDS

The 30- to 60-minute ferry trips to Lantau, Lamma, Cheung Chau, and Peng Chau take you far away from the urban hustle of Hong Kong and Kowloon. The Outlying Ferries Pier is a 15-minute walk west from Star Ferry on the Hong Kong side. Ferries leave about once an hour. The Hong Kong Tourist Association has exact schedules, but many tourists take pot luck for the first ferry going anywhere (see the Islands section of this guide).

Lantau

The largest island, even larger than Hong Kong. Many sections look like what Hong Kong must have looked like a century ago. Weekends are hell for ferries and buses (there are few taxis), but weekday outings are very interesting for the following sights.

Po Lin Monastery. Located 2,500 feet above sea level, Po Lin has over 100 resident monks and nuns who take care of an ornate temple, a number of chapels, hundreds of Buddhas, including a particularly attractive 30-foot Buddha. Many visitors eat in the Vegetarian Restaurant. The temple was built in 1905.

Tung Chung. This old town on the northern shore of Lantau has much atmospheric interest. Its fort, guarded by six cannons, is historically fascinating. It was built in the eighteenth century by the Chinese Emperor to guard against pirates, smugglers, and the occasional foreigner. The bus from Silvermine Bay stops here, but the most enjoyable way to arrive is by a three-hour walk down from Po Lin Monastery, passing many shrines and temples.

Lantau Tea Gardens. Founded a quarter of a century ago, the tea gardens have rooms for rent, barbecue facilities, ponies, camping, and, of course, tea. Telephone (5)985–8161 for information.

Trappist Monastery. Dedicated to a vow of silence, the Trappist monks do not welcome casual visitors (and once they politely turned away a young television journalist who wished to interview them). But they are happy to allow visitors to stroll through their grounds and visit the dairy, which supplies some of Hong Kong's fresh milk. To get to the monastery, take the ferry to *Peng Chau* Island (itself interesting for its porcelain factories and old alleys) and take a sampan across to Lantau.

Cheung Chau

Once a pirate hideout, Cheung Chau now houses many expatriates and is a delightful place to visit. There is no transportation on the island, but the walks are pleasant. The atmosphere and the secluded beaches are the main attractions, but there are two others as well.

Cheung Po Chai. A cave retreat reputedly used by Cheung Po Chai, one of the most famous pirates of the late eighteenth century. Some people say that Cheung Po Chai stashed his booty here.

Pak Tai Temple. Built in 1783 in honour of Pak Tai (who reputedly drove away a plague some 3,000 years ago), Pak Tai Temple is Cheung Chau's oldest and is the center of festivities for the Bun Festival (see the Seasonal Events section of this guide). Frequently, mystical monks come here and pray in "tongues."

Lamma

Mainly a rural island, where some of Hong Kong's oldest archeological remains have been found. (They can now be seen in Hong Kong's Museum of History.) The little Tin Hau Temple here is of no special importance, but it is the center of an interesting fishing community. The main attractions on Lamma Island are the chain of outdoor restaurants by the Sok Kwu Wan Pier, the unspoiled beaches, and the opportunities for a good stroll.

 PERFORMING ARTS. Until 1972, Hong Kong's performing arts were confined to a few visiting artists and some *ad hoc* Chinese musical ensembles. This last decade, though, the government and private enterprise have funded and instigated a series of year-round festivals, opened auditoriums, and promoted professional western-style ensembles, including a philharmonic orchestra, and several Chinese groups. On almost any evening you will be able to find a cultural event to attend.

Following are the major venues of performing arts. They display forthcoming events in their lobbies and usually advertise other events around Hong Kong.

VENUES

City Hall, Edinburgh Place by Star Ferry, Central Hong Kong; (5)229928 (box office). Most orchestral and musical groups. Large auditorium, recital hall, theater.

Arts Centre, 2 Harbor Rd., Wanchai, Hong Kong; (5)280626. Fifteen floors of auditoriums, rehearsal rooms, etc. Visiting groups, local drama, film-society movies, arts bookshop. Most programs are advertised on the Centre's main floor.

Queen Elizabeth Stadium, Oi Kwan Road, Wanchai; (5)756793. A sports stadium with seating capacity of 3,500 that frequently presents ballet, orchestral, and even disco events.

Hong Kong Coliseum, Hung Hom Railway Station, Hung Hom, Kowloon. (3)765–9234. Opened in 1983 with seating capacity of over 12,000. Everything from basketball to ballet.

Ko Shan Theatre, Hung Hom, Kowloon; (3)342331. The territory's first open-air theater, opened in 1983. Two thousand seats under cover, 1,500 outdoors. Chinese opera and orchestral, pop, and variety shows.

Tsuen Wan Town Hall, Tsuen Wan, New Territories; (0)440144. Off the beaten track, but this New Territories auditorium, seating 1,424, has a constant stream of performers, from the Hong Kong Philharmonic to Chinese acrobatic teams. Audiences are relatively unsophisticated, which makes viewing all the more fun.

Hong Kong Academy for Performing Arts, Harbor Road, Wanchai, Hong Kong; (5)823–1500. Near the Hong Kong Arts Centre. Facilities include two major theaters seating 1,600 people, plus a 200-seat studio theater and other studios.

Academic Community Hall, 224 Waterloo Rd., Kowloon Tong, Kowloon; (3)386121. A very modern auditorium that belongs to Baptist College. Mainly rock and pop recitals, but the Hong Kong Philharmonic and other groups frequently play here too. Take the M.T.R. to Kowloon Tong, then a taxi.

Lee Theatre, 99 Percival St., Causeway Bay, Hong Kong; (5)795–4433. Usually a movie theater, but visiting and Chinese pop stars often perform here.

INFORMATION

The best daily calendar to cultural events is the *South China Morning Post* newspaper (which lists events in very small print near the letters page), or the *Hong Kong Standard* newspaper. Weekly listings are in the *TV & Entertainment Times,* which is placed in hotels and on newsstands each Saturday but gives listings starting from the following Wednesday. Radio Hong Kong 3 gives listings of the day's events, including art exhibitions. The Hong Kong Tourist Association's monthly guidebook also lists upcoming events, as does the tourist newspaper *Hong Kong,* which is distributed in hotels.

FESTIVALS

Hong Kong has arts festivals in every season. Visitors here during these times are exceptionally fortunate as they can see some of the finest performing artists and films from Asia and Europe—if tickets are available. City Hall is the main venue. For detailed information, write beforehand to: Festivals Office, Urban Council, New World Centre, Tsimshatsui, Kowloon, Hong Kong.

Hong Kong Arts Festival (January–February). Four weeks of music and drama from around the world. Venues include City Hall, Arts Centre, the Academy for Performing Arts, the Coliseum, Ko Shan Theatre, and playgrounds throughout the colony.

Hong Kong International Film Festival (April). More than two weeks of films from up to three dozen countries. Quality varies, but since the festival is for non-commercial films, it's the best chance to see movies from all over Asia. Film displays are presented on second floor of Low Block, City Hall. Films are shown throughout the day in City Hall Recital Theatre and at other sites as well.

Festival of Asian Arts (October–November). Perhaps Asia's major cultural event. Over 150 artistic events from as far afield as Hawaii, Bhutan, and Australia. Most are staged at City Hall and Queen Elizabeth Stadium, but during the day lectures, exhibitions, and demonstrations are held throughout Hong Kong. Playgrounds often play host at night. Held biennially.

Mid-Autumn Festival (September–October). Also known as the Lantern Festival, this was once simply a family-outing night, but now the Government sponsors Chinese opera and singing in Victoria and Ko Shan parks (in Hong Kong and Kowloon, respectively); be prepared to brave crowds of up to 10,000 standing, shouting, singing people.

PERFORMING ARTS ENSEMBLES

Performing arts groups are sponsored by the government (usually the Urban Council or the Recreation and Culture Department); independent promoters, or *ad hoc* groups. Posters in City Hall usually give complete information on performances.

Hong Kong Philharmonic Orchestra. Almost 100 artists from Hong Kong, America, and Europe play eclectic programs (mainly Western, but often including works by outstanding Chinese composers) with soloists who have included Ashkenazy, Maxim Shostakovich, and Rudolph Firkusny. Performances mostly on Friday and Saturday at 8:00 P.M. in City Hall, Academic Community Hall, or Tsuen Wan Town Hall, with tickets available at City Hall Box Office. Telephone (5)832–7121 for further information.

Hong Kong Chinese Orchestra. Created in 1977 by the Urban Council, this group performs only Chinese works, although they sometimes transcribe Western music for their own instruments. The orchestra is divided into strings, plucked instruments, wind, and percussion. Each work must be arranged and orchestrated especially for the occasion. Weekly concerts are given in venues throughout Hong Kong and are especially popular in the New Territories. The orchestra represented Hong Kong at the Commonwealth Arts Festival in 1982.

CHINESE OPERA

Cantonese Opera. There are ten Cantonese opera troupes in Hong Kong, as well as over 100 amateur singing groups. Many perform "street opera," as in the Shanghai Street Night Market on Sundays, while others perform at temple fairs, in City Hall, or on playgrounds under the auspices of the Urban Council. While some visitors unfamiliar with the form are alienated by the strange sounds, you should realize that the symbolism of the hand gestures, waving costumes, and facial movements is a highly complex and extremely sophisticated art form. Every gesture has its own meaning—in fact there are 50 different gestures for the hand alone. Props attached to the costumes are similarly intricate and are used in exceptional ways. For example, the principal female role will often wear five-foot-long pheasant tails attached to the headdress. Anger is shown by dropping the head and shaking it in a circular fashion so the feathers move in a perfect circle. Surprise is shown by "nodding the feathers." One can also "dance with the feathers" to show a mixture of anger and determination. The orchestral instruments punctuate the singing. It is best to have a friend translate the gestures, since the stories are so complex that they make Wagner or Verdi libretti seem almost childlike.

Peking Opera. Some people like this less than Cantonese opera, because the voices are higher-pitched. But this is an older opera and more respected for its classical traditions. Several troupes visit Hong Kong from the People's Republic of China each year, and their immaculate and meticulous training is of a high degree. They perform in City Hall or at special temple ceremonies.

Soochow Lyrics. Not actually opera, but more a fourteenth-century nightclub show, Soochow Lyrics are performed frequently by the Su Chow Opera Association, a group of emigrants from that esteemed city. Only a single prop is used: the fan. Open, it can be a shy lady. Closed, it can represent a male speaker. It can also represent an opium pipe, flute, stick, or cigarette. Unlike those of other Chinese opera, the lyrics are touching even to the foreigner. The music is soft and charming. There are no sudden eruptions and no harsh grating sounds. The mood lacks the blatant tension of Western singing or the boisterous emotions of Cantonese opera. All is implied or hinted; the genius is in the nuance.

DANCE

Hong Kong Dance Company. The Urban Council created the Hong Kong Dance Company in 1981 with the goal of promoting the art of Chinese dance and to present newly choreographed work on Chinese historical themes. They give approximately three performances each month, and have appeared at the

Commonwealth Arts Festival in Australia. The 30 members are experts in folk and classical dance. They appear in venues throughout the colony.

Modern Dance Theatre of Hong Kong. Founded in 1977 by American dancer Daryl Ries, the group performs frequently, combining jazz, modern dance, Chinese dance, and *avant garde* innovations. Very much a Hong Kong phenomenon.

Hong Kong Ballet. There are about 30 members in the colony's first professional ballet company and vocational ballet school. Very little, except the dancers, is Chinese, and it is entirely Western-oriented. The dancers perform in schools, auditoriums, and at various festivals.

DRAMA

Chung Ying Theatre Company. A professional company with British and Chinese actors doing plays in English and Cantonese. Churches and schools are the main venues. The British Council can give detailed information on forthcoming works.

Hong Kong Repertory Theatre. Sixteen professional Cantonese actors, whose work is entirely in Cantonese. Frequently, they perform translated Western drama.

Actors Rep. A group of professional actors who perform in Hong Kong Arts Centre or City Hall.

Garrison Players/Hong Kong Stage Club. Amateur groups that perform in the Hong Kong Arts Centre. Around Christmas, they do the typical British pantomime.

OTHER ARTS GROUPS

The *Hong Kong Philharmonic Orchestra* soloists frequently offer chamber-music recitals. Additional information is available from the orchestra office, (5)832–7121. Radio Television Hong Kong also sponsors recitals.

Visiting drama groups appear during the Arts Festival or Asian Arts Festival. Infrequently, official cultural groups, such as British Council or United States Information Service, will bring them in as part of a Far East tour.

Outside of the International Film Festival, several film societies show movies at the Arts Centre and City Hall. Studio One is most prominent, but visitor's tickets are scarce. Telephone (5)202282 for possible guest tickets. The most interesting group is the *Film Culture Centre of Hong Kong,* to which many young filmmakers belong. Call (5)282572 to find out what's on. The Alliance Française, Goethe Institute, and British Council frequently show films at City Hall and the Space Museum.

Free Chinese Cultural Shows, sponsored by the Hong Kong Tourist Association, are performed in the Ocean Terminal, New World Centre, and Tsim Sha Tsui Centre, all in Kowloon, as well as The Landmark and Cityplaza on Hong Kong Island. A monthly schedule and program is published by the H.K.T.A.

SHOPPING. Hong Kong is such a superb shopping bazaar that even the most blasé buyer cannot fail to be impressed. The variety of places to shop—from huge Japanese and Chinese department stores, chic designer boutiques and vast, multi-storied, air-conditioned shopping arcades to tiny back-street stalls and huge street markets—offers visitors and residents some of the best shopping in the world.

As a duty-free port, Hong Kong has a distinct advantage over other cities. With the exception of alcohol, tobacco, perfumes, and certain petroleum products, no duties are levied on imported or locally manufactured goods. Hong Kong's free-enterprise trading policy also ensures keen competition, more room for bargaining over prices, and a chance of finding even the most bizarre item on your shopping list. (Military and diplomatic personnel can shop in the China Fleet Club's shops in Fleet House, 6 Arsenal Street, Wanchai, Hong Kong, where goods are between 10 percent to 25 percent cheaper than they are anywhere else in Hong Kong.)

But the bargains don't come easily. The heat and crowds have to be reckoned with, and a language problem, and, despite campaigns to eradicate it, a sometimes nonchalant and occasionally downright rude style of service. It helps to shop out of rush hours (1:00 P.M. to 2:00 P.M. and 5:00 P.M. to 7:00 P.M. weekdays, Saturday afternoons, and Sundays); to seek out specific areas for specific items, and to shop for short periods of time only. A list of reputable shops with agents' recommended retail prices for a wide range of items is published in *The Official Guide to Shopping, Eating Out and Services,* The H.K.T.A. also publishes two informative brochures: a *Shopping Guide to Video Equipment* and *Factory Outlets in Hong Kong (Ready-to-Wear & Jewelery)*. All are available free at the Hong Kong Tourist Association (H.K.T.A.) information centers. You can recognize one of these H.K.T.A. member shops by the H.K.T.A. decal (a red junk logo) on its door or window. If you have a legitimate complaint against one of these listed shops, contact the Association. The H.K.T.A., also runs a very useful shoppers' hotline, (5)244191, ext. 278, to deal with enquiries.

The golden rule for shopping in Hong Kong is to compare prices, especially if you are buying an expensive item. Get the card of each shop you visit and write down the price of the item in which you are interested. You can then compare all of the prices and have a record of which shop offers the best deal. The "silver" rule is common sense: you get what you pay for. If someone tries to sell you a solid gold "Rolex" for only US$100 because you are the first customer of the day, it is not likely to be the real thing.

The common practice of bargaining may intimidate newcomers, but you will soon find it pays to learn the skill. It can also be fun. You cannot, however, expect to bargain everywhere. The Chinese product stores, the large department stores, and many of the larger boutiques and shops have a fixed-price policy. But in small shops, stalls, and markets, start by offering about half the asking price and then play it by ear.

If you are into bargain buying, be careful not to leave shopping to the last minute at the airport. Prices there are generally a good deal higher than they are in shops and stores downtown. And don't be taken in by those duty-free signs in the airport. Everything, everywhere in Hong Kong is duty-free, except the aforementioned goods.

Credit Cards. In theory, most international credit cards are accepted in Hong Kong. In practice, however, especially in hi-fi and camera shops, shopkeepers are often unwilling to accept them because of the card fee they will have to pay the credit-card companies. They will say that the price you have spent hours bargaining over is only a "cash discount" price. The only thing you can really do is pay or leave. In other words, cash is usually quicker.

Guarantees. With the purchase of durable goods, such as electrical or photographic equipment, watches, lighters, and other high-value branded items, be sure to get a worldwide guarantee. This should bear the name or insignia of the sole agent in Hong Kong, a complete description (model and serial number) that matches the equipment purchased, date of purchase, address of the shop where the item was bought, and the stamp of the shop. Be sure that there is a servicing center near your home town so you can take full advantage of the guaranteed free servicing.

Receipts. A receipt is another bit of paper power that will come in handy, especially for after-sales complaints or negotiations, shipping and postage reference, insurance, and, of course, customs declarations. Be sure to ask for a detailed receipt, listed by item, including serial numbers, model numbers, gold content, accurate description of stones for jewelry, makers' warranty, etc. Hong Kong shopkeepers are well aware of the "made-for-customs" receipts—but so are the customs officials. When going through customs, keep your receipts separate from your checked luggage so you can readily declare your purchases.

Shipping Home. You will find that many shops can arrange to pack your goods and ship them directly to your home. Occasionally, of course, the goods never arrive. It will help if your purchase comes from a Hong Kong Tourist Association member shop so that you can refer your complaint to the Association for advice or action. For more serious complaints about a fraudulent sale, contact the Royal Hong Kong Police Force Fraud Squad at Commercial Crimes, c/o Criminal Investigations Department, Royal Hong Kong Police Force Headquarters, Arsenal Street, Wanchai, Hong Kong; (5)284511, ext. 25. If your complaint concerns the quality of your purchase, contact the Consumer Council, Asian House, 3rd fl., 1 Hennessy Rd., Hong Kong; (5)748297.

As for insurance, it is advisable to arrange with an insurance company for insurance against damage in transit, since insurance taken by shops covers only loss in transit. If you prefer to post small items yourself, you can find full details on weight and size limitations from any Hong Kong Post Office. Or call the Postal Enquiry Service at (5) 231072. Parcels usually take at least six to eight weeks to reach Europe and the United States by sea and about one week by air.

Opening Hours. Another advantage to shopping in Hong Kong is the late opening hours. With the exception of the Central business district on Hong Kong Island, where shopping hours are from 10:00 A.M. to 6:30 P.M., you will find that in the popular shopping areas of Causeway Bay in Hong Kong, and Tsimshatsui and Mongkok districts in Kowloon, shops will often stay open as late as 10:00 P.M. Many shops and markets are also open on Sunday. This includes some department stores, which will close on a weekday instead.

However, if you are in Hong Kong over the Chinese New Year (January or February), you will find that many shops and services close for at least the first two days and that prices for some goods escalate beforehand. Made-to-order items will also be difficult to obtain during this time. On the other hand, shops do a thriving business during such Western holidays as Christmas and New Year's Day, various bank holidays, and even on most Chinese festival days.

MAJOR SHOPPING AREAS

Hong Kong Island: Western District, from the edge of Central to Kennedy Town, is one of the oldest and most Chinese areas of Hong Kong, offering a fascinating experience in window shopping and the chance to buy that exotic something for the person who has everything. Here you can find craftsmen making mah-jong tiles, opera costumes, fans, and chops; Chinese herbalists selling ginseng, snake musk, and powdered lizards; rice shops, rattan dealers, and wholesalers in dried sharks' fins; cobblers, tinkers, and tailors, and numerous alleyways filled with knick-knacks and curios.

But for real shopping, Western also offers a huge *Chinese Merchandise Emporium,* opposite Central Market, in Queen's Road Central, with a vast display of made-in-China goods. And in Pottinger Street, just next to the Emporium where it meets Queen's Road Central, you can find stalls selling every kind of button and bow, zipper and sewing gadget. Farther west on Queen's Road are tea merchants, silversmiths and one of Hong Kong's largest swallows-nest merchants, at number 331. Cloth Alley, off Wing On Street, is nearby, and in the road above, Wellington Street, you'll find a variety of printers, picture framers, mah jong makers, and small boutiques. Going west, don't miss Man Wa Lane for your personal Chinese chop; almost opposite, on Connaught Road Central, you will find Western's two largest department stores: *Sincere* and *Wing On.*

But the backstreets behind Western Market are where you will really feel you are in "Chinatown." Wing Lok Street and Bonham Strand West are excellent browsing areas, with their herbalists' and snake gall-bladder wine shops (visit She Wong Yuen at 89–93 Bonham Strand for a taste). Some good, cheap printers are here, too, if you need stationery printed quickly. Farther up, off Queen's Road West, is Fat Hing Street, famous for baby clothes. Going back toward Central, don't miss the well known Ladder Street, zig-zagging from Caine Road to Hollywood Road and Queen's Road Central, with its stalls of bric-a-brac. The well known Hollywood Road is better for antiques, though. If you are in Western at night, try the Night Market by the Macau Ferry Pier.

Hong Kong: Central, the financial and business center of Hong Kong, offers an extraordinary contrast of chic boutiques, sophisticated department stores, hotel shopping arcades, narrow lanes in which vendors sell look-alike designer goods with no labels, and clothing alleys full of bargain buys.

Lane Crawford, on Queen's Road, just east of the Chinese Emporium, is Hong Kong's most luxurious department store. Other exclusive shops can be found in Central's major complex, the Landmark, and in adjoining Landmark East and Central Building and Swire House, as well as in the shopping arcades of the Mandarin, Hilton, and Furama Intercontinental hotels. On the corner of Queen's Road Central and Wyndham Street is a branch of *Chinese Arts & Crafts,* which has a small but excellent range of clothing, linens, jewelry, and *objets d'art.*

The two most interesting alleys in Central for clothing, cloth, and accessories are Li Yuen streets East and West (between Queen's Road and Des Voeux Road and just west of Queen's Theatre). Wyndham Street and On Lan Street have a good collection of embroidery and linen shops and D'Aguilar Street has some chic boutiques.

Hong Kong: Wanchai, more famous for the "Suzie Wong" nighttime meanderings than for daytime shopping, still has some interesting spots for the curious or adventurous shopper. Tattooes, for instance, are available in Jaffe Road, and traditional Chinese bamboo bird cages in Johnston Road. Wandering through the lanes between Johnston and Queen's Road East, with their fresh vegetable and fruit markets, you can find dozens of stalls selling buttons and bows, knickknacks, and cheap clothes. In tiny Spring Garden Lane, you will also find several small factory outlets. Queen's Road East (near its junction with Queensway) is famous for its shops that make blackwood and rosewood furniture and camphorwood chests. Follow it all the way up to Happy Valley and you will find plenty to tempt or interest you. In Wanchai Road, off Queen's Road East, there are more furniture shops and a branch of the Consumer Council (at number 188) that can help with any complaints or inquiries about products sold in Hong Kong; (5)748297.

Hong Kong: Happy Valley, the horse-racing venue, is also the popular haunt of shoe shoppers. Follow the road around the eastern edge of the race course and you will pass dozens of shoe shops. Many of them will make shoes or boots to order at reasonable cost. The nearby *Leighton Centre* has several fashionable boutiques, toy, and accessory shops. But prices are higher here than they are in the boutiques of Causeway Bay, Hong Kong Island's greatest shopping area.

Hong Kong: Causeway Bay is dominated by four large Japanese department stores: *Mitsukoshi* in Hennessy Centre, *Sogo* on Hennessy Road, and *Daimaru* and *Matsuzukaya,* both on Paterson Street. There is also the main branch of the *China Products* store, next to Victoria Park, and a branch of the prestigious *Lane Crawford* in nearby Windsor House. But all along Hennessy Road, which leads into Wanchai, are hi-fi, camera, and electronic shops (see Electronic Gear) and around the Lee Gardens Hotel are hundreds of small boutiques and tailors. Lockhart Road (parallel to Hennessy Road) has some good shoe shops and the Excelsior Hotel Shopping Centre features a range of art, gift, and souvenir shops. Don't miss *Jardine's Bazaar* with its bustle of stalls selling a wide range of cheap clothes.

Hong Kong: Eastern District, including the areas of North Point, Quarry Bay, and Shaukiwan, is more of a residential and Chinese-restaurant area than an exciting shopping area. There are a few large department stores along the main King's Road, but the best shopping is found farther east down King's Road in the huge shopping complexes of *Cityplaza I & II* at Taikooshing, which also houses Hong Kong's largest department store, *UNY.*

Hong Kong: Stanley is the best and most popular shopping area on the south of the island (take a number 6 bus from Exchange Square or 260 bus from Central). The *Stanley Market* is a mecca for bargain hunters in clothes and the whole area around Main Street has a trendy-arty ambience. *Witchcraft,* at 26B Stanley Main St., for instance, sells antique folkcraft collectibles, including Japanese tansu and screens, Filipino basketwear, and primitive *objets d'art.* For handicrafts, try *David Arts Co.* and *Stanley Chinese Products Co. Ltd.,* both in Stanley Main Street. (Some Hong Kong Island tours stop in Stanley for a brief shopping respite.)

Kowloon: Tsimshatsui, with its "Golden Mile" of shopping along Nathan Road, is justifiably popular with tourists for its hundreds of hi-fi, camera, jewelry, cosmetic, fashion, and souvenir shops. But investigate also the streets east of Nathan Road—for instance, Granville Road, with its factory outlets, embroidery, and porcelain shops, or Mody Road, with its souvenir alleys. To the west of Nathan Road is the more Chinese Canton Road and the camera enclave of Lock Road. In Tsimshatsui you'll also find three large and well stocked branches of *Chinese Arts & Crafts,* the Japanese *Isetan* department store (next to the Sheraton Hotel, with its own well-stocked shopping arcade), the multistoried maze of the *New World Shopping Centre,* and the vast, air-conditioned shopping complex of *Ocean Terminal-Ocean Centre-Harbour City-Hongkong Hotel* (next to the Star Ferry), plus a lovely row of shops on **Park Lane Shopper's Boulevard,** in Kowloon Park, facing Nathan Road. The new and quickly expanding shopping area of *Tsimshatsui East* provides other air-conditioned shopping complexes.

Kowloon: Jordan Road, where it crosses Nathan Road (just by the Jordan Mass Transit Railway station), offers two good China product stores: *Chinese Arts & Crafts* and *Yue Hwa Chinese Products.* Between Jordan and Yaumatei are some fascinating old streets, such as Shanghai, Saigon, Temple, and Reclamation. Practical rather than pretty, this area concentrates on hardware and spare parts for machinery, bicycle and furniture-repair shops, and even, in Battery Street, fishing-tackle stores. If you peer closer, however, you will also come across mah-jong set makers, brassware stalls, bamboo kitchen ware, and street stalls selling mirror gods and images.

Nathan Road goes all the way up to Mongkok and Shamshuipo areas. **Mongkok** with its many cinemas and restaurants, is a popular evening shopping area for locals. **Shamshuipo** has gained fame recently for its small shops and stalls and particularly its *Golden Shopping Centre* of "made-in-Hong Kong" computer goods (see Electronic Gear). It used to be famous for its second-hand electrical goods in Apliu Street but that street, as most in Shamshuipo, is now dominated by cloth factories and clothing outlets.

Hung Hom, near the airport, is another large factory area, with shops selling goods at factory prices. The center of Hong Kong's jewelry and textile-manufacturing industries, it offers a tremendous choice in designer and factory bargains. **Man Yue Street** (Kaiser Estate) is particularly popular with bargain hunters. (But check also in the back pages of the classified section of the *South China Morning Post* for addresses of other factories and the shopping guides recommended at the beginning of the chapter on page 30.)

SHOPPING CENTERS

The Landmark, conveniently situated above Central Mass Transit Railway station, is Central's most prestigious shopping site, a multi-story atrium and basement complex with designer fashion stores, such as Celine, Loewe, D'Urban, Bazaar, Joyce Boutique, and Hermes of Paris, classy art galleries, and exclusive jewelry shops. The information board giving lists of shops is located on the mezzanine floor, near the central fountain area, which is a favorite meeting place and is often converted into a stage for plays or other performances. Pick up a leaflet with the month's events listed at the Landmark or Hong Kong Tourist Association information centers. There is a pedestrian bridge link with *Swire House's* shopping arcade (which in turn is linked to Connaught Centre—with its basement arcade—and the General Post Office) on one side and an exit to Central Building's arcade on the other. The *Prince's Building Shopping Arcade* is also packed with name-brand shops and is connected by a pedestrian bridge to the Mandarin Hotel on the one side and Alexandra house on the other. (The latter is connected to both Landmark and the Swire Building, which brings you full circle.)

The next stop on the Mass Transit Railway, Admiralty, also features a large complex of shops. Queensway Plaza, United Centre, and Admiralty Centre are linked by an air-conditioned walkway of shops that leads to a series of pedestrian bridges, which in turn lead all the way to the Hilton Hotel in Central. *Queensway Plaza* features a branch of the expensive Japanese *Matsuzukaya* department store, while in *Admiralty Centre* you can find optical shops, men's tailors, real-estate agents, and electrical and TV shops. Along the internal walkways are small boutiques and art galleries, shoe shops, and toy shops. Take the M.T.R. one stop in the other direction (west) to Sheung Wan, and you'll find yourself at the *Shun Tak Centre Shopping Arcade.* (You can get almost all the way on foot by an elevated walkway starting at the General Post Office and Exchange, which is connected to Swire House.)

Cityplaza I & II, one of Hong Kong's shopping centers and a popular venue for weekend family outings, is located in Taikooshing, Quarry Bay. The major reasons for Cityplaza's popularity are its ice rink, the "Rollerworld" roller-skating rink, and a bowling alley. This is the perfect place to amuse the children while you browse through the six floors of shops, which feature, perhaps inevitably, a large number of children's clothing and toy shops (Les Enfants, Circles, Crocodile, Peter Pan, Crystal) as well as men's and women's fashions (Sunrose, Condor, Circles, Allegro, and Romano) and *UNY* and *Dodwell Department Stores.*

Ocean Terminal-Ocean Centre-Hong Kong Hotel-Harbour City, located right next to the Kowloon-side Star Ferry, is one of the largest complexes of shops in the world. Harbour City by itself is Asia's largest air-conditioned shopping, office, and residential complex, with about 122 fashion shops, 40 shoe and bag shops, 40 jewelry and watch stores, and 43 restaurants. It is connected by moving pavement to the *Ocean Terminal* and *Ocean Centre* complexes, which lead into the *Hong Kong Hotel Shopping Arcade.* You can find just about everything you want here, from costly antiques at *Charlotte Horstmann & Gerald Godfrey,* in both the Ocean Terminal and Centre, and Asian crafts and curios at *Amazing Grace Elephant Co.,* at 242 Ocean Terminal, to silk cheong-sams, cameras, and carpets. *Harbour City* has the largest *Dodwell Department Store,* which sells a good range of British brand goods. Prices are usually fixed so you will find items are more expensive than they are in the markets and small-town stores.

From the Kowloon Star Ferry, you can take a minibus to Tsimshatsui East, a fast-growing office, hotel, and shopping area. Already there is a *Wing On Plaza, Tsimshatsui Centre, Empire Centre, Houston Centre, South Seas Centre,* and *Energy Plaza,* and more shopping centers are being built. Pleasantly located along the harbor waterfront, the centers are exuberantly crammed with every kind of shop and store; prices are reasonable and the atmosphere lively.

Tsimshatsui East has rather overshadowed the other harbor-front shopping center next to the New World Hotel, the *New World Shopping Centre.* But New World still boasts more than 60 fashion shops, more than 20 leather shops, and some 20 jewelry shops, as well as restaurants, optical shops, tailors, hi-fi stores, arts and crafts shops, and the large Japanese *Tokyu Department Store.* The *Regent Hotel Shopping Arcade,* featuring some sophisticated shops, can be reached through the center.

DEPARTMENT STORES

The various Chinese product stores give shoppers some of the most unusual and spectacular buys in Hong Kong—and often at better prices than they would pay in mainland China. Whether you are looking for jade jewelry, silk mandarin coats, Chinese stationery, or simply a pair of chopsticks, you cannot go wrong with these stores. Most are open seven days a week, but avoid Sunday sale days, Saturdays, and weekday lunchtimes if you dislike mammoth crowds. The stores are particularly adept at packing, shipping, and mailing goods abroad but are not so talented in the finer arts of pleasant service.

Chinese Arts & Crafts (24 Queen's Rd. Central, Hong Kong; in Kowloon at Star House, near the Star Ferry; in New World Shopping Centre; in Silvercord Building, opposite Harbour City; and at 233 Nathan Rd.) is particularly good for silk embroidered fashions, jewelry, carpets, and *objets d'art,* but prices are somewhat higher than they are at other stores.

China Products Company (19–31 Yee Wo St., next to Victoria Park, in Causeway Bay, Hong Kong; and at 488 Hennessy Rd., Causeway Bay; and in

Kowloon at 73 Argyle St.) gives an excellent general selection of goods, particularly at the main Yee Wo Street store.

Chinese Merchandise Emporium (92–104 Queen's Rd. Central, Hong Kong) has a bustling local clientele on its way from Central Market. The material, toy, and stationery departments are particularly good here. *Yue Hwa Chinese Products Emporium* (301–309 Nathan Rd, Yaumatei, and 54–64 Nathan Rd., Tsimshatsui, both in Kowloon) features a broad selection of Chinese goods with a popular medicine counter. *Chung Kiu Chinese Products Emporium* (17 Hankow Road, and 530 Nathan Rd., Tsimshatsui, both in Kowloon) specializes in arts and crafts at its Tsimshatsui branch.

Japanese department stores are very popular in Hong Kong, especially those clustering in powerful proximity in Causeway Bay, Hong Kong: *Daimaru* and *Matsuzukaya* in Paterson Street and *Mitsukoshi* and *Sogo* in Hennessy Road, plus *UNY* in Cityplaza II, Taikoo Shing, Quarry Bay. On Kowloon side, *Isetan* in the Sheraton Hotel is smaller but equally popular. Opposite it, in the New World Shopping Centre, is *Tokyu Department Store*.

The *Taiwan Man Sang Product* stores (777 Nathan Rd., 17 Percival St., and 129 Tung Choi St., all in Kowloon) are the Taiwanese equivalent of the China product stores that stock mainland Chinese goods.

Hong Kong department stores, meanwhile, stock large selections of Western goods at fixed and usually fair prices. The oldest and largest chains are *Wing On* (eight branches throughout Hong Kong), *Sincere,* (173 Des Voeux Rd., Central, Hong Kong, and 83 Argyle St., Kowloon) and *Shui Hing* (23 Nathan Rd., Kowloon). *Lane Crawford* is the most prestigious department store of all, with prices to match its reputation. Sales here can be dangerous for both the physically and financially weak, as everyone, from secretaries to tai-tais (executive wives), pushes and shoves to find luxury bargains. (The main store in Queen's Road Central is the best; branches can be found in Windsor House, Causeway Bay, Hong Kong; and Manson House, Nathan Road, Kowloon.)

Some of these department stores hold Sunday sales, but these and the seasonal sales at all the department stores can be more exhausting than they are worth. Stay clear unless you love that sort of shopping.

MARKETS, BAZAARS, AND ALLEYS

These give you the best of Hong Kong shopping—good bargains, exciting atmosphere, and a fascinating setting. The once-famous Cat Street, the curio haunt in Upper Lascar Row, Hong Kong, with a reputation for selling stolen second-hand goods, has unfortunately fallen to office development, but there are still plenty of other alleys and markets to whet your appetite in bazaar buying. Some of the best are listed here.

Li Yuen Streets East and West, Central, Hong Kong (between Queen's Road Central and Des Voeux Road Central), offer some of the best bargains in cloth and cheap fashions (with or without famous brand names), trendy jewelry, and accessories. Leather bags of every variety, many in designer styles, are particularly good buys here. You may be warned by police loudspeakers to watch out for pick-pockets in these crowded and popular lanes, so let your eyes wander but keep your hands firmly on your handbag.

Cloth Alley (Wing On Street, just west of Central Market, past Jubilee Street) has some fantastic bargains in all kinds of cloth and material. *Baby Lane* (Fat Hing Street, off Queen's Road West, near Possession Street) is a unique market for traditional Chinese baby clothing, including red silk-embroidered capes, padded Chinese jackets and vests, and even Chinese backpacks. An excellent place for unusual gifts. *(The Welfare Handicraft Shops* in the Connaught Centre, Hong Kong, and in Kowloon on Salisbury Road and in the Ocean Terminal, also have a selection of these traditional baby items.)

Jardine's Bazaar, in Causeway Bay, Hong Kong (just behind Klasse Grand Department Store), merges a fresh fruit and vegetable market with a tightly packed cluster of clothing stalls that sell attractively priced fashions and sportswear.

Poor Man's Nightclub, in front of the China Ferry Terminal and the Shun Tak Centre (which houses the Macau Ferry Terminal), operates at night and is given its name from the cheap food stalls and goods available. Music from bargain-priced cassettes blares next to fortune tellers urging parakeets to pick out fortune cards, while hawkers yell out prices for jeans, T-shirts, and other fashion goods. A fun place to meander but it is advisable to avoid eating at the food stalls.

Temple Street in Kowloon (near the Jordan Mass Transit Railway station) is another nighttime marketplace, and is filled with a colorful collection of clothes, handbags, electrical goods, gadgets, and all sorts of household items. By the light of lamps strung up between stalls, hawkers try to catch the eye of shoppers by flinging fashions up from their stalls; Cantonese opera competes with pop music, and there's a constant clatter of goods being displayed and sold and a constant chatter of hawkers' cries and shoppers' bargaining. The market stretches for almost a mile and is one of Hong Kong's liveliest nighttime shopping experiences.

Jade Market, in Kansu Street (off Nathan Road) in Tsimshatsui is *the* place to see jade in every form, color, shape, and size. Open every morning from 10:00 A.M., the market is full of dealers carrying out intriguing deals and keen-witted sellers trying to lure tourists. Some trinkets are reasonably priced, but unless you know a lot about jade, don't be tempted into buying expensive items. *Kowloon City Market,* near the airport, Kowloon (take a number 1 or 1A bus from Star Ferry Kowloon and get off opposite the airport), is a favorite with local bargain hunters because of its huge array of cheap clothes, porcelain, household goods, and electrical gadgets.

Stanley Village Market in Stanley (take a number 6 or 260 bus from Central) is a popular haunt for Western residents and tourists seeking cheap designer fashions, jeans, jumpers, and T-shirts at factory prices and in Western sizes. There is also a number of shops featuring ethnic goods from Asia, including rattan and household goods. This is a pleasant place for meandering, but it's crowded at weekends.

WOMEN'S CLOTHING

Hong Kong surprises and disappoints many newcomers, who find it to be more Western than they expected. Nowhere is this more obvious than in the field of fashion. Nearly every woman in the street—especially in areas like Central—is wearing the latest Western fashions. Boutiques abound. And the variety of off-the-peg clothes available is astounding. It may come as a surprise, too, to learn that many big-name designers (Calvin Klein, Yves St. Laurent, Ralph Lauren, Charlotte Ford, Pierre Cardin, Levi, Britannia, and Gloria Vanderbilt, to name but a few) manufacture in Hong Kong. You can find such high fashion in places like the Landmark in Central, Hong Kong, in the chic boutiques of Wellington Street and D'Aguilar Street, Central, in the department stores, such as Wing On and Sincere, and in many hotel shopping arcades. But take note: prices will not necessarily be any cheaper than they are back home.

Some of the leading top fashion stores are *Green & Found,* in the Ocean Centre and the Landmark; *Joyce Boutique,* in the Landmark and Peninsula Hotel; *Issey Miyake,* in Swire House; *Boutique Bazaar,* in the Landmark, Peninsula Hotel, and Swire House, Peninsula Hotel *Celine Boutique,* in the Landmark, 56 Nathan Rd., Yaumatei, *Matsuzukaya,* Causeway Bay, and Tokyu Department Store, Kowloon; *Chanel Boutique,* in the Peninsula Hotel; *D'Urban,* in the Landmark, Matsuzukaya, Mitsukoshi, Daimaru, Hong Kong, and New World Centre, Kowloon; *Giorgio Armani,* in the Mandarin Hotel; *Christian Dior* in the Landmark; *Gucci,* in the Landmark and Peninsula Hotel; *Hermes of Paris,* in the Landmark and Peninsula Hotel; *Loewe,* in the Landmark; *Nina Ricci,* in the Regent Hotel; *Esprit,* in Auto Plaza, Tsimshatsui East, Chung Shung Building, Hing Fat Street, North Point and Prince's Bldg., Central.

For slightly more trendy or unusual fashions (though still fairly expensive), *Jenny Lewis* (for exquisite Asian-style modern fashions), in Swire House, Peninsula Hotel, Ocean Centre; *Pavlova,* in Swire House; *Diane Freis* (for delightful floral-patterned dresses), in Furama Hotel, Ocean Terminal, Prince's Bldg., Tsimshatsui Centre, and Harbour City; and *Michel Rene,* in the Landmark, Harbour City, New World Centre, 86 Nathan Rd., Ocean Centre, Paterson Plaza, China Building, and Harbour City. Laura Ashley's beautiful printed dresses can be found at *Kinsan Collections,* 29 Wyndham Street, Central.

Medium-priced fashions in the latest styles, for the young and young-at-heart, can be found in such popular stores as *Toppy,* in Mitsukoshi Department Store, and in Ocean Centre, New World Centre, the Landmark, and Harbour City; *Foxy Fashion,* in Ocean Centre and Landmark basement; *Birds,* in Excelsior Hotel in D'Aguilar Place, and 33 Carnarvon Rd.; the *Fashion Factory,* in Peak Tower; and *The Farmhouse,* 75 Stanley Main St., Stanley.

The colorful sports and casual wear of *Esprit* is stocked at several boutiques, but the firm's own three-floor store in Hing Fat Street, North Point, has a more extensive range. For dancers or exercisers and those who like the latest in sexy bathing suits, *Delilah* at shop 54, New World Centre, Kowloon, *La Plume,* shop

226, Edinburgh Tower, Central, and Cliche, shop 203, Holiday Inn-Golden Mile shopping arcade, stock all kinds of dance wear and "fancy feathers." For frothy negligées, *Caetla* at Bank of East Asia Building in Des Voeux Road, Central, has the stuff of your dreams—for a price. For cool cottons try *Design Selection* in Wyndham Street, Central, Harbour City, Kowloon, *The Cotton Collection,* with two locations in Kowloon and three in Hong Kong, and *Scruples* in Wilson House, 19–27 Wyndham Street, Central. For uniquely designed T-shirts, sweat shirts, plus a host of other designer goods, try the *Ben Sprout Shop,* inside the Kowloon terminal of the Star Ferry.

And for something fancy in the millinery line, or other types of accessories, try *Renomee,* shop 115, Melbourne Plaza, Queen's Road, Central.

If you are willing to go out of your way, you can pick up cheap designer fashions at various factory outlets (see below) that sell end-of-run or seconds (many of them are hardly damaged at all). And, of course, there are the many clothes markets that also sell these clothes (Stanley Market has a good choice in Western sizes) as well as the counterfeit versions (you may even find designer labels on items that the designer never actually makes, such as "Yves St. Laurent" jeans). The best places to find these cheap "designer" fashions are in the two clothing alleys of Central—Li Yuen streets East and West—in the streets of Causeway Bay, and in the bustling Kowloon City Market.

Factory Outlets. For the best of bargain buys in top-fashion clothes, take a trip to some of the factories manufacturing designer clothes and pick up high-fashion (almost indiscernible seconds or overruns) at a fraction of the price you would pay at home. One of the best areas for silk is Man Yue Street in Hung Hom, Kowloon, near the airport (take a taxi to *Kaiser Estate,* Phase I, II, and III), where such factories as *Camberley, Four Seasons, Genti Donna, Bonaventure,* and *Wintex* produce for the top fashion houses in Europe and the United States. (See list of publications and H.K.T.A. brochures at the beginning of this section.)

Tailor-Made Women's Clothing. Despite the plethora of boutiques, department stores, and off-the-peg fashion stores, you can still find Chinese tailors to make Western suits and dresses or evening gowns (and, of course, the traditional high-necked silk cheongsam). Silk fashions are probably the best buy in tailored clothing because the cloth is woven in China, while all other fabrics have to be imported.

Tips for men's tailored clothing apply to women, too. Be prepared to pay more for better, quicker service and a finer understanding of your needs. Bear in mind that traveling long distances is tiring and time-consuming. It's worth paying more for a tailor near or in your hotel. And allow plenty of time—at least three days—for a tailor to complete your job. The more rushed he is, the worse his work will be.

Larger branches of *Chinese Arts & Crafts* charge about HK$500 for tailoring, with an additional HK$200 or so for embroidered fastenings or satin trims.

CHILDREN'S CLOTHING

There are plenty of stores in Hong Kong that sell trendy, Western-style, ready-to-wear childrens' clothing. Among the best are *Charade* at the Regent Hotel and Landmark; *Circles* in the Landmark, Ocean Centre, and Cityplaza; *Crocodile* in Cityplaza, New World Centre, Ocean Centre, and many other locations; *Crystal* in the Ocean Terminal and Cityplaza; and *Children's Clothing Company* at Ocean Centre, Landmark, D'Aguilar Street, and Cityplaza. Britain's famous *Mothercare* is located at Windsor House, 311 Gloucester Rd., Causeway Bay, Hong Kong. You can also find some fabulous traditional Chinese clothing for younger tots in *"Baby Lane,"* Fat Hing Street, Western. Silk *mien lap* (padded jackets), a particularly good buy for winterwear and costing under HK$50 for baby sizes, can be found both in "Baby Lane" and in the two clothing alleys in Central, Li Yuen streets East and West.

TAILOR-MADE MEN'S CLOTHING

There are over 4,000 tailor shops in Hong Kong, and Shanghai tailors in many of them have justifiably given Hong Kong its reputation for fine tailor-made suits. But there are pitfalls to avoid if you want to receive the best of Hong Kong's tailoring talents.

First, give the tailor plenty of time—at least three days. Suits *can* be made in 24 hours (the famous Sam's once made a suit in a record two hours and six minutes) but at best they will probably be shoddy; at worst, they will fall apart within weeks.

Choose a tailor in a convenient location. Don't forget that you will have to go back at least twice for fittings. Prices of tailors located in hotel or other major shopping centers will, of course, be higher than those charged by other tailors, but you are paying for the convenience of a central location, better service, and a finer understanding of your needs.

It helps to have a good idea of what you want before you go to the tailor, perhaps aided by a picture clipped from a magazine. Go through every detail slowly and carefully, making sure it is all marked down on the order form. Take a swatch of material away with you to ensure that the final garment is in fact made from the same material you ordered. And when you pay a deposit (which should not be more than 50 percent of the final cost), make sure the receipt includes all relevant details: the date of delivery, the description of the material, and any other details. All tailors keep records of clients' measurements, so if you are truly satisfied with the efficiency of service and the style and cut of your suit, you can always order another one by mail. Keep a copy of the original measurements, however, in case you need to change them.

There are a number of reputable and long-established tailors in Hong Kong. *Sam's,* in Burlington Arcade, 94 Nathan Rd., Kowloon, has been patronized by members of the British Forces since it opened in 1957. And even a member of the Royal Family, the Duke of Kent, has his shirts made there. Prices for Sam's suits range from HK$1,100 to HK$3,500, and custom-made shirts from

HK$120 to HK$250. *Ascot Chang,* with shops in the Peninsula and Regent Hotels in Kowloon and Prince's Building in Central, has been putting shirts on the backs of the famous since 1949. Clients have included Lyndon Johnson, George Bush, Sammy Davis Jr., and Andy Williams. Prices range from HK$180 for a Dacron shirt to HK$280 for pure cotton, while silk shirts start at HK$580. Another illustrious shirt maker is *Mee Yee & Company,* at 28 Stanley St., Central, Hong Kong. Clients over the shop's 50-year history have included princes and politicians, comedians and artists (a check from Marlon Brando is framed in a place of honor on the wall). A terylene-cotton (English terminology for the American dacron-cotton) shirt will cost about HK$160, while pure cotton shirts start at HK$220. A personal monogram costs an extra HK$10 to HK$15.

LINENS, SILKS, EMBROIDERIES

Pure silk shantung, silk and gold brocade, silk velvet, pure silk damask, and printed pure silk crêpe de chine are just some of the exquisite silk materials available in Hong Kong at reasonable prices. The best selections are to be found in the *China Products Emporiums, Chinese Arts & Crafts,* and the *Yue Hwa* stores. (Made-up silk garments from mandarin coats to nightdresses are also good buys at Chinese Arts & Crafts, and stylish dresses, blouses, and pants are also available.)

Irish linens, Swiss cotton, Thai silks, and Indian, Malay, and Indonesian fabrics are among the imported cloths you can find in Hong Kong. Many of them are displayed in the cloth alleys of Central in Wing On Lane and Li Yuen streets East and West. *Vincent Sum Designs,* 5A Lyndhurst Terrace, Central, specializes in Indonesian batik, a small selection of which can also be found in *Mountain Folkcraft* in Ocean Terminal, Kowloon and 12 Wo On Lane, Central. Thai silks are part of the collection of Thai arts and crafts in *The Thailand Shop* in Silvercord, Canton Road, Kowloon. Chinese linens and cottons are a good value, but the best buys from China are undoubtedly the hand-embroidered and appliquéd linens and cottons.

You can find a magnificent range of hand-embroidered tablecloths, napkins, handkerchiefs, and placemats in the *China Products* stores and *Chinese Arts & Crafts,* as well as in various shops in Wyndham Street, Central, Hong Kong, and nearby On Lan Street. Shops on Upper Wyndham Street go in for Indian fabric and carpets. The art of embroidery is said to have originated in Swatow, and *Swatow Drawn Work,* G2–3 Worldwide House, Central, shows some of the best examples of this intricate and delicate art. When buying hand-embroidered items, make sure the edges are properly overcast; beware, too, of locally manufactured, machine-made versions.

FURS

It seems quite bizarre that Hong Kong, with its tropical climate, should host so many fur shops. However, high-quality skins, meticulous tailoring, and excellent hand-finishing, as well as competitive prices, make furs a good buy here.

Some of the largest and most popular stores are *Siberian Fur Store* at 21 Chatham Rd., Kowloon, and 29 Des Voeux Rd., Central, Hong Kong; *Stylette Models,* L2–38B New World Shopping Centre, Kowloon, and Excelsior Hotel, Hong Kong. *Jindo Fur Salon,* in World Finance Center, Harbour City, offers a wide range at factory prices.

PERFUME AND COSMETICS

Aromatic ointments were believed to have been used by the Egyptians over five thousand years ago. But the East made the major contributions to the art of perfumery. Today, however, Chinese cosmetics are hardly a match for the modern Western fragrances. Sandalwood soap is perhaps the exception (the "Maxam" label in China product stores is prettily packaged and costs HK$2.50 a bar). And if you like strong aromas in distinctly Chinese floral packaging, have a look at the Hong Kong-manufactured "Two Girls" range (Kwong Sang Hong's main shop in Harbour Commercial Building, next to Wing On and Korean House on Connaught Road Central, is as attractively decorated as its products). For Western perfumes, however, the best buys are in the big department stores such as *Wing On* and *Sincere,* or the main drugstores, *Manning* and *Watson's.*

SHOES

The place to buy shoes in Hong Kong is in Happy Valley, where a long line of shoe shops border the race course and Leighton Road. Another popular haunt is along Prince Edward Road, near the Mass Transit Railway station of the same name. These shops mostly stock locally made or Philippine-made shoes, so don't expect their bargain-priced varieties to offer much in the way of durability.

Large-footed customers may also have some trouble finding locally made shoes in their sizes. Top-name Italian and other European brands can sometimes be found in these shops and certainly in the major department stores and shopping centers, such as the Landmark, Central.

Custom-made shoes, for both men and women, are readily and quickly available. Cobblers—even those with such unfortunate names as Lee Kee Boot & Shoe Makers in Peking Road, Kowloon—are renowned for their skill in copying specific styles at a reasonable cost. You can order a pair of leather shoes, a copy of a famous designer brand, for example, for less than HK$500. If you are into cowboy boots in knee-high calfskin, try some of the Wanchai cobblers, such as *Kow Hoo Shoe Company* in the Hilton Hotel. The shops in Happy Valley will also make custom-made shoes and boots, but make sure you leave your size chart if you want to mail order from home.

JEWELRY

Jewelry is the most popular item among visitors to Hong Kong. It is not subject to tax or duty, so prices are normally much lower than they are in most other places of the world. Turnover is fast, competition fierce, and the selection fantastic. As one of the world's largest diamond-trading centers, Hong Kong offers these gems at prices that are at least 10 percent lower than world-market levels. Settings will also cost less here than in most Western capitals, but check with your country's customs regulations, as some countries charge a great deal more for imported set jewelry than for unset jewelry.

Although Hong Kong's jewelers are legally required to mark the gold content on each gold item sold, many are reluctant to do so. The Hong Kong Tourist Association, however, keeps a strict watch on its member shops to follow the law and requires all of its gold-trading members to mark every gold or gold-alloyed item displayed or offered for sale with marks indicating both the gold fineness of the article and the identity of the shop or manufacturer. If you have any complaints about a gold item purchased in one of these member shops, call the Association immediately; (5)244191. The Consumer Council, (5)748297, should also be able to help with complaints. Before buying, you might want to check the current gold prices, which most stores will have displayed, against the price of the gold item that you are thinking of buying.

When buying diamonds, check on the "Four C's"; carat weight, color, clarity, and cut. For more detailed information on diamonds or for making complaints, call the Diamond Importers Association; (5)235497. Pearls, another good buy in Hong Kong, should be checked for color (silvery white, light pink, darker pink, yellow, plain white); shape ((cultured pearls usually have a perfect round shape); luster (never found in synthetics); and size (cultured pearls from the South Seas range from 10 millimeters to 15 millimeters in diameter, Japanese pearls from three millimeters to 10 millimeters. A good place to have your gem's identity and value confirmed is the Gemmological Laboratory of Hong Kong, 802 Luk Hoi Ting Building, 31 Queen's Rd., Central, Hong Kong; (5)262422. Alternatively, try S.P.H. De Silva, 232 Worldwide Plaza, Central, Hong Kong; (5)268760.

Jade, of course, is Hong Kong's most famous stone, full of Oriental mystique. But beware: though you will see so-called "jade" trinkets, bracelets, adornments, and figurines everywhere in Hong Kong, the good-quality jade is rare and expensive. Two substances are called jade: nephrite and jadeite. Nephrite was the only type known in ancient times and was used for decorative *objets d'art;* jadeite is of more recent discovery and is the green Burmese type commonly used in jewelry.

But jade is not only green in color. You will find jade in shades of purple, orange, yellow, brown, white, and even violet; the most expensive color is a deep translucent emerald green. Just to complicate matters, there are other types of jade, such as aventurine, a green quartz; New Zealand greenstone; bowenite, a form of serpentine; and Australian jade, another form of green quartz.

The subject is obviously complex and, if your knowledge is limited, you would be well advised to buy only from reputable shops. A visit to the *Jade Market* in Kansu Street, Kowloon is, however, a must. Here you can watch the intricate and mysterious procedures of the jade merchants as they bid for rocks that—hopefully—contain jade. The street is packed with jade trinkets spread out onto the pavement. Walking down the street you will get an excellent idea of the range of jade's many colors, shapes, and forms.

If you are suitably attracted but sensibly wary of spending your money in Canton Road, visit *Jade House* in Regent Shopping Arcade, or *Jade Creations,* in Lane Crawford House, fourth floor, Queen's Road Central, Hong Kong, or shop 110, Ocean Terminal, for more reliable help in choosing a jade item.

The prestigious shopping area of Central, Hong Kong, features some of the more opulent, big-name jewelers, such as *Kevin Jewellery* at the Hilton Hotel; *Larry Jewelry* at the Landmark (and also 33 Nathan Rd.); *Dickson Watch and Jewellery,* in the Landmark, Peninsula, and Holiday Inn Golden Mile hotels, *De Silva's* in the Central Building and in Worldwide House; *Manchu Gems* in Ocean Terminal, and *Dabera* in Admiralty Centre. Other large and reputable jewelry stores are *King Fook* (various locations all over Hong Kong) and *House of Shen* in the Peninsula and Hongkong hotels. *Chinese Arts & Crafts* has a wide collection of jade and porcelain jewelry and enamelware, as well as antique Chinese and Tibetan jewelry. Famous international jewelers can also be found in Hong Kong: *Van Cleef & Arpels* in the Landmark and Peninsula Hotel; *Cartier* at The Peninsula Hotel and in Swire House, Central; and *Asprey of Bond St.* in Prince's Building, Central. *Ilias Lalaounis* is located in the Regent Hotel Lobby and Landmark; and for Oriental-influenced modern jewelry, take a look at the fabulous designs by *Kai Yin Lo,* 1602, 16th Fl., 2 Wellington St., Central.

WATCHES

You will have no trouble finding watches in Hong Kong. Street stalls, department stores, and shops overflow with every variety, style, and brand name of timepieces, many of them with irresistible gadgets. But remember Hong Kong's incorrigible talent for imitation when buying watches. A super bargain gold "Rolex" may have hidden flaws—cheap local or Russian mechanisms, for instance, or gold that begins to rust. Stick to reputable dealers if you want to be sure you are getting the real thing. When buying an expensive watch, check the serial number against the manufacturer's guarantee certificate and ask the salesman to open the case to check the movement serial number. And if an expensive band is attached, make sure the receipt states whether it is from the original manufacturer or is locally made. If in any doubt, telephone the authorized agent. You should obtain a detailed receipt, the maker's guarantee, and a worldwide warranty at all times.

LEATHER

From belts to bags, luggage to lighter cases—leather items are high on the list for the Hong Kong shopper. The best and most expensive leather goods come from Europe, but locally made leather bags in famous designer styles go for a song in Li Yuen streets East and West in Central, Hong Kong, and in other shopping lanes.

For the real, top-quality products, visit the department stores, such as *Lane Crawford* (Queen's Road Central main branch is the best); *Wing On* (Connaught

Road Central and many other branches); *Sincere* in Connaught Road Central; and the Japanese trio in Causeway Bay—*Daimaru, Mitsukoshi,* and *Matsuzukaya.* Expensive leather fashions are tempting buys at *Loewe,* in the Landmark, Central, Matsuzukaya, and Peninsula Hotel, while fine Italian shoes at *Carrano* in the Landmark and *Emanuel Ungaro* leather bags at *Duty Free Shoppers* and *Mitsukoshi* make the locally made versions seem vastly inferior. Other top brand names available in department stores or in their own shops are Nina Ricci, Cartier, Lancel, Il Bisonte, Comtesse, Guido Borelli, Caran d'Ache, Franco Pugi, and Christian Dior. Made-to-measure leather clothes, shoes, and luggage are also available in some of the larger stores, but allow plenty of time for such items to be made properly.

CERAMICS

Fine English porcelain dinner, tea, and coffee sets are popular buys in Hong Kong and are best found at *Craig's* in St. George's Building, Ice House Street, Hong Kong, or Ocean Centre, Kowloon. Royal Worcester and Royal Crown Derby are among the famous designers stocked at Craig's. *Rosenthal* in Prince's Building, Central, or Ocean Terminal, Kowloon, and *Wedgwood* in The Landmark, are other top-quality ceramic shops.

For a full range of made-in-China ceramics (the traditional tea set packed in a wicker basket makes an unusual gift) visit the various China Products stores, which offer fantastic bargains and attractive designs. Be warned, however, that it is often difficult to buy additional matching pieces. Other Chinese ceramic pieces, such as vases, huge bowls, and table lamps, can be found in the streets of Tsimshatsui, especially Granville Road, in the shopping centers of Tsimshatsui East and Ocean Terminal/Centre, and, for real bargains, in the street markets, such as Kowloon City Market.

The Hong Kong Tourist Association's pamphlet, *Arts, Crafts & Museums* provides a list of ceramic factories you can visit, as do the other factory outlet guides. Two of the most popular factories, offering fantastic ceramic bargains, are *Yuet Tung China Works,* Lot 3726, Tai Wo Ping, Kowloon, (3)778–1006; and *Ah Chow Factory,* 489a Castle Peak Road, Flat B1, seventh floor, Block B, (3)745–1511.

For the more unusual ceramic items, you might like to visit *Sheung Yu Ceramic Arts* showroom, South Seas Centre, Tsimshatsui East, Kowloon, (3)-739–2666, for ceramic replicas; and *Hong Kong Treasures,* 14 Wellington St., Central, for hand-painted porcelain platters on lacquered wood. For unusual Chinese vases and bowls try *Mei Ping,* twenty-first floor of Wilson House, 19–27 Wyndham Street, Central. Ceramic elephant stools from Vietnam make delightful tabletops, stools, or decorative items and can be found at the *Vietnamese Import-Export Shop,* Asian House Arcade, 1 Hennessy Rd., Hong Kong; at the *Men's Shop* in Ocean Centre, or at *Amazing Grace Elephant Co.,* Excelsior Shopping Centre, Cityplaza, Ocean Terminal, and Landmark basement.

ANTIQUES

Hong Kong can be very tempting to people seeking Asian antiques. From posh and expensive establishments to tiny, dilapidated junk stalls, there is a range of antique shops to suit every pocket and interest. As always, of course, beware of doling out the dollars unless you really know your market. Fakes can be extremely deceiving, especially when they are as well made as, say, the Taiwanese copies of beautiful Ch'ien Lung-era porcelain. Bargains and fantastic discoveries are much harder to find in Hong Kong these days than they were just ten years ago. If you want to be sure of your purchase, patronize reputable shops, such as *Charlotte Horstmann and Gerald Godfrey* at Ocean Terminal, with a warehouse at Harbour City; *Eileen Kershaw,* at the Peninsula Hotel and Landmark; *Ian McLean Antiques,* 73 Wyndham St.; or *Lane Crawford,* Queen's Road Central.

But these are your top-line establishments. For shoppers with less cash and more curiosity, *Hollywood Road* on Hong Kong is undeniably the best place for Asian antiques. Treasures are hidden away here among a jumble of old-family curio shops, sidewalk junk stalls, slick new display windows, and dilapidated warehouses. Behind this bewildering façade, Chinese and Western dealers carry on a multi-million dollar business in Asian antiques and reproduction art and furnishings.

Look for *Eastern Dreams* on the corner of Lyndhurst Terrace and Hollywood Road, which has two floors of antique and reproduction furniture, screens, and curios; *Yue Po Chai Curios Store,* next to Man Mo Temple, one of Hollywood Road's oldest shops, boasting one of the largest and most varied inventories in Hong Kong; *Schoeni Fine Arts,* 1 Hollywood Rd., which specializes in ivory carvings; *Honeychurch Antiques,* 29 Hollywood Rd., offering Japanese, Chinese, and Thai antiques and specializing in Chinese silverware, such as opium boxes, and in rare maps and cricket paraphernalia.

In the Cat Street area, once famous for its thieves' market of second-hand stolen goods, there is now almost nothing of antique interest. But among the high-rise office blocks that are the result of the area's redevelopment, *Cat Street Galleries,* 38 Lok Ku Rd., is an attempt to bring together various dealers in one building. Only opened recently, it has not yet managed to recapture the atmosphere of bygone days or even of present-day Hollywood Road, but some of the shops may be worth a visit.

If you cannot find anything to interest you in Hollywood Road (not likely), there are several other fascinating Aladdin's Caves that could probably handle your entire shopping list. *Amazing Grace Elephant Co.,* 242 Ocean Terminal, Ocean Centre, Excelsior Hotel, Cityplaza, and Landmark basement, has a wide range of Asian antiques, curios, and gifts at reasonable prices. *Eastern Fabrics,* 8–10 On Lan St., eighth floor, has some fine Japanese kimono and small Japanese decorative pieces. *Treasures of China,* 312 World Finance Centre, Harbour City, stocks both art and antiques from the Middle Kingdom.

There are other, less physically tiring ways to find antiques in Hong Kong. One of these is at the auction. *Lammert Brothers* in Sutherland House, second floor, Central, Hong Kong, and *Victoria Auctioneers,* 38 D'Aguilar St., Central, regularly advertise auctions in the local papers (check the classified section of the *South China Morning Post*). Admission is free. Persian carpets are some of the bargains you might be lucky to buy here, but, as always, the excitement of an auction is the mystery of what you might find.

ART

Like any other major city, Hong Kong has its school of sidewalk artists, painting the popular sights and scenes in gaudy oil colors. They frequent the streets and alleys of Tsimshatsui and the arcades, such as Chung King Mansions, off Nathan Road. Bargaining is usually accepted.

Chinese Arts & Crafts stocks a wide range of Chinese paintings on scrolls. An excellent buy here are the small square or round paintings on silk. Another bargain, in the print line, are the nineteenth-century Hong Kong and South China prints sold in the Government Publications Centre near the main Post Office, next to the Hong Kong Star Ferry.

Very much more up-market, with prices to match, are *Burlington Art Gallery* in the Admiralty Centre (above Admiralty Mass Transit Railway station); *Sally Jackson Art Gallery* in Ocean Terminal; and *The Asian Collector Gallery,* 19–27 Wyndham St., a highly regarded gallery specializing in Japanese prints, old maps and engravings, and nineteenth-century China trade paintings. (It also features an "Art for Offices" service.) On Lan Street, Wyndham Street, and nearby Wellington Street you'll find several other small art galleries and a good choice of framers who will frame your picture at prices usually much lower than in Europe and the United States. Try, for example, *Man Fong,* 41 Wellington St.; or *Wah Cheong,* 7 Wellington St.

If you are interested in seeing the latest exciting developments in the East-meets-West art of local painters, visit *Alvin Gallery,* 51 Wyndham St., Central; the Arts Centre in Wanchai, which often has exhibitions, with works for sale; or the Hong Kong Museum of Art, in City Hall High Block, Central, Hong Kong.

IVORY

Ivory, like jade, is highly revered by the Chinese and comes in all forms, from whole elephant tusks to tiny toothpicks. *Schoeni Fine Arts,* 1 Hollywood Rd; Hong Kong, specializes in ivory pieces, but you will find collections in many other shops as well, particularly in the Hollywood Road antique shops and in the arts and crafts shops of Wyndham Street-Wellington Street, Central. Beware of the old-looking yellow stain on some supposedly antique pieces—it is not necessarily an indication of antiquity, since unscrupulous dealers sometimes stain ivory deliberately.

As various restrictions have been placed on the importation of ivory items by governments of most European countries and the United States, it is advisable to check with your home customs office, consulate in Hong Kong, or with the Hong Kong *Trade Department;* (3)722–2491. The shop where you buy your ivory item should give you a Certificate of Origin issued by the Customs and Excise Department.

Factory outlets selling ivory are *Tsang King Kee Ivory Factory Ltd.,* 18–20 Wyndham Street, Central, (5)231985; *Kwong Fat Cheong Ivory and Mahjong Factory,* 27 Wellington St., Central, Hong Kong; (5)251533; and *Tack Cheung Ivory Factory,* 36 Wyndham St., Central, Hong Kong; (5)231786.

HANDICRAFTS AND CURIOS

The traditional crafts of China cover a fascinating range of items, such as Chinese lanterns, temple rubbings, screen paintings, paper cuttings, seal engravings, and wooden bird models. The Hong Kong Tourist Association publishes a useful pamphlet, "Arts and Crafts and Museums," which is available at all Association information centers. It lists places where you can buy these specialty items. On Sunday afternoons at the Landmark you can see these crafts being made.

The Welfare Handicrafts Shop in the Connaught Centre, Hong Kong, Ocean Terminal, and Salisbury Road, between the Y.M.C.A. and Star House, Kowloon, also stocks a good collection of inexpensive Chinese handicrafts, especially attractive for children. All profits go to charity. For more bizarre gifts, *Startram (HK) Ltd.,* in Star House by the Kowloon-side Star Ferry Concourse or up on The Peak in Peak Tower, Hong Kong side, offers Star Ferry fashions—sailor suits and caps—as well as Star Ferry crockery and china, along with many other items of interest.

Small and inexpensive curios from other parts of Asia are on sale at *Amazing Grace Elephant Co.,* 242 Ocean Terminal, Ocean Centre, Excelsior Hotel, Cityplaza, and Landmark basement, which offers a little bit of everything from India, Sikkim, Nepal, Sri Lanka, Thailand, and the Philippines. *Mountain Folkcraft* in Ocean Terminal and at 12 Wo On Lane (just off D'Aguilar Street, Central) is a great find and very popular with locals for its chock-a-block collection of fascinating curios. *Banyan Tree,* Harbour City and the Prince's Building, and *Nic Nac,* Edinburgh Tower, Central and Harbour City, Kowloon, feature slightly more pricey but equally varied items from Asia. More artifacts can be found in *Tribal Arts & Crafts,* 41 Wyndham St., Central. For exclusively Filipino goods, visit *Kon Tiki* in the Ocean Terminal; and for Indonesian goods, try the *Indonesian Shop,* also in Ocean Terminal, and *Ria Crafts Gallery* in Silvercord, Canton Road. *Gallery 69* in the Landmark, Edinburgh Tower, and Regent Hotel, has one of the best selections of Korean goods, while the *Vietnamese Import-Export Shop* in Asian House Arcade, 1 Hennessy Rd., Hong Kong, has a lovely range of Vietnamese porcelain and lacquerware. For Thai crafts, try *Thai Shop* in the Houston Centre, Tsimshatsui East, and Silvercord. Stanley Market is also worth visiting for ethnic goods. Some of the more interesting shops there are *Witchcraft,* 26B Stanley Main St., and *Ah Kam's Craft,* also on Main Street.

MISCELLANEOUS CHINESE GIFTS

If you are really stuck for a gift idea, think Chinese. Some of the most unusual gifts are often the simplest. How about a pair of chopsticks, in black lacquer and finely painted? They're available at China Product stores for only a few dollars. Alternatively, for about HK$30 you can buy a Chinese chop engraved with an appropriate name in Chinese (remember that the male calligraphic style carves out the background material; the female style the actual characters). Take a walk down Man Wa Lane in Central (opposite Wing On Department Store at 26 Des Voeux Rd., Central,) for some chop ideas. And then, of course, for cold climates, there are the wonderful *mien lap,* padded silk jackets that are sold in the alleys of Central or (a better quality) in the various China Product stores. Another unusual item for rainy weather—or even as a decorative display—is a beautifully hand-painted Chinese umbrella, available at Chinese Arts & Crafts and other China Product stores for less than HK$30.

CARPETS AND RUGS

Although the craft of carpet making did not originate in China (it probably came from India or Persia via Tibet), the Chinese, over the past thousand years, have adapted and refined the art to create a particularly Chinese style of carpet, with some magnificent colors and designs. The all-wool, silky Tientsian carpets are the best, but Sinkiang and Shanghai carpets are also very fine. Practical qualities are high priorities among Chinese manufacturers, who claim that their pure wool carpets will not burn, will not flatten with use, and will not gather into wool particles. The carpets are highly resilient and durable, with a lifespan of 60 years and are said to grow brighter and smoother with use. Though prices have shot up recently, carpets are still cheaper in Hong Kong than they are in Europe and the United States. The *China Product* stores and *Chinese Arts & Crafts* give the best selection and price range. For locally made carpets, *Tai Ping Carpets* are highly regarded for both off-the-floor and custom-made carpets. The store takes four to six weeks to make specially ordered carpets, for which customers can specify certain thicknesses and even the direction of the weave. As the firm has its own dye house, matching colors is no problem. There is a showroom in Hutchison House, Central, Hong Kong, and the factory is at Lot 1637, Ting Kok Road, Tai Po, New Territories; (0)656–5161. Tai Ping's occasional sales are well worth attending; check in the classified section of the *South China Morning Post* for dates. *Sammy Lee & Wang's Co.* at Windsor Mansions, 29 Chatham Rd., Kowloon, is another good local manufacturer. It also has a large collection of Pao Tou rugs.

In Upper Wyndham Street, Central, you will find several shops selling Persian, Turkish, and Afghan rugs—another good buy in Hong Kong, though don't expect any miraculously low prices. *Oriental Carpet Trading,* 42 Wyndham St., is probably the best in the area. You could also try your luck at *Persian Carpets,* 30 Queen's Rd. Central, Hong Kong, and *Tribal Rugs Ltd.,* Unit 66, Admiralty Centre, Hong Kong.

FURNITURE

Home décor has boomed tremendously in Hong Kong in recent years and manufacturers of furniture and home furnishings have been quick to expand their activities. *Interiors,* 38 D'Aguilar St., and *Maitland-Smith,* 30 Hollywood Rd., both in Central, plus *Furniture Boutique,* 3 Tin Hau Temple Rd., Causeway Bay, stock imported and locally made goods, many with the Oriental touch in Western-style rosewood dining sets, cabinets, etc.

Lower down the price range, *Design 2000* in the Ocean Centre stocks a wide range of both imported and locally made furniture. Other good places for locally made rattan can be found along Queen's Road East in Wanchai. Another good bet is Stanley Market.

For really fine furniture buys in Hong Kong, take a look at the famous blackwood Chinese furniture. Most of the chairs, chests, and couches in varnished and lacquered redwoods stained black are the products of the late nineteenth century and early twentieth century, made by craftsmen in Canton. The blackening of the wood was thought to give it more of a dignified look, as well as to provide protection against humidity. There are a number of old-style shops specializing in blackwood furniture in the Western end of Hollywood Road, near Man Mo Temple. Blackwood furniture is just one of the many styles in Chinese furniture, however. Northern Chinese furniture, for instance, is blonde, fashioned in such woods as elm. *Ian MacLean's,* 73 Wyndham St., Central, has one of the best collections of northern provincial furniture in Hong Kong.

Reproductions are common, so supposedly "antique" furniture should be looked at carefully to ascertain its real age. Some points to look for include: a mature sheen on the wood; large gaps at the joints that have resulted from natural drying; the signs of hand craftsmanship, such as curved surfaces instead of straight lines on the backs, arms, and legs, and the uneven and varied diameters of arms and legs (the more precise the edges of shaped pieces are, the less likely they were carved by hand); signs of former restorations; and signs of gradual wear, especially at leg bottoms.

Blackwood, like other woods such as rosewood and teak, must be properly dried, seasoned, and aged to prevent future cracking in climates that are less humid than Hong Kong's. With rosewood items make sure that there are floating panels to allow for natural shrinkage and expansion. Rosewood furniture is a popular buy in Hong Kong. Queen's Road East, the great furniture retail and manufacturing area, offers everything from full rosewood dining sets in Ming style to dozens of different styles of rosewood end tables with a varying number of drawers and shelves in French or Chinese style. Custom-made orders are accepted in most of the shops on this street. Try *Winful Furniture & Curios,* 12–22 Queen's Rd. East, for some of the best custom-made furniture items. Rosewood furniture dealers, such as *Cathay Arts,* can also be found in the Ocean Terminal complex.

For carved camphorwood chests, Queen's Road East and nearby Wanchai Road are again the best places in Hong Kong, with Canton Road in Kowloon a close follow-up. The Chinese Products stores and Chinese Arts & Crafts also sell a good selection of made-in-China chests, screens, and tables.

Luk's Furniture in Gee Chang Hong Centre, Wong Chuk Hang Road, Aberdeen, is a bit off the beaten track, but offers a huge range of rosewood, teakwood, and lacquer furniture at warehouse prices.

TEA

If you wanted to buy a ton of tea, you could probably do so in Hong Kong's most famous tea area—Western district in Hong Kong Island. Down Queen's Road West and Des Voeux Road West you come across dozens of tea merchants and dealers, such as *Cheng Leung Wing*, 526 Queen's Rd. West, *Ying Kee*, 8 Wing Kut Street, Central, or *Cheong Hing Tea House*, 242 Queen's Rd. West. In this area, too, and in the back streets of Central, you can quench your thirst at a traditional tea stall serving tea from gleaming silver urns. In Kowloon there's the *Win Wa Tea Co. Ltd.*, 45–47 Kimberly Road. But for more leisurely savoring of this revered beverage, which dates back more than 2,000 years, stroll along Stanley Street in Central, where Hong Kong's greatest selection of teas are served in traditional teahouses. The beautiful *Luk Yu Teahouse* is the oldest and best known. Alternatively, try the *Wan Lai*, 484 Shanghai St., Yaumatei, Kowloon, for an experience of having *yam cha* (tea with small snacks, called *dimsum*) in the company of "birdwalkers" who come here with their caged singing birds after taking them for a morning walk.

You can buy packages or small 190-gram tins of Chinese tea in the tea shops of the Western district or, more conveniently, at the various China Product stores and leading supermarkets, such as Park 'n Shop. There is a choice of three types: green, or unfermented; black, or fermented; and oolong, semi-fermented; Various flavors include jasmine, chrysanthemum, rose, and narcissus. Loong Ching Green Tea and Jasmine Green Tea are among the most popular, available in attractive tins that carry the salubrious reminder of the tea's "remarkable effect in quenching thirst, arousing spirit, relieving fatigue, dispersing heat, helping the digestion, and cleansing the bowels."

KUNG-FU SUPPLIES

There are, of course, hundreds of kung-fu schools and supply shops in Hong Hong, especially in the areas of Mongkok, Yaumatei, and Wanchai, but often they are hidden away in back streets and up narrow stairways. The two most convenient places to buy your drum, cymbal, pair of leather boots, sword, whip, double dagger, stretcher cizer, studded wrist bracelet, Bruce Lee kempo gloves, and other kung-fu exotica are *Kung Fu Supplies Co.*, 188 Johnston Road, Wanchai, and *Shang Wu Kung Fu Appliance Centre*, 322A Excelsior Hotel Shopping Arcade, Causeway Bay, Hong Kong.

CAMERAS/LENSES/BINOCULARS

Many of Hong Kong's thousands of camera shops are clustered on Lock Road-lower Nathan Road area of Tsimshatsui and in the back streets of Central and Hennessy Road, Causeway Bay. But as with all such purchases, it pays to shop around rather than settle on the first shop you come to. Mark down prices on the shop's card so that you know where to return for the best buy. If you are interested in buying a number of different items in the shop (most also stock binoculars, calculators, radios, and other electronic gadgets) you may find you can bargain a good discount.

The most reliable places to shop for such items are at Hong Kong Tourist Association member shops (pick up its useful *Official Guide to Shopping, Eating Out & Services* at any of its information centers) and authorized dealers (check the sole agent for a list). These shops should give you a one-year worldwide guarantee, unlike most unauthorized dealers, which will have obtained their camera gear—quite legally—from sources (such as outlets in Japan) other than the official agent. So if you don't mind not having a guarantee (and good equipment should not break down in a year, anyway) you may pick up better bargains at such unauthorized shops.

OPTICAL GOODS

There is a surprising number of optical shops in Hong Kong, and some surprising bargains, too. Soft contact lenses, for instance, cost about HK$600, hard lenses HK$300 or so; and frames for glasses go for as little as HK$65. All the latest styles and best quality frames, such as Yves St. Laurent, Rodenstock, Bausch & Lomb, and Christian Dior, are available at leading optical shops, at prices generally much lower than they are in the United States and Europe. *The Optical Shop* (branches throughout Hong Kong) is the fanciest and probably the most reliable store.

If you want lenses made as well, it is advisable to have your prescription with you, since opticians in Hong Kong do not have to be licensed and may not give as good a test as you will get at home. (This situation may soon change, as the Hong Kong Government is now drafting legislation requiring opticians to be licensed.)

HI-FIs, STEREOS AND TAPE RECORDERS

Hennessy Road in Causeway Bay has long been the mecca for people seeking hi-fi gear, although many of the small shops in Central's Queen Victoria Street and Stanley Street and in Tsimshatsui's Nathan Road offer a similar variety of goods. Be sure to compare prices before buying, as they can vary widely. Also make sure that guarantees are worldwide and applicable in your home town or country. It helps, too, if you know exactly what you want, since most shops don't have the room or inclination to give you the chance for testing, listening, and comparing. However, if you do want to hear the equipment before plonking down your credit card or travelers' checks, some of the major makers do have individual showrooms. The hi-fi shop will be able to direct you. Another tip: though most of the export gear sold in Hong Kong has fuses or dual wiring so it can be used in any country with any voltage, it does pay to double check.

Televisions and Video Recorders. Hong Kong uses the PAL system, as does Britain, Australia, and most other countries in Europe except France and Russia, which use the Seacam system. In the United States, the color system is NTSC. Therefore, make certain your purchase matches the equipment sold in your country. (It is not as difficult as it sounds: just tell the shopkeepers where you want to take your system and they'll make certain you get the right model.) But again, make certain before you walk out the door. (See H.K.T.A. brochure *Shopping Guide to Video Equipment.*)

COMPUTERS AND PERIPHERAL DEVICES

All of the big names—Apple, Sinclair, Osbourne, IBM, BBC/Acorn—sell in Hong Kong. Whether the equipment is any cheaper or not in Hong Kong is a moot point. If you are going to buy, make sure the machines will work on the voltage in your country—an IBM personal computer sold in Hong Kong will work on 220 volts, while the identical machine in the United States will work on 110 volts. Servicing is a major concern, too.

The real bargains in computers and their peripheral devices are the locally made versions of the most popular brands. But be warned: even though the bargains are superb when compared to U.S. or European prices, you may have trouble getting your Hong Kong computer past customs on your return.

The *Asia Computer Plaza* in Silvercord, Canton Road, has 40,000 square feet devoted solely to anything connected with computers. Most of the big names have outlets there. There are also three shopping centers in which dozens of small computer shops offering just about everything are crammed. On Hong Kong Island, the most accessible of the two is the *Ocean Shopping Arcade* at 140 Wanchai Road or Hong Kong Computer Centre, 54 Lockhart Rd. The *Golden Shopping Centre* in Shamshuipo (Kowloon) is more difficult to reach, so it is best to take the MTR to Shamshuipo Station and leave by the Fuk Wah Street exit. The shopping center is just across the street.

ELECTRONIC GIMMICKS AND GADGETS

For those electronic devices that shoppers just love to bring home, the *Special Interest Electronic Co.,* Hutchison House, 10 Harcourt Road, Central, has hundreds of strange and no-so-strange items.

 RESTAURANTS. It is almost impossible to write about restaurants in Hong Kong without lapsing into clichés. But most of the clichés are accurate. Hong Kong *is* the place where East meets West. Expatriate clubs are located cheek-by-jowl with noodle stalls. And Hong Kong is still the gastronomic capital of the Orient, although these days many of the great Chinese chefs have been lured away to San Francisco, New York, and London.

Restaurants and eating out play a vital part in the day-to-day life of Hong Kong. Chinese tradition dictates that one entertains in a restaurant rather than in the home, which is just as well, because most Chinese families living in Hong Kong's over-crowded apartment blocks have neither the space nor the facilities for the latter.

The statistics are amazing. The Yellow Pages of the Hong Kong telephone directory list more than 4,000 restaurants. This means you could eat out every night for eleven years and not go back to the same place twice. And in Hong Kong, you *could* eat out every night, because restaurants hardly ever close for Sundays or public holidays, except maybe for the first three days of Chinese New Year (a movable feast, which falls from the middle of January to early March).

Not all restaurants are listed in the Yellow Pages, which means that at a conservative estimate there may be another 1,000 down-market operations to explore. With a population of just over five million, Hong Kong therefore supports a staggering ratio of one restaurant for every 1,000 people!

Before you set out to eat, it might pay you to get a copy of the Hong Kong Tourist Association's *Hong Kong: The Great Eating Adventure.*

Apart from lavish Chinese banquets and *deluxe* Western restaurants, eating out in Hong Kong is a very informal affair. You can count on your fingers the number of establishments with a dress code of any sort, and although it may be wiser to do so, booking is not essential except at the most popular venues. Even so, no one minds if you hang around waiting for a table and it is accepted practice to wait behind the chairs of diners who are about to settle up and leave. Chinese people do not linger at the end of the meal as Westerners do, so do not feel put out by this habit.

Although there are certain points of etiquette involved in eating Chinese food, Westerners are not expected to know what these are, and no one will watch to see whether you handle your chopsticks with aplomb or listen to see if you slurp your soup. In fact, soup-slurping is *de rigueur.*

Most Chinese restaurants and many of the Western ones in Hong Kong welcome children and provide high chairs for babies and toddlers. You won't be expected to order a full meal for a child, and the staff will not take it amiss if you simply ask for an extra plate so your child can share your food. Hong Kong's younger visitors will be treated with a kindness and consideration they will be unlikely to receive back home. Even spilt drinks or dropped chopsticks are treated with friendly tolerance.

Eating out in Hong Kong is generally cheaper than it is in Japan or in the West. Our price categories are necessarily general, and prices will, of course, vary with the items you order. Obviously, Beluga caviar or a rare game dish might well push a meal from one price bracket into the next, but just to give you an idea of what you might expect to pay per person for food only, here is our rule-of-thumb guide. *Deluxe:* HK$300 and up; *Expensive:* HK$150 to HK$300; *Moderate:* HK$100 to HK$150; *Inexpensive:* HK$100 or less. You will see that there is a gratifyingly large number of restaurants in this last category.

In most Hong Kong restaurants, a 10-percent service charge will be added to your bill, and you will not be expected to leave an additional tip. However, when your change is brought to you on a tray, it is customary to leave the small change and take only the notes and HK$5 pieces. In the few establishments listed where there is no service charge, we have said so. Tip 10 percent under these conditions.

Although the major credit cards are widely accepted, many smaller establishments accept no cards at all. Do not assume that a restaurant will take your card unless you have checked it out. It is fair to say that more and more restaurants are taking more and more cards, but Chinese people are generally happier to deal in cash than with any sort of credit arrangement. As elsewhere, all first class hotels in Hong Kong take all major credit cards. These are the abbreviations we have used for credit cards: AE, American Express; CB, Carte Blanche; DC, Diners Club; MC, MasterCard; V, Visa; OTB, Overseas Trust Bank. In our notations, "No CB," for example, means that the restaurant will take all of the other cards except Carte Blanche.

Dimsum. Most larger Cantonese restaurants serve *dimsum,* the very tasty morsels that appear only from morning to mid-afternoon. The Hong Kong Tourist Association publishes an excellent leaflet, with pictures, to tell you what's what. The staff in these restaurants pushes trolleys around, calling out the names of the dishes and you just point to what you want. Some dishes, such as congealed blood and various giblets, are rather esoteric, but others, such as steamed pork buns or spring rolls, are readily acceptable to anyone.

Dimsum restaurants are always busy at lunch times, and reservations are not taken. Try to go as part of a group, and get there early. Be prepared to shout to make yourself heard above the cheerful chatter of your neighbors. When you arrive and place your first order, the trolley pusher will stamp your bill, and at the end of the meal the final reckoning will be made. Alternatively, if all dishes are the same price, as they often are, the number of plates on the table will indicate the total cost. Whichever way the bill is tallied, it will be modest.

Buffets and Bargains. Buffet meals seem to be gaining in popularity in Hong Kong. Buffets usually comprise a wide variety of hot and cold Western dishes and salads, standard Chinese dishes, curries, desserts, fruit, and cheese. There is usually a special price for children under the age of 12, about one third or one quarter less than the adult price.

A good way to eat at some of Hong Kong's best Western food outlets without breaking the bank is to go for the business lunch most of them offer. It usually consists of two or three courses, with choices, coffee or tea, and sometimes a glass of wine thrown in for good measure.

In Chinese restaurants, always check the prices of fresh fish, prawn, crab, and lobster dishes, particularly if a typhoon has been lurking in the area. Scarcity drives prices up at certain times of year, and fish prices are always higher after a typhoon because the fishermen are unable to leave harbor. Prices of local vegetables also rise after a typhoon, but this is not as likely to affect the restaurant diner.

In Chinese restaurants, game and other seasonal specials are seldom translated into English. Try to get the waiter to explain what they are, or better still, eat with a Chinese friend who can translate. Hong Kong's Chinese restaurants feature cuisines from every corner of China. For ease of understanding, we have grouped them into the six main categories: Cantonese, Hangchow, Shanghainese, Pekingese, Chiu Chow, and Szechuanese. Cantonese food comes from China's southernmost province, from where most of Hong Kong's population also hails, so naturally Cantonese restaurants are by far the most numerous.

If your only taste of Chinese food to date has been the fare at the neighborhood takeout, you have a surprise in store, and it should be a pleasant one. Try at least one new dish with each meal.

Street stalls are usually a good bet. It's unusual for anyone to suffer a stomach upset eating at Hong Kong's food stalls, as food tends to be cooked very quickly at very high temperatures. Noodle soup is always good, especially when topped by chicken or duck or Chinese sausage, but *congee,* a rice soup with finely chopped bits of meat or fish, might not be to Western tastes. *Pak choi* and *choi sum* are local green vegetables that make an excellent accompaniment for your main dish, and they are usually served in an oyster sauce, cooked *al dente* so you can really taste them.

Hong Kong has a substantial Indian population, which supports a string of Indian restaurants that range from the basic to the plush. With one vegetarian exception, they tend to specialize in north Indian fare, and tandooris figure prominently on menus.

Naturally, cuisines from neighboring countries within the region are also well represented: Japanese, which is always expensive, Korean, Thai, Burmese, Malaysian, Indonesian, Sri Lankan, Vietnamese, and Filipino.

Of western cuisines, French tends to dominate, despite the fact that most Hong Kong hoteliers are Swiss or Austrian. Italy is also strongly represented, and so, for some reason, is Mexican. This last phenomenon is recent, and spontaneous combustion seems to be the only explanation for four Mexican restaurants hitting a market where hitherto there was only one. Australian, Dutch, German, Hungarian, Jewish, Mediterranean, Middle Eastern, Scandinavian and Swiss foods are all represented, though sparsely. Hong Kong has only one Spanish restaurant, and the Filipino and Mexican restaurants serve some Spanish dishes, as does the Mediterranean restaurant; the Middle East is poorly represented, too, with two restaurants.

Nevertheless, variety is still the spice of life in Hong Kong. As well as the above national listings, we have listed coffee shops, grill rooms, and a number of other venues serving what could only be described as international fare.

Other fast indigenous foods are skewers of charcoal broiled *satay, won ton mee* (noodle soup), and fried and battered eggplant, green pepper, bean curd, octopus, and squid. Find a seller whose oil smells fresh.

The areas for street stalls are numerous. The Poor Man's Night Club (night market) in front of the Shun Tak Centre is the most obvious choice. The area also has more sophisticated operations, where you can actually sit down and eat clams, whelks, mussels, prawns, and crabs. In the winter, snake soup is a local favorite. It's supposed to be particularly fortifying against the cold north wind.

In Wanchai, Tonnochy Road and Marsh Road are established street-stall areas. As well as the sit-down operations, you'll find hawkers selling sweet soups and waffles that exude tantalizing smells.

On Kowloon side, the night markets on the west of Nathan Road near Jordan Road ferry pier are happy hunting grounds for adventurous eaters in search of broiled cuttlefish or plates of wok-fried noodles.

Our listings start with a section on Chinese restaurants, beginning with Cantonese and moving on, in alphabetical order, to Chiu Chow, Hangchow, Peking, Shanghai, Szechuanese. Then come the listings of other international cuisines, in alphabetical order, followed by coffee shops, grill rooms, international places, steakhouses, and vegetarian restaurants. Next come sections on pub food and offbeat eating. Within sections, you'll find the most expensive restaurants listed first, and within price brackets they are listed in alphabetical order.

A word about the décor of the average Chinese eatery. Though many are absolutely opulent, it does not follow that the food in these highly decorated palaces is good. Many, many of the best restaurants are basic—formica tables, neon lights, the odd picture or calendar on the plain or even slightly scruffy wall—and crowded. Their kitchens, which you will no doubt spot on the way to the toilet, may be downright rudimentary, to use polite terminology. But don't be put off. Some of the best meals in Asia, perhaps even the world, are served in this type of surroundings.

CANTONESE

Expensive

The Chinese Restaurant. Hyatt-Regency Hotel, 67 Nathan Rd., Tsimshatsui, Kowloon; (3)662321. One of the classiest restaurants in town, with *dimsum* rivaling that of the Regent (which is saying something), good seafood, fine poultry, and an elegant atmosphere. Open 11:00 A.M. to 3:00 P.M. 7:00 to 11:00 P.M. All major credit cards.

The Eagle's Nest. The Hilton Hotel, 2 Queen's Rd., Central, Hong Kong; (5)233111. This aptly named elegant venue on the 25th floor of the hotel offers spectacular views on three sides. Nor is the food upstaged by the scenery. One of the few places in Hong Kong where you can mix styles of Chinese cuisine. Superb Cantonese food as well as other classical Chinese dishes, such as Peking or Szechuan duck, beggar's or Shantung chicken. Smaller portions for single diners. *Dimsum* for lunch. For dinner, try the "unlimited dish special," virtually as much as you can eat for HK$195 per person plus service. Live music, dancing in the evenings. Open noon to 3:00 P.M., 7:00 P.M. to 1:00 A.M. All major credit cards.

Flower Lounge. Royal Garden Hotel, Mody Road, East Tsimshatsui, Kowloon; (3)722–1592; also at 441 Lockhart Rd., Wanchai, Hong Kong; (5)772212; 3 Peace Ave. (off Waterloo Road), Mongkok, Kowloon; (3)715–6557. The interiors at the Royal Garden are in a class of their own, and those of this basement restaurant are no exception. A Chinese pavilion set in a miniature lake and reached across a little bridge serves *dimsum* and inexpensive Cantonese specialties up through the price range to game and fish dishes. Open 11:00 A.M. to midnight. No CB.

Fook Lam Moon. 459 Lockhart Rd., Hong Kong; (5)772567; 31 Mody Rd., Tsimshatsui, Kowloon; (3)688755. Typical, conservative, up-market Cantonese restaurant with more emphasis on food than on décor. Don't be put off by the obscene-looking tanks of whelks outside. They're a great delicacy and a restaurant specialty. Other recommended dishes are tender sautéed frogs' legs and slightly gamey roast pigeon. Open noon to 11:00 P.M. V, MC, AE, OTB.

Shang Palace. Shangri-La Hotel, 64 Mody Rd., East Tsimshatsui, Kowloon; (3)721–2111. Palace is the operative word. A luxury restaurant, lavishly decorated in red and gold, with traditional motifs imported from Mainland China. Sweet and spicy barbecued meats and shark's fin soups in all their varieties are the specialties. *Dimsum* and special lunch menu from noon to 3:00 P.M., 11:00 A.M. to 3:00 P.M. Sundays and and public holidays; dinner from 7:00 P.M. to 11:30 P.M., when there are personalized matches and red roses for ladies. All major credit cards.

Spring Moon Chinese Restaurant. The Peninsula Hotel, Salisbury Rd., Tsimshatsui, Kowloon; (3)739–2332. A very chic Chinese restaurant, as befitting the Peninsula. Elegantly basketed *dimsum* with honest originality (chive dumplings), as well as the usuals. The à la carte menu has wonderful sautéed prawns and beef rolls with golden mushrooms. All is prepared perfectly. All major credit cards.

Sun Tung Lok Shark's Fin Restaurant. Ground floor, Phase 3, Harbour City, Canton Road, Tsimshatsui, Kowloon; (3)722–0288; 137 Connaught Rd. West, Hong Kong; (5)462718; 39 Mody Rd., Tsimshatsui, Kowloon; (3)670806. The latest of a short chain of lavish restaurants specializing in seafood. Choose your quality of shark's fin (premium, superior, superlative, or supreme) according to taste or bank balance. Other rare delicacies include double-boiled deer penis, five kinds of snake with chrysanthemum petals, and braised conpoy with garlic and sea moss. (Don't be put off, they have regular Cantonese food, too!) From noon to midnight. DC,V.

Luk Yu Tea House. 24 Stanley St., Central, Hong Kong; (5)235463. Time has virtually stood still at this traditional Chinese tea house tucked away on a narrow street parallel to Queen's Road. The wooden ceiling fans, vast wall mirrors, and brass spittoons haven't changed since World War II. No doubt many of the regulars date back just as far. Service for Westerners can be offhand, so find a Chinese friend to bring you here. Tea and some of Hong Kong's best *dimsum* starts at 7:00 A.M. Later in the day, try the mouth-watering baked chicken with ginger and scallions or bamboo shoots with shrimps. Open until 10:00 P.M. No credit cards.

Man Wah. The Mandarin, Connaught Road, Central, Hong Kong; (5)220111. Very restrained décor for a Chinese restaurant, and a lack of ostentation characterizes the Man Wah's food. There's only one grade of bird's nest, for example, and at HK$100 for a bowl of soup, it has to be the best. On the other hand, a party of six to eight people could eat very well for around HK$200 per head, provided they avoided bird's nest and shark's fin. Open noon to 3:00 P.M., 6:30 P.M. to 11:00 P.M. All major credit cards.

Sunning Unicorn. 1 Sunning Rd., Happy Valley, Hong Kong; (5)776620. An interesting counterpoint of East and West. The décor is undeniably Western, and not bad at that, and although the majority of the clientele is local, the food is tailored toward Western taste. Still, the fish dishes are particularly good, and it's all very civilized. Open noon to midnight. V,AE, MC, OTB.

Moderate

Boil and Boil Wonderful. Food Street, Causeway Bay, Hong Kong; (5) 779788. The extraordinary name indicates that the restaurant specializes in Cantonese casserole cooking, a type of fare traditionally reserved for winter months. Reckon on one casserole per person, and try a variety of fish, meat, and vegetables. More conservative Cantonese fare is also available. European wine list, traditional décor. Lunch and dinner daily; reservations advisable for both. Open 11:00 A.M. to midnight. No CB.

East Ocean Seafood. East Ocean Centre, 98 Granville Rd., East Tsimshatsui, Kowloon; (3)723–8128. Yet another new restaurant in this newest area of Hong Kong. Up-market décor and such classics as shark's fin soup and abalone. Open 11:00 A.M. to midnight. V, AE, MC.

Fat Siu Lau Seafood. Third floor, Houston Centre, Mody Road, East Tsimshatsui, Kowloon; (3)686291. As the name implies, seafood, and in particular, the baked stuffed whelks, is the thing to go for here. Open 11:30 A.M. to midnight. All major credit cards.

Floating Restaurants (Aberdeen). There are three—The Jumbo, (5)539111; the Sea Palace, (5)527340; and Tai Pak, (5)525933—and collectively they are one of the territory's most famous landmarks. And they all have the ability to serve superb and fresh Cantonese seafood. That's the good news. The bad news is that the waiters and captains, for the most part, seem to be an intolerant and rude bunch, intent on making life as difficult as possible for the visitor who does not speak Cantonese or read Chinese. The Jumbo is the largest, as the name implies, and is probably the most famous, in spite of being the youngest of the three. It seems to be the main destination of the harbor cruises intent on pressuring the guests to stay on for an awful set meal. We'd skip the experience, but if you feel you have to try one of the restaurants because they are so famous (infamous), try to go with a friend. Failing that, do not let them stick you upstairs (eat with the Chinese fishermen and businessmen downstairs). Be tough and hang in there and it will eventually work out. Oh yes, be certain to check all the prices beforehand, particularly those marked "seasonal." *Dimsum* is available at lunch. Open 7:00 A.M. to 11:00 P.M. All major credit cards.

King Bun. 158 Queen's Rd., Central, Hong Kong; (5)430300. Opinions vary as to which is the best Cantonese restaurant in Hong Kong, but King Bun is high on most people's lists. It is reputed to be the only place to eschew M.S.G., apart from other considerations. Specialties change with the season, but game and fish, killed minutes before they get to the table, are taste sensations. Sand-pot mutton casserole is available year-round at a more modest price, depending on the number of diners. *Dimsum.* Open 7:30 A.M. to 11:00 P.M. AE.

Lychee Village. 9–11A Cameron Rd., Tsimshatsui, Kowloon; (3)685907; also at 15D Wellington St., Central, Hong Kong; (5)245613. A rare combination of a Cantonese restaurant that serves excellent food in surroundings that don't make you wonder a little uneasily what the kitchen's like. Casseroles and soups are both good; ask about seasonal specialties. Open 8:00 A.M. to midnight. AE, V.

Maxim's Palace. World Trade Centre (adjacent to the Excelsior Hotel) Causeway Bay; (5)760288; A former convention center that looks like one, with wall-to-wall carpet and stackable chairs. Food is mostly Cantonese, although famous dishes from other cuisines, such as beggar's chicken and Peking duck, are included. A bland place in most respects, but convenient. *Dimsum* from 8:00 A.M. to 6:00 P.M., dinner from 6:00 P.M. to midnight. All major credit cards.

Orchid Garden. 37 Hankow Rd., Tsimshatsui, Kowloon; (3)682970; Once a contender for the title of best Cantonese restaurant, this one holds the distinction of being relatively sympathetic toward novices. Waiters will even provide forks upon request, but an impressive number of Chinese banquets testifies to its authenticity. Groups of two and four should avoid banquet food and go for humbler, tasty stuff, such as chicken in a paper bag, fried cuttlefish with vegetables, and double-boiled soups, or *dimsum* at lunch. Open 8:00 A.M. to midnight. No credit cards. **Orchid Village.** 341 Lockhart Rd., Hong Kong; (5)756891 (called Orchid Village; same company, different name).

Patek. 2–4 Kingston St., Causeway Bay, Hong Kong; (5)790–5060. A clean, carpeted restaurant, where winter time is snake time. If the thought does not appeal, try deep-fried snake with bamboo shoots. The rest of the year, the menu is more conventional. Most would find pan-fried minced pigeon with lettuce leaves more than acceptable, and the double-boiled black mushroom soup has a biting but not unpleasant flavor. Open 7:30 A.M. to midnight. V, MC, AE, OTB.

Regal Seafood Restaurant. Hotel Regal Meridien Hong Kong, Mody Road, East Tsimshatsui, Kowloon; (3)722–1818. Like all up-market Cantonese restaurants, this one is difficult to classify for price because it depends on the quality of shark's fin or abalone you choose. This restaurant does three grades of each, as well as bird's nest, pigeon, conpoy, fish maws, and frogs. Waiters will walk novices through the meal, but seafood and various soups rarely fail to please, with the exception of abalone. Chinese adore it, most Westerners abhor it. Hotpots of seasonal game are out of this world. Open 9:00 A.M. to midnight. All major credit cards.

South Villa Restaurant. 58 Cameron Rd., Kowloon; (3)721–5431. Conveniently situated for East Tsimshatsui hotels, South Villa caters to tourists and locals alike. Seasonal dishes are the ones to go for, although shark's fin, bird's nest, abalone, and minced pigeon are available year round. Chinese décor both inside and out. Clever use of screens evokes intimacy without totally obscuring the view. Open 11:00 A.M. to midnight daily. AE,V, MC, OTB.

Unicorn. 11 Kingston St., Causeway Bay, Hong Kong; (5)779117. Adjacent to Food Street. Elegant backdrop to some unusual Cantonese dishes, such as lamb hotpot, frogs legs fried in an almond batter, and stuffed bean curd. Open 11:30 A.M. to midnight, with *dimsum* to 6:00 P.M. AE, V, DC, OTB.

Yaik Sang. 454 Lockhart Rd., Causeway Bay, Hong Kong; (5)766211. Famed for its much-imitated lemon chicken, Yaik Sang produces a number of other truly excellent dishes. Soyed pigeon, baked chicken in salt, and sautéed lobster are both carefully cooked and presented, and will appeal to Western as well as to Chinese palates. V, OTB.

Yung Kee. 32 Wellington St., Central, Hong Kong; (5)232343. Yung Kee has never quite recovered from the shock of being included in *Fortune's* top-ten restaurants in the world a couple of decades ago, but it's still well worth a visit. This is the place to try 1,000-year-old eggs with pickled ginger, and the roast goose is justly famed. Walnut cookies are a nice change from sweet soups for dessert. Open 11:00 A.M. to midnight. AE, DC, V.

Moderate to Inexpensive

Jade Garden. 53 Paterson St., Causeway Bay, Hong Kong; (5)258246; also at fourth floor, Star House, Salisbury Road, Kowloon; (3)661326; and many other branches on both sides of the harbor. A consistently reliable restaurant chain that can cope with foreigners. Small parties of one, two, or three can get small portions so they can try a variety of dishes. Beggar's chicken must be ordered ahead, but it's worth the trouble. Open 11:30 A.M. to 11:30 P.M. All major credit cards.

Inexpensive

Fung Shing. 28 Irving St. (one street back from Yee Wo Street and parallel to it), Causeway Bay, Hong Kong; (5)762345. Truly gourmet food in this unlikely little restaurant, with dishes you don't find everywhere. For instance, *gum chen gi* (gold coin chicken) and chicken livers skewered between bits of pork fat and roasted. Even *chow fan* (fried rice) is something special here. Open noon to 11:00 P.M. Booking advisable. Service not included. No credit cards.

Lamma Hilton. (Also known as **Shum Kee Seafood Restaurant**) 26 First St., Sok Kwu Wan, Lamma Island; (5)982–0241. Take a three-decker ferry from Central or a smaller *kai do* (local ferry) from Aberdeen to Sok Kwu Wan. Turn right and walk past other restaurants until you come to a large orange awning. (There is a sign, too.) Try baked crab in ginger sauce or salted prawns, for a fraction of their price back home. The Lamma Hilton is actually no better nor worse than other Sok Kwu Wan restaurants lining the quay, but it's the one foreigners head for. The menu includes just four meat dishes. Reservations advisable on summer evenings. Wine available, or B.Y.O.B. (no corkage). No credit cards.

Peak Café. 121 Peak Rd., Hong Kong; (5)96168. The Peak Café, directly over the road from the top station of the Peak Tram, looks more like a Swiss chalet than a Cantonese restaurant. The food isn't anything to write home about, but a tray of Hainan chicken with rice, soup, and glass of tea, taken on the terrace with views of Aberdeen and the islands, is a bargain nevertheless. Open 11:00 A.M. to 11:00 P.M. No credit cards.

Pearl City Restaurant. 36 Paterson St., Causeway Bay, Hong Kong; (5)-778226. A Cantonese restaurant (and nightclub at night), Pearl City is a good place for the visitor to try *dimsum,* as the waiters here speak English. Roasts are available, as well as the traditional steamed or fried *dimsum,* and the contrast in textures may well be appreciated by non-Chinese. Dimsum until 5:00 P.M. daily. Regular Cantonese menu and floor show nightly. No credit cards.

Tung Hing. 41 Praya Road, Cheung Chau Island; (5)981–0412. One of the best waterfront restaurants. Fun at 4:00 A.M., when the fishermen dine on dimsum. Convenient for lunch or dinner. Marvelous lemon duck, chicken with black bean sauce, and luscious fresh prawns. Open 4 A.M.–11 P.M. No credit cards.

CHIU CHOW

Moderate

Carrianna Chiu Chow. First floor, Carrian Centre, 151 Gloucester Rd., Wanchai, Hong Kong; (5)741282. Smart, modern Chinese surroundings and good value Chiu Chow dishes, such as roast goose or fried pomfret in black bean sauce, washed down with the strong and bitter "Iron Goddess" tea. Well patronized at lunch times. Open 11:00 A.M. to 11:30 P.M. No CB.

Chiuchow Garden. Second floor, Tsimshatsui Centre, Salisbury Road, Kowloon; (3)687266. Seasonal specials printed in Chinese only, so consult the waiters for help—they won't mind at all. Standard Chiu Chow menu, plus imaginative soup dishes. Open 11:30 A.M. to midnight. No CB.

Siam Bird's Nest. 55 Paterson St., Causeway Bay, Hong Kong; (5)775436. Only the bird's nests come from Thailand, where the owner, so legend has it, rents a mountain from the government for the sake of the nests the swallows build there. Try bird's nest in soup, either savory or sweet, or with mashed chicken. Highly nutritious. Open 11:30 P.M. to 1:00 A.M. No credit cards.

Universal. 249 Des Voeux Rd., Central, Hong Kong; (5)452182. Ornate, Chinese-style eating house serving gutsy Chiu Chow food to locals. Minced pigeon with ham and lettuce leaves is a favorite, as is fried chicken with chinjew sauce. Open 11:30 A.M. to 11:30 P.M. OTB, V.

Inexpensive

Golden Red Chiu Chow Restaurant. 13 Prat Ave., Tsimshatsui, Kowloon; (3)666822. Off Chatham Road. Down-market décor, but good food. Start with a Fried Four Delicious Combination (prawns, spring rolls, shrimp ball, and sea blubber). After that, do your own thing. Prices permit experimentation. Open 11:00 A.M. to 4:00 A.M. No credit cards.

Pak Lok Chiu Chow. 23–25 Hysan Ave., Hong Kong; (5)768886. Around the corner from the Lee Gardens Hotel. Large whelks in a tank outside lure or repel the diner (check the price before you order them). Other items are entirely reasonable. Open 11:00 A.M. to 2:00 A.M. No credit cards.

HANGCHOW

Expensive

Tien Heung Lau. 18C Austin Ave., Tsimshatsui, Kowloon; (3)662414. Reputedly, this is Hong Kong's only restaurant with this type of cuisine. The *piece de résistance* here is begger's chicken, which can be obtained in other restaurants—but this is probably the best in town. This dish should be ordered the day before or no later than the early morning of planned evening meal. Other Hangchow dishes include smoked duck, a special sweet-and-sour fish, and the restaurant's famed fried shrimps with tea leaves. Excellent tea and wine also come from this region. Open noon to 2:30 P.M., 6:00 P.M. to 10:30 P.M. No CB.

PEKING/MONGOLIAN

Moderate

Genghis Khan Mongolian Grill. 20 Luard Road, Wanchai, Hong Kong; (5)282212. The do-it-yourself attitude prevails as you prepare your own seafood, meat, and vegetables. The Peking menu has some excellent choices too. Open noon to 3:00 P.M. and 6:00 P.M. to midnight. All major credit cards.

Ocean City Peking Restaurant. New World Centre, Salisbury Road, Tsimshatsui, Kowloon; (3)722–5500. The fact that this is part of such a massive food complex might put some people off, but the food does not seem to suffer from the size of the operation. The menu is catholic, with beggar's chicken and Szechuan bean curd served alongside Peking duck. Surroundings are comfortable but noisy, and the staff is helpful. Open 11:00 A.M. to midnight, Monday through Saturday, 10:00 A.M. to midnight, Sundays and public holidays. No CB.

Peking Garden. Excelsior Hotel Arcade, Causeway Bay, Hong Kong; (5)777–231; also at Alexandra House, Chater Road, Central, Hong Kong; (5) 266456; Star House, Salisbury Road, Kowloon; (3)686863; Empire Centre, Mody Road, Tsimshatsui East, Kowloon; (3)721–8868. Owned by a chain that never skimps on the Oriental décor, with a noodle maker who exhibits his dexterity every evening. The food is unremarkable, except for snake soup in winter (don't ask whether it's fresh), but the place is good at helping strangers conquer a menu. Open 11:30 A.M. to midnight, Monday through Saturday, 10:30 A.M. to midnight Sundays and public holidays. No CB.

Inexpensive

American. 23 Lockhart Rd., Hong Kong; (5)277277. This isn't actually one of the restaurants famed for its Peking duck, although it is available and popular with foreigners. Instead, try sizzling beef served on a hot, iron platter, prawns with chilli sauce, and paper-wrapped chicken. In winter (November through April), Mongolian hotpot, slivers of meat and fish in stock, is the specialty. Open 11:00 A.M. to midnight. No credit cards.

Mongolian Barbecue. 58 Leighton Rd., Happy Valley, Hong Kong; (5)761986. Everyone loves a Mongolian barbecue. Order a selection of meat, fish, and vegetables, and grill your own assortment with sesame oil. Push the cooked concoction into a hollow sesame seed roll and munch away. The waiters are helpful to first timers, and there are alternative dishes (but no one ever orders them). Reservations advisable. Open 11:00 A.M. to midnight. No credit cards.

North China Restaurant. 7 Hart Ave., Tsimshatsui, Kowloon; (3)668239. English-speaking waiters here, as 35 percent of the clientele are tourists. Typical Peking menu. Try fried smoked chicken, cabbage and ham soup, minced beef with pickled cabbage, and Peking Duck. Open 11:00 A.M. to 11:00 P.M. No CB.

Pine and Bamboo. (a.k.a. Chung Chuk Lau) 30 Leighton Rd., Happy Valley, Hong Kong; (5)772859; also at 13 Sai Yeung Choi St., Mongkok, Kowloon; (3)947195. In winter (November to April), this is the place for Mongolian hotpot, a cook-it-yourself feast of slivers of meat, fish, and vegetables, which are immersed in a central pot of steaming stock. In summer, try stuffed pancakes, yellow fish in white wine, and prawns in chilli sauce. Open noon to 11:30 P.M. No service added. No credit cards.

Spring Deer. 42 Mody Rd., Tsimshatsui, Kowloon; (3)664012. Hong Kong residents tend to think Spring Deer when they think Peking duck, but the restaurant also specializes in handmade noodles and produces superb steamed dumplings with pork. Crispy toffee bananas round out the meal. Open 11:00 A.M. to 11:00 P.M. V only.

SHANGHAI

Moderate

Sanno. 3 Cornwall Ave., Tsimshatsui, Kowloon; (3)671421. Unpretentious, but comfortable, with tablecloths and air conditioning. Nibble soyed spiced beef with peanuts and pickled cabbage, and don't miss out on buns-in-a-bite. In autumn, live fresh-water "hairy" crabs are declared to be "plumpy in roe, tender in meat, rich in nutrition, delicious in taste." What more could anyone want? Open 11:00 A.M. to 11:30 P.M. No credit cards.

Inexpensive

Great Shanghai. 26 Prat Ave. (off Chatham Road), Tsimshatsui, Kowloon; (3)668158. Gourmets declare this to be *the* place to eat eels, particularly sautéed in garlic or braised with bamboo shoots. But not everyone can cope with wriggling live shrimps that have to be peeled and dipped in bean sauce. Open 11:00 A.M. to midnight. AE,V.

Shanghai Yat Pan Hong. 38 Kimberley New St., Tsimshatsui, Kowloon; (3)678452. A favorite with local Shanghainese businessmen who come for a taste of old Shanghai. Don't miss the special steamed bread or the aromatic smoked fish. Between October and December, try the freshwater "hairy" crabs—pricey, but a much-rated delicacy. Open noon to 4:00 A.M. No credit cards.

SZECHUAN

Expensive

Lotus Pond. Harbour City, Canton Road, Tsimshatsui, Kowloon; (3)724–1088. A luxury restaurant with food as good as the prices. The atmosphere is very classy, complete with silk-bound menus. Diced chicken with garlic and smoked pigeon. Open 11:00 A.M. to midnight. All credit cards.

Prince Court. Shop 115, Sutton Court, Harbour City, 21 Canton Road, Tsimshatsui, Kowloon; (3)668939. The only *nouvelle cuisine seu-tchouanaise,* with very original recipes. Not as spicy as most Szechuan restaurants, but the original confections of meat and fruits together are an indication of the future. Open 11:00 A.M. to midnight. All major credit cards.

Sichuan Garden. Third floor, The Landmark, Central, Hong Kong; (5)214433. A bright, clean, very professional operation, as you'd expect in this prime location. Good food, but not outstanding, with the exception of the smoked duck. Very busy at lunch time. Open 11:30 A.M. to 3:00 P.M., 6:00 P.M. to midnight. All major credit cards.

Moderate

Cleveland Szechuen. 6 Cleveland St., Causeway Bay, Hong Kong; (5)763876. This restaurant's excellent reputation is founded on two Szechuan specialties—smoked duck and king prawns with chilli and garlic sauce. Business is almost always brisk. Open 11:00 A.M. to midnight. AE, V, DC, OTB.

Pep 'n Chilli. 12–22 Blue Pool Rd., Happy Valley, Hong Kong; (5)738251. A restaurant cannot live by tourists alone, although rumor had it that when this restaurant opened in 1981, it was trying to do just that. It's found favor with sufficient locals to stay in business, with sophisticated interiors and waiters who'll walk you through the menu. A must is spiced beef with kumquat (tangerines), and Westerners like to finish with toffee apples or toffee bananas. Open for lunch and dinner daily, reservations recommended for dinner. All major credit cards.

Red Pepper. 7 Lan Fong Rd., Causeway Bay, Hong Kong; (5)768046. This Szechuan restaurant, which many residents patronize, is tucked away behind the Lee Gardens Hotel. And busy though it is, it's good. Eggplant in garlic sauce is pungent and warming. Contrast taste and texture with spicey minced beef with vermicelli (called "ants climbing a tree" in the vernacular). Reservations are advisable. Open noon to midnight. AE, DC, V.

Sze Chuen Lau. 446 Lockhart Rd., Causeway Bay, Hong Kong; (5)790–2571. Dragons twine up the outside, while inside, the only concession made to Westerners is to indicate the chilli hot dishes on the menu. Smoked duck is a specialty, albeit sometimes disappointing. Instead, try hot-and-sour soup, prawns in chilli, aubergines in garlic sauce, and crispy beef. Wash it all down with beer. Make reservations at weekends. Open 11:00 A.M. to midnight. V, AE, MC, OTB.

TAIWANESE

Inexpensive

Ching Yip Restaurant. Food Street, Causeway Bay, Hong Kong; (5)778018. Taiwanese fare is a cross between Cantonese and Chiu Chow, and it is somewhat rare outside Taiwan. Limited menu, but photographs of dishes facilitate choosing. Relaxed ambience. Lunch and dinner daily. AE, V, OTB.

VEGETARIAN

Bodhi Vegetarian Restaurant. 388 Lockhart Rd., Wanchai, Hong Kong; (5)732155 and 56 Cameron Rd., Tsimshatsui, Kowloon; (3)7213561. One of the classiest Chinese vegetarian restaurants, with specials like "Pastoral Tang" (bean curd with chili, sesame, and mushrooms) and "Heavenly Blossom," made with broccoli and fresh mushrooms. Good taste, very cheap. Open 11:00 A.M. to 11:00 P.M. AE, MC, V.

Vegi-Food Kitchen. 8 Cleveland St., Causeway Bay, Hong Kong; (5)8906660. Wonderfully evocative names for classic mushroom-beancurd-peppery dishes in a delicious atmosphere. Open 11:30 A.M. to midnight. No credit cards.

Wishful Cottage. 336 Lockhart Rd., Wanchai, Hong Kong; (5)735645. The Chinese/English language menu here is based fungus, bean curd, and any number of other esoteric vegetables, such as heart-of-leaf mustard and hairy water weed. This restaurant is for genuine seekers of gustatory experience at around HK$30 to HK$40 per head. Not even a drop of beer in the place. Open 9:00 A.M. to 10:00 P.M. No credit cards.

AUSTRALIAN

Inexpensive

The Stoned Crow. 12 Minden Ave., Tsimshatsui, Kowloon; (3)668494. The simple fare at this Wagga Wagga of the Orient deserves to be classed as pub food, but the menu is a bit more extensive than in most pubs, and it's set up like a restaurant, with a small bar and men and women sitting around tables. The only place in town for kangaroo tail soup. There is a limited dessert menu. Open 11:30 A.M. to midnight. AE, DC, V.

AUSTRIAN

Expensive

Mozart Stub'n. 8 Glenealy Road, Central, Hong Kong; (5)221763. A tiny "Tyrolean" bistro in the Orient. Very fresh food. Keep an eye out for the chalkboard specials. Open noon to 2:00 P.M. and 7:00 P.M. to 10:30 P.M. Major credit cards.

BURMESE

Moderate

Khin's Burmese Kitchen. Wah Kwong Regent Centre, twenty-fourth floor, 88 Queen's Road Central, Hong Kong; (5) 235380. Would you believe a luxurious Burmese restaurant? Cheery and cozy, and has a bar. Food includes khaukswe, a blend of chicken and egg noodles in coconut milk; mohinga, made of fish, noodles, and herbs in a spicy soup; and sanwinmakin, a blend of sesame seeds, ground farina, raisins, and coconut. None is very hot. Open noon–3 P.M., 6:00 P.M.–11:30 P.M. except Sunday. All major credit cards.

Inexpensive

Rangoon Restaurant. 265 Gloucester Rd., Causeway Bay, Hong Kong; (5)-893–2281. If you've never had grilled tea leaves with peanuts, or glass noodles with tiny shrimp, this is your type of restaurant. Authentic Burmese cuisine from Mandalay and Rangoon in a light, bright atmosphere. Open 11:00 A.M. to 11:00 P.M. AE, MC, V.

DUTCH

Moderate

Dutch Kitchen. King's Theatre Building, Wyndham Street, Central, Hong Kong; (5)233770. An attractive restaurant, the only really Dutch one in town. The menu concentrates on North sea fish (haddock, eel, and herring), veal, chicken, and the famous Dutch pea soup. Reservations necessary for lunch time. Open 11:30 A.M. to 11:00 P.M. All major credit cards.

FRENCH

Deluxe

Amigo. 79A Wong Nei Chung Rd., Happy Valley, Hong Kong; (5)772202. A Spanish-style villa across from the race track, this is the only restaurant outside a hotel to make it into the top bracket on price, and local gourmets out for a celebration swear by it. Those easily embarrassed by strolling minstrels should avoid it, however. A basically Mediterranean menu, with such additions as Macau sole, Scotch salmon, and Sydney rock oysters. Good wine list, personalized matches if you book ahead, and red roses for ladies on leaving (they think of everything). Executive lunches. Open noon to midnight. All major credit cards.

Gaddi's. The Peninsula Hotel, Salisbury Road, Tsimshatsui, Kowloon; (3)-666251. Once famed as "the best restaurant east of Suez," Gaddi's is hard-pressed to maintain its reputation since a bevy of deluxe restaurants in top hotels came on-line. But for a glimpse of Colonial splendor, Gaddi's named after a pre-war maitre d', is hard to beat. Whenever you go, dress. Dance music at night. Reservations imperative. Open noon to 3:00 P.M., 7:00 P.M. to midnight. All major credit cards.

Margaux. Shangri-La Hotel, 64 Mody Rd., East Tsimshatsui, Kowloon; (3)721–8588. Undeniably one of the best of the new hotel restaurants to emerge in Hong Kong in the last couple of years. Undeniably *haute cuisine,* too; it's a venue for wedding anniversaries and birthdays, with a string quartet suitably muted in the background. In deference to the restaurant's name, it boasts an excellent but pricey wine list. Jacket and tie or national dress. Open noon to 3:00 P.M. (except Sunday) and 7:00 P.M. to 11:30 P.M. All major credit cards.

Pierrot. The Mandarin Hotel, Connaught Road, Central, Hong Kong; (5)-220111. The Pierrot reflects the Mandarin's frequent international rating as one of the top hotels in the world. The most famous of the grand chefs always manage to put in in periodic appearances to do their stuff, and a unique and classic *à la carte* selection follows. Smaller than you'd expect, so reservations are essential. Don't try for pre-dinner drinks at the Chinnery Bar on the first floor if you have women in your party; there's a men-only rule. Open noon to 3:00 P.M.; closed Sunday and at lunch time on public holidays. All major credit cards.

Plume. The Regent Hotel, Salisbury Road, Kowloon; (3)721-1211. Glide down the carpeted staircase like royalty and dine on *nouvelle cuisine* in unashamed luxury against the spectacular backdrop of Hong Kong's harbor. Jacket and tie. Booking essential. Open 7:00 P.M. to 2:00 A.M. nightly. All major credit cards.

Le Restaurant de France. Hotel Regal Meridien, 71 Mody Rd., East Tsimshatsui, Kowloon; (3)722-1818. The food is splendidly elegant, with prices to match and mouth-watering menus from the best ingredients money can buy. Try guinea fowl terrine with truffles and pistachios, lobster pâté with Pouilly Fuisse, or salt-baked lamb with a vegetable *gateau.* Open 7:00 P.M. to midnight. Closed on Sundays. All major credit cards.

Expensive

Belvedere. Holiday Inn Harbour View, Mody Road, East Tsimshatsui, Kowloon; (3)721-5161. Excellent food in tasteful surroundings. Enjoy the view and enjoy the food. There's a melting starter of lobster pearls in champagne aspic, or the richer pigeon breast and mango cocktail, and unusual main courses such as pheasant morin and braised boneless goose. For desserts, the usual gâteaux, soufflés, and other diet wreckers. Open noon to 3:00 P.M., 7:00 P.M. to midnight. All major credit cards.

The Five Continents. Regal Meridien Airport Hotel, Sa Po Road, Kowloon; (3)718-0333. Probably because of its location, this restaurant was slow to take off when it opened in 1982. But the word has spread, and it has grown in popularity. In sound-proofed comfort you can watch the jumbos land at Kai Tak, while you sample the *haute cuisine à la carte* or such daily specials as cassoulet or bouillabaisse. Open noon to 3:00 P.M., 7:00 P.M. to midnight. All major credit cards.

Hugo's. Hyatt Regency Hong Kong, 67 Nathan Rd., Tsimshatsui, Hong Kong; (3)662321. Hugo's is unashamedly old-fashioned, both in terms of ambience and food, and no one's complaining. As well as a well composed *à la carte* selection and lunch-time roast beef, there's the bargain Executive Luncheon, with three courses (plenty of choices) for HK$120. On Sundays and public holidays, there's a brunch buffet. Jacket and tie for dinner. Open noon to 3:00 P.M., 7:00 P.M. to 11:00 P.M. All major credit cards.

Lalique. Royal Garden Hotel, Mody Road, East Tsimshatsui, Kowloon; (3)721-5215. The Royal Garden has the most spectacular interiors in town, and Lalique is no disappointment. Art deco etched glass, Champagne bar, and sumptious settees set the scene for a *nouvelle cuisine* experience you won't forget. It's not cheap, but memories—especially of the soufflés—seldom are. Open 6:30 P.M. to midnight. All major credit cards.

Parc 27. Park Lane Hotel, 310 Gloucester Rd., Causeway Bay, Hong Kong; (5)790-1021. Casually elegant and very spacious dining in a very relaxed atmosphere augmented by one of the best views in town. Some *nouvelle cuisine* selections, but balaced nicely with table-bending buffets. Executive luncheons as well. The lovely presentation of food is almost Asian in appearance. Music in the evening. Open noon to 3:00 P.M., 7:00 to 11:00 P.M. All major credit cards.

Park Lane. New World Hotel, Salisbury Road, Tsimshatsui, Kowloon; (3)-694111. A smart, comfortable venue with the atmosphere of a London club. It isn't cheap, but nevertheless offers good value for money, with complementary *crudités* and *petit fours*. Daily *table d'hôte* for both lunch and dinner, as well as *à la carte.* Open noon to 2:30 P.M., 7:00 P.M. to 11 P.M. All major credit cards.

Rotisserie. Hotel Furama Inter-Continental, 1 Connaught Rd., Central, Hong Kong (5)255111. In dark paneled comfort, the Rotisserie does sterling work serving *cuisine du marché* to appreciative guests. The strolling Filipino band puts in an appearance after 8:00 P.M. It's not the same band everywhere, but visitors are excused for assuming otherwise. Open noon to 3:00 P.M., 7:00 P.M. to 11:00 P.M. All major credit cards.

Stanley's. 86 Stanley Main St., Stanley, Hong Kong; (5)938873. Take a break from shopping for a civilized lunch at this intimate restaurant with a cuisine that leans toward French. For a romantic dinner for two, book a table on the balcony overlooking the South China Sea, but only when the humidity is low. Blackboard specials, *à la carte* menu, and an excellent wine list. Weekend reservations are essential. Open Tuesday through Sunday, 9:00 A.M. to midnight. No AE.

Verandah. The Peninsula, Salisbury Road, Kowloon; (3)666251. If you can't decide whether to eat French or Chinese, this is the place for you. What used to be an open-air restaurant years ago is now glassed in and air-conditioned and serves traditional French dishes side by side with grilled steaks, rack of lamb, and Chinese specialties. The Chinese selection is catholic but limited. Desserts are melt-in-the-mouth sorbets, soufflés, and magnificent flaming dishes. Leave room for them. If you can't choose from the *à la carte,* compromise on the Marco Polo buffet lunch. He should have been so lucky. Open 7:00 A.M. to 11:00 A.M., noon to 3:00 P.M., 6:00 P.M. to 11:00 P.M. All major credit cards.

Moderate

Au Trou Normand. 6 Carnarvon Rd., Tsimshatsui, Kowloon; (3)668754. A French provincial restaurant with a good reputation, although standards seem to vary. Pâtés, charcuterie, and soups are reliable, and in deference to the Normandy origins of *le patron,* whose portrait gazes down at diners, a great deal of trouble is taken with fish. Tarte Isigny and crêpes Normandes are delicious regional desserts with which to finish the meal on a high note. And don't forget the complementary "Trou" (a glass of Calvados). A three-course business lunch is served each weekday, as is the usual *à la carte.* Open noon to 11:00 P.M. daily. Book for dinner at weekends. No CB.

La Brasserie. Hotel Regal Meridien, Hong Kong, Mody Road, East Tsimshatsui, Kowloon; (3)722–1818. One of two Brasseries in Hong Kong; both are pleasant. Good, rich, traditional French fare in a smart but informal setting. Menu features such classics as *escargots de Bourgogne, moules farcies,* steak *au poivre,* and *rognons de veau,* and the dessert trolley is guaranteed to knock holes in a diet regime. Open noon to 3:00 P.M., 7:00 P.M. to midnight. All major credit cards.

La Brasserie. Marco Polo Hotel, Canton Rd., Tsimshatsui, Kowloon; (3)721 –5111. Daily specials are painted on a mirror, but all the old favorites—snails, steaks, terrines—are there all the time. The atmosphere is calculated to be informal, with gingham tablecloths and waiters in long aprons. Open noon to 3:00 P.M., 7:00 P.M. to midnight. All major credit cards.

La Rose Noire. 1st floor, 8–13 Woo On Lane, Central, Hong Kong; (5)-265965. A superb French restaurant, known only to the few. Elegant, modest but with fine food. This could be the equivalent of French *dimsum*. Small portions of steak tartare or *pâté gras d'oie,* roasted goat's cheese, scrambled eggs with smoked salmon and caviar. Quail eggs, chocolate mousse . . . obviously this restaurant is a labor of love. Piano music at night. Open 12:30 to 3:00 P.M., 5:30 P.M. to 3:00 A.M. AE, DC, V.

Le Tire Bouchon. 9 Old Baily Street, Central, Hong Kong; (5)235459. The name means "corkscrew," and it is well worth the effort to get to this tiny bistro if only to sample some of the 60 different wines. Rather a smallish selection of dishes on the menu, so the main attraction is the *vin.* Nice place to linger over a glass or three. Open noon to 3:00 P.M., 7:00 P.M. to midnight. MC, V.

GERMAN

Expensive

Baron's Table. Holiday Inn Golden Mile, 50 Nathan Rd., Tsimshatsui, Kowloon; (3)693111. The specialty of this Teutonic eatery is game, so the arrival of autumn usually means fresh grouse, hare, or venison. The restaurant is superbly Germanic, so it is rather like dining in a medieval castle on the Rhine. Excellent smoked food from the hotel's own smokehouse. Open noon to 3:00 P.M., 7:00 P.M. to midnight. All major credit cards.

Moderate

Schnurrbart. 29 D'Aguilar St., Central, Hong Kong; (5)234700 and 6 Hart Ave., Tsimshatsui, Kowloon; (3)723–9827. The "original German beer pub" is the self-styled billing, but from a non-German point of view, it seems more of a restaurant than a pub. Excellent *Wurst,* as you would expect, plus an extensive range of German meals and snacks. Fixed lunches and dinners are good value. Open 11:00 A.M. to 2:00 A.M. AE, DC, V.

Old Heidelberg. First floor, Astoria Building, 24–30 Ashley Rd., Tsimshatsui, Kowloon; (3)723–3666. Tiled floors, wood panels, and a welcoming atmosphere combine with country-style German cooking to make this restaurant worth a visit. Imported Thuringer bratwurst brings back memories of what sausages used to be. Three-course set lunch, HK$30. Filipino guitarist and organist in the evenings. Open noon to 3:00 P.M., 5:00 P.M. to midnight. All major credit cards.

INDIAN

Moderate

Gaylord. 6–6A Mody Commercial Building, 2–4 Hart Ave., Tsimshatsui, Kowloon; (3)724–3222. Schmaltzy décor with plush settees to settle into, this Gaylord is somehow less piquant than the original Indian chain. And so is the food. Nevertheless, reservations are recommended for weekends. Lunch and dinner daily, with a Sunday lunch buffet. Open noon to 3:00 P.M., 6:30 P.M. to 11:30 P.M. All major credit cards.

Maharaja Restaurant. 222 Wanchai Rd., Hong Kong; (5)749838; also at 1–3A Granville Circuit, off Granville Road, Tsimshatsui, Kowloon; (3)666671. Northern Indian fare, which means tandooris and rich Moghlai specialties that don't blow your head off. No pork or beef, in deference to Muslims and Hindus, but fish and lamb dishes that are well worth waiting for. And you do have to wait. If your party consists of more than one, emphasize that you all want to eat at the same time. Reservations recommended for buffet lunches and dinners on weekends. Open noon to 2:30 P.M., 7:00 P.M. to 11:00 P.M. No CB.

New Delhi. Ground floor, Bank of America Building, Central, Hong Kong; (5)244655 and 52 Cameron Road, Tsimshatsui, Kowloon; (3)664611. Mild North Indian and Kashmiri curries. The lamb curry and tandoori are famous here, and *Palak Kashmiri Kofta*—spinach and homemade cheese in curry sauce —is another specialty. Open (Central) 11:00 A.M. to 3 P.M., 6:00 to 11:00 P.M., (Tsimshatsui) noon to 2:30 P.M., 6:30 to 11:00 P.M. V only.

Viceroy of India. Sun Hung Kai Centre, Harbour Road, Wanchai, Hong Kong; (5)727227. An uncharacteristic, rather opulent Indian restaurant with pink and beige interior décor and not a poster of the Taj Mahal in sight. There's even a house wine. The food is north Indian, with tandooris figuring prominently. Open noon to 2:30 P.M., 6:30 P.M. to 11:30 P.M. No CB.

Inexpensive

Bombay. 15 Leighton Rd., Happy Valley, Hong Kong; (5)795–0370. Originally situated at the top of Wyndham Street, the Bombay disappeared for a while and re-emerged on this site, none the worse for the trip. Someone once said you judge a good north Indian restaurant by the rogan ghosh (a rich, spicy mutton dish) and by that yardstick the Bombay comes out rather well. A real tandoor produces genuine tandooris, and you can watch the chef make parathas and naan (bread). Wine list, but beer or lassi (yoghurt drink) are more appropriate. Open noon to 11:00 P.M. No CB.

Maharani Mess. 40–42 Wyndham St., Central, Hong Kong; (5) 232778. This tiny little North Indian bistro is a hidden treat for business executives in the area. Tandooris, biryanis, tiggas, and, of course, curries and samosas. Open 7:00 A.M. to 11:00 P.M. No credit cards.

Mayur. 13th floor, BCC Building, 25–31 Carnarvon Rd., Tsimshatsui, Kowloon; (3)675044. Vegetarian and non-vegetarian set meals, tandoori dishes, and halal curries, as well as regional favorites. Also serves Szechuan food, which makes it the first Indian restaurant to serve Chinese food. Live Indian music. Open noon to 3:00 P.M., 6:00 P.M. to midnight. No CB.

Woodlands. 8 Minden Ave., Tsimshatsui, Kowloon; (3)693718. If you are considering turning vegetarian, turn Indian vegetarian. Woodlands proves that Indian cuisine can provide zest, variety, and satisfaction without meat or fish. The menu is extensive, but rotates so that only a small number of dishes is available each day. Helpful staff will put you right, or go for the Madras thali (combination meal) for a taste of all sorts. Open 11:30 A.M. to 3:30 P.M., 6:00 P.M. to 11:00 P.M. No credit cards. (At these prices, no one would dare.)

INDONESIAN

Inexpensive

Indonesian. 26 Leighton Rd., Hong Kong; (5)779981; also at 66 Granville Rd., Tsimshatsui, Kowloon; (3)673287. A bright and cheery family restaurant that is popular with expatriate Indonesians for *rijstaffel* Sunday lunch. Everyone always starts with the delicious *satay*, but it's not obligatory. As an alternative to *gado gado* salad, try *sajur lodeh* (vegetables in coconut milk). Mild mutton curry falls off the bone, and spiced dried beef is a favorite. But everyone should try *brengkis ikan* at least once. It's fish in chilli paste wrapped and baked in banana leaves, and it's one of the hottest dishes ever to blister a diner's palate. No wine list; beer, tea, or *chendol* (coconut milk with worms of green bean jelly). Open noon to 11:00 P.M. V, DC, OTB.

Java Rijstaffel. 38 Hankow Rd., Tsimshatsui, Kowloon; (3)671230. Aussies who remember Royal Interocean Lines, a Dutch shipping company based in Indonesia, will be interested to know that this restaurant was founded by the wife of an R.I.L. executive who missed her favorite tucker. *Rijstaffel* is the Indonesian version of buffet, and it's an ideal way to try a new cuisine. Balance your meal as you would normally, with meat and/or fish, vegetables or salad, and rice or noodles. *Sambals* are side dishes that cool or add zest if necessary. Or order *nasi goreng* (fried rice), *kerrie ajam* (chicken curry), and *babi kecap* (pork in soy sauce) *à la carte*. Open 11:30 A.M. to 11:00 P.M. No credit cards.

Ramayana. Basement 2, Houston Centre, Mody Road, East Tsimshatsui, Kowloon; (3)721–7029. Not the place for a discreet rendezvous, since it's situated below an atrium shopping center with bubble elevators gliding up and down the sides. However, the food has not been unduly watered down, with the exception of the peanut sauce for satays, which is rather bland. Set meals are a good bet for novices. Open noon to 11:00 P.M. No CB.

ITALIAN

Expensive

Pizzeria. Kowloon hotel, 19–21 Nathan Rd., Tsimshatsui, Kowloon; (3)-698698. Much more than tasty pizza graces this very up-market and delicious Italian eatery. Lovely salad bar. Luncheon buffet. Open 11:45 A.M. to 3:00 P.M., 6:00 to 11:00 P.M. All major credit cards.

Moderate

Rigoletto. 14 Fenwick St., Wanchai, Hong Kong; (5)277144. A romantically lit bistro-style restaurant with picture windows facing onto a couple of Wanchai's more colorful bars. Inside, you can watch the fish swim around a bust of Mozart in the tank. The most memorable dish is the Vatican fish soup, a zestful first course that's more like a main course. Pizzas are highly rated. Reasonable Italian house wine and good coffee. Open noon to 3:00 P.M., 6:00 P.M. to midnight daily. AE, V.

La Taverna. 1 On Hing Terrace, Central, Hong Kong; (5)228904; 36–38 Ashley Rd., Kowloon; (3)691945. The Central branch is the most difficult to find (turn left off Wyndham Street up a broad, steep flight of steps opposite the start of Wellington Street). But once there, seated on the glassed-in verandah with a glass of house vino, you are almost in Italy. These restaurants do rather suffer from the assumption that Italian food is all pizza and pasta, but the pizzas are deliciously light and crisp; much nicer than the heavy pan variety with which Hong Kong abounds these days. Try *fritto misto* or *ossobuco* for a change. Superb coffee. Lunch and dinner daily. V, DC, AE.

Inexpensive

La Bella Donna. 51 Gloucester Rd., Wanchai, Hong Kong; (5)228904. Hitting the market somewhere between romance and fast food, La Bella Donna serves good pizzas and *zuppa di pesce* (fish soup). It's nice and informal, the sort of place a single can feel comfortable, and as any Italian restaurant worth its name should, it serves decent house wine and coffee. Open noon to midnight. AE, DC.

Spaghetti House. Harbour City, Canton Rd., Tsimshatsui, Kowloon; (3)721 –9357; 85B Hennessy Rd., Wanchai, Hong Kong; (5)290901; 38 Cameron Rd., Tsimshatsui, Kowloon; (3)686635; 5 Sharp Street East (near Lee Theatre), Causeway Bay, Hong Kong; (5)895–2245. The closest thing to American-style pizzas, as well as a few pastas. A touch of home. Winter "hot pots" (seafood, goulash, etc.) are very popular. Open 11:00 A.M. to midnight. No credit cards.

JAPANESE

Deluxe

Nadaman. Shangri-La Hotel, 64 Mody Rd., East Tsimshatsui, Kowloon; (3)721–2111. All Japanese restaurants are aesthetically appealing, and this one more so than most. Bamboo screens, rock gardens, and Bonsai trees calm the nerves and aid the digestion. There are three tatami rooms for those who want to go native, and a sushi bar, as well as conventional tables. Open noon to 3:00 P.M., 6:30 P.M. to 11:00 P.M. All major credit cards.

Unkai. Sheraton Hotel, 20 Nathan Rd., Tsimshatsui, Kowloon; (3)691111. A famous name in Osaka, this version has passed muster with the Japanese locals. Sushi, Teppan Yaki, and Kaiseki are the specialties; a special menu is available for those who want to sample a little of everything. Open noon to 3:00 P.M. and 6:30 to 11:00 P.M. All major credit cards.

Expensive

Ah-So. World Finance Centre, Harbour City, Canton Road, Tsimshatsui, Kowloon; (3) 683392. Billed as Hong Kong's only "floating sushi bar"—the *sushi, sashimi*, etc. float by on little boats. Open noon to 3:00 P.M. and 6:00 P.M. to midnight. All major credit cards.

Benkay. Basement, Gloucester Tower, The Landmark, Central, Hong Kong; (5)213344. The teppanyaki and sushi bars, as well as regular tables, are all very busy at lunch times. The food is superb quality. Open noon to 3:00 P.M., 6:00 P.M. to 10:30 P.M. All major credit cards.

Hooraiya Teppanyaki. Food St., Causeway Bay, Hong Kong; (5)778797. Teppanyaki always comes pretty pricey because it just can't be made with frozen or second-class raw material. Non-Japanese may want to take a set meal, which includes all the necessary accompaniments, and supplement it with extras from the *à la carte* menu. As usual for a Japanese restaurant, the environment is exquisite. Hot sake from lovely little flasks. Lunch and dinner daily. Reservations advisable after 7:00 P.M. AE, DC, V, MC, OTB.

Matsubishi. Ground floor, Lockhart House, 440 Jaffe Rd., Causeway Bay, Hong Kong; (5)795–0850. A teppanyaki restaurant with *table d'hôte* set meals and *à la carte* selection. Half the fun is watching the performance as the cook deftly chops and slices and places works of art on plates. Open noon to 3:00 P.M., 6:00 P.M. to 11:30 P.M. All major credit cards.

Okahan. Lee Gardens Hotel, Hysan Avenue, Causeway Bay, Hong Kong; (5) 765393. The aesthetic surroundings one takes for granted in Japanese restaurants, and to some extent, the quality of food, too. Parties here can sit around the teppanyaki grill. Matsuzaka beef melts in the mouth. Okahan special, an unusual combination of beef and fish, fetchingly presented, is justly famous. Open noon to 3:00 P.M., 7:00 P.M. to 11:30 P.M. AE, V, DC, OTB.

Moderate

Ozeki. Towning Mansion, Paterson Street, Causeway Bay, Hong Kong; (5)790–4888; also at New World Centre, Chatham Road, Kowloon; (3) 695795. Sample the bland yet fragrant delights of Japanese cuisine in simple, elegant surroundings. Drink warm sake from arty little stone flasks or wash down the delicately presented dishes with light Sapporo beer. Open noon to 3:00 P.M., 6:00 P.M. to 11:30 P.M. AE, OTB.

Yamato. Matsuzakaya basement, Great George Street, Causeway Bay, Hong Kong; (5)796316. More hustle and bustle than in the average Japanese restaurant, because this one is in the basement of a Japanese department store. Half-size portions are served for children, and lunch time encourages indigestion. Lovely, light *tempura* (battered items) and tasty *yakitori* (skewered chicken). Open 11:00 A.M. to 11:00 P.M. No credit cards.

JEWISH

Moderate

Beverly Hills Deli. #55 New World Centre, Tsimshatsui, Kowloon; (3)-698695/6 and 2–3 Lan Kwai Fong Basement, Central, Hong Kong, (5)265809. Kowloon's "deli" is located in a mammoth shopping arcade, while Central's is in the "Greenwich Village" district and is packed with Central business folk at lunchtime. Both claim to be the only authentic delis, with kosher and non-kosher food. Smart, tiled interiors with blow-ups of eating scenes from the movies, and a carry-out counter, serving more than 50 types of sandwiches, blintzes, stuffed cabbage, smoked fish, and spare ribs. Deliveries direct to your hotel room. (Ring the one on your side of the harbor.) Open daily, 7:00 A.M. to 1:00 A.M. All major credit cards.

KOREAN

Moderate

Arirang. 76 Morrison Hill Rd., Happy Valley, Hong Kong; (5)723027; also at Hyatt Regency Hotel, Nathan Road, Tsimshatsui, Kowloon; (3)665551. Arirang, a Korean barbecue restaurant that has been on its present site for twelve years, is across the road from the race course. It's cheerful and spacious with eight tables; on each of two floors all with a barbecue hot plate and extractor chimney. Newcomers should try a combination barbecue of several dishes. Old hands can do their own thing, always remembering to use one pair of chopsticks to cook and one to eat. Or let the waiter do it. Open 11:00 A.M. to 11:00 P.M. Reservations advisable. No CB.

Go Gu Jang Korean Restaurant. Second floor, Lee Gardens Shopping Arcade, Hysan Avenue, Causeway Bay, Hong Kong; (5)772021. This one's a cut above your average Korean restaurants and actually has a wine list. Most people go for *shabu-shabu,* a do-it-yourself hotpot of seafood, meat, and vegetables, with side dishes of pickles. Order extras depending on your appetite, but beware of over-ordering. Open noon to 11:00 P.M. AE, V, DC.

MALAYSIAN

Inexpensive

Malaya Restaurant. 158 Wellington St., Central, Hong Kong; (5) 251580. A vast menu with Malaysian, Chinese, and European dishes. At last count there were more than 20 different curries alone and half a dozen different *satays.* Open 11:00 A.M. to midnight. No CB.

MEDITERRANEAN

Moderate

The Mistral. Harbour View Holiday Inn, 10 Mody Rd., East Tsimshatsui, Kowloon; (3)721–5161. Lovers of zesty southern European food will love this place. Go for the old favorites; *paella, moussaka,* stuffed vine leaves, and fresh dates and figs. This is the only place in town for swordfish kebab. Wash down the lot with robust house wines and strong coffee. Open noon to 3:00 P.M. and 7:00 P.M. to 11:00 P.M. All major credit cards.

MEXICAN

Moderate

Casa Mexicana. Victoria Centre, Watson Road, North Point, Hong Kong; (5)665560; also at *La Tortilla,* 28 Cameron Rd., Tsimshatsui, Kowloon; (3)-723870. An unlikely location, so get someone to write the address in Chinese for the taxi driver. Wholesome, toothsome tacos, burrittos, enchiladas, and guacamole at reasonable prices in a casual atmosphere. Mexican artifacts create that South-of-the-border feeling, and Margaritas (by the liter) also help. Open noon to midnight. No CB.

HK Mexican Association. Block C, C–4, 11th floor, Hankow Centre, 1C Middle Rd., Tsimshatsui, Kowloon; (3)674535. The original "Mexican Club" for those who have been coming to Hong Kong long enough to remember. Tex-Mex style Mexican food. Open noon to midnight. MC, V.

Someplace Else. Sheraton Hotel, 20 Nathan Rd., Tsimshatsui, Kowloon; (3)721–6151. A New York, T.G.I.F.-type restaurant, in a two-level arrangement with lots of Tiffany lampshades, brass, and wood. The food is mainly Mexican, with Terlingua chili, nachos, and potacos, and much, much more. Sunday brunch at HK$75 per head. Live guitar and piano music in the evenings. Open 11:00 A.M. to midnight Sunday through Thursday, 11:00 A.M. to 2:00 A.M. Friday and Saturday. All major credit cards.

MIDDLE EASTERN

Expensive

Casablanca Supper Club. Marina Tower, ninth floor, Shum Wan Road, Aberdeen, Hong Kong; (5)540044. Many tourists head to Aberdeen for seafood. Should you long for *mezze* instead of mussels or lamb in place of lobster, or perhaps a bit of romance (complete with piano music), this place is for you. Western food is also available. Dinner is served until 11:00 P.M., when the restaurant changes into a disco. Open noon to 3:00 P.M. and 6:30 P.M. to 2:30 A.M. All major credit cards.

Moderate

Omar Khayyam Middle Eastern Restaurant. New World Centre, Tsimshatsui, Kowloon; (3)668243. A trendy new restaurant, decorated in pseudo-Arabic, with plentiful dips, sauces, yoghurts, main courses, and of course a complete supply of araks and Greek ouzo. Luncheon buffet. With the right ordering, very moderate prices. Noon to 3 P.M., 7 to 10:30 P.M. AE, DC, MC, V.

NEPALESE

Moderate

Godown. Sutherland House Basement, Club Rd., Central; Hong Kong; (5)-221608. The Godown is known for jazz, light food, basic bohemia. Little known except to the Gurhka community, Godown also has a Nepalese curry buffet every Wednesday and Saturday. Curries, sweets, with an admixture of Tibetan dishes. Open noon to 2:00 A.M. AE, MC, V.

PHILIPPINES

Inexpensive

Little Manila. 9 Minden Ave, Tsimshatsui, Kowloon; (3)669919. An easygoing, noisy haunt of the local Filipino community. The standard menu items, such as *lumpia* (spring rolls), *sinigang* (sour soup), and *adobo* (meat marinated in soy and vinegar), are all here, but try stuffed eggplant, crispy *pata* (fried pork), and *ginatan* (sweet potatoes, banana, and jackfruit in coconut milk). Open 10:00 A.M. to 2:00 A.M. No credit cards.

Mabuhay. 11 Minden Ave., Tsimshatsui, Kowloon; (3)673762. Tucked away on a dead-end street that runs parallel to Mody Road. On Saturdays and Sundays you won't make yourself heard above the rattle of Tegalog from Hong Kong's 14,000-strong Filipino population, who all seem to be here or in the other Filipino restaurant down the street. As well as classics like pork *adobo* (marinated in soy sauce) and *sinigang* (sour soup), there are such Spanish dishes as *paella* and *calamares*. Open 11:00 A.M. to 11:00 P.M. All major credit cards.

PORTUGUESE

Moderate

Pinocchio. Island Centre, eighth floor, 1 Great George St., Causeway Bay, Hong Kong; (5)790–9111. No relation to the Macau restaurant of the same name, but the spicy African chicken and prawns *piri-piri,* pan-fried sardines, and *lechon* (suckling pig) will satisfy you if you do not have time to get over to Macau. Open 11:00 A.M. to midnight. All major credit cards.

RUSSIAN

Inexpensive

Czarina. 25 Bonham Rd., Hong Kong; (5)402874. It is not exactly what your long lost *bubba* would call home cooking, but then again, there are very few White Russians left in Hong Kong. Good borscht hot or cold. Other Russian dishes include Veal Jarbarka, Chicken Duchess, Pelemeni, and, of course, the obligatory "à la Kiev." The menu is not exclusively Russian should your companion tire of the trek to the old country. Open 10:00 A.M. to 11:00 P.M.

SOUTHEAST ASIAN

Expensive

Spices. Repulse Bay, Hong Kong; (5)812–2711. On the site of the old Repulse Bay Hotel, this is a Penninsula Group operation, so you know it is going to be up-market and good. As the name implies, the restaurant features a melange of Eastern food under one roof—from spicy *vindaloos* Goan-style to Indonesian *rendengs* and Thai *tom yam kung.* Open 10:30 A.M. to 11:00 P.M. All major credit cards.

Moderate

Asian Delights. Riverside Plaza Hotel, Ta Chung Kiu Road, Shatin, New Territories; (0)649–7878. Thai, Indonesian, and Singaporean foods mixed with a touch of Japanese in one menu. Luncheon and dinner buffets. Open noon to 11:00 P.M. All major credit cards.

Inexpensive

Satay Hut. 144–148 Houston Centre, Mody Road, East Tsimshatsui, Kowloon; (3)723–3681. *Satays* are almost fast food in this shopping center operation. Singapore-style noodles and Thai soups are a welcome, though inexpensive, change from hamburgers. Open 11:00 A.M. to 10.30 P.M. No credit cards.

SMI. 85 Lockhart Rd., Wanchai, Hong Kong. No less than 80 different curries, from India to Indonesia, with specials from Malaysia. Quite an amazing menu. Inexpensive. 11 A.M.–11:30 P.M.. DC, V.

SEAFOOD

Expensive

Bentley's Seafood Restaurant and Oyster Bar. Prince's Building, Chater Rd., Hong Kong; (5)868–0881. Its namesake in London is famous. Elegant crabs, oysters, scallops, smoked salmon, and fish. Eschewing the goodies of the South China Sea, Bentley's brings in 80 percent of their fish from Blighty (the olde English name for England.) Open noon to 3:00 P.M., 6:30 to 11:30 P.M. AE, DC, V.

Moderate

Market Street. Basement, Wilson House, 19 Wyndham Street, Central Hong Kong; (5)8107566. Fresh seafood and U.S. beef are displayed on central counter. You choose what you like, pay a small charge for cooking in any style, or have a set lunch or dinner. A new concept based on the Chinese outdoor fish market, but very popular. Open 10:30 A.M. to 3:00 P.M. (lunch), 3:00 to 6:00 P.M. (*dim-sum*), 6:00 P.M. to midnight (dinner). All credit cards.

SPANISH

Moderate

Adriadico. 89 Kimberly Rd., Tsimshatsui, Kowloon. A branch of Adriadico in Washington, D.C. and Manila. This out-of-the-way restaurant has lovely decor, classical music, and a splendid selection of beef tenderloin with garlic, lamb stew, two different paellas, and of course a wide selection of Spanish wines. Moderate prices.

SRI LANKAN

Moderate

Club Sri Lanka. 17 Hollywood Rd., Central, Hong Kong; (5) 247341. A homey little restaurant with a full list of Ceylonese and Tamil foods. Hot curries, Dutch-inspired poppers, regional specials like Galle-style beef and tamarind, and a full list of unique Ceylon sweets. Very moderate prices. No credit cards.

SWISS

Expensive

Chesa. The Peninsula, Salisbury Road, Tsimshatsui, Kowloon; (3)666251. An intimate, wood-paneled delight of a venue for *tête à tête* over fondue in the winter, or a light business lunch that's a welcome change from the heavier fare elsewhere. Frequently changing specialties from the Swiss cantons include fresh-water fish, cheeses, veal, and charcuterie. Reservations strongly recommended. Open noon to 3:00 P.M., 6:30 P.M. to 11:00 P.M. All major credit cards.

THAI

Moderate

Chili Club. First floor, 68–70 Lockhart Rd., Wanchai, Hong Kong; (5)272872. Really authentic Thai food, as well as Laotian specials. Totally unprepossessing, very crowded at lunchtime, but extremely helpful staff, very spicy, cheap, and great fun. Open noon to 3:00 P.M., 6:00 to 11:00 P.M. V.

Sawadee. 1 Hillwood Rd., Tsimshatsui, Kowloon; (3)7225577. Managed by Thais, with authentic hot curries, salads and soups in a beautiful atmosphere. 11:30 A.M.–11 P.M. AE,V.

Silks. Ground and first floors, 4–6 On Lan Street, Central, Hong Kong; (5)242567. The classiest-looking Thai restaurant in Hong Kong. The trendies go there for food which isn't terribly spicy, but the Thai chefs who work in the kitchen can dish up the finest dishes with special requests. Open noon to 3:00 P.M., 6:00 to 11:00 P.M. AE, MC, V.

VIETNAMESE

Moderate

Golden Bull. Level One, New World Centre, Salisbury Road, Tsimshatsui, Kowloon; (3)694617; also at 9 Hart Ave., Tsimshatsui, Kowloon; (3)670531. A jungle retreat set in a shopping center. Regrettably, not all the menu is Vietnamese, although the dishes that are seem authentic enough. Try sliced beef in hot vinegar hot-pot style, which you cook yourself, or hot-and-sour fish soup and delicious fresh bread. Open noon to 11:30 P.M. All major credit cards.

Inexpensive

Café de la Paix. 17 Hillwood Rd. (opposite Kowloon Park, off Nathan Road), Kowloon; (3)721–2747; also *La Campagne*, 11 Hillwood Rd., Kowloon; (3)671871 (no credit cards). Unpretentious Vietnamese venue, with the usual range of pork and seafood dishes, noodles, and soups. Open noon to 11:00 P.M. All major credit cards.

Perfume River. 51 Hennessy Rd., Wanchai, Hong Kong; (5)278644; also at 89 Percival St., Causeway Bay, Hong Kong; (5)762240. Cheap and cheerful with do-it-yourself Viet hot pots, spring rolls, salads, and noodle dishes. Couldn't be more convenient. Open noon to midnight. All major credit cards.

Rainbow. 34–36 Stanley St., Central, Hong Kong; (5)226323. Vietnamese food with a Chinese accent. Try a steamed pork roll for breakfast, just for a change. Open 8:00 A.M. to 11:00 P.M. No Credit cards.

Saigon Beach. 66 Lockhart Rd., Wanchai, Hong Kong; (5)273383. Another fun venue with *nuoc mam* (spring rolls dipped in pungent fish sauce), spicy fish and pork dishes, and soups. Eccentric closing on the 15th and last day of every month. Otherwise, open noon to 10:00 P.M. No credit cards.

COFFEE SHOPS

Café Rendezvous. Holiday Inn Harbour View, 70 Mody Rd., East Tsimshatsui, Kowloon; (3)721–5161. The *à la carte* is very much the norm for a hotel coffee shop, but a couple of special features deserve a mention. First, there's a special children's menu. Second, there's a no-smoking area. Third, there are buffets for lunch *and* breakfast. Last, there are harbor views. Open 7:00 A.M. to 1:00 A.M. All major credit cards.

Cafe Terrace. Victoria Hotel, Shun Tak Centre, Hong Kong; (5)407228. Great view at coffee-shop prices. Open 6 A.M. to 2 A.M. All major credit cards.

Café Vienna. Holiday Inn Golden Mile, 50 Nathan Rd., Tsimshatsui, Kowloon; (3)693111. What distinguishes this coffee shop from the others is the special afternoon taste treats. For example, from 3:00 P.M. to 6:00 P.M. daily, the café serves the "pancake parade" (they are really crêpes), marvelous diet wreckers such as crêpes filled with chocolate, strawberries, or fresh fruit or . . . you get the idea. Periodic promotions include selected Chinese snacks (to see how the Chinese satiate a sweet tooth) and ice creams. Oh yes—the only things

"Viennese" are the pastries and coffee. Open 6:30 to 2:30 A.M. All major credit cards.

California. 30–32 D'Aguilar St., Central, Hong Kong; (5)211345. Such a trendy place as this would probably resent being classified as a coffee shop, but the short-order American cooking is its specialty. It is designed to be like America/California of the 1950s. Weekend disco and occasional shows. Open noon to 3:00 P.M. and 7:00 P.M. to 11:30 P.M. Disco nights till 3:00 A.M. All major credit cards.

Cat Street. The Hilton Hotel, 2 Queen's Rd., Central, Hong Kong; (5)233111. With access from the hotel or the street, Cat Street is always busy, and lunch-time booking is advisable unless you want to wait. The usual coffee-shop menu is supplemented by an admirable number of Asian specialties. High chairs for tots and friendly service. No-smoking area. Open 6:00 A.M. to 3:00 A.M. All major credit cards.

Clipper Lounge. Mandarin Hotel, 1 Connaught Rd., Central, Hong Kong; (5)220111. Not really a coffeeshop *per se,* but the food is short order-ish and excellent. Lovely cakes and sweets to go with high tea. What makes this place so popular is its superb people-watching location on the mezzanine floor over-looking the lobby. The lounge is also quite popular with businessmen who sink into the deep leather lounges with their briefcases spread out beside them. Expensive. Open 8:30 A.M. to midnight. All major credit cards.

Coffee Garden. Shangri-La Hotel, 64 Mody Rd., East Tsimshatsui, Kow-loon; (3)721–2111. Skylights and masses of lush greenery make this a very pleasant place for a light lunch. There's a coffee shop menu with Asian specials, a lunch buffet, and a choice of Kosher dishes—most unusual for Hong Kong. Open 6:00 A.M. to 2:00 A.M. All major credit cards.

Delicatessen Corner. Holiday Inn Golden Mile, 50 Nathan Rd., Tsimshatsui, Kowloon; (3)693111. If only all coffee shops or carry-out places could be like this. Not kosher or kosher-style, but nevertheless superb meats, sausages, and fish, much of it smoked in the hotel's own smokehouse—reputedly the only one in Hong Kong. (Health aficionados, please take note: no preservatives or addi-tives are added to the smoked food.) The main deli in the hotel has tables, the small branch in Hutchison House has only a small bar along the wall with stools, and the branch on The Peak is only carry out. Open 7:30 A.M. to midnight. All credit cards.

Expresso. Hilton Hotel, 2 Queen's Rd. Central, Hong Kong; (5)233111. Hidden away on the ground floor, this tiny hole-in-the-wall does not have all the hustle and bustle of the Cat Street coffee shop, but it is still a pleasant place to have a moderately priced meal. Though the overall impression is Italian, there are plenty of other items on the menu, including daily specials. Mind you, this is not the place to go for a quick sandwiches, because there aren't any. Lovely Italian coffees. Good selection of pastries. Open 7:30 A.M. to 10:00 P.M. All major credit cards.

Le Grand Café. Hotel Regal Meridien, Mody Road, East Tsimshatsui, Kow-loon; (3)722–1818. The usual international coffee-shop selection with a Chinese section in deference to the local populace. Open 6:00 A.M. to 2:00 A.M., with a Sunday lunch buffet. All major cards.

The Greenery. The Royal Garden, Mody Road, East Tsimshatsui, Kowloon; (3)721–5215. The Greenery really lives up to its name, with plants everywhere, even overhead. Usual coffee shop menu with soups and hamburgers and more substantial dishes. Open 7:00 A.M. to 1:00 A.M. All major credit cards.

Harbour Side. The Regent Hotel, Salisbury Road, Tsimshatsui, Kowloon; (3)721–1211. Just grab a hamburger, or treat yourself to a three-course bonanza that will push this coffee shop into the moderate-price bracket. The harbor view is so good you almost get wet feet. Daily specials and a fixed menu. Open 6:00 A.M. to 1:00 A.M. All major credit cards.

Lobby of the Peninsula Hotel. Salisbury Road, Tsimshatsui, Kowloon; (3)-666251. It's almost sacrilege to classify The Pen's fabled lobby with its gilded columns as a mere "coffee shop," but as good as the food is, that is basically the style. Everything from a very uncolonial hamburger to cucumber sandwiches while you sit back and watch the world go by. When the hotel was but a mere railway hotel, its lobby was one of the few crossroads for Westerners traveling in the Orient. Today, it is just one of the most popular. High tea with silver service is *de rigueur.* On a more mundane level, there is a three-course roast beef luncheon daily. Open 7:00 A.M. to 1:00 A.M. All major credit cards.

Mandarin Coffee Shop. The Mandarin, Connaught Road, Central, Hong Kong; (5)220111. Recently moved to a lighter, more spacious environment within the hotel, and now more popular than ever. The best breakfast specialty is cinnamon toast, and you have to ask for it because it is not on the menu. Somehow even the coffee shop retains all the "poshness" for which the hotel is famous. Reserve for lunch or afternoon tea (real tea, of course, not teabags). Open 6:30 A.M. to 1:00 A.M. All major credit cards.

Peak Tower Coffee Shop. Upper Peak Tram Terminal, Victoria Peak, Hong Kong; (5) 97262. After you've got off the Peak Tram, take the lift up still farther to the coffee shop. Never mind the food, look at the views! Open 9:30 A.M. to 11:00 P.M. All major credit cards.

La Plantation. Regal Meridien Airport Hotel, Sa Po Road, Kowloon; (3)718 –0333. If your flight is delayed, forget the awful airport restaurant. Instead, cross the air-conditioned footbridge to an oasis of cool green with slow ceiling fans. Daily roasts for lunch and dinner and a Sunday buffet, as well as the usual salads, hamburgers, pasta, and fried rice. There's also a selection of the food you never dared to try: from a Chinese-style hawker trolley, ox tripe, braised sinew with herbs, and scalded pig's liver. Open from 6:00 A.M. to midnight daily. All major credit cards.

Seasons. 17 On Lan Street, Central, Hong Kong; (5)268429. Tiny menu but charming atmosphere. Specials include fresh seafood chowder in pastry shell, salmon, and other daily dishes. Excellent live music in the evenings. Open 11:00 A.M. to 3:00 P.M., 5:00 to 11:00 P.M. AE, DC, V.

Terrazza. The Landmark, Des Vouex Road, Central, Hong Kong; (5)264200. There's nothing Italian except the name. Bargain breakfasts and set lunches are the mainstays of this balcony over the atrium of Hong Kong's smartest shopping mall. As often as not, there's lunch-time entertainment of some kind in the atrium, and even when there's not, there's a fountain. Open 8:00 A.M. to 7:00 P.M. No CB.

Windmill. The Excelsior Hotel, 281 Gloucester Rd., Causeway Bay, Hong Kong; (5)767365. Delftware, copper kettles, and prints of Dutch masters are inevitable in a coffee shop with such a name. The food is average but the ambience pleasant, with views over the Royal Hong Kong Yacht Club marina. Open 7:00 A.M. to 12:30 A.M. All major credit cards.

GRILL ROOMS

Expensive

Bocarinos Grill. Victoria Hotel, Shun Tak Centre, Hong Kong; (5)407228. Done in a light, Mediterranean style with ceramic tiles and white stucco walls, and arches and columns dividing the booths. Open grill with a traditional grillroom menu plus salad wagon. Open 11:00 A.M. to 3:00 P.M., 6:00 P.M. to 11:00 P.M. All major credit cards.

Excelsior Grill. The Excelsior Hotel, 281 Gloucester Rd., Causeway Bay, Hong Kong; (5)767365. An open charcoal grill is the focus of this restaurant, but the menu is full of rewards for the more adventurous diner. Superbly discreet service and lots of space between tables. Sunday buffet brunch. Open noon to 3:00 P.M., 7:00 P.M. to 11:00 P.M. All major credit cards.

Grandstand Grill. Sheraton Hotel, 20 Nathan Rd., Tsimshatsui, Kowloon; (3)691111. Gourmet food in race-course setting, with a good-value, set-price roast beef lunch for HK$85. A strolling guitarist does the rounds in the evenings. Open 7:00 A.M. to 11:00 A.M., noon to 3:00 P.M., 6:30 P.M. to 11:30 P.M. All major credit cards.

Grill. The Hilton Hotel, 2 Queen's Rd., Central, Hong Kong; (5)233111. Consistently busy at lunch times when tycoons and bankers munch their charcoal broiled steaks, chops, seafood, and roast beef. Dinner is a little more sophisticated, and *haute cuisine* comes into its own. Open noon to 3:00 P.M., 7:00 P.M. to midnight. All major credit cards.

Mandarin Grill. The Mandarin, Connaught Road, Central, Hong Kong; (5)220111. Restrained yet sophisticated. The menu is simple: steaks, chops, daily roasts, and emphasis on seafood. Live flute and guitar music nightly. Open 7:00 A.M. to 11:00 A.M., noon to 3:00 P.M., 6:30 P.M. to 11:00 P.M. All major credit cards.

Rib Room. Prince Hotel, Harbour City, Canton Road, Tsimshatsui, Kowloon; (3)723–7788. Though a grill room, there is a heavy emphasis on steaks, not only the favorite American ones and the backups from Australia and New Zealand, but Kobe beef from Japan and Angus beef from Scotland. Champagne and steak specials. Open noon to 3:00 P.M. and 6:30 P.M. to 11:00 P.M. All major credit cards.

Taipan Grill. Hongkong Hotel, Canton Road, Tsimshatsui, Kowloon; (3)-676011. An ambitious menu for what is basically a grill room. As well as the usual grills and roasts, there's a nice range of fish dishes (sole filled with salmon mousse, sautéed prawns in spicy herb and tomato sauce), and tempting soufflés. The ambience is intimate and romantic, with more Filipino musicians doing the rounds. Open noon to 3:00 P.M., 6:00 P.M. to midnight. All major credit cards.

INTERNATIONAL/CONTINENTAL

Expensive

Pink Giraffe. Sheraton Hotel, 20 Nathan Rd., Tsimshatsui, Kowloon; (3)-691111. Perched atop of the Sheraton Hotel, the Pink Giraffe is at its best at night, although it's also open for breakfast and lunch. Oysters, lobster, pepper steak, and roast duck are predictably popular items on a menu that is highly predictable. A live jazz band plays in the evenings, unless there's a star performer flown in from the United States or Australia. Open 7:00 A.M. to 10:00 A.M., noon to 3:00 P.M., 6:30 P.M. to 1:00 A.M. All major credit cards.

Verandah. Repulse Bay, Hong Kong; (5)812–2722. This is the one and only classic Verandah Restaurant of the famed Repulse Bay Hotel—except that there is no more Repulse Bay Hotel. It was torn down during the building boom of the early 1980's. The restaurant, and the adjacent Bamboo Bar, are replicas of the 50-year-old classic (minus the wonderful alfresco dining of yore). It still looks good, has a splendid wine cellar and all the old classics of before. Homemade goose liver terrine with truffles, medallions of veal, fine sweets. If one misses the great buffets, this is still the new Hong Kong, and one can still relish the great driveway, the fine service, and a good meal in an atmosphere that reeks of Noel Coward, Ernest Hemingway, and other old Repulse Bay Hotel guests. Open noon to 2:30 P.M., 7:00 to 10:30 P.M. Weekend breakfast between 8:00 and 10:30 A.M. All major credit cards.

Moderate

Bauhinia Room. Hongkong Hotel, Canton Road, Tsimshatsui, Kowloon; (3)676011. This restaurant is actually worth a mention for its harbor views alone (out over Ocean Terminal), but the food is also pretty good, as befits a member of the Peninsula Group. It's less pretentious than the Taipan Grill in the same hotel. Open 6:00 A.M. to 11:00 A.M., noon to 3:00 P.M., 6:00 P.M. to midnight. All major credit cards.

Jimmy's Kitchen. South China Building, 1–3 Wyndham St., Hong Kong; (5)265293; also at Kowloon Centre, 29 Ashley Rd., Tsimshatsui, Kowloon; (3)684027. A popular Hong Kong restaurant for more than 50 years. The extensive menu is supplemented by seasonal specials and daily roasts. Something for everyone, from crabmeat canelloni to prawn sari, with pig's knuckle and goulash in between. Satellite, a deep-fried ice cream, is a much favored dessert, as is the apple strudel. The pleasant service and informal atmosphere keep the crowds rolling in. Open 11:00 A.M. to 11:00 P.M. All major credit cards.

Landau's. (5) 893–5867 Gloucester Rd., Hong Kong; (5)790–5867. Ceiling fans and sepia-colored photographs of old Hong Kong set the scene at this relaxed eatery run by the Jimmy's Kitchen people. Fish and grills are almost always good. Blackboard seasonals, such as lobster thermidor and fresh artichoke with butter sauce, are as good as you'd get anywhere. If you still have room, try a tangy crêpe suzette or a strawberry omelette with Cointreau for dessert. Lunch and dinner daily. All major credit cards.

Nathan's. Hyatt-Regency Hotel, 67 Nathan Rd., Tsimshatsui, Kowloon; (3)662321. This unusual restaurant is named for the road it overlooks, not for its Coney Island namesake. Serves breakfast, lunch, afternoon tea, cocktails, and dinner (with live entertainment), and the decor seems to blend perfectly with each change of mood. At lunch, tandoori buffet, carved roast, or California treats like crayfish and artichoke salad. Open 6:00 A.M. to 2:00 A.M. All major credit cards.

Peak Tower. Upper Peak Tram Terminal, Victoria Peak, Hong Kong; (5)972 -60. A circular restaurant with views right round Hong Kong Island, across to Kowloon and the New Territories, and on a clear day, to the hills of China. The food tries very hard, but it isn't great. It could never upstage the view, anyway. Weekend lunch buffets. Open 11:30 A.M. to midnight. Reservations recommended. All major credit cards.

La Ronda. Hotel Furama Inter-Continental, 1 Connaught Rd., Central, Hong Kong; (5)255111. This restaurant sticks to buffets, since the management decided that *à la carte* dining and a revolving restaurant with kitchens on the floor below were incompatible. Mind you, it can be disconcerting to try to find your moving table again after you've served yourself at the buffet, which stands still. The tables are numbered, which helps. It's a good buffet, and the views of Hong Kong and Kowloon are great. Open noon to 2:30 P.M., 7:00 P.M. to 11:00 P.M. All major credit cards.

Inexpensive

Balcony. The Royal Garden, Mody Road, East Tsimshatsui, Kowloon; (3)-721–5215. Overlooking the most spectacular atrium in town, with hanging plants and running water tinkling away. Buffet lunch noon until 3:00 P.M., pastries and sandwich snacks until midnight. All major credit cards.

Sammy's. 204–6 Queen's Rd. West, Hong Kong; (5)488400. Tucked away in Western District, this eatery, which is now going into its fourth decade, is a budget travelers' secret. Large helpings and many ethnic specialties. 8:00 A.M. to midnight.

Susanna's. 70 Po Tung Rd., Sai Kung, New Territories; (3)281–2139. Good and heaping portions of European and Cantonese food, everything from Russian borscht to Chinese clams in a spicy sauce. Good and inexpensive wine list, too. Open noon to midnight, seven days a week. No credit cards.

STEAK HOUSES

Expensive

Palm. 38 Lock Rd., Tsimshatsui, Kowloon; (3)721–1721. Named after the New York original. Hong Kong's jetsetters are caricatured on the walls, and local talents are given free rein with felt-tipped pens. Gimmicks aside, the Palm serves prime U.S. steaks, lobster, and daily specials. Limited wine list and endless coffee. Lunch and dinner daily. V, AE.

San Francisco Steak House. First floor, Barnton Court, Harbour City, Canton Road, Kowloon; (3)722–7576. A bit like an old railway carriage, with red plush upholstery and lots of wood, but the San Francisco Steak House claims to do the best steak and lobster in town. That's a debatable point, but the extras are very good—onion rings, big baked potatos, garlic bread, and fresh salads with sharp dressings. Open noon to 3:00 P.M., 5:30 P.M. to midnight. AE, V.

Steak House. Regent Hotel, Salisbury Road, Kowloon; (3)721–1211. Simplicity is the keyword, with bentwood chairs and charcoal-broiled steaks from 6 to 16 ounces. Meat is prime U.S. beef, chilled not frozen. Mix your own salads. Fresh berries are always available. Pricey but popular, so reservations are necessary. Open for lunch and dinner every day. All major credit cards.

Steak Place. Shangri-La Hotel, 64 Mody Rd., East Tsimshatsui, Kowloon; (3)721–2111. The simplest menu in town offers a choice of four steaks (choose your size), roast beef, or lamb chops with a baked potato, corn on the cob, and mix-your-own salads. Open 7:00 P.M. to 11:00 P.M. All major credit cards.

WINE BARS AND PUBS

Pub food is the fare that is served in British (or Australian or New Zealand) public houses without the elaborate table settings or table service usually found in restaurants. It's the sort of food that can be produced in bulk and kept hot without spoiling—pies, quiches, soups, or such cold foods as Scotch eggs, salads, and sandwiches.

In terms of quality, pub food is variable, but it is generally a cut above fast food and is eaten in more congenial surroundings, almost always with a drink of some sort in front of you.

Some pubs go to town and collect quite a healthy proportion of their profits from the food they serve, particularly at lunch time. The Dickens Bar, The Jockey, and the Royal Falcon fall into this category. Others are content to serve food purely to supplement drinking. The Old China Hand and Ned Kelly's Last Stand are examples of this genre. It's extremely rare to find desserts on a pub menu, unless there's a buffet arrangement. Cynics would suggest that this is because you drink more if you are eating savory food. As pub food is cheap, most pubs don't take credit cards, unless they happen to be housed in an international hotel. Usually you pay as you go along.

Expensive

Brown's Wine Bar. 104-206 Tower 2, Exchange Square, Central, Hong Kong; (5) 237003. Not only can you buy wine by the bottle from a fine list, but you can taste two dozen wines by the glass (2½ or 5 oz) from a special dispenser. A favorite haunt of stockbrokers, particularly after the exchange's closing at 3:00 P.M. Eight house wines and an exquisite menu. Open 8:00 A.M. to midnight. Closed weekends. Visa, MC.

Royal Falcon. The Royal Garden, Mody Road, East Tsimshatsui, Kowloon; (3)721–5215. Relax in an atmosphere of duplex Victoriana at Hong Kong's most up-market pub. Lunch-time buffet, salad bar, and roasts. At nights, there's a disco, resident band, and light show, but no food. Open noon to 3:00 P.M., 5:30 P.M. to 1:00 A.M., 2:00 A.M. Friday, Saturday and prior to public holidays. All major credit cards.

Moderate

Beefy's Cabin. 70 Canton Rd., Tsimshatsui, Kowloon; (3)663397; also at *Beefy's Tavern,* 76 Canton Rd., Tsimshatsui, Kowloon; (3)674697. Cheap, cheerful, clean, and bright; Beefy's fish and chips and shepherd's pie will restore wilting tastes buds after a surfeit of gourmet meals. Singer and electric organ at night. Open noon to 5:00 A.M.

Bull and Bear. Hutchison House, 10 Harcourt Rd., Central, Hong Kong; (5)257436. Reservations are necessary at lunch time, as this pub fills with expatriate bankers and younger employees of the hongs (business houses). Salads and sandwiches served at lunchtime only. Open 11:30 A.M. to 2:00 A.M.

Dickens Bar. The Excelsior Hotel, 281 Gloucester Rd., Causeway Bay, Hong Kong; (5)767365. Dark wood, prints of Dickens characters, and Chinese waitresses in pseudo-Victorian dress are elements of the theme of this not very British pub, which serves a great value curry buffet lunch on Monday, Wednesday, Friday, and Sunday, and Mexican on Tuesday and Thursday. HK$35 includes a beer. Shepherd's pie, Scotch eggs, and steak-and-kidney pie are available for traditionalists. Live jazz on Sunday afternoons. Open 11:00 A.M. to 2:00 A.M., 11:00 A.M. to 3:00 P.M. Saturday and before holidays. All major credit cards.

Friar Tuck. 053 World Shipping Centre, Harbour City, Canton Road, Tsimshatsui, Kowloon; (3)723–3298; Edko Tower, 32 Ice House St., Central, Hong Kong; (5)242332. A bit more ambitious in terms of food than most other pubs, but the bar is large and the décor leans to the olde English. Open noon to 1:00 A.M. daily.

Jockey. First floor, Swire House, Connaught Road, Central, Hong Kong; (5)261834. Busy at lunch times, when there's steak-and-kidney pie, ploughman's lunch, soups, and sandwiches. Disco and dancing in the evening. Open 11:30 A.M. to midnight.

Joe Bananas. 23 Luard Rd., Wanchai, Hong Kong; (5)291811. A jump back to America of the 50's and 60's, but certainly up market (in style and price). Would you believe 32 different brands of bottled beer plus six on tap? Open 11:30 A.M. to 1:00 A.M.

Mad Dogs. 33 Wyndham St., Central, Hong Kong; (5)252383. The name, of course, refers to Noel Coward's famous refrain, "only mad dogs and Englishmen go out in the noon day sun." This is the colony's only Scottish pub, though for the rest of world it would be British. Good pub fare—Scottish and English—including pies and, of course, haggis. Open 11:30 A.M. to 1:00 A.M., Fridays and Saturdays till 2:00 A.M.

Ned Kelly's Last Stand. 11A Ashley Rd., Tsimshatsui, Kowloon; (3)660562. Dixieland jazz—played nightly from 9:00 P.M.—is the lifeblood of this 'fair dinkum' Aussie pub. Food is simple and filling—Australian meat pies, hefty sandwiches, and steaks—and there's Foster's Aussie lager, as well as local brews. Open 11:30 A.M. to 2:00 A.M.

Nineteen 97. 9 Lan Kwai Fong, Central, Hong Kong; (5)260303. The food is just average here and the Austrian co-owner has managed to put on a few Austrian specialties. The main attraction is the bar and late-night eating, which seems to attract a great many nightowls. This place is about as close as Hong Kong has come to a singles bar. Open noon to 1:00 A.M. (or later if the customers stay on). No CB, OTB.

The Old China Hand. 104 Lockhart Rd., Wanchai, Hong Kong; (5)279174. A darts pub with limited food—ploughman's lunch, meat pies, sausage and beans, and the like. Beer by the jug. Open 11:30 A.M. to 2:00 A.M.

Le Tire Bouchon. 9 Old Baily Street, Central, Hong Kong; (5)235459. With 60 different wines to choose from, the bistro lives up to its name (which means corkscrew in English). Open noon to 3:00 P.M., 7:00 P.M. to midnight. MC, V.

Traps. Valley Centre, 82 Morrison Hill Rd., Happy Valley, Hong Kong; (5)740800. The *raison d'être* for this bar across from the race course and football club is sport. A giant TV screen allows you to watch live racing or action replays while you enjoy a pie and a pint. Saturday lunch is a roast beef special; Sunday lunch is a curry special. Also, pâté, pasties, quiche, etc. Open 11:30 A.M. to late on weekends, 7:00 P.M. to late during the week. All major credit cards.

Waltzing Matilda. 9 Cornwall Ave., Tsimshatsui, Kowloon; (3)676874. A boozey home-away-from-home for homesick Aussies, with the cheapest T-bone steak in town. Open all the hours when anyone could possibly drink cold Fosters: 10:30 A.M. to 5:30 A.M. No credit cards.

OFF-BEAT EATING

If you tire of eating in Hong Kong's more conventional restaurants, or you want to get one up on those folks next door who've been absolutely everywhere and done everything, head away from the urban areas and sample seafood delights off the beaten track.

Head north from Kowloon, through the Lion Rock Tunnel, to Shatin. Here you'll find the *Shatin Floating Restaurant.* It's owned by the same company that owns the *Jumbo,* but it caters to a larger proportion of locals than its Aberdeen counterpart does, so you don't feel so much like one of the herd.

Also in Shatin, close to the railway station and the main road, is the *Lung Wah Hotel.* The hotel restaurant specializes in pigeon in every possibly guise—baked, sautéed, steamed, or in soup, and has been cooking pigeons, as well as pigeon's eggs, hearts, and giblets, for something like 30 years.

Up the road towards Tai Po, across the road from the Chinese University there's a very pleasant spot called *Yucca de Lac.* At lunch times you can enjoy superb views across Tolo Harbour while you eat a leisurely meal on the terrace, or if you're there on a fine evening, sit below trees festooned with fairy lights. The food is Cantonese, as it is in almost all of the restaurants outside of town.

In the northwest corner of the New Territories, there's a place called Laofaoshan, which is famous, at least locally, for its oysters. Although the traditional stir-frying method used in much Cantonese cooking calls for minimal cooking times, Chinese people generally eschew raw food, so you won't get oysters newly opened served in shells on a bed of crushed ice. The products of the Laofaoshan oyster beds are sautéed, steamed, or made into soup, and cairns of shells by the roadside testify to the vast number of oysters the Laofaoshan restaurants get through. Of course, you can eat other things here, and fish once more predominates. You choose your fish from the market stalls and take it to a nearby restaurant.

Avoid Sunday and public holidays, as these are the times the population of Tsuen Wan and Yuen Long flock to Laofaushan *en famille;* and check the prices of seafood and oysters before you order, as they tend to vary with the season and the weather. Fish, prawns, and oysters are cooked to order by the catty (about two pounds).

Sai Kung on a Sunday is a fine place for walking or sailing. The place to eat is *Pebbles,* at 13 Sha Tsui Path, (3)2816388, with a wide variety of cuisines, mainly European.

Lei Yue Mun (or Lyemun or Leimun) is a tiny fishing village huddled at the edge of the sea across from Shaukiwan, which is at the eastern end of Hong Kong Island. Here you choose your own live seafood from the many fishmongers, and, after bargaining with the vendor, take it to the restaurant of your choice and have it cooked. It's better if you do this in a party of between six and twelve, as this way you can sample more dishes.

The easiest way to get there is to take the MTR to Kwun Tong Station and a taxi to the tiny pier that serves the village. If there are no taxis on the return trip, take a minibus to the Kwun Tong Station. The food is worth the effort.

Another colorful way to eat your way through an evening is to head for Causeway Bay typhoon shelter (April through October only) and hire a sampan (complete with tables and chairs) from one of the ladies who'll immediately accost you and insist that she has the best sampan in the whole of Hong Kong. The object of the exercise is to float round the typhoon shelter for a couple of hours, choosing dishes from the floating kitchens of other sampans you meet. Alternatively, of course, you could just stay in one place and let them all come to you.

As well as *congee,* rice, noodles, and endless combinations of meat, fish, and vegetables with black-bean sauce, ginger, chilli, garlic, or oyster sauce, there are also bar sampans, orchestra sampans, and, rumor has it, floating brothels for appetites unsated by food and drink.

Conditions are primitive, and wine drinkers should bring their own. The restroom is a hold cut in the stern of a sampan with a curtain round it, which might give a clue to the smell that pervades the air on warm nights.

The outlying islands all have good restaurants that are not that difficult to reach. On Lantau, there are a couple that are just a step away from the ferry terminal at Silvermine Bay, but it's more rewarding to be just a bit more adventurous and catch a bus to Cheung Chau, where there are a number of good, cheap eating places right on the beach. And it's the best beach in Hong Kong, according to Lantauians. The "Lantau Hilton"—real name Charlie's—in the village of Tong Fuk is a welcome gastronomic respite, as is *The Gallery.* Also on Lantau, visitors to *Po Lin Monastery* can sample vegetarian food in the visitor's restaurant attached to the monastery.

The waterfront at Cheung Chau is lined with restaurants that do a brisk trade in all types of Chinese food, as well as one or two spots that provide basic

Western fare. But walk across the narrow neck of the island (Cheung Chau has no motorized transport) to the beach and *Cheung Chau Country Club.*

Despite its name, it is not a club but an ordinary restaurant. The food is very reasonable, both in terms of cost and quality, but go for a table on the balcony rather than inside, where it's a bit like eating in a barn.

Lamma is another island that is well known for its fish restaurants. As well as the *Lamma Hilton,* which is listed in the Cantonese section, *Peach Garden, Fu Kee Seafood Restaurant,* and *Chow Kee Seafood Restaurant* are also worth a visit. Different restaurants have their own strengths and weaknesses, although they almost all have the same menu. The Lamma Hilton has better prawns than the Peach Garden, but the Peach Garden is great for lobster.

There are also a couple of very good fish restaurants out at the only village on remote Po Toi Island. A hoverferry service at hourly intervals on Sunday is the only way to get there, unless you happen to have friends with a pleasure junk.

If you get down to Shek O, a very attractive village on a peninsula at the southwest corner of Hong Kong Island, the eating choice is between a bowl of hot and delicious noodle soup, which is improved by the addition of judicious quantities of chilli sauce, and *Shek O Village Restaurant.* The latter is a friendly little place with the usual fish tanks outside, and you'll find all manner of fish and vegetable dishes on the menu.

Less far afield is Repulse Bay, where you have to move a body in order to get on the beach in summer. Almost everything, from film for your camera to a cold can of beer, costs more on the beach at Repulse Bay than it does anywhere else in Hong Kong. But there is one exception. The *Sea View Restaurant,* which sits right on the beach. It's also one of the few Hong Kong restaurants in which you can sit and eat in a swimsuit.

For those who want to do something different that feels safe or vice versa, there's the brigantine owned by the Hilton Hotel, the *Wan Fu.* The brigantine still has all its masts, but these days it runs on engines rather than depending on the vagaries of the wind. It runs to a schedule that includes lunch buffets and evening barbecues—you eat while moored in Junk Bay or Repulse Bay—and prices for these include all the wine you can put away.

Finally, for those who want to try the place which is probably the farthest afield, head for the *Frog and Toad Pub* (it serves snacks, too) in Dai Lo Wan (Bay), Lantau Island, accessible by a two-and-a-half hour march from Chimawan beach or by hired sampan (HK$30 round trip, from Cheung Chau Island. Just be sure to tell them when to pick you up.)

 NIGHTLIFE. Hong Kong's nightlife offers something for everybody. It ranges from elegant piano bars and dining rooms to rollicking British and Australian pubs, to jazz jam sessions, to high-tech, super-strobed discos, topless bars and "Suzie Wong" girlie bars.

There are several hundred entertainment places in Hong Kong. For every 100, at least 99 are for men. These establishments can be roughly divided into girlie bars, topless bars, hostess clubs, ballrooms, and massage parlors, and are, for the most part, devoted to the entertainment of Chinese males. The majority of them are "invisible" to tourists, as the signs are not translated into English. However, there is still plenty of nightlife to interest the male tourist, with or without his wife or lady friend.

Establishments with female companionship are very much an accepted part of (male) life in the Far East, and U.S. and U.K. measures don't quite fit here. Hong Kong is not Boston.

The high-class hostess clubs with Japanese names attract expense account executives from Japan but also welcome anyone with money to spare.

Listed here are those few places that cater, at least partly, to non-Oriental customers. Some, particularly in the "Suzie Wong" topless bar category, have been omitted. And in those places listed, watch your bill carefully.

By the way the legal age for drinking in Hong Kong is 18, and there is no closing time in the colony.

COCKTAIL AND PIANO BARS

Visitors to Hong Kong usually frequent their hotel's bars first, especially if they do not know the city. The hotels here have done themselves proud and there are a number of piano bars, happy leftovers from more relaxed times.

Excelsior Hotel. The piano player in the *Noon Gun Bar,* overlooking the colorful Causeway Bay Typhoon Shelter, plays each evening.

Holiday Inn-Golden Mile. The *Inn Bar,* just off the lobby, is this hotel's hideway.

Holiday Inn-Harbour View. Laid-back sounds nightly in the *Golden Carp Bar.*

Hong Kong Hotel. The famous *Gun Bar,* with its hilarious cartoons of Hong Kong's colonial life-style on the walls, is off the lobby.

Hyatt-Regency. Just off the lobby is the *Chin Chin Bar,* which is not only popular with guests, but has a following from local residents too.

Mandarin Hotel. The *Captain's Bar* off the lobby is a gathering place for businessmen of Central District (after 6:00 P.M.) and is one of the few places where a tie is required. In the evenings, the *Harlequin Bar* on the twenty-fifth floor is quietly elegant and offers magnificent views.

The Miramar. *The Princess Bar,* with one of the last remaining piano bars on Nathan Road, is off the lobby.

Shangri-La Hotel. There is easy piano-listening in the *Tiara Lounge* from 6:30 P.M. on, along with a superb view. The *Music Room* brings you back to the era of romance.

The Sheraton. *The Great Wall Bar,* off the lobby, is so popular that several dozen tables have been added to the lobby. A small band plays from 6:00 P.M. to 11:00 P.M.

PUBS AND BARS

The liveliest Hong Kong pubs often have an Australian theme: **Ned Kelly's Last Stand,** 11A Ashley Rd., **Waltzing Matilda Inn,** 9 Cornwall Ave., the Waltzing Matilda Arms, 22 Cameron Rd., **The Stoned Crow,** 12 Minden Ave., the **Kangaroo Pub,** 15 Chatham Rd. (next to the Empress Hotel) and **Harry's Bar,** 8 Pratt Ave.; all in Tsimshatsui, Kowloon.

Then there are the British pubs. In Tsimshatsui, Kowloon, you will find the **Blacksmith's Arms,** 16 Minden Ave., and the **Friar Tuck,** 053 World Shipping Centre, Harbour City, plus the **China Coast Pub** in the Regal Meridien Airport Hotel.

On Hong Kong Island there is the **Bull & Bear** on Lambeth Walk in Central District and the **Godown** in the basement of Sutherland House, next to the Furama Hotel, plus **The Jockey Pub** in Swire House. At the top of Wyndham Street, number 33, **Mad Dogs** takes the prize for the most British-style (although it's really Scottish) pub in town. Also in this area is the **Friar Tuck** at Edko Tower, 32–38 Ice House St. There is also the **Horse & Groom,** 126 Lockhart Rd., Wanchai and the **China Hand,** 104 Lockhart Rd. In Causeway Bay you'll find the **Dickens Bar** in the Excelsior Hotel and **The Shakespeare** on Cannon Street. A septet of bars on Hong Kong Island which are very popular meeting places are **Rumours,** Sunning Plaza, Hysan Ave. (across from Lee Gardens Hotel), one of the only places with an outdoor beer barden; **Traps** in Valley Centre, 82 Morrison Hill Rd., Happy Valley (next door to Caravelle Hotel), which attracts footballers (soccer and rugby players) and the horse-racing crowd; and **1997,** a more up-market drinking establishment which attracts young professionals of both sexes from the territory's faced-paced business community and is very popular for the late nightcap, at 9 Lan Kwai Fong, Central District. Nearby is **California** at 30–32 D'Aguilar St. (but fronting on Lan Kwai Fong), also an up-market drinking hole with a lot of offer, as is **Joe Bananas,** 23 Luard Rd., Wanchai. **Scotties,** on Lan Kwai Fong, is a place to bend an elbow.

The territory's top German pub, **Schnurrbar,** is located on both sides of the harbor; 6 Hart Ave., in Tsimshatsui, Kowloon, and 29 D'Aguilar Street in Central. German beer, snacks, music, and atmosphere. And for convivial English drinking with the hard-core, try **Tattersall's,** in the back of the Godown, Sutherland House, Central.

WINE BARS

If you feel like a drop of the grape and a quiet chat, try **La Rose Noire,** 1st. fl, 8–13 Wo On Lane, Central District, Hong Kong, a French bistro with a modest menu whose patrons sip long into the evening (the owner is an excellent pianist and his wife a fine chanteuse), and if the mood takes them. . . . Another French bistro with a fine sipping atmosphere is **Le Tire Bouchon** (the corkscrew) at 9 Old Bailey St., Central, which has more than 60 wines available for your tasting pleasure. **Brown's Wine Bar,** 104–206, Tower 2, Exchange Square,

Central, is different from the two French ones. Located in the heart of the business district and adjacent to the stock exchange, it attracts more hard-nosed professionals than romantics.

DISCOS

The young and energetic will be glad to know that Hong Kong's discos are far from fading. In fact, new ones, some of them super-sophisticated, are opening. Entry, including two drinks, ranges from HK$66 to HK$105. (The higher weekend/public holiday prices are quoted below.)

Just about every hotel has a disco, but a few deserve special mention. **Faces** is a Juliana's operation in the New World Hotel, with a cover of HK$105. **The Royal Falcon,** designed as an English country pub in the day, turns into a classy disco at night, and is often packed with young people. It is in the basement of the Royal Garden Hotel in Tsimshatsui East (cover HK$99). Nearby, in the Regal Meridien Hotel, is **Hollywood East,** which changes its decor to a new theme every three months. Cover is HK$99 for two drinks. **Canton** in Harbour City, Kowloon, is spread over two floors and holds 1,000 writhing patrons. HK$88 for two drinks. (Free entrance for Prince Hotel guests.) **Hot Gossip,** just next door, combines dancing with dining and cocktails. HD$88 for two drinks. **Apollo 18,** across the street in Silvercord, is similar in price. The **Future** in the Miramar Hotel hits you for HK$77 upon entry, while the **Cosmos** in the Riverside Plaza charges HK$88. The **Shesado** in Bar City, New World Centre, is the only Japanese high-tech disco in town. HK$77 for two drinks. Across the harbor is the **Talk of the Town** (cover HK$99) in the Excelsior Hotel, with its marvelous views, and **Casablanca Supper Club** in the Aberdeen Marina Club Building. **Shum Wan Road,** Aberdeen, becomes a very classy disco from 11:00 P.M. (HK$99). **California,** in Central's D'Aguilar St./Lan Kwai Fong area, a restaurant by day, becomes a disco Wednesday, Friday, and Saturday nights (cover HK$85). The disco music also flows Friday and Saturday nights at **Rumours** (no cover charge) at Sunning Plaza, Hysan Ave. (opposite Lee Gardens Hotel), Causeway Bay, Hong Kong. Music, live and recorded, also permeates the atmosphere in **Joe Bananas,** 23 Luard Rd., Wanchai. The ever-popular **Godown** in the basement of Sutherland House, 3 Chater Rd., Central, changes from a restaurant to a disco each evening. No cover.

JAZZ AND C&W

Ned Kelly's Last Stand. 11A Ashley Rd., Tsimshatsui. As the name implies, it is an Austrialian-style pub, but is better known as a traditional (Dixieland) jazz spot with nightly sets. And the place is jam-packed, too.

Dickens Bar. This pseudo-British pub in the basement of the Excelsior Hotel becomes a jazz spot on Sunday afternoons.

Rick's Café. 4 Hart Ave., Tsimshatsui; (3)672939. The place is decorated on the theme of the Bogart movie *Casablanca,* complete with long bar and potted palms. Live jazz Wednesday, Friday, Saturday, and Sunday.

Holiday Inn-Harbour View. The jazz champagne brunch (11:30 A.M. to 3:30 P.M.) in the Belvedere each Sunday has become a Hong Kong tradition. Also laid-back sounds in the *Golden Carp Bar* each evening.

Excelsior. Sunday afternoon in the *Dickens Bar,* jazz from 3:00 P.M. to 6:00 P.M. is internationally known and visiting musicians often sit in.

Godown. Basement, Sutherland House, 3 Chater Rd., Central. Jazz every Wednesday night with big band sounds on the first Sunday of every month.

Mandarin. *The Captain's Bar.* Monday to Saturday, jazz every evening.

Seasons. 17 On Lan St., Central, Hong Kong. Every Monday and Wednesday evening.

Country & Western. *Bar City,* 2nd Basement, New World Centre, Tsimshatsui, Kowloon. The only place in town to hear Country & Western and Bluegrass sounds. HK$50 minimum Friday and Saturday nights.

DINNER THEATER

Some of the hotels have dinner shows on a now-and-then basis, and the Hilton and the Sheraton occasionally bring in some really big names.

Hilton. Two or three times a year, the Hilton brings in British stage plays, usually Noel Coward-style three-act comedies. The evening's entertainment includes a four-course dinner and costs HK$325.

GIRLIE BARS

For a taste of the 1950s and 1960s, there are still a few old-fashioned "girlie" bars in Hong Kong. Expect to pay about HK$12 to HK$20 for your own beer and upwards of HK$40–50 for a "girlie" drink. Keep a grip on your emotions and also your tab. Stories abound of foolish visitors tucking in without checking the price first and having to deal with hefty bouncers as they sign away a few hundred bucks or pounds on their credit card. Any arguments call for the cops, who are quite accustomed to this problem. Even after you've signed an exorbitant tab on your card, go to the police. You'd be surprised how they manage to get bills reduced. Best to pay as you go.

Kowloon

The Two Dragons, 5A Humphreys Ave., is one of the starkest of the leftovers, with little wooden booths along the wall that are typical of the Salons de Thé on Saigon's Tudo Street, a juke box with golden oldies at the back, and the girls operating exactly as they did so long ago. "No monee, no talkee" is the rule, no matter how many drinks you buy. And when you stop you are a "Cheap Charlie."

Bloom Bar, 16 Carnarvon Rd., is the only leftover from rest-and-recreation days with girls who come out on the street and haul customers inside.

Four Sisters Bar, 1 Minden Row, is an ex-girlie bar that through some mysterious process has become a favorite spot for locals of all nationalities.

The New Canticler, 28A Hankow Rd., is another golden oldie, where the girls sometimes stand on the doorstep to lure customers in or the *mamasan* stands and calls to passers-by.

Red Lips, off Lock Road across from the entrance to the Hyatt Regency, is an absolute must for aficionados of the genre. What sets it apart from the other places left over from Vietnam's R&R days is that the same "girls" are still working there. (And there are those that swear they were there during the Korean war!) Prices are accordingly low, and well worth the time-warp "camp" experience.

Red Lion Inn, 15 Ashley Rd., just keeps on going, year after year. You can still see the juke box at the back and occasionally a girl walks up to a lonely customer, but it is all very subdued now.

Hong Kong

Pussycat Bar, 36 Lockhart Rd., Wanchai, has had several transitions, and is still popular with visiting troops and locals. There's live music, a dance floor, a few struggling girls called "Public Relations Assistants." On Saturday night and Sunday Hong Kong's Filipinas descend on the bar looking for action.

Makati Inn, 15 Luard Rd., Wanchai, is a nightclub with dance floor and lots of Filipinas, is also popular with troops and locals.

HOSTESS CLUBS

The hostess bar is an Oriental tradition, a modern version of the original pleasure houses, and Hong Kong is full of them.

One of the interesting trends in the past two years has been the opening of larger and more lavish hostess clubs, in a city that was already teeming with them.

Hostess clubs are designed for groups of men to enjoy drinks and the company of pretty girls. Some only sell liquor by the bottle. Many will offer a private room, if there are four or five men in a group, at no extra charge.

The luxury hostess clubs of Hong Kong have a style and grace not found in other cities of Southeast Asia. All are very pricey, and designed for the affluent businessmen who entertains with the help of a generous expense account. Here are some of the better ones, but before charging off, read the warning about "bills" under the "Girlie Bars" section.

Hong Kong

Club Celebrity, 171–191 Lockhart Rd., Wanchai. Every customer feels like a celebrity from 8:00 P.M. to 3:00 A.M. while surrounded by 150 gorgeous hostesses. Decor is excellent, with thousands of tiny, soft lights winking like stars, and waterfalls and plants to keep your ions up and add oxygen to the ambience. Mirrors, statues, draperies, and mini-aquaria add to the setting.

The minimum charge should be HK$150, but this won't happen with all those ladies from Hong Kong, Korea, Taiwan, and Japan vying to sit with you. The hostess charge is HK$5 per five minutes.

Club Dai-Ichi, 257 Gloucester Rd., near the Excelsior Hotel, is one of the long-established clubs. This luxurious nightspot has 300 hostesses and is a haven for visiting executives. Most of the girls are Chinese, but others are Korean and there are a few Europeans. Dance music is from two bands, and in the evenings three female singers add to the entertainment.

The club opens at 1:00 P.M., a handy attraction for the last afternoon after a conference, when you have already checked out of the hotel and have to wait for your flight. Minimum charge is HK$100 if you sit alone. English, Japanese, Cantonese, Shanghainese, plus other dialects, are spoken.

For each hour a lady sits with you, HK$100 (day), or HK$150 (night) will be added to your bill. Groups of gentlemen usually buy a bottle of whisky or brandy to keep on the table, at HK$300 for regular brands.

If you decide to take your companion out to a dinner, movie, theater, or dancing, you pay HK$340 for a minimum of three hours during the day or HK$300 for two hours at night.

Kowloon

Club Cabaret, New World Centre on Salisbury Road. The Cabaret, in the first basement, is an unusual hostess club. It was originally designed as an international nightclub, with a big bandstand and large dance floor, but was later changed to a hostess club, the only one in town with upholstered ceilings.

Cabaret has 50 hostesses, mostly English-speaking, from Hong Kong, Korea, the Philippines, Thailand, Singapore, England, and Australia. Hostess charges are HK$64 per hour, hostess drinks are HK$25–$40, the same as your own. Minimum charge—perish the thought—is HK$88. Escort charges are HK$400 for a three hour minimum.

Chinese Palace Nightclub, next door to the Imperial Hotel, in the basement of Chungking Mansions. Hours are from 1:00 P.M. to 4:00 A.M., and there are different rates for "day," up to 9:00 P.M., and "night," from 9:00 P.M. to closing. Tired executives from overseas are welcomed by 350 lovely hostesses who speak English, Cantonese, Mandarin, Shanghainese, and Fukien. The "day" minimum charge is HK$75 and drinks start at HK$12. After 9:00 P.M. the minimum is HK$120. Daytime hostess charges are HK$75 per hour; after 9:00, they are HK$120.

Escort charges are HK$231 for a minimum three hours in the daytime. After 9:00, the charge is HK$470 for "full escort" from 9:00 P.M. to 4:00 A.M.

Club DeLuxe, first floor, New World Centre, is almost unbelievably lavish. You enter a softly lit room with plush chairs and a view over the Regent Hotel gardens and the harbor. Green foliage hangs from the ceiling and the carpet is so deep it tickles your ankles. There are trees, shrubs, flowers, glasswork, and brasswork, plus the mingle of music and the tinkle of waterfalls. And this is only the bar and cocktail lounge.

The minimum charge is HK$30 for the customer who wants to relax on his own. Neither are hostess charges exorbitant, at HK$108 per hour, considering that early-evening customers get to pick from 150 dazzling girls from Hong Kong, Korea, Japan, the Philippines, England, and Australia. Eight out of every ten of them speak English. A drink for a hostess costs HK$25, and they do make it last.

Volvo Nightclub, Mandarin Plaza, East Tsimshatsui, Kowloon. Some of the poshest surroundings you can imagine. An antique Rolls-Royce, converted to electric drive, delivers drinks along a "highway" which cuts a swath through the club. The ladies really do drink tea here. Ordinary drinks range from HK$25 to $40 during the day (2:00 P.M. to 9:00 P.M.) and HK$30 to $45 during the evening (9:00 P.M. to 4:00 A.M.). The girls will pass the time next to you at HK$17 per 10 minutes during the day and HK$27 per quarter hour at night.

China City Nightclub, Peninsula Centre, fourth floor, 67 Mody Road, East Tsimshatsui, Kowloon. Would you believe 1,000 ladies waiting to please? Another of the very posh hostess clubs. Same details as Volvo.

In all of the places mentioned the standard 10 percent service charge is added to every price, except for some of the "full escort" prices, which include the service charge.

Payment for escort services, although made in advance, entitles you only to the company of the lady. This does not rule out more intimate relations, but it means the two must be considered separately. To avoid problems, make *all* arrangements before you leave the club with the hostess.

On the Kowloon side of the harbor, on Nathan Road and Peking Road, you'll find several well-established hostess clubs, with Japanese names, that are quite popular with tourists. They are called the **Danshaku, Club Ginza, Hollywood Club,** and **Kokusai.** The names are similar, and so are the decors, so that it is sometimes difficult to tell which of these establishments you are enjoying.

MACAU

MACAU

by
SHANN DAVIES

Shann Davies, a widely traveled British freelance writer, has edited several guides to Chinese cities. She has written about Macau for over 20 years and is the author of two books: Viva Macau! *and* Chronicles in Stone.

From Hong Kong, Macau is only 40 miles away by sea. Its attractions, from casinos to historic buildings to Portuguese restaurants, are remarkably different from anything to be found in Hong Kong. What could be more appropriate for a Western traveler than a trip to the first European settlement on the Asian mainland?

Macau, 90 miles down river from Canton, was founded in 1557, by Portuguese merchants who for almost a century controlled the fabulously rich trade between China and Japan because direct trade was banned by both countries. Some of the profits went to build churches, forts, and fine mansions, while the rest was invested in Oriental luxuries for the markets of Europe.

This golden age ended abruptly with the closure of Japan and the loss of mercantile power to the Dutch and British traders. Macau became a home and entrepot for international commerce, as well as headquarters for the scholar-missionaries who served as advisers to the rulers of China.

In the eighteenth century, the religious orders were expelled, and soon after its founding in 1841 Hong Kong took away the traders. So Macau was forced to survive on legalized gambling and opium sales. Earlier in this century the city became known as a den of sex, sin, and spies. In truth, in these regards it was a pale shadow of Shanghai and Hong Kong, and during the Pacific War, when Macau remained neutral Portuguese territory, it showed its true colors by welcoming refugees from all over China.

Macau's modern prosperity comes from revenues from taxes on gambling franchises and the export of textiles, toys, electronics, fireworks, and artificial flowers. Like Hong Kong, it is a duty-free port with a *laissez-faire* economic policy. Everyone is free to set up a business with minimal taxation and government interference. And the city's annual budget usually balances.

In the past few years major building projects have been undertaken, such as the trotting track, the University of East Asia, and several luxury hotels. At the same time, many of the city's oldest buildings have been beautifully restored.

Relations with China are excellent, with increasing two-way trade and joint business ventures in Zhongshan, the neighboring Chinese county. Macau's close proximity to the People's Republic also makes it the most popular gateway for one-day China tours.

Politically, Macau has, since 1974, been officially a Chinese "territory under Portuguese administration." Lisbon appoints a governor and cabinet to work with a legislative assembly of locally elected and appointed members to handle the operations of the city. In 1987, Portugal agreed to hand back Macau to China on December 20, 1999, with the territory promised 50 more years of its own economic and social systems.

Macau's population of about 400,000 is markedly more tolerant and easy-going than that of Hong Kong, although it is just as densely packed into generally substandard housing. Most people live in the 2.5 square miles of the peninsula, although there are a few settlements on the rural islands of Taipa and Coloane, which cover a little less than four square miles. About 95 percent of the people in Macau are Chinese. Of the remainder, about 7,000 speak Portuguese as their first language, but only a few come from Portugal, the others being Macanese from old established Eurasian families. In addition, there are expatriate Europeans, Americans, and Australasians, plus several thousand Vietnamese refugees and "hostesses" from Thailand and the Philippines. Although Portuguese is the official language and Cantonese the most widely spoken, English is widely understood.

Exploring Macau

If history were a good accountant, nobody would be skimming over the forty-mile waterway from Hong Kong to Macau today. After all, the city lost all economic significance a century and a half ago, and a Portuguese-administered enclave of six square miles in modern China must be a classic geo-political anachronism. How and why has it survived into its fifth century?

For new visitors, the first clue is found on the vessel en route to Macau. Most of the passengers will be Chinese from Hong Kong on their way to the casinos, which have provided the territory with the bulk of its revenue since gambling was legalized in the 1840s to compensate for the loss of trade to newly founded Hong Kong. Also on board will be Portuguese civil servants, on four-year tours of duty from a mother country that lost all practical interest in Macau in the mid-seventeenth century.

Other fellow passengers are Jesuit priests and Catholic nuns, Chinese and European, who run vital, centuries-old charities and tend to one of Asia's oldest and more devout Christian communities. Frequently there are also Buddhist priests, who help maintain Macau's firm faith in its Chinese traditions. And in recent years, these regular commuters have been joined by tourists—more than 600,000 a year—international businessmen, Australian jockeys, British engineers, Swiss chefs, French showgirls, and dance hostesses from Southeast Asia. In their own ways they all prove that there's plenty of life left in the *grande dame* of the China coast.

The voyage, which is technically a flight on a Jetfoil, is a pleasant progress through scattered hilly green islands, some part of Hong Kong, some Chinese, and most uninhabited. Macau, when it appears on the skyline, jolts the imagination. Hills crowned with a lighthouse and a church spire, a blur of white buildings and tree-lined avenues confirm that this is a bit of Iberia, settled by the Portuguese in 1557 and the first European outpost on the China coast. For almost 300 years, it was the only entrepot for China trade, and its waters were often crowded, first with Portuguese caravels, later with British Indiamen and American clippers, and always with Chinese junks, which transhipped silk, porcelain, and tea from China and clocks, telescopes, ginseng, woolens, and opium to China.

Within minutes the water changes color as the vessel enters the muddy estuary of the Pearl River. Ninety miles upstream is Canton, the traditional traders' entrance to China. Clearly visible across the border with Macau is the new, special economic zone of Zhuhai, booming with industry and tourism sponsored by China in cooperation with Macau, Hong Kong, and Western countries. The image of a sleepy, Mediterranean town is replaced as visitors draw near. Now appear modern high rises, huge factory projects, and the graceful bridge to the outlying islands, arching to the height of the largest of the bat–wing-sailed junks, which are based in the neighboring Chinese island of Lappa.

Oldtimers see Macau's special character as being spoiled by the concrete evidence of economic progress, and certainly the city is noisier, dirtier, and more crowded than ever before. Yet the Macanese way prevails, as it has through good times and bad. For a century after its founding in 1557, Macau was possibly the richest place on earth, the linchpin of trade between China and Japan, Asia and Europe. When Japan was closed and the Dutch took over the vital sea lanes in the 1640s, Macau adapted to the status of a convenient headquarters for other Western traders. And when these traders moved to Hong Kong in 1841, the tiny territory survived in genteel poverty by providing rest and recreation for the business folk of Hong Kong.

Survival, however, has never meant conformity to logic, and there is a looking-glass quality to Macau. For the visitor this is illustrated at the ferry terminal, built from the back to the front at a considerable expense. Arrivals have to cross a bridge to the far side of the road to join a taxi line that points against the traffic, which means making a detour to get to town.

The Outer Harbor

The history of Portuguese Macau almost came to an end at this spot in 1622, when the Dutch fleet landed a large invasion force to capture the rich entrepot. From here the troops attacked Guia and Monte forts, only to be defeated by a ragtag army of Jesuit priests, Portuguese soldiers, and African slaves.

Today the outer harbor is designed to welcome all arrivals. On the mile-long avenue from the wharf are the Oriental, Presidente, and Lisboa hotels, the Jai Alai Stadium and its casino, the new Macau Forum for conferences and sports events, and the grandstand for the annual motor and motorcycle Grand Prix events. Usually the avenue is a pleasant promenade or scenic drive by taxi or pedicab, but for the

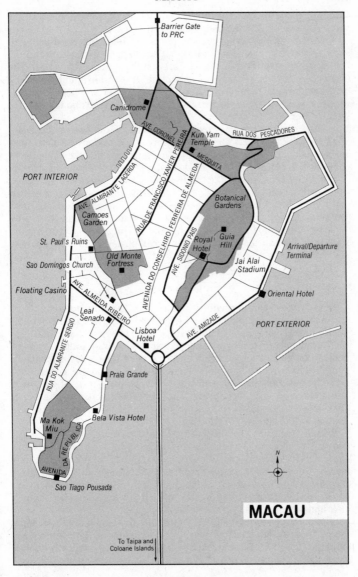

Barrier Gate
to PRC

Canidrome

AVE. CORONEL

RUA DOS PESCADORES

Kun Yam
Temple

MESQUITA

PORT INTERIOR

AVE. ALMIRANTE LACERDA

RUA DE FRANCISCO XAVIER PEREIRA

AVENIDA DO CONSELHEIRO FERREIRA DE ALMEIDA

Botanical
Gardens

Camoes
Garden

AVE. SIDÓNIO PAIS

Royal
Hotel

Guia
Hill

St. Paul's Ruins

Old Monte
Fortress

Jai Alai
Stadium

Arrival/Departure
Terminal

Sao Domingos Church

Floating Casino

AVE. ALMEIDA RIBEIRO

Oriental Hotel

Leal
Senado

Lisboa
Hotel

AVE. AMIZADE

PORT EXTERIOR

RUA DO ALMIRANTE SERGIO

Praia Grande

Bela Vista Hotel

Ma Kok
Miu

DA REPUBLICA

AVENIDA

Sao Tiago Pousada

N

MACAU

To Taipa and
Coloane Islands

third weekend in November it is the first and final straightaway for motorcycles, production cars, and Formula cars.

Overlooking the harbor are the slopes of Guia Hill, embossed with new homes, a convent, and a hospital and topped with a fort and the oldest lighthouse on the China coast, still a beacon for ships. The seascape presents a changing panorama with fishing junks bobbing through the quiet ocher water, ferries chugging to Canton, and the arcs of white wake as foil-borne vessels and hovercraft land and take off like giant waterfowl.

Another kind of aircraft used to appear in the outer harbor: the flying clippers of Pan American Airways, which gave Macau a brief, and accidental, place in aviation history. On April 28, 1937, the Hong Kong Clipper left Manila on a flight that would inaugurate air service between the West Coast of the United States and China. The plane was supposed to land in Hong Kong but at the last minute the British authorities held back landing permission, to gain rights for their own Imperial Airways. The seaplane landed in Macau and was greeted by most of the population before flying on to Hong Kong. The service continued intermittently until the outbreak of war; the Pan Am terminal stood on the site now occupied by the Oriental Hotel.

Downtown

In theory, Macau is small enough to allow a visitor to cover all of the main attractions in a day, and with unswerving determination you could do it. However, it's almost impossible to resist the casual pace of Macau, where meals are enjoyed at leisure and traffic slows to pedicab or pedestrian speed in many parts of town. For a relatively straightforward introduction to the many-layered and often contradictory character of the city, you can stroll the mile or so of the main street, Avenida Almeida Ribeiro, generally known by its Chinese name, "Sanmalo." It begins a short walk from the Lisboa and ends at the floating casino in the inner harbor.

Within this short distance you find colonial Portugal, traditional China, and modern Asia locked in architectural and social embrace. Logically, it is an unworkable misalliance; in Macau it's an enduring marriage of convenience. One reason is that buildings, institutions, and even life styles have survived because enough people wanted them to, not because their preservation was officially decreed. Sanmalo might look and sound casually chaotic, but it works.

Like a European city, the focal point of this downtown is a large square, with a fountain and plaza surrounded by several impressive buildings. The Leal Senado, or Loyal Senate, has a classically simple façade, garden courtyard, and Edwardian council chambers. The Senate acts as a municipal government, taking care of parks, garbage collection, the police force, and traffic regulations.

Its president is by tradition the president of the Santa Casa da Misericordia, or Holy House of Mercy, the oldest Christian charity on the China coast. Its headquarters occupy a handsome baroque building in the square, and its offices administer old peoples' homes, kitchens for the poor, clinics, and a leprosarium. Behind the Santa Casa is the beautiful São Domingos church, with a magnificent altar.

The central Post Office and telephone exchange, as well as some handsome old commercial buildings with arcades at street level, are also in the square. The São Domingos produce market, its narrow streets packed with stalls selling fruit, vegetables, and wholesale-priced clothing from local factories leads off the square.

Sanmalo has some regular clothing stores, but the majority of shoppers come here for gold jewelry, watches, and clocks, Chinese and Western medicines, brandy, biscuits, and salted fish. Interspersed are banks, lawyers' offices, and the Central Hotel. Now a rather dingy, inexpensive place to stay, the Central used to contain the city's only casinos, where the *fan tan* button game attracted the high rollers and the top-floor brothel did a thriving business.

The heart of the old red-light district was Rua da Felicidade (it appropriately means "Street of Happiness"), which runs off Sanmalo. Few brothels have survived competition from sauna and massage parlors, but you can still see the large picture-windows (some now boarded up) where the girls once displayed themselves. The area does preserve the atmosphere of a pre-war China coast community, especially in the evening. After sunset, foodstalls with stools and tiny tables are set out. Lights blaze from open-fronted restaurants, laundries, tailor shops, and family living rooms. The pungent smell of cooking pervades the streets, and it seems as if most of Macau's 400,000 people had fled their tiny apartments to eat out, relax, and socialize.

Another side street off Sanmalo that is worth a detour is Rua Cinco do Outubro. It contains one of the best-looking traditional Chinese medicine shops anywhere. The Farmacia Tai Ning Tong has an elaborately carved wooden façade and a cavernous interior, its walls lined with huge apothecary jars of medicinal roots, deer horn, and other assorted marvels. In a corner are mortars and pestles for making potions to order.

On the opposite side of the street is the Loc Koc teahouse. It looks undistinguished from the outside, but climb up to the third floor and discover an incredible room with pyramid-vaulted wooden ceilings, skylights, brightly carved pillars, stained-glass windows, and walls hung with scrolls and mirrors. It is open from 4:00 A.M. to mid-afternoon and caters to a wide cross-section of the population, from wharf workers to bankers, market porters to students.

The Old Citadel

When the Portuguese arrived in Macau, there was a small population of fishermen on the coast, and the first European buildings were set up along the fine bay where the trading ships anchored. These ships made an annual voyage to Nagasaki to trade Chinese silk and porcelain for Japanese silver. The governments of both Japan and China banned direct trade, and the Portuguese made fabulous profits from their monopoly.

The most remarkable early buildings in Macau were on Monte Hill. Built by the Jesuits, they included a fort, a college, and the collegiate church of the Mother of God, commonly known as St. Paul's. By the early seventeenth century, the college had become a university for scholar-missionaries en route to the courts of China and Japan. The church was declared the most magnificent in Asia, and a small town of merchants, clerics, and craftsmen grew up around the Monte.

Today this area is the heart of old Macau for visitors, and is easily reached from Senate Square via Rua da S. Domingos. The college was destroyed in a disastrous fire in 1835, and the ruins of the fort are now a quiet belvedere. Of the church, only the great stone façade remains, but it is less a ruin than a dramatic symbol of Macau and certainly the leading tourist attraction.

Traditional craftsmen, still in business carving camphorwood chests and family shrines, hand-beating metal utensils, making barrels and mattresses, and weaving bird cages, still occupy the jumble of narrow streets below the church. Tercena and Estalagens are the most interesting streets.

Following either Rua de S. Paulo or Tercena, you reach the Camões Museum, which was formerly the home of the President of the British East India Company. It is a superb example of colonial architecture and contains a collection of Chinese antiques, nineteenth-century furniture and artifacts, exportware porcelain, and works by the British artist George Chinnery and others.

The house's private grounds are now the most popular public gardens in the city. From dawn to dusk they are frequented by people practicing *tai chi chuan* shadow-boxing, men carrying their caged songbirds for a country walk, young lovers, students, and silent groups huddling over games of Chinese chess. The garden contains a courtyard shaded by liana-draped banyan trees, a grotto enshrining the bronze bust of poet Camoes, steep wooded paths, and lookouts over the inner harbor and China across the bay.

The Old Protestant Cemetery, a "corner of some foreign field" for over 150 Americans and British, is opposite the entrance to the garden. It is a well-kept and tranquil retreat, where tombstones recall the troubles and triumphs of Westerners in nineteenth-century China. Some of the names are familiar: George Chinnery; Captain Henry Churchill, great grand uncle of Sir Winston; Joseph Adams, grandson of the second U.S. president; Robert Morrison, translater of the Bible into Chinese; Thomas Beale, the opium king; traders James B. Endicott and Samuel Proctor. In addition, there are the graves of sailors who were the victims of battle, accident, or disease. Several were members of Commodore Perry's historic fleet and died while he wintered in Macau and Hong Kong, before returning to Japan to forcibly open it up for trade in 1854.

Restoration Row

One of the most incredible, and illogical, aspects of Macau is the physical survival of so much of its past. Given the city's shortage of land, revenue, and investment possibilities, it would have made economic sense to follow Hong Kong's lead and replace old buildings and gardens with high-rise office and apartment blocks. It's true that this has happened, the most glaring example being the Praia Grande, but history is more than holding its own. One reason is the Macanese power of positive procrastination, which infuriates businessmen today as it has doubtless done the would-be developers of the past. It's not that the government and public enterprises are not enthusiastic about development projects—such as the recent plan to reclaim land for an international airport and a two-square-mile industrial zone—but they rarely get past the discussion stages.

Happily for Macau's heritage, when it is a question of maintaining public buildings, procrastination is overcome by family pride, and every year or two buildings are given a new coat of white or pastel wash and generally spruced up. In some cases, such as the governor's residence and the government palace, the interiors have recently been redecorated and air-conditioned. Following suit, all of the churches and Chinese temples have also recently been restored to their old splendor.

Conservation and common sense don't always go together, but there is an outstanding example of such a match in Macau's Restoration Row. Actually it is a row of houses built in the 1920s in symmetrical arcadian style, on the Avenida do Conselheiro Ferreira de Almeida, a block or so from the Royal and Estoril hotels. The owners of the houses were persuaded to forego huge profits and sell to the government. The houses were then converted into homes for the Archives, the National

Library, the Education Department, and university offices. The exteriors were extensively repaired and the interiors transformed. In the case of the library, the building had to be completely gutted to accommodate the stacks and rooms for the vast collection of old books. The Archives building has space for researchers and a small auditorium.

Continuing along the avenue, you come to the marvelously restored Lou Lim Ioc garden, which nicely balances European architecture and classical Chinese horticulture. It was created in the Soochow style by a wealthy merchant in the last century, but fell into ruins when the family moved out in 1938. It was bought by the government in the 1960s and, after massive restoration of the shrub "forests," sculptured concrete "mountain," pond, zigzag bridge, and Chinese gateways, the beautiful facsimile of a Soochow garden was opened to the public in 1974.

Other places of interest in this area are the Memorial House of Sun Yat-sen, with memorabilia of the leader of the 1911 Chinese Revolution, and St. Michael's Catholic Cemetery. This contains a beautiful, immaculately maintained chapel, and graves of some of Macau's famous sons, including Nicolau Mesquita, the colonel who defeated a Chinese invasion force with enormous daring in 1849.

On the Doorstep of China

The date of Mesquita's victory and a solemn quotation from Camões—"Honor your country for it looks after you"—are inscribed on the stone gate—Portas do Cerco—that leads to China. Today the gate is closed at night, but throughout the day it is used by a steady stream of two-way traffic. From China come farmers carrying morning-fresh produce in bamboo baskets or on trucks, along with Chinese officials involved in joint business ventures and Macau and Hong Kong residents returning from visits with their families. From Macau the traffic consists of bus loads of tourists and groups of businessmen.

Close by the border are two very different attractions. On one side is the Canidrome, where greyhound races are enthusiastically followed. On the other side of the road is the Lin Fung Miu, or Temple of the Lotus. In the old days this used to provide overnight accommodation for mandarins traveling between Macau and Canton. Today it is visited for its exquisite façade of clay bas-reliefs and classic architecture.

Kun Iam temple, nearby on the Avenida do Coronel Mesquita, should not be missed. The Buddhist temple has a wealth of statuary and decoration and a courtyard with a stone table where the first Sino-American treaty was signed in 1844 by the Viceroy of Canton and President John Tyler's envoy, Caleb Cushing. The treaty, which followed the ceding of Hong Kong to the British, marked the beginning of China's Western-dominated century.

Behind Kun Iam is Areia Preta, Macau's new industrial zone, built mostly on reclaimed land. The textile factories here produce quality sports and leisurewear for the United States and Europe, as well as toys, electronics, and artificial flowers.

Peninsula Macau

The narrow, hilly peninsula, stretching from the main street to Barra Point and the Pousada de Sao Tiago, is quintessential Macau, very Portuguese and very Chinese, ancient and uncomfortably modern. It is bounded on one side by the Praia Grande and its extension Avenida da Republica, a graceful, banyan-shaded boulevard where people fish from the seawall or play Chinese chess. Parts of the promenade unfortunately have been taken over by parked cars, but there are also plenty of benches, and the traffic is well diluted by pedicabs.

The cargo and fishing wharfs of the inner harbor, with their traditional Chinese shop houses—with the ground floors occupied by ship's chandlers, net makers, ironmongers, and shops selling spices and salted fish—are on the opposite side of the peninsula.

In between there are several areas of historic or scenic interest. One is Largo de Sto. Agostinho, or St. Augustine Square, which is reached by climbing the steep street next to the Senate, or from the Praia Grande and the pink-and-white Palacio, which houses government offices.

Taking the Travessa do Paiva to the right of the Palacio you pass the trimly restored headquarters of the Department of Tourism. Beyond is the dimple-stoned ramp to the square, which looks as if it came all of a piece from nineteenth-century Portugal. To the left is the Dom Pedro V theater, modeled on a European court theater. Opposite is the imposing church of St. Augustine, with its life-sized statue of Christ carrying the cross, which is paraded through the streets on the first day of Lent. Next door is Casa Ricci, offices for one of the most active Catholic charities in Macau. Across the square is the Seminary of St. Joseph's, home of preeminent local historian and living legend Father Manuel Teixeira, and a collection of religious art by seventeenth-century European and Japanese painters. Completing the scene is the Memorial home of Sir Robert Hotung, the Hong Kong millionaire, who gave his house to the city in thanks for giving him refuge during the Pacific War. It is now headquarters for the new Cultural Institute.

Retracing your steps down the ramp, and continuing along the Rua de São Lourenco, you reach the elegant twin-towered church of St. Lawrence and the Salesian Institute, a technical school that stands on part of the site of the headquarters of the British East India Company. From here you can take the Rua do Pe. Antonio to the Bela Vista Hotel, or return to the Praia Grande and follow it to the Calcada do Bom Parto. Either way you'll want to stop and visit the Bela Vista, a century-old landmark hotel that is still in business. It has had a rather checkered existence and looks the worst for it, but remains a favorite with many travelers. The rooms are big, cheap, and in need of renovation, and the restaurant has known better days, but for a truly Macau experience, have a coffee or drink on the splendid terrace and survey the city and seascape.

Farther up the hill is one of the best lookouts in Macau, the courtyard of the Bishop's Palace and Penha Chapel. The Palace is always closed and the Chapel is opened only on the feast day of Our Lady of Penha, patroness of seafarers, and on the Feast of Fatima.

At the far end of the peninsula is Barra Point and the marvelous Pousada de São Tiago, a twenty-three-room Portuguese inn built into the ruined foundations of a seventeenth-century fort. It has the original staircase entrance, a terrace with ancient trees and a fountain, a chapel, hand-made mahogany furniture, blue-and-white tiled walls, an indoor waterfall from a natural spring, and so much more you have to see it for yourself.

A short walk around the point brings you to the place where Macau's history and probable settlement began. This was where the Taoist goddess A-Ma (also known as Tin Hau) is said to have brought a junk of poor fishermen safely ashore during a typhoon. In gratitude they built a temple in her honor, and today it stands among huge boulders decorated with red characters and a carving of the junk. It consists of prayer halls on four different levels, connected by winding steps and tree-shaded resting spots. One of the early names for this area was A-Ma-Gao, Bay of A-Ma, which the Portuguese made into Macau.

Taipa Island

Linked to the city by the graceful 1.6-mile bridge, Taipa can be reached by bus (including a double-decker with open-topped roof deck) or taxi. Some residents jog over it daily. Up until the end of the nineteenth century, Taipa was two islands and provided a sheltered anchorage where clipper ships and East Indiamen could load and unload cargoes, which were then carried by junks and barges to and from Canton. Gradually the islands were joined by river silt and land reclamation, but there is a reminder of the old days on the small Taipa Praia, where an early 20th-century mansion has been restored to become the Taipa Folk Museum.

Taipa and Coloane, its neighbor, are Macau's New Territories, having been ceded by China only in 1887. Until the building of the bridge both islands led a somnolent existence, interrupted only by occasional pirate raids. Taipa's economy depended on the raising of ducks and the manufacture of firecrackers. There are still some duck farms to be seen, as well as some firecracker factories, which look like ancestral Chinese villages but now produce fireworks for the American and European markets.

The village of Taipa is a tight maze of houses and shops in the traditional mold, but it is changing due to the island's new prosperity and now boasts banks, a two-story municipal market, air-conditioned shops, and several excellent restaurants. Other old institutions of Taipa have also undergone changes. The Pou Tai Un Temple, a little behind the Hyatt Regency Hotel, is still famed for its vegetarian restaurant (the vegetables are grown in an adjoining garden) but it has been embellished with a new yellow-tiled pavilion and statue of the Buddhist Goddess of Mercy.

For Buddhists, Taoists, and Confucians, Taipa is a favored last earthly address. They are buried or their bones stored in the massive United Chinese Cemetery, which covers the cliff on the northeastern coast of the island. It is lavishly decorated with colored tiles and assorted religious images.

The northeast section of Taipa provides a stunning contrast, thanks to a recent building boom. Just across the bridge is the luxurious Hyatt Hotel and the hilltop University of East Asia. Directly facing the bridge is a zig-zag wall sculpted with images from Macau's history, with a path alongside and a park above.

On the western side of the island is the Raceway of the Macau Trotting Club, fifty acres of reclaimed land with an ultra-modern, five-story grandstand, a five-furlong trotting oval, and air-conditioned stables for 480 horses. The Raceway is also used for acrobatic shows and might in the future feature flat racing.

Coloane Island

Situated at the end of a 1.5-mile causeway from Taipa, the larger, hillier island of Coloane has so far been spared from development. It is about a twenty-five minutes drive from the city, and so is generally considered to be remote. This makes it a popular spot for relaxed holidays, and the attractive 22-room Pousada de Coloane, with a pool, great restaurant, and magnificent terrace, is filled with Hong Kong families during the summer.

There is a long beach below the *pousada,* and another one at Hac Sa (Black Sands). Both are clean, although the water is Pearl River ocher, and there are plenty of cafés for food and drink. The village of Coloane, with its old tiled-roofed houses, the Tam Kong Temple, and the Chapel of St. Francis Xavier, is more interesting for overseas visitors.

The picturesque chapel, with its cream-and-white façade and bell tower, was built in 1928. Outside its door is a monument surrounded by cannon balls commemorating the local defeat of a pirate band in 1910, Macau's last encounter with old-style pirates. There are some important relics inside the chapel. The most sacred is an arm bone of St. Francis Xavier, who died in 1552 on an island fifty miles from here while waiting to begin his mission in China. The bone, now in an ornate silver reliquary, was destined for his church in Japan, but by then the Japanese had closed their doors on the Christian church. So the relic was kept in Macau, first in St. Paul's, later in St. Joseph's, and since 1976 in this chapel.

Other relics are the bones of the martyrs of Nagasaki and those of Vietnamese Christians executed in the early seventeenth century. By a strange irony, although it is not so strange for Macau, Coloane has a sizable Vietnamese community of boat people who fled their country and now await resettlement in a large, open camp administered by the Catholic church.

The newest development on the island is a finely landscaped park run by the forestry department. Its major attraction is a large aviary containing many exotic species. It is located on the western coast road, a short distance from the village.

PRACTICAL INFORMATION FOR MACAU

HOW TO GET THERE. Considering that the Hong Kong–Macau route is possibly the busiest international water highway in the world—with more than four million round-trip passages a year, or a daily average of almost 11,000—the procedure is very efficient. This is not to say it's problem free. Tickets are hard to get at weekends and on public holidays, when the Hong Kong gamblers travel *en masse.* And services are disrupted when typhoons are in the area. Added to that is Hong Kong Immigration, which is ever on the alert for illegal immigrants, is painstakingly slow. In Macau there are not enough immigration channels for foreign visitors, but most visitors no longer need visas so the immigration process is faster.

Travel documents: Visas are NOT required by nationals of the U.S., Philippines, Japan, Australia, Canada, New Zealand, Malaysia, Thailand, Brazil, Austria, Belgium, Denmark, Spain, France, Greece, Italy, Norway, the Netherlands, the U.K., West Germany, Sweden, and Switzerland (up to six months stay), or Hong Kong residents with passports for up to 20 days. Other nationals need visas, available upon arrival; HK$50 for individuals, HK$75 for a family, and HK$25 for group members. The standard visa, for an individual or husband traveling with wife and/or children under 14, allows a stay of up to 20 days or two visits within 20 days.

Tickets: Travel agents arrange tickets, as can many hotels. Otherwise, there are 11 Ticketmate computer-booking outlets that sell Jetfoil tickets up to 28 days in advance. In addition to the wharf, these outlets are located in Exchange Square and many of the Mass Transit Railway's main stations. It's best to get the return ticket at the same time. These can be changed at the Macau wharf if necessary. Jetfoil tickets can be booked by phone, (5)859–3288, with major credit cards. Tickets for Hong Kong Macao Company's hydrofoils and Jetcats can be booked with an American Express or Visa card by phone (5)232136. There is a HK$15 departure tax from Hong Kong, none from Macau.

By sea. A fleet of Boeing *Jetfoils* operate the most popular service to Macau. Carrying about 260 passengers, these craft ride comfortably on jet-propelled hulls at 40 knots and make the 40-mile trip in just under one hour. Beer, soft drinks, and snacks are available on board, as are telephones. They leave every half hour between 7:00 A.M. and dusk, with hourly departures between 7:00 P.M. and 1:30 A.M. The top deck of each vessel is special class.

Fares for the first class upper deck are HK$66 on weekdays, HK$72 on weekends and public holidays, HK$88 on the night service. Lower deck economy fares are HK$57 weekdays, HK$63 weekends, and HK$77 at night. The Jetfoils are operated by the Far East Hydrofoil Company, a division of Shun Tak Shipping, which runs three conventional *ferries* on the route. They provide a pleasant, leisurely way of getting to Macau and take about three hours. They make three round trips a day—morning, afternoon and night—with extra sailings on holidays. The fares range from HK$30 for aircraft-type seats to HK$150 for a deluxe VIP double cabin.

The other long-established company on the route is Hong Kong Macau Hydrofoil. It operates three jet-propelled catamarans called *Jetcats.* They carry 215 passengers and make the trip in about 70 minutes, with 10 round trips a day. Fares are HK$46 on weekdays, HK$58 on weekends and holidays. As befits its name, H.M.H. also has a fleet of *hydrofoils,* which take about 75 minutes and make 22 round trips a day between 8:00 A.M. and dusk. Hydrofoils can be uncomfortable in choppy seas, but they have the advantage of small, open decks for picture-taking and wind-swept rides. Fares are HK$46 on weekdays, HK$58 on weekends and holidays. American Express cardholders (only) can book by phone, (5)232136.

The latest transport to Macau is by *high-speed ferries,* which take 90 minutes and make six sailings a day. They have comfortable seats, snack bars, and poker machines plus a sun-deck for VIP lounge passengers. Fares range from HK$35 to HK$55, bookable at the Macau wharf.

Another service to Macau is by *hover-ferry.* Operated by Sealink Ferries, these craft carry 250 passengers each and take just over an hour. Fares are HK$45 weekdays, HK$56 weekends and holidays. Currently they make six round trips a day, sailing from Shamshuipo's Taikokshui ferry pier on the Kowloon peninsula. The pier is also served by some Jetfoils, hydrofoils, and Jetcats. The Kowloon service is designed for residents of the New Territories and Kowloon and is not really convenient for tourists in Kowloon hotels.

 CURRENCY. The Macau pataca, which consists of 100 avos, is worth three or four cents less than the Hong Kong dollar, which is freely negotiable in Macau.

 CLIMATE. Hong Kong residents like to spend some of the hottest part of summer in Macau, because it is a little cooler, less humid, and more exposed to sea breezes.

In general, late fall and winter are dry, sunny, and pleasant, with temperatures in the 60s and low 70s, with cooler nights. Spring weather tends to be humid, rainy, and unpredictable, with temperatures to the 80s. Summers are hot and tropical, with rains that flood low-lying areas.

 TELEPHONES. Macau's antiquated telephone system has been totally overhauled, but it still leaves something to be desired. All local calls are free and equipment is scarce, so many people rely on telephones in restaurants and shops—rather a nice bonus for visitors. Numbers are often changed and lines do get snarled, but one successful recent innovation is direct dialing to Hong Kong. (Hotels insist guests call via the operator.) International Direct

Dialing to most foreign countries has become available. Calls to Macau from Hong Kong have to go through the exchange, unless you have an IDD number.

To call Taipa and Coloane from Macau use the area code "2." For emergencies, call 999 for police, 573366 for an ambulance, 572222 for fire, and 573001 for directory assistance.

LANGUAGE. Portuguese is the official language, but most people speak Cantonese. English is widely understood.

BUSINESS HOURS. Most government and private offices are open 9:00 A.M. to 1:00 P.M. and 3:00 P.M. to 5:30 P.M. on weekdays, 9:00 A.M. to 1:00 P.M. on Saturdays.

CONSULATES. All foreign consulates accredited to Macau are based in Hong Kong. They include the United States, Japan, Canada, Germany, France, Italy, and Brazil. The British Trade Commissioner acts as consul to Macau.

ELECTRICITY AND WATER. There is both 110 and 220 voltage in use in Macau, but in major hotels there are adaptor plugs for both. Tap water is quite safe and comes either from China or from Macau's own reservoir.

TIPPING. Only the smallest restaurants do not include a service charge on the bill. However, adding a small tip is generally accepted, although less than the amount in Hong Kong, and no one will be made to feel uncomfortable if he doesn't tip.

HOTELS AND INNS. Until fairly recently, Macau's accommodations were, at best, merely adequate. But the situation has changed dramatically with the opening of several hotels that are of international first class standard. These can be booked through offices overseas or in Hong Kong. Macau's hotels depend on visitors from Hong Kong, who often make plans at the last moment, so room rates fluctuate with weather conditions and holiday periods. This usually means that sizable discounts are offered for mid-week stays. Discounts are best obtained in Hong Kong or at the hotel.

Macau also has two Portuguese inns, known as *pousadas,* modeled on the national inns of Portugal, with distinctive Macanese elements incorporated. These are listed separately.

In general, hotels listed as luxury are of the highest international standard, with pools and health clubs, public areas that are showcases of design, and guest rooms equipped with all modern comforts. Those in the moderate category are efficient, clean, and comfortable, with air-conditioning, color TV (with English and Chinese programs from Hong Kong), room service, and restaurants. They cater to gamblers, regular visitors, and medium-priced tours. Inexpensive hotels tend to be old and run-down. The rates quoted are per room, double occupancy, exclusive of 10 percent service and 5 percent tax. *Luxury:* 300–650 patacas; *Moderate:* 290–480 patacas; *Inexpensive:* 50–250 patacas. All major credit cards are accepted, unless otherwise stated.

LUXURY

Hyatt Regency and Taipa Island Resort. Taipa Island, at the end of the Macau-Taipa bridge; (2)7000; for reservations from Hong Kong, call (5)463773; from overseas, use Hyatt Hotels Reservations. Opened in early 1983, the Hyatt is the first in Asia to have guest rooms that were fully prefabricated (in the United States) and shipped as modules. They therefore conform to Hyatt Regency's high standards, with all modern conveniences and attractive furnishings. The public areas were built in Macau to designs by Dale Keller, and they combine the best of Iberian architecture and Chinese décor. The foyer is a spacious lounge with white arches, masses of potted plants, and fabulous Chinese lacquer panels. Beyond is the *coffee shop,* a lounge aptly named *The Greenhouse, Afonso's* Portuguese restaurant, and the Japanese teppanyaki grill. The hotel also has a Macanese restaurant, the *Flamingo.* The hotel has a complete sports and recreation resort on its grounds. The Hyatt is close to the trotting track and to some good jogging routes, but it is inconveniently located for the casinos and city center. There is a free shuttle bus to and from the wharf and the Lisboa Hotel. As a result, the Hyatt is for relaxed holidays in scenic, peaceful surroundings. 365 rooms.

Oriental. Avenida da Amizade, the Outer Harbour road, convenient to both the wharf and the Lisboa; 567888. For reservations: from Hong Kong, call (5)476188; overseas through offices of Mandarin Oriental. Built on the site of the old Pan Am seaplane terminal, with marvelous views of the Pearl River and islands, and conveniently located, this hotel has proved to be very popular. Most of its public rooms, such as the grill room and *Café Girassol,* face the sea. There is also the *Dynasty* Cantonese restaurant, the *Bar da Guia,* with a Grand Prix motif, an elegant casino, and sports facilities including a pool, tennis and squash courts, and a health club. The guest rooms have marble bathrooms, teak furniture, and all first-class appointments. 438 rooms.

Presidente. Avenida da Amizade, along the harbor road from the wharf and close to the casinos; 55388. For reservations in Hong Kong, call (5)266873; overseas through Utell International reservations offices. The Presidente is not really a luxury hotel, but it is first class in the standard of its rooms and its convenient location. It has a pleasant lobby bar/lounge; Continental, Chinese, and Korean restaurants; a disco with a skylight roof; and a sauna. The hotel is popular with business visitors, gamblers, and tourists. 340 rooms.

Royal. 2 Estrada da Vitoria, beside the Vasco da Gama Garden, at the foot of Guia Hill, in the residential district; 55222; for reservations from Hong Kong, call (5)422033; overseas through offices of Dai-Ichi Hotels. The Royal has an excellent location, with superb views of Guia Hill, the city, and the Inner Harbour. It has a marble-clad lobby with a marble fountain and a lobby lounge under huge chandeliers. Health club, squash court, and sauna rooms are in the basement. Upstairs is a glass-roofed swimming pool and three restaurants: the *Royal Canton,* serving Cantonese food; the *Japanese Ginza;* and the *Vasco da Gama,* with continental fare. The hotel has shuttle bus service to the casinos and the wharf. The Royal is managed by Japan's Dai-Ichi hotel chain and is reminiscent of other Dai-Ichi properties. 380 rooms.

MODERATE

Metropole. 63 Rua da Praia Grande, close to the city center and casinos; 88166; for reservations from Hong Kong, call (5)406333. The Metropole, which is managed by the China Travel Service, is located over the CTS office, where bookings can be made for trips to China. It has pleasant, comfortable rooms, and an excellent Continental restaurant which becomes a nightclub in the evening. The hotel is popular with business travelers and younger visitors. 109 rooms. Visa only.

Lisboa. Avenida da Amizade; 77666; for reservations from Hong Kong, call (5)591028. Rising above two floors of casinos, the mustard-colored tiles, frilly white window frames, and giant circus mandarin-hat roof of the Lisboa hotel tower make it an inescapable landmark. The architecture is fanciful to say the least, but the hotel is strictly business, which means gambling. Most of the guests spend their waking hours at the casinos, which can make for noisy corridors at all hours of the night. The guest rooms are first class, however, but be prepared to pay for any room service in cash. Similarly, you can't sign on your room at the elegant *A Galera Grill, Noite e Dia* coffee shop, or any of the various Chinese and Japanese restaurants in the hotel. With the completion of a new matching tower, the Crazy Paris Show has moved into a special auditorium in the hotel. Apart from the casinos, there is an arcade of space-invader machines, a four-lane bowling center, an attractive pool terrace, and saunas.

Sintra. Avenida Dom Joao IV; 85111; for reservations from Hong Kong, call (5)408028. A sister hotel to the Lisboa, the Sintra is quiet and comfortable. On the Praia Grande bayside, close to the casinos and downtown, it is popular with regular visitors and medium-priced tour groups. It has a 24-hour dining room and bar, plus an evenings-only Chinese restaurant, with a singer. 260 rooms.

INEXPENSIVE

Bela Vista. Rua Comendador Kou Ho Neng; 573821. This landmark, century-old colonial hotel has great charm and a marvelous terrace, but it is badly in need of renovation. Guest rooms are huge but draughty, and the restaurant food and service are not up to the setting. 26 rooms. Visa only.

Estoril. Avenida Sidonia Pais, in the residential district. This hotel caters to patrons of the Paris Nightclub on the ground floor. It has a good Chinese restaurant and sauna. 89 rooms.

In addition to the hotels, there are many small *villas,* which are basically guesthouses with communal television, refrigerator, and sometimes bathroom. Most of them cater to Hong Kong Chinese and the staffs usually don't speak English.

PORTUGUESE INNS (POUSADAS)

Pousada de São Tiago. *Luxury.* Avenida da Republica, at the tip of the peninsula, distant from the casinos and wharf; 78111; for reservations from Hong Kong, (5)261288. This *pousada* is as much a tourist attraction as it is an accommodation. It is a classic Portuguese inn built into the ruins of the seventeenth-century Barra Fort with enormous imagination and hard work. The roots of ancient trees dictated the shape of the terrace and coffee shop; the fountain was built from the original water cistern, and the small chapel of St. James (or São Tiago) was perfectly restored. Blue-and-white tiles, crystal lamp shades, mahogany period furniture, and much of the other furnishings and tableware were all specially made in Portugal, the carpets in Hong Kong, and the rest by local craftsmen. The entrance is the original entrance to the fort, and natural springs have been trained down the walls of mossy stones. There is a swimming pool with great views and the *Fortaleza Restaurant,* with arched windows framing the trees and sea. Reserve rooms well in advance for weekends. 23 rooms.

Pousada de Coloane. *Moderate.* Praia de Cheoc Van, Coloane Island, 30 minutes from the city and wharf; (2)8144; for reservations from Hong Kong, call (5)455626. This *pousada* is a small, delightful resort inn. Among the delights are the huge terrace overlooking a good sandy beach, a pool, and superb restaurant with some of the best Portuguese food in Macau. The Sunday buffets are renowned and, at 45 patacas per person, a great bargain. The rooms have balconies and stocked ice boxes. The *pousada* is strictly for lazy vacations, although there is a shuttle bus into town. During the summer Hong Kong families tend to fill the place. 22 rooms. MasterCard, Visa only

HOW TO GET AROUND. In the old parts of town and shopping areas, walking is the best means of transportation. The side streets are narrow and usually crowded with sidewalk businesses and people, but pedestrians make better progress than vehicles. Otherwise, transport is quite varied.

By pedicab. The tricycle-drawn, two-seater carriage has been in business as long as there have been bicycles and paved roads in Macau, and some look like originals, as do their drivers. The pedicabs cluster at the wharf and their drivers hustle their guide services. Unless it's raining, a pedicab ride along the Outer Harbour road or around the Praia Grande is a pleasant, relaxed way to appreciate the city. A ride along the busy main streets is not, and since it's impossible for pedicabs to climb the hills, touring in them is not recommended. The drivers tend to be garrulous and cheerful types, who speak some English. Fares have to be negotiated, with the driver asking at least double what he'll settle for. Short trips should cost 5 to 10 patacas, an hour's hire about 30 patacas.

By taxi. There are always taxis at the wharf, outside hotels, and cruising the streets. All are metered and most are air-conditioned and reasonably comfortable, but the cabbies speak little English and probably won't know the English or Portuguese names for places. It is highly recommended that you carry a map or name card with destinations in Chinese. Flagfall is 4 patacas for the first mile and 40 avos for each additional fifth of a mile. A few avos tip is suggested. They get a 5 pataca surcharge to Taipa, and 10 patacas to Coloane.

By bus. The buses that rattle around the city are cheap at 50 avos, but crowded and uncomfortable. Public minibuses, which serve a few routes, are slightly better. Most useful for visitors are the buses that operate from the city, via the Lisboa hotel, over the bridge to the islands of Taipa and Coloane. Open-topped, double-deck buses serve Taipa. The fare to Taipa is 1 pataca, to Coloane Village 1.50 patacas, and to Hac Sa beach 2 patacas. Replicas of 1920s London buses ply regular tourist routes and make transfers. Known as "Tour Machines," tickets cost 20 patacas, or 200 patacas for an hour's hire, and you can get on and off at will on the same ticket.

By bicycle. Bicycles are for hire at about 8 patacas an hour. In the city they are available from shops on Ave. Dom Joao 1V, or near the Taipa bus terminal. The Hyatt and Oriental have newer bikes for a higher rental fee.

By hire car. Self-drive mini-mokes are fun and ideal for touring. Most national driving licenses are valid. (Hong Kong driving licenses are not valid.) Rates are HK$250 for 24 hours weekdays, HK$280 weekends; special packages are also available from Hyatt, Royal and São Tiago pousada. Book in Hong Kong (5)434190 or Ticketmate, in Macau at the wharf office of Macau Mokes, 78851. All major credit cards.

 SEASONAL EVENTS. Macau is probably unrivaled in the number and variety of its holidays. The territory celebrates Catholic fast and feast days, Chinese festivals, historic anniversaries, and annual sports events. There are currently 24 public holidays a year and twice as many days when a greater or lesser part of the population takes time off. For visitors this profusion of holidays is a bonus attraction. It's also usually a surprise bonus, since many of Macau's annual events are movable feasts, set according to the Chinese calendar or the calculations of the Catholic church. For exact dates you need lunar tables and a missal, or information from the Macau tourist office. Some of the festivals of both East and West are very colorful and intriguing, but they can also be difficult to enjoy because of large, noisy crowds, so be prepared.

January. *New Year's Day* is a public holiday. Special winter dishes, such as hot-pot, are available in restaurants.

February. The first day of the first moon some time between mid-January and early March is *Chinese New Year,* and Macau celebrates for three days, with cannonades of firecrackers, family banquets, dragon dances, temple visits, and magnificent flower and plant markets. On the 15th day of the new year the *Lantern Festival* is held, and the full moon is greeted by thousands of candle-lit lanterns shaped like animals or boats or spaceships, carried by families and their children. In general, Chinese New Year in Macau is far more accessible to visitors than it is in Hong Kong.

March. The *Procession of Our Lord of Passos* is unique to Macau and one of the city's most spectacular events. On the first weekend of Lent, the statue of Jesus carrying the cross is taken from St. Augustine's altar in a shroud to the cathedral and, after Sunday High Mass, carried back to the church via stations of the cross set up across town. It is accompanied by the church hierarchy dressed in purple, children's choirs in white, the police band, and several thousand Catholic and non-Catholic residents. A much smaller group pays homage to the father of the 1911 Chinese Revolution on the 12th, the *Anniversary of the Death of Sun Yat-sen,* by visiting Sun's Memorial Home, close to where he once lived.

April. On the 22nd day of the second moon, the Chinese do honor to their ancestors at the *Ching Ming Festival.* Traditionally minded Macau celebrates by offering joss and food at family graves, followed by feasting with the souls of the dead. This is a public holiday and enables people to visit ancestral graves in China. *Easter* weekend is also a public holiday, when Macau's Catholics crowd the churches and parade holy images around the streets. The most popular Chinese deity in Macau is worshipped at the *A-Ma Festival,* on the 23rd day of the third moon. Though not a public holiday, it is the occasion for thousands of Taoists to visit the A-Ma Temple to pray and give offerings of food and joss, an immensely exciting but chaotic scene. In contrast, the public holiday on the 25th, celebrating the *Anniversary of the Portuguese Revolution* in 1974, is a time for most people to stay home, socialize in restaurants, or go shopping.

May. *Labourers' Day,* on the first, is celebrated as a public holiday with workers' rallies and speeches, or as a time to relax. On the 13th, devout Catholics remember the Portuguese shepherd children with the *Procession of Our Lady of Fatima.* An image of the Virgin is carried from St. Dominic's to the chapel on Penha Hill in the evening. On Coloane island, a week-long celebration takes place with the *Festival of Tam Kong,* the favorite local Taoist god of seafarers. And throughout the territory this is a time for *Bathing of the Buddha,* when Buddhist shrines are washed and purified.

June. Probably the most exciting event for visitors on Macau's calendar is the *Dragon Boat Festival* on the fifth day of the fifth moon. Based on ancient legend, it has become a local and international sporting contest, in which long, sleek dragon boats from different fishing communities in Macau and overseas race in the Outer Harbour, watched by most of the city from the the waterfront or from decorated junks. Firecrackers, drums, silk banners, sweet rice cakes, and valuable prizes make this a noisy, colorful and stunning affair. On the 10th, everyone is again on holiday for *Camoes and Portuguese Communities Day.* Government officials pay homage to the national poet in Camoes Gardens and in the evening hold a National Day reception in the pink-and-white Palacio on the Praia Grande. *Corpus Christi* is another public holiday, with church services and crowded beaches. Special masses are sung for the *Feast of St. John the Baptist* on the 23rd and 24th. He is the patron saint of Macau, but more significantly, on June 24, 1622, a vastly outnumbered Macau force repelled an invasion by the Dutch.

July. This is a quiet month for holidays, though not for holiday-making (many residents go away on vacation), but there is a very Macanese celebration on Taipa and Coloane islands, the *Feast of the Battle of July 13*. The battle took place in 1910, when the Macanese scored a decisive victory over pirates who had been treating the offshore islands as their own territory. There are church services, dragon dances, and general festivities during this public holiday.

August. This is another vacation month with only two special events. The *Feast of Assumption of Our Lady* is celebrated on the 15th as a public holiday. The *Feast of Maidens* takes place on the seventh night of the seventh moon. Formerly the occasion for street markets, it is now a family festival when unmarried girls pray for husbands to the legendary cowherd and weaver—lovers who were literally star-crossed when in anger the gods turned them into stars that met only once a year in heaven.

September. The Autumn Equinox is celebrated in Macau as the *Mooncake Festival,* and families go to high areas to light lanterns and eat mooncakes made of ground lotus, sesame, and duck eggs, while they admire the moon at its brightest. The following day is a public holiday. Food also plays a part in the *Feast of the Hungry Ghosts,* when the Chinese make offerings to their ancestors in order to please them.

October. The *National Day of the People's Republic of China* on the first is an unofficial public holiday with many offices closed. There are rallies, masses of firecrackers, and special receptions by local Chinese leaders. On the fifth the Portuguese celebrate *Republic Day,* marking the birth of the republic in 1910. The ninth day of the ninth moon is *Cheung Yeung,* when Chinese once again visit family graves and give offerings.

November. *All Saints* and *All Souls* days, on the first two days of the month, are public holidays. Early in the month the all-comers 26-mile Marathon is run. Then it is time for the finishing touches to preparations for the *Macau Grand Prix,* held on the third or fourth weekend of the month. Following a week of trials, a jam-packed city watches motorcycle, production, and Formula car races on the 3.8 mile Guia Circuit, which, with Monaco, is one of the few road circuits to wind through city streets. Straightaway speeds have reached 140 miles per hour.

December. There are plenty of public holidays this month. On the first is *Independence Day,* commemorating Portugal's independence from Spain in 1640. The *Feast of the Immaculate Conception* is on the eighth. The *Winter Solstice* takes place on the 22nd. Then, of course, there are the holidays of *Christmas Eve* and *Christmas Day.*

TOURIST INFORMATION. In Macau, the *Department of Tourism* (D.T.M.) offers information, advice, and a wide variety of free maps, books, and brochures about services and attractions in the territory. The D.T.M. has an office at the arrival terminal, open 9 A.M. to 6 P.M. every day, and the main office at Travessa do Paiva next to Government Palace, open office hours. Telephone, 77218.

In Hong Kong, the *Macau Tourist Information Bureau* (M.T.I.B.) has brochures, maps, and hotel and transport information. The staff will help visitors plan their trips. The office is located at 305 Shun Tak Centre, 3rd floor, 200 Connaught Road Central, Hong Kong; (5)408180, and after office hours (5)-408198. An information desk has been set up in Hong Kong's Kai Tak Airport, at the "Buffer Hall" between "Customs" and "Arrivals." The office is open from 8 A.M. to 10 P.M. daily.

The M.T.I.B. has worldwide offices that offer similar services. (See the Tourist Office section of this guide.) Further information can be obtained from reservation offices of Hyatt-Regency Hotels and Mandarin Oriental Hotels.

Macau might be small and relatively compact, but it is also complex, so it's a good idea to study the map and information material before arriving. It's also useful to carry the Chinese names of restaurants and out-of-the-way attractions.

Visitors in Macau on business can get information about any aspect of local commercial conditions from the *Macau Business Centre,* Edificio Ribeiro, at the city end of the Praia Grande; telephone 86462.

TOURS. Regular and customized tours, for individuals or groups, by bus or car, are easily arranged in Macau and provide the maximum amount of sightseeing in a short space of time. There are two basic tours. One covers mainland Macau with stops at the border, Kun Iam Temple, St. Paul's, and Penha Hill. It lasts about three and a half hours and, by bus, costs HK$67 for one to three passengers, HK$62 each for four or more, and is inclusive of a three-course lunch. By car, the cost is HK$150 for one, HK$100 each for two or more.

The other standard tour consists of a two-hour trip across the bridge to the islands of Taipa and Coloane to see old Chinese villages, firework factories, temples, beaches, the trotting track, and the new university. The bus tour costs HK$15 each for four or more.

The most comfortable way to tour is by car. For a maximum of four passengers it costs HK$100 an hour. Taxis are available for hire by the hour. Depending on your bargaining powers, the cost is HK$80 or more. Best of all are the self-drive mini-mokes. (See "How To Get Around" section.)

Most people book tours with Macau agents while in Hong Kong, or through travel agents before leaving home. If you do it this way, transport from Hong Kong to Macau will be arranged for you and guides will be waiting for you in the arrival hall in Macau. There are many licensed tour operators in Macau. Among those who specialize in handling English-speaking visitors and have offices in Hong Kong are: *Able Tours,* Hoi Kwong Building, Travessa do Pe. Narciso, Macau; 89798 (8 Connaught Rd. West, Hong Kong; (5)459993); *Estoril Tours,* Lisboa Hotel, Macau; 73614 (Macau Wharf, Hong Kong; (5)591028. *International Tourism,* 9 Travessa do Pe. Narciso, Macau; 86522 (143 Connaught Rd., Hong Kong; (5)412011); *Macau Tours,* 9 Ave. da Amizade, Macau; 85555 (287 Des Voeux Rd., Hong Kong; (5)422338); and *Sintra Tours,* Sintra Hotel, Macau; 86394 (3rd floor, Shun Tak Centrer, Hong Kong; (5)408028).

These agents also sell tours to China (see China Tours section of this guide).

 PARKS AND GARDENS. According to statistics Macau is one of the most crowded places on earth, yet tucked into the city you'll find gardens and mini-parks that provide residents with space for *tai chi* exercises, the airing of caged pet birds, study, and children's play. All are open from dawn to dusk and are meticulously tended by municipal gardeners. Except for Lou Lim Ioc (entrance fee, 50 cents) all parks are admission free.

Camoes Grotto, behind the Camões Museum and a short walk from St. Paul's façade, is Macau's oldest and most interesting garden. Named for Portugal's greatest poet, who is popularly believed to have lived in Macau in 1557, the garden once belonged to the colonial mansion that is now the Camões Museum. In 1785 La Perouse, the French cartographer, set up a small observatory here to peer into China. It was taken over by the city in 1886, when a bronze bust of Camões was installed in a rocky alcove. Nearby a wall of stone slabs was inscribed with poems praising Camões and Macau. The garden consists of heavily wooded hillocks, a belvedere with stone tables and benches, and a simple Chinese pavilion, all of which are popular with chess players and gossiping housewives. The entrance to the garden is laid out with flower beds and ancient, liana-draped banyan trees.

Flora Gardens, on Ave. de Sidonio Pais, a few blocks beyond the Estoril Hotel, are all that remain of the Flora Palace, a stately home that burned to the ground in the 1920s. It is the most European of Macau's gardens, with landscaped avenues of exotic trees, a pond with waterfowl, and an extensive nursery for flowers and shrubs. A small, rather ramshackle zoo with monkeys and birds occupies the site of the mansion, as do an ornamental fountain and the bust of a past governor. The gardens extend into the semi-wilderness of the slopes of Guia Hill.

Lou Lim Ioc Garden, on Estrada de Adolfo Loureiro, just beyond "Restoration Row," is a classic Chinese garden modeled on those of old Soochow. The garden and a large Victorian house were built in the nineteenth century by a wealthy Chinese merchant. With the decline of the Lou family fortunes, the house was sold and became a school. The garden was taken over by the city in 1974 and totally restored. Enclosed by a wall, it is a miniaturized landscape with mini-forests of bamboo and flowering bushes, a mountain of sculpted concrete, and a small lake filled with lotus and golden carp. A traditional nine-turn bridge zigzags (to deter evil spirits, which move only in a straight line) across the lake to a colonial pavilion with a wide verandah. Exhibitions are sometimes staged here.

Other gardens are the *Montanha Russa,* a forested hill north of the city; *Carmel Garden* on Taipa Island; and the roadside parks of *Vasco de Gama, Victory, S. Francisco* gardens, and *Coloane Park* with its aviary.

 SPECTATOR SPORTS. For most regular visitors to Macau, the sporting life means playing the casinos, but there are plenty of other sports, too, albeit with gambling on the sidelines. The Macanese are keen on team sports and give creditable performances at Interport soccer and field hockey matches with Hong Kong. Jogging has become very popular and the city has some excellent routes, especially on Taipa and along the Praia Grande.

Horse Racing. Harness racing at the *Macau Trotting Club,* Taipa Island— (2)7211 in Macau, (5)212346 in Hong Kong—is the newest spectator sport. The raceway, with Asia's first trotting track, is located on three million square feet of reclaimed land, close to the Hyatt Regency Hotel. The oval track is five furlongs and races are one mile or 10.5 furlongs. Mobile starting gates from the United States are used, and the rules are a mixture of Australian and American. The horses are usually from New Zealand and Australia, while the trainers and drivers hail from North America, Australia, and Macau.

The Macau Trotting Club spared no expense in building the facility. The five-story grandstand can accommodate 15,000 people, 6,000 of them in air-conditioned comfort. There are Chinese and European restaurants and several bars, plus, of course, convenient betting windows with the latest computerized totalizator. To give the punter maximum choice, bets are for win, place, quinella, forecast, trifecta, treble, quartet, quadrella, and double quinella. The minimum bet is HK$2. To help you follow your money, a gigantic Video Matrix screen, made up of 32,000 individual lamps, faces the grandstand so the spectators can follow the leaders from start to finish. Alongside is the tote board with lights flashing up the odds and results.

Special race meetings are held periodically. The Hyatt offers the Hyatt-Regency Cup in June. The club's anniversary Cup series, worth 2 million patacas to the winners, is held in September. The event is a celebrity-studded affair, with guests—Cary Grant, Gregory Peck, Mohammed Ali, Jack Klugman, and Miss Universe, to name a few from the recent past—flown in from the United States.

There are races throughout the year, starting at 2:00 P.M. on Sunday. Admission to the public stands is HK$3, with passes to the members' stands usually available (call (5)212346 or (5)260015 in Hong Kong). A fleet of buses commutes between the Lisboa Hotel and the track from two hours before post time. Tickets are sold on the buses.

Greyhound Racing. Greyhound racing has proved to be very popular with residents and Hong Kong punters for many years. The races are held at the scenic, open-air *Canidrome,* Avenida General Castelo Branco, close to the border. Most dogs are imported from Australia. The 10,000-seat stadium has rows and rows of betting windows and stalls for food and drink. Races are held on weekends and on Hong Kong public holidays year round, with additional meetings on the second and fourth Wednesday of the month during the summer. They begin at 8:00 P.M. Admission is 2 patacas for the public stand, 5 patacas for the members' stand, and 80 patacas for a box for six people. The minimum bet is HK$2.

Jai Alai. Jai Alai, played in the handsome stadium opposite the ferry wharf, has never really caught on in Macau, but does offer an exciting spectacle for those interested in this Basque game, which is said to be the fastest ball game in the world. The *pelotarios,* who hurl the ball along the 60-yard court at up to 150 miles per hour, are usually from the Basque country, with a few local players. A large electronic board lights up with the odds and results of each game, and the bettors have plenty of windows to choose from. The minimum bet is HK$2. The stadium also contains a casino, restaurant/nightclub, bar, coffee shop, and—in the gallery overlooking the jai alai court—half a dozen billiard tables for hire.

Jai Alai games begin at 7:30 P.M every night and last until midnight. There are other contests at 2:00 P.M. Saturday and Sunday. Admission is 1 pataca and boxes are 18 patacas for six people.

Motor Racing. The *Macau Grand Prix* takes place on the third or fourth weekend in November, and from the beginning of the week the city is shattered with super-charged engines being driven around the 3.8-mile Guia Circuit, which follows the city roads along the Outer Harbour to Guia Hill and around the reservoir. The route is as challenging as that of Monaco, with rapid gear changes demanded at the near right angle Statue Corner (behind the Lisboa Hotel), Solitude Esses, and the Dona Maria Bend.

The Grand Prix was first staged in 1953 and the standard of performance has now reached world class. Today, cars achieve speeds of 140 miles per hour on the straight, with the lap record approaching 2 minutes 20 seconds. The premier event is the Formula Three championship, with cars brought in from around the world. There are races for motorcycles (including a grand prix) and production cars (before the big Formula race). Many internationally famous drivers have taken part, including former world champion (1980) Alan Jones, Ricardo Patrese, and Keke Rosberg.

Hotel bookings for the Grand Prix have to be made long in advance, and the weekend should be avoided by anyone not interested in motor racing. Also be warned that for days after the event local aspirant champs make menaces of themselves on the roads.

Running. The 26-mile *Macau Marathon* usually takes place in late November. All runners are welcome to try the fairly grueling course beginning and ending with the Macau-Taipa bridge and including the roads around the islands.

Dragon-Boat Racing. Dragon-Boat Racing has become the newest international sport in Asia. It derives from an ancient Chinese festival in which fishing communities would compete in long, shallow boats with dragon heads and tails, in honor of a poet who drowned himself to protest official corruption. At the time, about 2,000 years ago, his friends took to boats and pounded their oars while beating drums to scare the fish away from his body. In recent years, contests between Hong Kong, Singapore, Nagasaki, Penang, and Macau have expanded to include teams from Australia, Britain, the United States, and China's Guangdong Province, and the winners now show professional form. The festival takes place on the fifth day of the fifth moon (usually some time in June) when there are races in the harbor and bay. International races are held a few days later. The waterfront road provides a natural grandstand for spectators, and the event is immensely colorful with decorated junks, noisy with firecrackers and drums, and exciting with furiously paddled dragon boats. In addition to the experts, there are teams from local companies and government departments.

Cricket Fighting. Cricket fighting used to be a popular sport in Macau, with huge wagers on favorite insects. The city was even the venue for "world championships," with crickets brought in from China and Hong Kong to compete with local champions. On one occasion, it is said, the overall winner was flown to Honolulu to fight Hawaii's best, only to meet an untimely end at the hands of the Department of Agriculture. The sport still survives among a few Chinese aficionados, and fights are arranged during the summer months, usually at private houses. The crickets fight in a small ring and "trainers" stimulate them to action by tickling their abdomens with prods of mouse whiskers. It isn't easy to locate the venues, but the Department of Tourism may be able to help.

 CASINOS. The glamorous images summoned up by the word "casino" should be checked at the door, along with any cameras, before you enter a Macau casino. Here you'll find no opulent floor shows, no free champagne, no jet-setters in evening dress, no suave croupiers. What you will find is gambling. Open 24 hours a day, the rooms are noisy, smoky, and shabby. The gamblers, mostly Hong Kong Chinese, are businessmen, housewives, concubines, servants, factory workers, and students, united in their passion—and what a passion it is. There is almost certainly more money wagered, lost, and won in Macau's casinos than in any other casinos in the world. The total amount is unknown except to the syndicate, Sociedade de Turismo e Diversões de Macau (S.T.D.M.), which has the legal franchise. (In return for the franchise, S.T.D.M. is paying the government a premium of HK$1.3 billion (US $162.5 million) over a 10-year period plus 26 percent—rising to 30 percent—of gross income, plus the money to build homes for 2,000 families, new passenger ferries, and a new dredger to clear the harbor. The boss of the syndicate "is pleased" with the agreement, so judge the profits for yourself.)

There are five casinos in Macau, but for foreign visitors only four count: those in the **Lisboa** and **Oriental** hotels, the **Jai Alai Stadium,** and the **Palacio de Macau,** known usually as the floating casino. The busiest is the two-story casino in the Lisboa, where the games are roulette, boule, Black Jack, Baccarat, craps, and the Chinese games *fan tan* and big and small. There are also banks of slot machines, known in Chinese as "hungry tigers."

There are few limitations to gambling in Macau. No one under 18 is allowed, although no identity checks are made. Most gamblers use Hong Kong dollars and get any pay-off in the same currency. There are bars in the Lisboa and floating casinos, which provide ringside seats on the action.

The mass of punters in the casinos might look unsophisticated but, whether tycoons or housemaids, they are as knowledgeable as any gamblers in the world. They are also more single-minded than most, eschewing alcohol and all but essential food when at the tables. And, of course, they are superstitious. Which all adds up to certain "Macau Rules" and customs, which any visitor should know. The rules are printed out and available at the casino, and then there are two good books on the subject: *Gamblers Guide to Macau,* by Bert Okuley and Frederck King-Poole, and the *Macau Gambling Handbook,* by A-O-A publishers, both available in Hong Kong.

Black Jack is enormously popular in Macau and there are dozens of tables in the three casinos. There are also frequently dozens of people crowded around the players, often placing side bets. An uninitiated player might feel flattered by this faith in his skill or luck—until he learns that by Macau Rules anyone betting higher than him on his hand can call that hand. Otherwise the rules are based on American ones. The dealers, all women, must draw on 16 or less and stand on 17 or more. "Insurance" bets are encouraged and any pairs can be split, but Macau permits doubling down only on two cards totaling 11. Minimum bets are HK$10 or HK$100 depending on the table. Macau gamblers have their foibles. For instance, a player might refuse a card against all odds because he or she believes it will break some mystical sequence. At other times, players will gang up and help one of their number to win. As for the dealers, they are allowed to play hands for customers who request it, and they regularly and aggressively urge players to take foolish chances. The dealers, like their colleagues at the other tables and the slot machines, are generally rude, surly, and greedy. They take a cut of any winnings automatically as a tip, and it's a battle to refuse to tip. There is, however, one rule that favors the players: No matter how bad a run of luck any dealer is having, she has to sit out her hour's stint.

Roulette in Macau is based on the European system, with a single zero, but with some American touches. Players are given different colored chips at an American-shaped table, and bets are collected rather than frozen when the zero appears. The minimum bet is HK$10.

Baccarat has, in recent years, become a status game for well heeled gamblers from Hong Kong, who brag about losing a million as much as they brag about winning one. An admiring, envying crowd usually surrounds the baccarat tables, which are separated from the rest of the tables. Minimum bets are HK$100 and HK$500 and the maximum of HK$60,000 is raised on special request. In Macau the player cannot take the bank, and the fixed rules on drawing and standing are complex, so read the rules first.

Craps has yet to catch on with Chinese gamblers in Macau. It follows American rules and the minimum bet is HK$10.

Fan Tan is an ancient Chinese game, which has surprisingly survived Western competition—surprising because it seems so boringly simple. A pile of porcelain buttons is divided on the table and the croupier removes four at a time until one, two, three, or four remain. Players wager on one or the other, with minimum bets of HK$10, and some are so good at counting that they leave the table long before the end of the game.

Big and Small, or *Dai Siu* in Chinese, is another traditional game, and scarcely more complicated. It is basically a question of betting on the total on three dice shaken in a glass dome. You bet, again with a minimum of HK$10, on small numbers up to 10 or a large number over 10 or a range of combinations. Most bets on *dai siu* and *fan tan* are in cash rather than chips, and the players are the least affluent of the casino's customers. They are fascinating to watch.

Slot machines line the walls of the three casinos, and these "hungry tigers are never without nourishment. In fact their life span is probably far less than those in Vegas or Reno, as punters crash down the arms and pummel uncooperative machines. Most of these machines take Hong Kong dollars.

The casinos of Macau offer more than gambling for a Western visitor. The Lisboa complex really has to be seen to be believed and explored to bolster belief. It contains numerous restaurants and bars, electronic games, shops, and a constant cavalcade of people.

In contrast, the new casino in the Oriental is small and elegant, designed for gamblers who like some Continental chic. Games include roulette, blackjack, baccarat, and craps. It is open noon to 4 A.M.

The floating casino is a marvelous clash of styles. When the old ferry was converted it was decorated with all the curlicues, golden panels, red banners, and fripperies of modern Chinoiserie. Since then it has lost its sheen and is a noisy, no-nonsense casino and restaurant.

The casino in the Jai Alai Stadium is best visited in combination with the jai alai games or nightclub.

 HISTORIC SITES. With more than four centuries of history-making—as the first European settlement in China, sole entrepôt for Chinese trade, and headquarters for international merchants and missionaries—it's not surprising that Macau has a wealth of historic buildings. What is remarkable is how well they have survived the assault of time, climate, and schemes for modernization. One reason is that they have all been in constant and practical use. They are also valued as part of a proud heritage and so are regularly restored and redecorated, even as they are obscured by graceless skyscrapers and gimcrack architecture.

St. Paul's (São Paulo) has long been a popular symbol of Macau. The richly carved baroque façade is all that remains of what was called "the greatest church in Asia." Built between 1602 and 1627 by exiled Japanese Christians and local craftsmen under the direction of the Jesuits, St. Paul's was the collegiate church for the Jesuit college, which was the first Western-style university in Asia. Such scholars as Matteo Ricci and Adam Van Schall studied here before going to the court in Peking. The church fell into disuse when the Jesuits were expelled in

1762. Later, the army was billetted in the college and in 1835 a fire destroyed everything except the façade.

Monte Fort, on the hill overlooking St. Paul's, was also built by the Jesuits, completed in 1623. In 1622, the year before it was completed, the fort was the scene of Macau's most famous battle. The Dutch, jealous of Portugal's power in Asia, invaded the territory, which was protected by a small force of soldiers, African slaves, and priests. As the Dutch closed on Monte, a lucky cannon shot, fired by one of the priests, hit the enemy's powder supply and in the ensuing confusion the Dutch were driven back to sea. In 1626, the first full-time governor of Macau evicted the Jesuits from the fort and for the next century and a half it was the residence and office of Macau's governors. The fort's buildings were destroyed in the 1835 fire, but the great walls, with their cannons, remain. Today the meteorological office maintains a station here, and the fort is a popular belvedere for residents and tourists. Its gates are open from 7:00 A.M. to dusk.

The Loyal Senate (Leal Senado) stands in the heart of the city, on the main street facing a European-style square. It is a superb example of colonial architecture, with a simple, elegant façade dating from 1876. The main building was constructed in the late eighteenth century, to house the senate of leading citizens who were at the time far more powerful than the governors, who served their short terms and then returned to Portugal. Today the senate, with some elected and some appointed members, acts as the municipal government, with its president holding the same power as a mayor. Inside the building, a beautiful stone staircase leads to a wrought-iron gate and a charming garden. The upper floor contains the senate chambers and the original national library, modeled on that of Mafra in Portugal. The foyer and garden are open during working hours, and there are occasional art and history exhibitions in the chambers and the foyer.

Holy House of Mercy (Santa Casa da Misericordia) stands in the square opposite the senate. Behind the imposing white façade are the headquarters of the first western charity in Asia. Founded in 1569 it established orphanages, clinics, homes for the aged, free food supplies for the poor, and a leprosarium. On the second floor (open during office hours) is a reception room with paintings of benefactress Marta Merop and Macau's first bishop, Dom Belchior, as well as the latter's cross and skull.

St. Dominic's (São Domingos), Largo de São Domingos, adjoining senate square, is possibly the most beautiful church in Macau, with a magnificent cream-and-white baroque altar of graceful columns, fine statues, and a forest of candles and flower vases. It was built in the seventeenth century by the Dominicans and has a stormy history. In 1644 a Portuguese officer involved in civil strife was murdered by a mob at the altar during mass. In 1707 the church was besieged by the governor's troops when the Dominicans sided with the Pope against the Jesuits over a controversy as to whether or not ancestor worship should be permitted among Chinese Christian converts. After three days, the soldiers broke down the doors and briefly imprisoned the priests. Today those doors are open only during services; at other times, visitors should ring the bell on the green gate next to the entrance.

Guia Fort and Lighthouse, built in the 1630s, is on the highest point in Macau. Several roads lead up to the fort. The gate is open from 7:00 A.M. to dusk, and the views from the fort's platform are truly panoramic. Within the fort is the lighthouse, erected in 1865 and the oldest on the China coast, and a small, simple, white-stone chapel, built in 1707 and dedicated to Our Lady of Guia. The fort is used by the Marine Police. When there are typhoons in the area, typhoon signals in the form of specially shaped black bamboo baskets are hoisted on a yardarm on the platform. Permission is needed to enter the lighthouse and chapel (not easy, but you can ask the Department of Tourism to try).

The Border Gate (Portas do Cerco) marks the traditional boundary of Macau. Beyond is an isthmus leading to the Chinese border town of Gongbei. The present gate was built in 1870 and bears the arms of Portugal's navy and artillery, along with a quotation from Camões, which reads, in translation: "Honor your country for it looks after you." On either side of the gate is written the date 1849. This commemorates the year when the governor, Ferreira do Amaral (whose statue stands outside the Lisboa Hotel), was assassinated by the Chinese. The local warlord planned to invade Macau but a Macanese colonel, Nicolau Mesquita, with thirty-seven men, slipped across the border and captured the Chinese fort. Today there is a steady flow of vegetable farmers, businessmen, and tourists at the gate. It is open from 7:00 A.M. to 9:00 P.M. daily.

Temple of the Lotus (Lin Fung Miu), Ave. do Almirante Lacerda, is close to the border gate. This superb temple, dedicated to both Buddhist and Taoist deities, was built in 1592 and used for overnight accommodation by mandarins traveling between Macau and Canton. It is famous for its façade of intricate clay bas-reliefs depicting mythological and historical scenes and an interior frieze of colorful writhing dragons. Open dawn to dusk.

Kun Iam Temple (Kun Iam Tong), Ave. do Coronel Mesquita, is in the north of the city. This Buddhist temple, dedicated to Kun Iam (also known as Kwan Yin), the Goddess of Mercy, was founded in the thirteenth century. The present buildings, which are richly endowed with carvings, porcelain figurines, statues, old scrolls, antique furniture, and ritual objects. It is best known among Western visitors for the stone table in the courtyard, where, on July 3, 1844, the first Sino-American treaty was signed by the Viceroy of Canton and United States envoy Caleb Cushing. The temple has a large number of funeral chapels, where you can see the offerings of paper cars, airplanes, luggage and money, which are burned to accompany the souls of the dead. Open dawn to dusk.

Dom Pedro V Theater, Largo de Sto. Agostinho, is on the hill above the Praia Grande and behind the Loyal Senate. The oldest Western theater on the China coast, it was built in 1859 in the style of a European court theater. Until the Second World War it was in regular use with local performers and international artists. In recent years it has been extensively restored and equipped with sophisticated stage lighting. It is now used for concerts and other entertainment, such as plays in Macanese. Although not officially open to visitors during the day, one of the doors is usually open and no one objects to people looking around at the marvelously Victorian foyer and auditorium. The façade is also very fine.

St. Augustine's (Sto. Agostinho) is in the Largo de Sto. Agostinho, opposite the theater. This superb baroque building dates from 1814, when it replaced the burnt-out seventeenth-century original. In the marble-clad high altar is the large statue of Our Lord of Passos, which is carried through the streets on the first day of Lent. Among the tombs in the church is that of Maria de Moura, a romantic heroine who in 1710 married the man she loved, even though he had lost an arm when attacked by another suitor. She died in childbirth and is buried with her baby and her husband's arm. Open daily.

St. Joseph's (São Jose), also in Largo de Sto. Agostinho, was once an important seminary with a superb church. Today it is in great need of repair and houses only Father Manuel Teixeira, Macau's resident historian, and some brilliantly restored 16th-century paintings. It is closed to the public.

Government Palace, Praia Grande, a distinctive pink-and-white mansion that contains the offices of the governor and his ministers, was built in 1849 by Macau's greatest architect Tomas de Aquino. Unfortunately the public is not permitted inside to see the regal banquet hall and dining room. The exterior is very impressive, especially since recent restoration.

Government House (Palacio de Santa Sancha), on the hill above the praya, was also built by Aquino, and shows the same mastery of elegant but simple lines. Surrounded by attractive gardens, it is the residence of the governor, so is closed to the public. But it can be easily seen from the road or the Bela Vista Hotel.

Penha Hill, above the Bela Vista, on the highest point of the narrow peninsula, is the dominant landmark for arrivals by sea. At one time it was crowned with a church, where seafarers would worship before setting out. The present building is the bishop's residence and includes a small chapel, built in 1935 (it is usually closed to the public).

Temple of A-Ma (A-Ma Miu) is at the far end of the peninsula. Dating from the early sixteenth century, this is the most picturesque temple in Macau, with ornate prayer halls and pavilions built among the giant boulders of the waterfront hillside. The rocks are inscribed with red calligraphy telling the story of A-Ma (also known as Tin Hau), the favorite goddess of fishermen, who allegedly saved a humble junk from a storm. One of the many Chinese names for the area was Bay of A-Ma, or A-Ma Gau, and when the Portuguese arrived they adopted it as Macau. Open dawn to dusk.

Old Protestant Cemetery is beside the Camões Museum on Praca Luis de Camões. Established in 1814, this was the first piece of land in Macau to be owned by foreigners. It was bought at the insistence of missionary-sinologue Robert Morrison and the British merchants who spent half the year in Macau. Before this time Protestants were buried outside the city walls and their graves were often desecrated. The cemetery has just over 150 graves, 50 of them are of Americans, including diplomats, traders, and sailors from Commodore Perry's historic fleet. The cemetery is meticulously maintained, albeit with some misspellings on repaired stones. Open from dawn to dusk.

MUSEUMS AND LIBRARIES. As happened with other colonial settlements around the world, many of the records and much of the portable treasure of historic Macau was taken "home" by Portuguese, British, Americans, and other expatriates, as well as by Chinese visitors. Fortunately plenty was left behind, and, with charming irony, some of it is now housed in the former homes of the expatriates.

Camoes Museum. Praca Luis de Camões, next to Camões Gardens and the Old Protestant Cemetery; 73500. The chief exhibit of this museum, named for Portugal's greatest poet, is the building itself. Built in the 1770s, it is a superb example of Iberian colonial architecture, with spacious, high-ceilinged rooms and tall windows shaded by louvered shutters. In the late eighteenth and early nineteenth centuries is was rented by the British East India Company as a residence for the men who controlled much of the contemporary China trade. Two of the museum's rooms recall this era, with Chinese four-poster beds and other period furniture and ornaments. Other rooms have displays of ancient Chinese pottery, Buddhist statues, and some very fine exportware vases and dinner sets, decorated with the Portuguese coat of arms. The museum's lower floor has galleries with paintings, drawings, and lithographs by Borget, Chinnery, and Chinese artists. There are regular exhibitions by modern artists from Macau and Hong Kong. Open daily except Wednesday, 10:00 A.M. to 5:00 P.M. Entrance 1 pataca, free on Fridays.

Memorial Home of Sun Yat-sen. Rua Ferreira do Amaral 1, close to Lou Lim Ioc Gardens. A must for anyone interested in the father of the 1911 Chinese Revolution, which overthrew the Manchu Empire. Dr. Sun, who is still revered in both Peking and Taipei, was born a few miles north of Macau and lived here from 1892 to 1894, during his long exile. The Memorial Home was built to replace his actual house, which burned down in the 1930s. It is a strange building in mock-Moorish style, and its collection of Sun memorabilia is haphazardly arranged and lacks a catalogue, although it does have English labels. Nevertheless, the photographs of Sun with old colleagues, copies of his books, and some of the first Nationalist flags ever to fly over the Chinese Republic all evoke something of the man and his times. Open from 10:00 A.M. to 1:00 P.M. Monday, Wednesday, Thursday, Friday; 10:00 A.M. to 1:00 P.M. and 3:00 P.M. to 5:00 P.M. weekends; closed Tuesday. Entrance 1 pataca.

Folk Museum. Taipa Praia. A fine early 20th-century mansion has been converted into a folk museum with authentic furniture and artifacts from old Macau.

National Archives and Library. Ave. do Conselheiro Ferreira de Almeida. Two beautifully restored buildings contain some of the oldest books about Macau and the Portuguese presence in the Far East. Scholars are welcome to browse; there is a photocopying machine available. Open from 2:00 P.M. to 8 P.M. Monday through Saturday.

Military Museum. S. Francisco Barracks, behind the Lisboa Hotel. This small but interesting museum has a collection of spears and swords from all over the old Portuguese empire and beyond, plus arms and ammunition from the

First World War and flags from old battles. Open from 2:00 P.M. to 5:00 P.M. weekdays. Free.

 SHOPPING. At first glance, Macau is a poor country cousin to Hong Kong when it comes to shopping. Most stores are small and open to the street, the clerks might well be eating snacks at the counters, and merchandise is haphazardly arranged. There is very little for sale here that isn't available in far greater abundance and variety in Hong Kong.

So why shop in Macau? First, the shopping areas are more compact. Second, sales staff are in general much more pleasant and relaxed, although their command of English isn't as good. And most important, most goods are cheaper. Like Hong Kong, Macau is a duty-free port for most items. Unlike the British territory, rents are reasonable and wages low, keeping overheads to a minimum.

Macau's shops are open every day of the year except for a short holiday during or just after Chinese New Year. Opening hours vary according to the type of shop, but usually extend into early evening. Credit cards are generally accepted, but not for the best discounts. Bargaining is expected, and is best done by asking for the "best price," which produces discounts of up to 10 percent. Larger discounts on expensive items should be treated with suspicion. Macau has its share of phony antiques, fake name-brand watches, and other rip-offs. Be sure to shop around, check the guarantee on name brands, and be sure to get receipts for expensive items.

The major shopping areas of Macau are the main street, Avenida Almeida Ribeiro, commonly known by its Chinese name Sanmalo, and the cluster of narrow streets bordered by Mercadores (alongside the Central Hotel), Tercena, Estalagens and Cinco de Outubro. This area is very colorful, noisy, and crowded with shop with names that charmingly reflect Macau's dual heritage: Pastelarias Mei Mun, Quinqilharias Fan Wing, Relojoaria Tat On, Sapatarias Joao Leong, for example.

GOLD AND JEWELRY

Macau's jewelry stores are not as lavish as those in Hong Kong, but they offer better prices because of low overheads. Each store displays the current price of gold per *tael* (1.2 troy ounces), which changes from day to day or hour to hour according to the Hong Kong Gold Exchange. Some counters contain 14 and 18 carat jewelry, such as chains, earrings, pendants, brooches, rings, and bangles. There are also items set with pearls or precious stones (usually made in Hong Kong), as well as pieces of costume jewelry and traditional Chinese pieces. One section of a shop is usually devoted to 24-carat gold jewelry and gold in the form of Krugerrand coins, *taels,* or tiny bars of a few grams, which come with assay certificates from Credit Suisse. These gold items are popular with the Chinese as investments. The shops also display some elaborate ornaments, such as wedding jewelry of beaten gold, dragons of gold filigree set with precious stones, or animals cast in gold.

Prices for gold items are based on the day's gold price plus a charge for workmanship and profit, so a limited amount of bargaining is possible. Interested customers can also ask to see the very best items, which are kept in the back room. There are occasional instances of fraud in which the gold is found to be less than the stated carat value. To combat this, the Department of Tourism issues a gold sticker for reputable jewelers to show in their windows. It reads "Centro de Informacao e Turismo Macau" and the Department will handle any complaints from customers, so check the shop window and keep your receipts.

All of the following recommended stores are covered by this guarantee. They are open from 9:00 A.M. to 7:00 P.M. and employ knowledgeable, helpful, English-speaking staff. Some have branches in the hotels, but these tend to be more expensive and to have a limited range of goods. *Tai Fung,* 36 Ave. Almeida Ribeiro, is a spacious, cool shop with a wide selection of gold jewelry and ornaments; all major credit cards. *Chow Sang Sang,* 58 Ave. Almeida Ribeiro, has a digital display of buying-and-selling-gold prices for the day and the previous day and a good stock of jewelry; all major credit cards. *Pou Fong,* 91 Ave. Almeida Ribeiro, is small but pleasant, with a collection of gold jewelry inset with opals, pearls, emeralds, and diamonds, plus some ornate clocks; all major credit cards. *Sheong Hei,* 29–31 Ave. Almeida Ribeiro, has a large selection of gold pieces, gem-set jewelry, and fancy ornaments; all major credit cards.

ANTIQUES

The days of discovering treasures of the Ming and T'ang among the Ching Chinoiserie in Macau's antique shops are long gone, but there are still plenty of old and interesting pieces available. Collectors of old porcelain can find some well-preserved bowls and other simple household ware from the Ming Dynasty or earlier. Prices for such genuine items prices run in the hundreds or thousands of U.S. dollars. Far cheaper are the ornate vases, stools and dishware from the late Ching period, China's Victorian era, which is now coming into vogue. This style of pottery is still popular among the Chinese and a lot of so-called Ching is faithfully produced today in China, Hong Kong, and Macau. Many of these reproductions are excellent and hard to distinguish from the genuine articles.

Over the years, experts and dealers have made profitable trips to Macau, so it's interesting to ask where new supplies of antiques are originating. The standard answer used to be "from an old Macau family," and after the war many long-established Macanese did have to sell their treasures. Today there is another explanation: they were brought out of China by legal and illegal immigrants in lieu of capital or foreign currency. Most of these smuggled items are small and some are certainly bargains. Among them are 2,000-year-old bronze money in the shape of knives, later types of coins with holes in the middle, jade pi (discs) and netsuke, ivory figurines, and old jewelry. In addition you can still sometimes fine exportware porcelain, made for the European market in nineteenth-century China, and old bonds from the early twentieth century.

The following antique shops are among the best known and most reliable. However, good sense and some research should be applied. These shops usually open from about 11:00 A.M. to 5:30 P.M. daily. *Veng Meng*, a veteran art dealer, has shops at 114 Ave. Almeida Ribeiro and 8 Travessa do Pagode, a small street off Estalagens. He has old porcelain, Ching pots, jade ornaments, old silver jewelry, and a good selection of ancient money; Mr. Meng speaks good English and knows his business. AE, CB, MC. *Wing Tai*, 1M Ave. Almeida Ribeiro, is known for its old furniture of blackwood inlaid with marble. It also has some fine blue-and-white porcelain, Chinese scrolls, old jewelry, and jade netsuke. The shop is open from 9:30 A.M. to 7:00 P.M. and the staff speaks good English; AE, DC, CB, MC, V. *The Antique House*, 11-G Ave. Coronel Mesquita (opposite Kun Iam Temple), has fine porcelain and Chinese antiques. AE, DC, MC, V.

CLOTHING

There are many shops in Macau that sell casual and sports clothes for men and women at bargain prices. Most are made in Macau or Hong Kong, and many carry big-name labels. In some cases these are fakes, but there are genuine overruns and rejects from local factories that manufacture, under license, garments for Yves Saint Laurent, Cacharel, Van Heusen, Adidas, and Gloria Vanderbilt. Levi and Lawman jeans cost about HK$100 and Vincent shirts about HK$75. There are also sweaters, padded jackets, and a good selection of very reasonably priced clothes for infants and children. The best prices are found at sidewalk stalls at the S. Domingos market and along Cinco de Outubro, Palha and Mercadores roads; no credit cards.

CRAFTS

Many traditional Chinese crafts are followed in Macau, and the best place to watch the craftsmen at work and buy their products is along Tercena and Estalagens. These old streets are lined with three-story shop-houses with openfront workshops on the ground floor. Some shops produce beautifully carved and inlaid furniture of mahogany, camphorwood, and redwood. The workers will refer interested customers to the agents who handle orders and shipping. On a more modest scale there are exquisite bird cages of bamboo with tiny porcelain bowls and decorations, red-painted family altars, lucky door plaques, and colorful wooden sandals made to measure on the spot.

 RESTAURANTS. Although East and West have clashed in many respects, when it came to cooking there was an instant rapprochement, and it happened in Macau. By the time the Portuguese arrived, they had learned a lot about the eating habits of their new empire and had adopted many of the ingredients. The Portuguese were the first to introduce China to peanuts, green beans, pineapples, lettuce, sweet potatoes, and shrimp paste, as well as a variety of spices from Africa and India. In China, the Portuguese discovered tea, rhubarb, tangerines, ginger, soy sauce, and the Cantonese art of fast frying to seal in the flavor.

Over the centuries a unique Macanese cuisine has developed, with dishes adapted from Portugal, Brazil, Mozambique, Goa, Malacca and, of course, China. Some ingredients are imported, but most are available, fresh each day, from the bountiful waters south of Macau and the rich farmland just across the China border. A good example of Macanese food is the strangely named Portuguese chicken, which would be an exotic stranger in Europe. It consists of chunks of chicken baked with potatoes, coconut, tomato, curry, olive oil, olives, and saffron. Extremely popular family dishes include *minchi* (minced pork and diced potatoes panfried with soy), pork baked with tamarind, and duckling cooked in its own blood, all of which are served with rice.

The favorites of Portuguese cuisine are regular menu items. The beloved codfish, *bacalhau,* is served baked, boiled, grilled, or stewed with onion, garlic, and eggs. Portuguese sardines, country soups such as *caldo verde* and *sopa alentejana,* and dishes of *coelho* (rabbit) are often served in restaurants. Colonial fare spans the world, from Brazilian *feijoadas* of beans, pork, spicy sausage, and vegetables to African chicken, baked or grilled in fiery *piri-piri* peppers and Goanese chicken with chilis. In addition, some restaurants offer baked quail and the delectable Macau sole. And then there are the giant prawns (weighing about a pound each), which are served in spicy sauce—one of Macau's outstanding dining pleasures.

Naturally the largest number of eating places in Macau serve Chinese food, and there are several restaurants offering first-class Japanese, Vietnamese, Indonesian, Thai, and even Italian meals, not to mention Chinese snack stalls and fast-food outlets. However, all of this fare is better, or at least as good, in Hong Kong, and a visit to Macau should be regarded as the opportunity to take lunch or dinner Macau-style. Food prices in Macau are generally so reasonable that it is difficult to categorize restaurants by price except at the top and bottom of the market. In the Macau context, *expensive* means more than 130 patacas per person, including wine; *inexpensive* is less than 40 patacas; and *moderate* is the majority in between. All restaurants add 5 percent government tax and most add 10 percent for service. Tipping is not universal, but service is usually so good you'll want to leave a few patacas extra. (The pataca is almost the same as the HK dollar.)

One of the best bargains in Macau is wine, particularly the delicious Portuguese *vinho verde,* a slightly sparkling wine, and still whites and reds such as Dão. Restaurant wine prices range from 20 patacas for a bottle (about 15 patacas in shops) at the *Riquexo* to 90 patacas for a bottle at the *Oriental Grill.* The standard price is 55 patacas, or 25 for a half bottle. Except in hotels, beer and spirits cost considerably less than they do in Hong Kong.

All restaurants are open every day of the year except for a few days' holiday after Chinese New Year. Both lunch and dinner tend to be leisurely affairs, and no one is hustled to eat and leave. Most people order wine, relax, look at the menu, note what other diners are eating, talk to the waiter, and then decide. There is a generally high standard of cleanliness in the kitchens. Dress is informal, and nowhere are jackets and ties required. The Department of Tourism's brochure, *Eating Out in Macau,* is very useful.

MACANESE-CONTINENTAL

Expensive

A Galera Grill Room. Lisboa Hotel; 77666. Long regarded as one of Macau's best restaurants; both Portuguese and Intercontinental grill fare are offered. Open noon to 3:00 P.M. and 7:00 P.M. to midnight. All major credit cards.

The Grill. Oriental Hotel; 567888. This beautifully designed room, with polished wooden pillars and archways, has great harbor views and an excellent menu with Portuguese specialties such as stuffed squid and seafood casserole, plus African chicken and steaks. Open noon to 2:30 P.M. and 7:00 P.M. to 11:30 P.M. All major credit cards.

Restaurante Fortaleza. Pousada de São Tiago, Ave. Republica; 78111. The setting alone would be reason enough to eat at the Fortaleza. It is located in the beautiful traditional Portuguese inn built into the old Barra fort and looks out over the trees and fountain on the terrace to the seascape of sailing junks and green islands beyond. The décor is exactly right, with crystal lamps, dark wood furniture, blue-and-white tiles, and dishware decorated in summery patterns. The food is almost as fabulous, with a good selection of such classic Macanese dishes as African chicken, baked codfish, quail, and pig's knuckle. Service is superb. Open noon to 11:30 P.M. AE, CB, DC, MC.

Moderate

Alfonso's. Hyatt-Regency Hotel, Taipa Island, (2)7000. In keeping with the décor and atmosphere of the hotel, this restaurant is a beauty. It is horseshoe-shaped with Portuguese décor, including rattan chairs and cheerful floral cushions. Picture windows look out onto the landscaped resort. The dishware and glasses are the best that Europe has to offer, and the menu is as imaginative and delicious as any in Portugal. The service is faultless. Open noon to 3:00 P.M. and 7:00 P.M. to 11:00 P.M. All major credit cards.

Estrela do Mar. 11 Travessa do Paiva, next to the Government Palace; 81270. Rather cramped and often resounding to Radio Macau, this is a great restaurant for rabbit, either baked, stewed, or grilled. It also serves very good *bacalhau,* Portuguese chicken, and *feijoadas.* The waiters are very attentive, though their command of English is hit-or-miss. Prices, however, are a hit, with an average meal with wine costing about 60 patacas. Open 11:00 A.M. to midnight. No credit cards.

Fat Siu Lau. 64 Rua da Felicidade, off the main street and close to the Inner Harbour; 573585. Opened in 1903, this is the oldest European restaurant in Macau and one of the most famous. It is located in the old red-light district but is a well designed and sophisticated place since it's extensive redecoration. You'll find gleaming white tablecloths, uniformed waiters, and relative tranquility. Fat Siu Lau, which is Chinese for House of the Smiling Buddha, is renowned for its roast quail and pigeon, but it offers equally good *bacalhau,* oxtail, seafood, and steaks. Service is superlative, and the price of a meal will average 70 to 90 patacas per person. Open noon to 1:30 A.M. No credit cards.

Flamingo. Taipa Island Resort, Hyatt-Regency Hotel; 27000. The wide, airy verandahs jutting out onto a lake, colonial ceiling fans, and a super-casual atmosphere add to the reasonably priced Macanese food. Open noon to midnight. All major credit cards.

Henri's Galley. 4 Ave. Republica; 76207. Situated on the banyan-lined waterfront, with a few extra tables on the sidewalk, Henri's is a firm favorite with local residents and European visitors from Hong Kong. One very good reason is that Henri Wong, the owner, *maitre d'*, food buyer, and ever genial host, is usually around to make sure that customers are well fed and helped in any way. The food is always up to the highest standard. House specialties include big servings of African chicken smothered in piquant sauce, curry crab, and huge prawns cooked in a spicy sauce to a secret recipe for a price based on the day's market price for prawns, on average 80 patacas per large platter. Henri's Portuguese fried rice, with chorizo hot sausage added, is another special treat. Macau sole for 42 patacas, soups for 12 patacas, and bacalhau for 35 patacas are also on the menu. Wine here is 39 patacas a bottle. Open 11:00 A.M. to 11:00 P.M. MC, V.

Metropole. Metropole Hotel, Praia Grande; 570231. The restaurant of the Metropole is big, busy, and of excellent value. It has a menu of Macanese and Continental dishes. The service is friendly and the decor, tastefully elegant. At night there is live music. Open 8:00 A.M. to 2:00 A.M. V.

Pinocchio's. 4 Rua do Sol, Taipa Island; (2)7128. Until the opening of the Hyatt Hotel, the best and often the only reason to go across the bridge to Taipa was to eat at Pinocchio's, located off the main street of Taipa village—not easy to find but well worth it. Owned by a former marine policeman, it consists of three air-conditioned rooms and a large-covered courtyard full of basic furniture with no tablecloths, harsh strip lighting at night, and a casual, noisy crowd of diners most of the time. The food, however, is impossible to fault. Among the best dishes are chili-crab, baked quail, and steamed shrimp. With a little advance warning the cook will also prepare superlative leg of lamb or whole roast suckling pig. Service tends to be casual, with little English spoken, except when the boss is around. Open noon to 11:30 P.M., closed the first Monday and Tuesday of the month. No credit cards.

Portugues. 16 Rua do Campo, a few blocks inland from the Sintra; 75445. Unpretentious, clean, reliable, and very agreeable, the Portugues is a relaxed and very reasonably priced restaurant. It serves fine *bacalhau,* Portuguese pork chops, pepper steak, and one of the best *caldo verdes* in town. The average price for a meal is about 60 patacas, including wine. Open 11:00 A.M. to 1:00 A.M. MC, V.

Pousada de Coloane. Praia de Cheoc Van, Coloane Island, 20 minutes by car from the city. (2)8144. By Macau standards, this is a long, long trip, but the restaurant at this inn has one of the best kitchens in town. The setting is also superb, with an attractive air-conditioned dining room and spacious outdoor terrace overlooking the beach. The menu specialties include imported Portuguese sardines, exquisite *caldo verde,* Brazilian *feijoadas, bacalhau,* and stuffed squid. On Sundays there is a sumptuous buffet for only 45 patacas per person. Other meals cost about 80 patacas per person, including wine. Open 8:00 A.M. to 10:00 P.M. MC, V.

Roma. 34A Rua Nova a Guia, close to the Royal Hotel; 81799. The sign outside says Giuliano's, after the owner, but he changed the name after opening this delightful Italian restaurant where the emphasis is on authentic home cooking and a relaxed and friendly atmosphere. Favorite dishes include mussels in garlic, steak in green peppercorns, and sweet and sour pork Italian style. Open noon to 2:30 P.M. and 7 P.M. to midnight. Closed Mondays. No credit cards.

Solmar. 11 Praia Grande, opposite the Metropole Hotel; 574391. For many, many years the Solmar was the most popular restaurant for local Portuguese and western visitors, but it now shows its age with slow service and occasionally disappointing meals. The best bets are the Portuguese chicken, seafood platter, grilled spicy sausage, and pork chops with hot sauce. The Solmar is pleasantly leisurely and inexpensive. Open 11:00 A.M. to 10:30 P.M. No credit cards.

Inexpensive

Riquexo. 69 Sidonio Pais, in the Park 'n Shop supermarket; 76294. This self-service café was created by and for lovers of authentic Macanese food at family prices. Each day half a dozen dishes are prepared in private kitchens and brought to the Riquexo (Portuguese for rickshaw and pronounced the same) in large bins, which are kept heated in the restaurant. There is beer and wine, at shop prices, as well as soups, salads, and desserts. The atmosphere is very much like a family get-together and the staff is cheerful and helpful. Prices average 30 patacas for three courses and wine. The best or most popular entrées are the first to go so, it's best to eat early. Open 11:00 A.M. to 3:00 P.M. No credit cards.

ASIAN

Expensive

Furusato. Lisboa Hotel; 81581. This is a branch of the famous Japanese chain and serves superb *sukiyaki, sushi, tempura,* and other Japanese delights in an authentic Japanese setting. Service and atmosphere are both marvelous. Open noon to 3:00 P.M., 6:00 P.M. to 11:00 P.M. All major credit cards.

Ginza. Royal Hotel; 55222. As befits a hotel of the Dai-Ichi group, the Japanese food is superb and varied, with *sashimi, yakimono,* and *teppanyaki* meals in a tastefully decorated restaurant. Open noon to 3 P.M. and 6 P.M. to 11 P.M. All major credit cards.

Kamogawa. Hyatt Hotel; 27000. The specials at this very pleasant and beautifully designed Japanese restaurant are cooked on the *teppanyaki* grill table. They include steak, shrimps, oysters, and other seafood. The beef *teppanyaki,* including soup and vegetables, costs 100 patacas. Other selections will add up to about 160 patacas per person. Open 7:00 P.M. to 11:00 P.M., closed Mondays. All major credit cards.

Moderate

Chiu Chau. Lisboa Hotel; 77666, ext. 83001. This is probably the best, and certainly most glamorous, restaurant in Macau that serves the *chiu chau* cuisine of Swatow, original home of many Southeast Asian Chinese. It's richer than Cantonese and more spicy. Open 11:00 A.M. to midnight. All major credit cards.

East Garden. 11 Rua Dr. P.J. Lobo, near Sintra Hotel; 562328. Reputed to have some of the best *dimsum* and other Cantonese fare in Macau. Open 8:00 A.M. to midnight. All major credit cards.

Four Five Six. Lisboa Hotel; 77666, ext. 2090. This restaurant draws lovers of Shanghainese food. The specialties are Shanghai lacquered duck, braised eel, and chicken boiled in rice wine. Open 11:00 A.M. to 1:00 A.M. All major credit cards.

Long Kei. 7-Largo do Senado, heart of town; 573970. One of the most popular Cantonese restaurants in Macau, with a comprehensive menu. Open 11:00 A.M. to 11:00 P.M. No credit cards.

Royal Canton. Royal Hotel; 55222. This large, attractive Cantonese restaurant has become very popular with locals and visitors. The menu is very extensive and the service friendly and efficient. Open 8:00 A.M. to midnight. All major credit cards.

 NIGHTLIFE. According to old movies and books about the China coast, Macau was a city of opium dens, brothels, casinos, and spy cells. In truth, the city was never so romantically sinful, but the myth endures and some visitors will be disappointed by the general somnolence of Macau by night. Most people spend their evenings at the casinos or over long dinners. There is, however, some interesting action.

THEATER

Apart from occasional concerts and recitals, theater in Macau means **Hotel Lisboa** and the *Crazy Paris Show,* a highly professional and sophisticated strip-tease spectacle, with girls imported from the Folies Bergere, Monte Carlo Sporting Club, and other five-star establishments. There are two shows, which are tastefully risque, at 8:30 P.M. and 10:00 P.M. daily, with an additional show at 11:30 P.M. on weekends and public holidays. Tickets, available at hotel counters, the ferry wharf, and the theater, are HK$90 weekdays, HK$100 weekends and holidays.

DISCOTHEQUES

Macau's first disco was the **Green Parrot** in the Hyatt Regency Hotel. It is the creation of Hong Kong's Manhattan Discotheques and is both elegant and fun, with a good selection of music and a very professional disc jockey. Entrance including a drink is 40 patacas weekdays, 70 patacas weekends and holidays.

The **Skylight** in the Presidente Hotel has a marvelous skylight roof, great views, and topless ballet shows. Entrance is HK$48, which includes a drink. The Lisboa's new **Mikado** disco charges HK$90, which includes two drinks. All of these discos have excellent music and lighting effects. All are open until 4 A.M. and take major credit cards. (Entrance fees are subject to fluctuation due to competition.)

NIGHTCLUBS

Most clubs have Thai or Filipina hostesses and some good music. Nightclubs usually display photos of the hostesses, with numbers, at the entrance so that customers can pre-order a companion.

Among locals the most popular nightclub is the *Paris,* in the Estoril Hotel. It has an attractive décor, good dance floor, and excellent band. It is open from 9:30 P.M. to 4:00 A.M. and the minimum is HK$33 weekdays, HK$45 weekends and holidays. The hostesses cost HK$15 per quarter of an hour; HK$60 an hour to take out. Drinks are HK$22 to HK$30. DC, MC, V.

There are dozens of smaller nightclubs around town, most of them displaying prices and photos, so the adventurous visitor has plenty of choice. But be prepared to run into clubs that prefer Asian clients.

For those who want to dance, and maybe have a meal, there are two recommended night spots. One is the **Portos do Sol** in the Lisboa. It has dance music from 8:00 P.M. to midnight. The minimum charge is HK$35 on weekdays, HK$42 on weekends, and extra if there is a floorshow. Dinner is good Continental fare. All major credit cards.

The European restaurant in the **Jai Alai Stadium** has a very good dance floor and strobe light effects, as well as a good band. There are set dinners for 68 patacas and *à la carte* meals for about 75 patacas per person. All major credit cards.

 SIDE TRIPS TO CHINA. One of the most popular tours of the region in recent years has been a day trip of China's Zhongshan County, often combined with a day and night in Macau. Zhongshan offers a neat microcosm of modern rural China, along with some interesting history, and it is only a fifteen-minute drive from the Macau wharf across a border where formalities are fast and easy. The area is of special interest to Westerners, since it was the home of many nineteenth-century Chinese migrants to the United States, Australia, and Europe. Some of them returned with wealth and built extraordinary tower-like houses or Western-style homes. The most famous of the latter is now revered as the home of Sun Yat-sen, who led the 1911 revolution that brought in the Chinese Republic.

The *China Travel Service* (C.T.S.) handles all tours to China, but travel agents in Macau and Hong Kong package and sell them competitively. The most active travel agent is *International Tourism,* which has expanded the original tour to include two days with an overnight stay in Shiqi, three days with an extension to the ancient cultural town of Foshan and a day in Canton before returning by train to Hong Kong, or four days with extra time in Macau.

Other travel agents selling Zhongshan tours are *Sintra,* next to the Sintra Hotel in Macau, 86394, and in the Shun Tak Centre; (5)408028; *Able Tours;* and *Macau Tours* (see Tours section of this guide).

For a one-day tour, which is available every day, tourists need to book 24 hours in advance, or, if in Macau, before noon on the proceding day. The procedure is simple and only passport numbers are required. For overnight stays you will need a visa—which means one photo and 24 hours' notice.

The basic one-day excursion to Zhongshan includes a visit to the ancestral home of Sun Yat-sen at Cuiheng, where visitors tour the house be built and a memorial school and museum; a visit to a commune or a kindergarten; and a Chinese lunch at a hotel in Zhuhai or Chungshan, or in Shiqi, the ancient market town and inland port that is the capital of the country. The tour costs HK$450 weekdays, HK$475 weekends, including transport between Hong Kong and Macau and lunch, including beer and wine.

This tour is often combined with a day and night in Macau, with a tour of the territory and a Chinese dinner. The cost is HK$683–733 weekdays, HK$750 –785 weekends, depending on the hotel used.

The newest tours to be introduced combine Macau and Zhongshan with Foshan and the provincial capital, Canton, and conclude with a train ride from Canton and Hong Kong. The three-day itinerary costs HK$1,400. The four-day tour, which adds a day in Macau, is HK$1,640. Other tours are being developed, so check with International Tourism for details.

Golfers can arrange a visit to Zhongshan with an overnight stay at the Chung Shan resort, which has become a popular spot for locals and visiting Chinese. It is an interesting, if rather unlikely mixture, of a proletarian country club and a cozy hideaway for roving males. The large site contains hot-spring baths, Chinese and Western restaurants, gardens, an international golf course designed by Arnold Palmer, a shooting range, stables, and shops. Visas are needed and are available in Macau in 24 hours. Green fees are HK$200 for 18 holes weekdays, HK$250 weekends. Caddies are HK$50 for 18 holes and a rented set of gold clubs costs the same amount. For details of the Chung Shan club, call the Hong Kong office, (5)210377.

There is another golf course in the area which is becoming popular. The Zhuhai International Club's championship 18-hole course is an challenging as it is attractive. Green fees are HK$150 weekdays, HK$250 weekends, and club rental is HK$15. Two-day packages are available for HK$699 from Hong Kong. Call (5)232136 (Hong Kong) for details.

INDEX

Index

**The letter H indicates hotels & other accommodations.
The letter R indicates restaurants.**

General Information for Hong Kong and Macau

See also indexes below for additional details

HONG KONG

Geographical and Practical Information

283

MACAU
Geographical and Practical Information

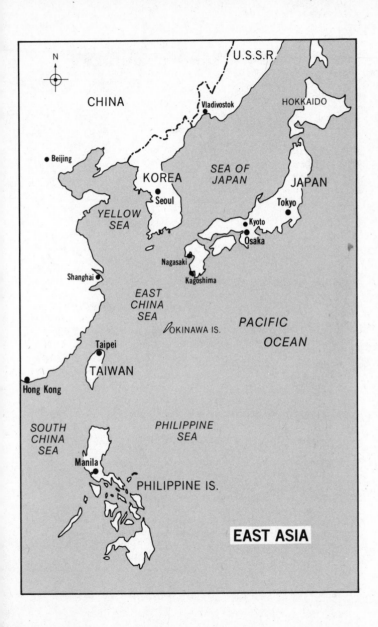

FODOR'S TRAVEL GUIDES

Here is a complete list of Fodor's Travel Guides, available in current editions; most are also available in a
British edition published by Hodder & Stoughton.

U.S. GUIDES

Alaska
American Cities (Great Travel
 Values)
Arizona including the Grand
 Canyon
Atlantic City & the New
 Jersey Shore
Boston
California
Cape Cod & the Islands of
 Martha's Vineyard &
 Nantucket
Carolinas & the Georgia
 Coast
Chesapeake
Chicago
Colorado
Dallas/Fort Worth
Disney World & the Orlando
 Area (Fun in)
Far West
Florida
Fort Worth (see Dallas)
Galveston (see Houston)
Georgia (see Carolinas)
Grand Canyon (see Arizona)
Greater Miami & the Gold
 Coast
Hawaii
Hawaii (Great Travel Values)
Houston & Galveston
I-10: California to Florida
I-55: Chicago to New Orleans
I-75: Michigan to Florida
I-80: San Francisco to New
 York
I-95: Maine to Miami
Jamestown (see Williamsburg)
Las Vegas including Reno &
 Lake Tahoe (Fun in)
Los Angeles & Nearby
 Attractions
Martha's Vineyard (see Cape
 Cod)
Maui (Fun in)
Nantucket (see Cape Cod)
New England
New Jersey (see Atlantic City)
New Mexico
New Orleans
New Orleans (Fun in)
New York City
New York City (Fun in)
New York State
Orlando (see Disney World)
Pacific North Coast
Philadelphia
Reno (see Las Vegas)
Rockies
San Diego & Nearby
 Attractions
San Francisco (Fun in)
San Francisco plus Marin
 County & the Wine Country
The South
Texas
U.S.A.

Virgin Islands (U.S. & British)
Virginia
Waikiki (Fun in)
Washington, D.C.
Williamsburg, Jamestown &
 Yorktown

FOREIGN GUIDES

Acapulco (see Mexico City)
Acapulco (Fun in)
Amsterdam
Australia, New Zealand & the
 South Pacific
Austria
The Bahamas
The Bahamas (Fun in)
Barbados (Fun in)
Beijing, Guangzhou &
 Shanghai
Belgium & Luxembourg
Bermuda
Brazil
Britain (Great Travel Values)
Canada
Canada (Great Travel Values)
Canada's Maritime Provinces
 plus Newfoundland &
 Labrador
Cancún, Cozumel, Mérida &
 the Yucatán
Caribbean
Caribbean (Great Travel
 Values)
Central America
Copenhagen (see Stockholm)
Cozumel (see Cancún)
Eastern Europe
Egypt
Europe
Europe (Budget)
France
France (Great Travel Values)
Germany: East & West
Germany (Great Travel
 Values)
Great Britain
Greece
Guangzhou (see Beijing)
Helsinki (see Stockholm)
Holland
Hong Kong & Macau
Hungary
India, Nepal & Sri Lanka
Ireland
Israel
Italy
Italy (Great Travel Values)
Jamaica (Fun in)
Japan
Japan (Great Travel Values)
Jordan & the Holy Land
Kenya
Korea
Labrador (see Canada's
 Maritime Provinces)
Lisbon
Loire Valley

London
London (Fun in)
London (Great Travel Values)
Luxembourg (see Belgium)
Macau (see Hong Kong)
Madrid
Mazatlan (see Mexico's Baja)
Mexico
Mexico (Great Travel Values)
Mexico City & Acapulco
Mexico's Baja & Puerto
 Vallarta, Mazatlan,
 Manzanillo, Copper Canyon
Montreal (Fun in)
Munich
Nepal (see India)
New Zealand
Newfoundland (see Canada's
 Maritime Provinces)
1936 . . . on the Continent
North Africa
Oslo (see Stockholm)
Paris
Paris (Fun in)
People's Republic of China
Portugal
Province of Quebec
Puerto Vallarta (see Mexico's
 Baja)
Reykjavik (see Stockholm)
Rio (Fun in)
The Riviera (Fun on)
Rome
St. Martin/St. Maarten
 (Fun in)
Scandinavia
Scotland
Shanghai (see Beijing)
Singapore
South America
South Pacific
Southeast Asia
Soviet Union
Spain
Spain (Great Travel Values)
Sri Lanka (see India)
Stockholm, Copenhagen, Oslo,
 Helsinki & Reykjavik
Sweden
Switzerland
Sydney
Tokyo
Toronto
Turkey
Vienna
Yucatán (see Cancún)
Yugoslavia

SPECIAL-INTEREST GUIDES

Bed & Breakfast Guide: North
 America
Royalty Watching
Selected Hotels of Europe
Selected Resorts and Hotels of
 the U.S.
Ski Resorts of North America
Views to Dine by around the
 World

AVAILABLE AT YOUR LOCAL BOOKSTORE OR WRITE TO
FODOR'S TRAVEL PUBLICATIONS, INC., 201 EAST 50th STREET, NEW YORK, NY 10022.